Using PageMaker®

Macintosh® Version

2nd Edition

C.J. Weigand

CORPORATION
LEADING COMPUTER KNOWLEDGE

Using PageMaker®

Macintosh® Version

2nd Edition

Library of Congress Catalog No.: 90-62066

ISBN 0-88022-607-2

93 92 91   4 3 2

Interpretation of the printing code: the rightmost double-digit number is the year of the book's printing; the rightmost single-digit number, the number of the book's printing. For example, a printing code of 90-1 shows that the first printing of the book occurred in 1990.

Using PageMaker: Macintosh Version, 2nd Edition is based on PageMaker Version 4.0 and earlier.

DEDICATION

To our country's Founding Fathers, whose far-reaching vision guaranteed our fundamental rights to freedom of speech and freedom of the press.

Publishing Director

Lloyd J. Short

Acquisitions Editor

Karen A. Bluestein

Project Manager

Paul Boger

Product Director

Shelley O'Hara

Senior Production Editor

Kelly D. Dobbs

Editors

Lori A. Lyons
Heidi Weas Muller
Gregory Robertson

Technical Editor

Laurence H. Loeb, D.D.S.,
*Exchange editor for the
Macintosh exchange on BIX*

Indexer

Hilary Adams

Book Design and Production

Tom Emrick
Bob LaRoche
Joe Ramon
Dennis Sheehan

Composed in Times Roman and Excellent #47
by Que Corporation. Desktop published using PageMaker 4.0.

ABOUT THE AUTHOR

C.J. Weigand

C.J. Weigand is a popular author, speaker, and consultant on the Macintosh and desktop publishing. He has written many articles and reviews that have appeared in *MacWeek, Macintosh Today, Computer Graphic, MACazine, Personal Publishing Magazine,* and other publications. For more than two years, Weigand served as senior editor for *MACazine* and *Personal Publishing.* He currently is editor and publisher of *The Weigand Report: the Working Newsletter for Macintosh Professionals,* an information resource for communicators, desktop publishers, and small-business users.

CONTENTS AT A GLANCE

TABLE OF CONTENTS

I   The Basics

II   Working with Text

III   Graphics and Printing Techniques

7   Graphics Basics 197

IV Creating Different Types of Publications

10 Planning Page Layouts 285

11   Designing a Newsletter 313

12   Designing Other Publications 327

Additional Tips and Techniques 343

ACKNOWLEDGMENTS

This book wouldn't have been possible without the loving and generous support of my wife Carol and my daughter Jennifer. A special, heartfelt thanks to them both.

Special thanks also go to Douglas "Sandy" MacKay of Packer Printing in Mystic, Connecticut, for always being on call and willing to share so many valuable insights.

Finally, many thanks to Karen Bluestein of Que Corporation who fought so vigorously for this project and then helped see it through to fruition.

TRADEMARK ACKNOWLEDGMENTS

CONVENTIONS USED IN THIS BOOK

The conventions used in this book have been established to help you learn to use the program quickly and easily. As much as possible, the conventions correspond with those used in the PageMaker documentation.

Commands, menu names, and dialog boxes are written with initial capital letters.

Words and letters that the user types are written in *italic* or set off on a separate line.

Options in dialog boxes and on-screen messages are written in **bold** and capitalized as they appear on-screen.

FOREWORD

I have known C. J. Weigand for a long time—first as senior editor for me when I was editor-in-chief of *MACazine*, later as senior editor at *Personal Publishing Magazine*, and most recently as editor and publisher of *The Weigand Report*. I also am proud to claim him as a friend. He is one of the most knowledgeable writers in the field of desktop publishing and one of the best Macintosh writers working today.

One of the hardest things for a writer to do, particularly when dealing with sophisticated concepts like typesetting and page-layout software, is to explain specific methods for accomplishing a particular task. This area is where C. J. shines his brightest. As his editor, I frequently used his work as an example to my other writers. He has a special talent for being clear and concise and a wonderful ability to explain complicated concepts without confusing the reader.

In the years since *MACazine's* demise, I have followed C. J.'s work in *Personal Publishing* and his newsletter. As a user of PageMaker, I have come to depend on him to ferret out shortcuts and secrets that help make my work easier. I have never been disappointed.

With *Using PageMaker: Macintosh Version*, he has hit his stride. Not only is this book filled with helpful hints for using PageMaker more efficiently, the text also offers good information you just cannot find elsewhere. Although other books on the subject and the documentation you receive with PageMaker often tell you how to use a specific feature, C. J. explains why you need that feature.

Pay particular attention to the tips, which you will find sprinkled throughout the book. They are mostly short, but oh-so-sweet; I think the tips are the best part of the book. They alone are worth the price of admission.

This book is one of the best—it is packed to the brim with helpful insights that spring from C. J.'s long association with PageMaker and page-layout techniques. No matter what your level of expertise, there is sure to be something here that will save you time and effort.

Enjoy it. I know I did.

Bob LeVitus
Summer 1990

Introduction

Desktop Publishing—What Is It?

Some people consider desktop publishing to be a passing fad; others view desktop programs as harbingers of things to come. Whatever your thoughts on the subject, desktop publishing has dramatically changed the way written communications are prepared. Today, almost anyone can become an instant publisher with a personal computer like the Macintosh, appropriate software to create text and graphics, a page-makeup program like PageMaker to bring the various page elements together, and a laser printer to print the final results.

Desktop publishing is doing it yourself—whether you are putting together a mail-order catalog for potential customers or an informal newsletter for company employees. Managing the entire publishing cycle from beginning to end means that you are in control. No longer must you suffer typesetters who introduce errors into your work or printers who habitually miss deadlines. No longer do you have to pay extra for incorporating last minute changes into your publications or turn away a client who needs an important document produced the same day.

Besides the control offered by desktop programs, desktop publishing's phenomenal growth has been fueled by a second consideration—doing it yourself costs less. Running stencils on a mimeograph machine also is an economical way to publish your ideas, but the inferior print quality visibly detracts from your attempt to get your message across. Desktop publishing with a laser printer, however, yields near-typeset quality documents. If you use a Linotronic ImageSetter, the results are indistinguishable from the results obtained with traditional typesetting methods.

In the Information Age, the proliferation of new publications sometimes seems overwhelming. More material than ever before is being published from the desktop. Each person has an insatiable desire to communicate thoughts and ideas to others, and desktop publishing enables you to do so more quickly and less expensively than ever before.

1

Why PageMaker?

PageMaker is the standard against which other page-layout software must be compared. The program is the first choice for most desktop publishers, primarily because of the friendly, intuitive user interface. If an item on the page doesn't look quite right, you grab the item using the mouse and move or manipulate it—just like working on a real desktop where you can pick up and rearrange items without having to think through the mechanics of what you are doing.

PageMaker is more flexible and easier to use than other page-layout programs. PageMaker possesses an exceptional array of features that makes the program attractive to professionals and novices. For example, you can flow text throughout a document with a click of the mouse, and you can format text automatically—two features that help save time when assembling your publications. You can edit text the same way you do when using a word processor. You can spell-check your stories, and you can search for and replace text attributes like font type, size, and style. You also can wrap text around irregularly shaped graphics, change the contrast and brightness of scanned images by using built-in controls, and apply spot color to text and graphics. Other features enable you to hyphenate and justify text, kern letter pairs and adjust overall tracking, generate indexes and tables of contents automatically, and much more.

With PageMaker, you get quality without complexity. The new features in the current release of PageMaker were added because they were requested by users like you. Each one is included for a reason, and each is important. These features help you perform publishing tasks that previously were considered impossible on a personal computer.

By comparison, many of the advanced features found in other programs are features you most likely do not need. For example, one program enables you to adjust leading (the amount of white space between successive lines of type) to within 0.001 point. The best the LaserWriter can do is 1/300 of an inch, or 0.24 point. You would have to print your documents using a high-end typesetting machine and examine incremental changes with a loupe. Most users don't need to go to such extremes when putting together publications like an annual business report or product sales catalog. PageMaker, however, can position text and graphics, for example, with an accuracy of 1/2880 of an inch. This is precise enough to handle the most sophisticated publishing tasks.

PageMaker is an excellent productivity-enhancing tool. You will find yourself relying upon this program for many tasks. You can use PageMaker to prepare newsletters, fliers, greeting cards, catalogs, sales ads, business documents, technical reports, books, pamphlets, menus, theater programs, and so on. PageMaker's uses are limited only by your imagination. If you do manual paste-up, PageMaker is a great time-saver. Minor alterations are easy to do, and you can create alternate layouts in just minutes. Major publication changes that previously would have taken days to do can be executed in just hours.

Besides being practical, PageMaker also is fun. You can take chances and experiment with new ideas, layouts, and designs. PageMaker encourages you to be creative, and creative communications is what desktop publishing is all about.

Who Should Use This Book?

Whether you own PageMaker, use the program at work, or plan to buy it soon, you should consider reading this book. If you are new to desktop publishing and feel somewhat intimidated by the complexity of PageMaker's multiple-volume documentation, this book helps you quickly master the basics. Despite PageMaker's apparent friendliness, most first-time users tend to flounder when attempting the simplest publishing tasks. They do not understand how to use PageMaker effectively. *Using PageMaker: Macintosh Version*, 2nd Edition quickly gives you the knowledge and skills you need to produce professional-looking publications every time.

If you are an experienced PageMaker user and want to hone your desktop publishing skills, this book helps you develop the proficiency needed to tackle the toughest assignments. Even the most experienced PageMaker users occasionally have difficulty achieving publishing goals. *Using PageMaker* contains step-by-step procedures to help you master new techniques quickly, plus an abundance of hints and tips to help you develop advanced skills.

A Few Words about Versions

This edition of *Using PageMaker* covers through Version 4. Since PageMaker first appeared on the market, many changes have been made. Each new version introduced capabilities requested by users. PageMaker Version 4 continues this tradition by adding many capabilities not contained in Version 3. If you are using an earlier version of PageMaker, however, this book still helps you master using the program. The basic features and overall approach to desktop publishing remain unchanged. The information you need can be found on these pages.

PageMaker Version 4 contains all features found in earlier versions. A few of the menu commands are rearranged, and several keyboard shortcuts are modified. But these changes, for the most part, are cosmetic. If you are comfortable using an earlier version of PageMaker, you can start working in PageMaker Version 4 and immediately feel at home. The added power of enhancements such as the Story Editor, document linking, and the table of contents and index generators, for example, remain hidden until you need them.

PageMaker Version 4 is bigger, faster, and sleeker than earlier versions. Some of its many new enhancements include the following:

❑ A Story Editor for faster text processing. You can open any story in the Story Editor and edit your text quickly and easily, without having to wait for your screen display to update. You also can open several stories simultaneously for editing.

❑ A 100,000-word spelling checker. You can check a selected range of text, your current story, or all stories in your publication at the same time.

❑ The capability to search for and replace text, including finding and changing passages by paragraph styles and text attributes

❑ The capability to set type size and leading in increments as small as a tenth of a point. Type sizes can vary from 4 to 650 points.

❑ Track kerning over any range of text. The amount of tracking is proportional to type size.

❑ Automatic and manual kerning over any range of text in as small as 0.01-em increments

❑ Word, letter, and paragraph spacing applied as paragraph attributes

❑ The capability to condense or expand type from 5 to 250 percent

❑ Text rotation in 90-degree increments

❑ Single publications can be up to 999 pages in length (limited only by available disk space).

❑ Automatic table of contents and index generation. These features effectively merge multiple publications into single volumes. Page-Maker also supports chain-printing of multiple publications from book lists.

❑ The capability to set paragraph, column, and page breaks

❑ User-definable widow and orphan controls

❑ A "Next style" feature for assigning following paragraph styles

❑ Inline graphics and paragraph rules that remain tied to your text as the text flows through your publications

❑ Automatic updating of imported text and graphics through the magic of links. You also can store all graphics outside your documents to keep publication sizes small and easily manageable.

❑ The capability to display graphic images grayed-out, at low-resolution, or at high-resolution

❑ Importing and displaying full 24-bit color TIFF and EPS images

❑ The capability to assign PANTONE colors

❑ On-line, context-sensitive Help

❑ A separate Table Editor utility

PageMaker Version 4 also contains dozens of other new features and improvements. You learn about and work with each of them in the following chapters.

How To Use This Book

The recommended way to use this book is to parallel each chapter's lessons with a project you currently are working on. Experiment on a backup copy of your project file and try the different concepts and techniques you learn. Begin each session by gathering all your materials and try to develop a clear idea beforehand of where your publication is going. That way, you have a much better chance of getting there.

Start at the beginning and read through to the end. You will benefit from the logical progression of ideas and can assimilate new concepts as they are introduced. Experienced users may want to skim quickly through the basic material presented in Chapters 2, 3, and 4 and delve right into Part II, "Working with Text." All users, however, should read Chapter 1, "The Publishing Process—an Overview," to gain a more complete understanding of desktop publishing. This chapter gives you a solid foundation upon which to build your publishing skills.

Using PageMaker assumes that you are familiar with basic Macintosh terms like "click," "double-click," and "drag." This book also assumes that you have read the user's manual that came with your Macintosh. If you are not comfortable working with menus, windows, dialog boxes, and so on, take time to learn more about them before starting Chapter 1. Inexperienced users can find extra help in Appendix B, "Installing PageMaker and Configuring Your System."

What Is in This Book?

Using PageMaker is divided into four main sections, plus two appendixes. There also is an additional tips and techniques section, and a quick reference section.

Part I, "The Basics," highlights the overall publishing process and explains the fundamentals of document preparation.

Chapter 1, "The Publishing Process—an Overview," provides an overview of the entire publishing process, including Planning, Preparing, Proofing, and Printing your publication.

Chapter 2, "PageMaker Basics," introduces you to PageMaker's basic working tools, explains the different parts of the PageMaker desktop display, and shows you how to access and use PageMaker's Help commands.

Chapter 3, "Creating a Document," teaches you how to set document defaults, use master pages, and lay a solid foundation for your documents.

Chapter 4, "Quick Start: Creating a Newsletter," introduces and reinforces some key concepts. After you complete the sample newsletter, you should have enough confidence to get started producing your own publications, even as you continue working through the remaining chapters.

Part II, "Working with Text," teaches you everything you need to know about using text in PageMaker.

Chapter 5, "Text Basics," discusses text sources, preparation, importation, and the proper selection of fonts. You also learn how to use PageMaker's story editor to create and edit text, to check your spelling, and to find and replace text by searching for assigned attributes.

Chapter 6, "Formatting Text," demonstrates the correct application of style sheets. You learn how to format your publications, including how to use columns, arrange individual elements on the page, and manage white space. You also learn how to create indexes and tables of contents, and how to prepare tables using the Table Editor.

Part III, "Graphics and Printing Techniques," examines PageMaker's graphic-handling capabilities and shows you how to harness the power of visual imagery in ways that add impact to your documents.

Chapter 7, "Graphics Basics," introduces you to different types of graphics. You learn how to use each of PageMaker's drawing tools. You also learn how to import, export, and link graphics, and how to modify Tiff and Paint pictures using PageMaker's Image Control commands.

Chapter 8, "Formatting and Enhancing Graphics," demonstrates working with scanned images, wrapping text around graphics for special effects, and adding color to your pages.

Chapter 9, "Printing Techniques," discusses all aspects of printing. Printing is the one area that causes the most problems for desktop publishers. You discover what the most common errors are and what steps you can take to avoid them.

Part IV, "Creating Different Types of Publications," ties everything together. You explore various ways to get your message across effectively by using PageMaker.

You also gain a deeper understanding of what good design is all about. This section introduces several proven concepts that help you produce publications that attract and hold reader interest.

Chapter 10, "Planning Page Layouts," explains how to communicate ideas effectively and lists 10 common mistakes that you should avoid. This chapter also discusses contrast and symmetry and how to achieve just the right look for your documents. You learn how to match different layout requirements with different types of publications. You also learn how to use and create templates.

Chapter 11, "Designing a Newsletter," shows you how to choose the right format, design a masthead, and add visual effects to your newsletters. You also gain insight into the use of photographs.

Chapter 12, "Designing Other Publications," presents information on creating overhead transparencies, brochures, mailers, certificates, and personal stationery. You study design concepts for ads, greeting cards, and other short documents. You also learn document-management techniques for longer publications, such as books, business reports, catalogs, and directories.

"Additional Tips and Techniques" contains many more useful insights about PageMaker and desktop publishing.

The "Quick Reference" section presents step-by-step instructions for using PageMaker. Use this section to refresh your memory or to quickly find out how to do something in PageMaker.

Appendix A, "Dealing with a Commercial Printer," provides a checklist that helps ensure that your printing jobs get done successfully—the first time.

Appendix B, "Installing PageMaker and Configuring Your System," is for the benefit of new Macintosh users who need extra help setting up PageMaker.

Using PageMaker is a straightforward guide to the satisfying and rewarding world of desktop publishing. This book helps you master all the skills you need to create successful publications using PageMaker.

I

The Basics

The Publishing Process —an Overview

Desktop publishing has been hailed as the perfect solution to nearly every publishing problem. Because of such exaggerations, new PageMaker users often become discouraged when their first attempts at desktop publishing yield less-than-desirable results. That "something magical" doesn't always happen on the first, or even the tenth try.

Homework is required if you want to produce professional-looking documents. You can become proficient, even with little or no prior experience, but first you must learn the basics. The purpose of this chapter is to give you the fundamentals you need, both practical and philosophical. These fundamentals help you better understand the mechanics of working with your PageMaker software.

Desktop Publishing

Desktop publishing can be divided into the following five steps:

1. Planning
2. Writing
3. Producing layouts
4. Reviewing
5. Printing

Examining each step briefly will help you understand how to take a typical publication from initial conception to final printing and distribution.

Planning

Planning is the idea stage in which you set the scope and tone of your publication. The first question you always should ask yourself is, "Who will be reading my publication?" Every subsequent decision you make follows, to some degree, the answer to that first question. Other questions to ask include: What is the purpose of the publication? How long should each article be? Should the writing style be formal or informal? Are illustrations called for? If so, how many, and how detailed should the illustrations be? Are photographs needed? Is color an option? How should the material be organized and presented? All these questions and more can be answered readily if you know your audience.

Determining your target audience is not always easy. You have to know something about your individual readers—their likes, dislikes, interests, prejudices, and ambitions. Are they small-business people or Fortune 500 executives? Are they goal-driven, always seeking new challenges or acquisitions, or are they content with what they have? What is their education level? What are their hobbies? And why should they want to read your publication instead of some other publication?

The planning stage is the place to get these answers. Do your research beforehand, and you become better equipped to serve the needs of your readers. Your publication is more likely to succeed. Whether you are preparing a simple flier for a church bazaar or a detailed book about investing in the commodities market, knowing your readers is the key to successful publishing.

The planning stage also includes delegating tasks. You have to determine who will write, edit, proofread, do the artwork, deal with the printer, track the budget, and be in charge of the coffee and donuts. Assigning responsibilities before you start avoids confusion later and makes the entire publishing cycle go more smoothly.

You learn more about planning later in this chapter, under "Planning Your Publication."

Writing

Writing quality often determines whether a publication succeeds or fails. Graphics are important, but graphics usually need accompanying text. You may capture a reader's interest with clever illustrations, but if the words don't hold that interest, you lose any chance you may have of getting your message across. The writing stage is the place to organize your ideas into words.

The writing stage also includes the preparation of graphics. Do not let the word "graphics" scare you. A graphic is simply a picture. A graphic can be a hand-drawn illustration, a piece of clip art, a scanned photograph, a design, a fill pattern, or any number of other visual enhancements.

Because graphics heighten interest in the written word, they should complement your text. Remember that you want to capture and hold reader interest. To make that happen, your text and graphics should work together. If purely decorative touches are called for, use them sparingly. The mark of an amateur desktop publisher is the overabundant use of graphic embellishments that fail to add to a publication's content.

For an introduction to some practical aspects of writing and graphics preparation, see "Preparing Your Publication" later in this chapter.

Producing Layouts

Planning and writing are essential, but these steps are only preliminary. The most important step in producing your publication is doing the layout. During the layout phase, you assemble all the disparate pieces into a complete whole by importing text and graphics into your page-makeup program and arranging the elements on your pages.

Much of your publication's design is set early in the planning stage. Not until you enter the layout phase, however, do you discover the best way to execute that design. Your choices may depend as much on content as on style. For example, although you may have anticipated using an informal single-column layout for a political newsletter, you may find that the conservative typeface and small pen-and-ink illustrations you selected go better with a formal two-column approach. Although the layout phase requires a certain amount of planning and discipline to achieve good results, this phase also presents an opportunity for creative spontaneity. You can experiment with new ideas, but remember that your ultimate goal is to match your publication's design to your audience's requirements.

Later in this chapter, in "Bringing It All Together," you are introduced to several key concepts indispensable to creating effective layouts.

Reviewing

The critical editing is done during the review stage. Although the review cycle begins during the writing stage and continues until your publication is printed, the definitive review is done during this stage. Any publication changes you make afterward can lead to unacceptable delays and result in increased production costs.

The final review should be undertaken by someone not directly responsible for the writing or layout. The closer you are to the preparation and assembly of a publication, the more likely you are to skip over typing, spelling, and punctuation errors. If you have to proof your work, read the text out loud to force yourself to go more slowly and focus on each word. Also explain your layout in detail to someone to help check your work. You may be surprised at how many errors you catch that you may have missed during earlier reviews.

The review cycle also is a time to ask whether you have met the goals set during the planning stage. You want to know whether your material works, whether you will reach your intended audience, and whether readers will respond appropriately. Ask a few people who match your audience profile to evaluate your rough layout. They may suggest changes that improve your publication's chances for success.

Under "Proofing Your Publication" in this chapter, you are introduced to a step-by-step approach for making sure that you don't overlook anything during your final review.

Printing

When you reach the printing stage, you are nearly finished. Even if you have done well so far, things still can go wrong. The printing stage is fraught with potential disasters. Many perfectly prepared publications have turned out badly because desktop publishers thought their work was done when their job was ready to be printed.

The quality of a print job directly affects how readers perceive a publication. Surprisingly, many desktop publishers are willing to settle for poor or marginal printing quality. This approach is like getting dressed up in fine evening clothes only to leave the house wearing soiled tennis shoes. You may not create the impression you had hoped for.

You learn more about printing later in this chapter, under "Printing Your Publication." You also find a detailed discussion about printing in Chapter 9.

Planning Your Publication

Planning your publication can be a team or an individual effort. Whether you work within a group or alone, for a client or for yourself, the essential planning steps are the same:

1. *Determine the size of your publication.*

   In addition to page count, determining the size includes selecting page dimensions and defining the image area. The image area is the portion of your page that lies within the margin boundaries. Your text and graphics appear in this area. The wider your margins, the less image area you have to work with and the more pages your publication may require to hold the same amount of text and graphics. Because the size of your publication is directly related to the final production costs, determining page count and size beforehand and then creating your text and illustrations to fit is a good idea.

2. *Prepare a preliminary layout.*

   Your preliminary layout doesn't have to be elaborate. Its purpose is to give you a rough idea of how your publication goes together. A preliminary layout is more important for lengthy or complex publications than for short ones in which most of your work can be done on-screen. When doing preliminary layouts, use a pencil to sketch each page on a separate sheet of paper. Simple boxes can be used to show the general arrangement of text and graphics. Think of your preliminary layout as a storyboard. Use the layout as a working guide and feel free to make changes as you work.

3. *Decide what you need to produce your publication.*

   Determine what software and hardware you need to edit and process text and graphics. Decide whether you need outside assistance to produce your publication; then seek out and hire qualified individuals. List all deadlines and plan how to meet them. Estimate overall production costs and set up a detailed publishing schedule before getting started. Consult with your commercial printer before deciding on a final schedule.

   You also should decide whether to scan in photographs, use spot color for artwork, or opt for typeset-quality Linotronic output. Obtain a rough cost estimate from your commercial printer. Make sure that the estimate includes the type of paper, method of binding, and total number of copies. Knowing your printing costs ahead of time helps you plan and manage your budget.

4. *Make a schedule and stick to it.*

   Of all the advice contained in this book, this is probably the most important. Without a schedule, you continually come up against deadlines without accomplishing what you originally set out to do. A schedule keeps you on track and within budget. If you have a team of people working with you, each person should be given an individual schedule based on the overall master schedule. This scheduling helps formalize individual responsibilities and ensures that nothing gets overlooked.

Planning the Layout

Your layout is a page-by-page arrangement of all the elements in your publication. Executing an effective layout, like producing a memorable piece of music, can be challenging. Adhering to a few well-established principles, however, can make doing layouts easier and still allow you the freedom of individual creativity.

Be consistent. For example, don't switch arbitrarily from three columns on one page to two columns on the next page to four columns on the next. With PageMaker, you can modify, change, and vary your layouts, but too much inconsistency turns readers away.

Don't confuse consistency with staidness. Type and graphics can be strewn across your pages with wild abandonment, but even then, you should seek a uniform style. Try to be interesting without being amateurish.

Err on the conservative side. Mixing too many design elements or overworking any one technique—for example, continually wrapping text around images—can detract from the professional look of your publication.

If you are not sure how to get started, try using commercially supplied templates like the ones from Aldus. Templates are pre-formatted documents you use to create your own publications. The layouts are already done for you. You supply only the text and graphics.

Use white space as a design element to make your pages seem more inviting. Clean, uncluttered pages are easy on the eyes. White space helps to focus reader attention.

Developing a Style

Style is equivalent to personality. You can do several things to give your publications a winning style.

- *Pick a typeface appropriate to the task.*

  If you are preparing an ad for fine china, for example, you would never choose a display face that looks like stenciled lettering. A stenciled typeface suggests the roughness of boxed cargo. You also would not select a block headline type to announce a church wedding. Instead, you would use an elegant script face that complements the formality of the occasion. Every typeface has a unique personality. Even subtle differences between selected typefaces can influence the look of a publication. Get to know what typefaces are available. Make sure that the typefaces you use do not clash with your intended message.

- *Strive for uniformity in your use of illustrations.*

  Avoid mixing different kinds of images on the same page. A low-resolution bit-mapped file, for example, doesn't normally sit well next to a high-resolution encapsulated PostScript file. Because artwork and photographs generally reflect the personalities of their creators, take extra care in choosing your illustrations. Be sure that they complement the perceived style of your publication.

- *When you find a layout that works, don't tamper with it.*

  This rule is especially true if you publish a periodical like a newsletter or catalog. Readers find the familiar reassuring. They tend to react negatively to sudden and abrupt changes unless there is a good reason.

If you must make alterations, try to make them gradually. Slight variations in the arrangement of text and graphics between publication issues may help create interest, but radical departures from the norm reduce reader acceptance of most publications.

- *Select an appropriate paper for your publication.*

  The color, texture, shape, and size of the paper you choose greatly influences reader perception. For example, you would not want to use ordinary tabloid newsprint to prepare a mail-order catalog that showcases expensive evening gowns. Tabloid newsprint, however, may be just the thing for announcing a bargain-basement sale on children's play clothes.

- *Keep in mind that style is based on the nature of a publication.*

  Study successful publications to learn and adapt new design techniques, but don't just copy those layouts that appeal to you. If you copy the works of others, your publications never will develop their own unique style.

If you have difficulty finding a style that works, experiment with a variety of approaches. Use different fonts and graphics or try different writing styles. Show your work to others and ask for honest opinions. Critical feedback can help you tailor your publications to meet the needs and expectations of your readers.

Evaluating the Cost

The cost of producing a publication varies greatly depending on how long you take to create each page. Only you can decide how much your time is worth. Assign an hourly rate to yourself and multiply the rate by the number of hours you plan to spend on a project. This formula gives you some idea of your labor costs. Don't forget to include training time as appropriate.

Up-front expenses for equipment, amortized over a reasonable period of time, should be included in your total. Even if you already own the necessary hardware and software, tack on an appropriate rental fee. Otherwise, your cost estimate will be artificially low.

Paper and printing are likely to be your biggest expenses. Together, they often equal or exceed all other expenses combined. Using a Linotronic ImageSetter adds $10 to $15 per page. Still, that is considerably less than the roughly $30 to $150 per page you may pay to have your publication typeset in the traditional manner.

When you first do desktop publishing, you may not save much money. New equipment, software, and training represent major investments that greatly increase the cost of producing your first few publications. Eventually, however, you recover your original investment. In time, your publishing costs will decrease dramatically.

Preparing Your Publication

Most of the preliminary steps needed to get your publication ready for layout are done outside of PageMaker. Although you may choose to do some of the work in PageMaker, the bulk of your writing, editing, and graphics preparation are best done using supplemental software. PageMaker is primarily a layout and assembly tool. PageMaker is a program for bringing together and integrating the many diverse elements that make up a publication.

PageMaker enables you to edit stories, do spell-checks, find and replace text (including searching by attributes), and many other word-processing chores. However, PageMaker lacks many of the capabilities of full-featured authoring tools like Microsoft Word or NISUS. PageMaker also contains simple drawing tools, but you cannot use them to prepare detailed artwork. Most graphics work must be done beforehand in programs specifically designed for such tasks.

Software You Need

As a minimum, you need a good word processor for processing text and one or more graphics programs (Paint, Draw, EPS, Tiff) for creating and editing illustrations. If you plan to include photographs in your documents, you want a program that enables you to edit scanned TIFF (Tag Image File Format) images. If you plan to work with display (decorative) type, for example, to prepare ads or promotional pieces, you also may want to acquire some third-party decorative laser fonts.

Word Processing Software

Any capable word processor that enables you to save files as text-only or ASCII (American Standard Code for Information Interchange) is ideal for use with PageMaker. Text-only files are stripped of all formatting information, including font types, sizes, and styles.

In addition to text-only files, PageMaker imports formatted files from several popular Macintosh word processors, including Microsoft Word, Microsoft Works, WriteNow, WordPerfect, Acta Advantage, and MacWrite. PageMaker retains most of the original formatting, including paragraph indents and assigned type styles.

PageMaker also supports Microsoft's Rich Text Format (RTF). The ASCII and RTF filters that come with PageMaker enable you to place documents created by IBM PC-compatible applications.

Text-only files placed within PageMaker are formatted automatically according to publication default settings and any conversions you select using PageMaker's Smart ASCII Import Filter. In Part II, you learn how to reformat text within PageMaker. You also learn how to use PageMaker's style sheets to assign subsequent formatting to paragraphs.

Graphics Software

A graphic in PageMaker is anything except text. A graphic can be a picture, photograph, or design element like a box or rule. PageMaker can import several different graphic formats, including Paint (bitmap), Draw (PICT and PICT 2), EPS (Encapsulated PostScript), and TIFF (Tag Image File Format). Each of these formats has distinct advantages and disadvantages. Figure 1.1 shows examples of these formats.

Fig. 1.1

A sampling of different graphic formats printed on a 300 dpi laser printer.

The Paint format, for example, yields a 72 dpi (dots per inch) black-and-white image that matches the bit-mapped (pixel) display of your Macintosh screen. Paint images are easy to create and edit, but their resolution is fixed at 72 dpi, and the images do not reproduce well when resized. When scaled up in size, they acquire a chunky appearance because each dot making up the image gets resized. When scaled down in size, the dots shrink only to 72 dpi and then start to drop out. Consequently, the images tend to become muddy looking. Paint images, however, can contain a lot of detail. Much of today's clip art comes in Paint format. Examples of popular Paint programs include MacPaint from Claris, SuperPaint from Silicon Beach Software, DeskPaint from Zedcor, and Canvas from Deneba.

The PICT and PICT 2 formats are standards for transferring draw-type files between applications. Draw-type images are described geometrically using mathematical vector notation. Instead of individual dots, these images consist of lines and shapes. They are treated as objects. Draw-type images reproduce well when scaled, but, if too detailed, can sometimes overload a laser printer's memory. Draw images are easier to create and edit than paint images. Popular drawing programs include MacDraw and MacDraw II from Claris Corporation, SuperPaint from Silicon Beach Software, MacDraft from Innovative Data Design, and DeskDraw from Zedcor. Most other Macintosh drawing programs, including programs intended for CAD (Computer Aided Design) work, also enable you to save files in PICT or PICT 2 format. (PICT 2 is an enhanced version of PICT and includes refinements like color and incremental rotation of objects.)

The EPS format permits transfer of high-resolution, device-independent PostScript files between applications. PostScript graphics can contain subtle gradations in object shading, curved and pattern-filled text, and other special effects. Macintosh EPS files come in two forms. The first uses a PICT or TIFF screen-display image piggybacked onto the EPS data, which enables you to see and manipulate your graphic on-screen. The second type is a generic EPS file that, when placed in PageMaker, shows only a shaded bounding box. The box contains the file title, creator, and creation date. Two excellent programs for creating and editing EPS graphics are Adobe Illustrator from Adobe Systems and Aldus FreeHand from Aldus Corporation. These programs are difficult to master, but the results you can get far exceed the capabilities of most draw programs.

TIFF files are designed primarily to handle scanned images. Like paint files, TIFF files are composed of tiny dots, but they are not limited to 72 dpi. TIFF files generally contain up to 300 dpi and simulate gray shading by arranging dots in irregular patterns. Unfortunately, a single TIFF standard has yet to gain universal acceptance. Several dozen formats are in existence. Every scanner manufacturer seems to have introduced a variation to prevent cross-usage of their company's software. PageMaker, however, imports and displays most TIFF files without difficulty. To edit gray-scale TIFF files, you need to use a program such as ImageStudio from Letraset or Digital Darkroom from Silicon Beach Software. Black-and-white TIFF files can be edited using any of the many popular paint programs that accommodate 300 dpi images. Editing color Tiff images requires more specialized and expensive color graphics software.

Creating or editing graphics requires that you use a separate software program. PageMaker cannot edit imported images—the drawing tools are limited to creating simple design elements. PageMaker, however, does enable you to adjust the contrast and brightness of paint and TIFF files. You also can change TIFF gray-scale levels and apply custom line screens for special effects. You learn more about these image-control features in Chapter 8.

Text Considerations

A story is a continuous body of text. A story can be a short article tucked away in the corner of a page or a feature-length piece that runs like a thread throughout your entire publication. The story is the heart of your publication—where your message meets the reader. When preparing stories for layout, you should consider several important factors.

Story Length and Publication Content

The number of allotted pages dictates how long your stories can be. You have to decide what to say and how to say it, and you have to make the story fit. In traditional publishing environments, a copyfitter juggles story lengths, resizes graphics, and somehow crams everything together with enough room left over for ads. A copyfitter's layouts often end up a compromise between what he wants to see included and what he can afford to include.

You probably do your own copyfitting. If your documents are straightforward, balancing story length and content is easy. If you are publishing a multi-page newsletter containing dozens of stories and graphics, this balancing act gets tougher. If stories run a little long or a little short, you can use certain tricks to make the stories fit without altering the layout. You learn some of these tricks in Chapter 10.

Selecting a Typeface

The Apple LaserWriter and most other Macintosh laser printers come with a set of built-in PostScript fonts for high-quality document printing. A font represents a specific typeface, style, and size. For example, Helvetica is a typeface, and Helvetica Bold 12-point is a font. Most fonts consist of the basic alphanumeric character set with upper- and lowercase letters, a selection of diacritics and punctuation marks, and a few typesetting symbols.

Most built-in LaserWriter fonts are suitable for preparing conservative business documents, but fall short when used to create publications like leaflets, theater programs, greeting cards, and announcements. For these kinds of publications, you want to use one or more commercial display faces available from companies like Adobe Systems, Casady & Greene, The Electric Typographer, and Dubl-Click Software. Figure 1.2 shows three kinds of fonts you may use in your publications.

The most important criterion for choosing any font is that the font not be so noticeable that your message gets missed. You want your words to be read. If, instead, the font you use becomes the focus of interest, your message may get overlooked. Selecting the right fonts for presenting your material is critical to get your ideas across. Fonts should complement your message by directing reader interest to what you have to say. Fonts and type styles are covered more thoroughly in Chapter 5.

Fig. 1.2

Different typefaces are required for different publishing tasks.

Garamond—A serif bookface that makes excellent body copy. It boasts exceptional legibility.

Helvetica Bold—A popular non-serif font used mainly for headlines and subheads.

Flourish—A display face that's ideal for extra-special occasions calling for a touch of elegance.

Graphics Considerations

Graphics in desktop publishing include illustrations (artwork and photographs) and design elements (rules, boxes, and printer's ornaments). Graphics encompass everything in a publication not thought of as text.

The graphics you use and their placement are critical to the success of your publication. Too often, graphics are used indiscriminately, without much thought being given to how they interplay with other graphics or stories. Professional publishers know that each graphic must count, just as each word in a story or headline must count.

Using Artwork

Without graphics, publications may appear flat and uninteresting. For example, a typical hand-typed business letter is not much of an attention-getter. If you browse through most popular magazines, however, you see graphics used everywhere to illustrate stories, sell products, and highlight information. The text carries the message; the graphics are used to arouse interest.

PageMaker is the quintessential medium for assembling documents that include graphics. In later chapters, you explore dozens of ways to use graphics to enliven your publications and make them stand out from competing publications.

Clip Art—Pros and Cons

The term "clip art" comes from the practice of clipping illustrations from books of commercially supplied artwork. These clippings are pasted onto mechanicals (hand-assembled proofs of final layouts) to create camera-ready copy. Most clip art available to desktop publishers comes prepackaged as digital images. These images come in various graphic formats. You generally can edit digital clip art to satisfy different publishing requirements.

Clip art is mainly for people who cannot afford to hire an artist or illustrator or who don't want to take the time and trouble to create artwork themselves.

Even if you have a whole team of artists working for you, however, clip art still can come in handy. Tight publication schedules sometimes mean that you don't have time to wait for artwork to be created from scratch. Prepackaged clip art offers a convenient shortcut. On-disk clip art, however, is expensive, and the artwork sometimes is limited in applicability. You may be better off creating your own drawings or scanning existing images, especially if your graphic needs are varied.

Scanned Images

The advent of high-resolution, low-cost scanners for personal computers has made scanning artwork more feasible than relying on disk-based clip art. The advantages of using scanned images are many. You can scan everything from hand-drawn sketches to photographs, and you need scan only what you intend to use. You also have complete control over scan quality. If minor tweaking of a scanned image's contrast or brightness is needed, you can do that within PageMaker. If you need to clean up or modify an image, however, you still need a program capable of editing Paint or TIFF graphics.

Most scanned images consist of line art or photographs. Line art is composed of simple lines and curves. The shapes are devoid of fill patterns, like cross-hatching or gray shading. Line art generally is used to emphasize or expand upon a theme or idea. Technical drawings included in equipment maintenance manuals, for example, are one type of line art.

PageMaker enables you to import scanned photos directly into your publications. After placing a photo, you can adjust its contrast, brightness, and gray shading. You also can create special line screens for heightened or dramatic effect.

A Few Words about Copyright

You can scan artwork and photos easily, and good material for illustrations is available from many sources. But keep in mind that copyright restrictions may exist on the use of some material. Owning a scanner does not give you license to copy the works of others, unless those works are known to be copyright free and in the public domain.

Commercially supplied clip art that you buy generally can be used in any way you like. You are not permitted to republish or resell clip art separately as artwork, however, without prior contractual arrangement with the publisher. Because the laws are sometimes subtle and complex on this issue, erring on the conservative side is best.

For example, a legitimate way to use clip art is to publish a greeting card for friends, relatives, clients, and business associates. You may face a courtroom encounter, however, if you use that same clip art to design a greeting card to be sold nationwide in stores or by mail order. Check with the original publisher whenever in doubt.

Original Artwork

The most satisfying artwork is the work you create yourself. Even if you cannot draw a straight line, you may discover hidden talents when you try using one of the many graphic software packages available for the Macintosh. These programs make drawing straight lines and curves easy. Some of these packages even have spray can tools (if you are into graffiti, you can be creative instantly). Creating your own artwork means that you can produce just the right illustrations for each job. No more searching endlessly through files of images that don't quite fit your publishing needs. An example of how to create artwork is shown in figure 1.3.

Fig. 1.3

With a scanner and graphics software, you can produce finished artwork from rough sketches.

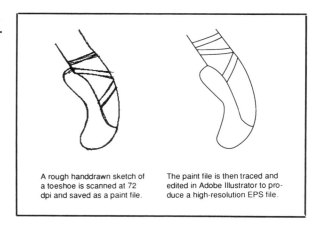

A rough handdrawn sketch of a toeshoe is scanned at 72 dpi and saved as a paint file.

The paint file is then traced and edited in Adobe Illustrator to produce a high-resolution EPS file.

The same copyright considerations apply to photographs. You would do well, therefore, to buy a camera and take your own pictures. Amateur photographs scan just as well as the ones you buy from professionals, and they don't cost nearly as much. Plus, if you own a camera, you can take photographs whenever and wherever you need them. You also can arrange your photo compositions to match the style requirements of your publication. You are not limited to choosing from a fixed selection of images from a stock photo agency that may not be quite what you had in mind. Shooting a couple of rolls of film to get one useful photo costs less than $25. Buying the same photograph from a stock photo agency can cost you as much as $150.

Bringing It All Together

You probably are anxious to begin assembling your pages, but you may be a bit nervous. Don't worry. Successful layouts can be done by anyone. Understanding that desktop publishing is primarily a vehicle for communicating ideas is the key to mastering page layout. Every step in the design of your pages should be aimed at communicating effectively with your readers. You may want to persuade, entertain, enlighten, or chastise. It doesn't matter. Your goal should be to get your message across.

Arranging Three Key Elements

Every page in a publication represents an arrangement of three key elements:

1. Headlines

2. Text

3. Graphics

Not all three elements always have to be present. For example, a novel may not have any pictures, and a travel guide may contain many pages of photographs unaccompanied by text.

Which elements you use and how you arrange them determine how effectively you communicate your ideas. A stockholders' annual report, for example, may lead off the fiscal section with a bold headline stating "Profits Are up This Year." This headline, followed by a large chart showing steadily increasing revenues, quickly conveys the following message: "The company is doing well, and your investments are safe." Any elaboration about how profits were obtained may be deemed secondary and printed in small type at the bottom of the page. In this case, the headline and graphic do all the work.

Many different combinations of these three key elements are possible. Knowing how to arrange these key elements successfully on your pages, however, depends first on understanding their differing roles.

Headlines

Think of your main headline as your show opener. A headline deserves prominent display because a headline is read first. If your readers find your headlines interesting, they read on. If not, they may not even glance at the text that follows.

Every day, readers get bombarded with information from every direction. Headlines help readers decide what to read and what not to read. Your headlines, therefore, should be designed to attract and hold attention. Informative, eye-catching headlines can give your publication a competitive edge.

In Chapter 10, you learn how to design headlines to help you communicate your message more effectively.

Text

Text is words. Words make it possible to express ideas, offer arguments, state opinions, and draw conclusions. Your pages frequently may consist of nothing but text—balanced, of course, by headers, footers, and a few ruled elements (especially with books, pamphlets, and scholarly journals). As a design element, text often shares equal billing with graphics (especially in catalogs and brochures). Text, however, always defers to headlines and graphics in sales ads, leaflets, product announcements, and other promotional materials.

You can wrap text around irregularly shaped graphics for eye-catching effect. You also can mask text within a graphic shape. Small blocks of strategically placed text, set in bold or italic type, can serve as "pull quotes" to heighten story awareness. Curved or rotated text can be used to draw the reader's eye toward a particular item of interest. You also can use text as a link between diverse elements on a page. And you can have text provide continuity in a publication in which the main focus is on pictures, as in illustrated how-to manuals or bound collections of artwork and photographs.

Regardless of how good your headlines or graphics are, after you capture a reader's interest, the body copy must take over. Your text should read well and should look good. Pay careful attention to formatting—proper kerning, word and line spacing, hyphenation, justification, and so on. All are essential to making body copy look presentable. You learn more about text formatting in Part II.

Graphics

In many ways, the graphic is the most important of the three key elements. Graphics usually get noticed first, even before the headline. Weak graphics give the impression of a weak publication.

Illustrations should suggest themes further expanded on in your text. They should help stimulate interest in what you have to say. Graphics that don't add meaning to a publication generally wind up detracting from that publication. Exceptions are design elements like rules and boxes that help balance or highlight other items on a page. Be careful not to overuse rules and boxes, however, or your publications may take on a cluttered look that also detracts from the appearance of your publication.

High-contrast graphics and simple line art usually work best. As the level of detail in an illustration goes up, so does the amount of effort required to understand the illustration. For example, compare the universal skull-and-crossbones symbol on containers of poisonous substances with a complicated electronic schematic. The meaning of the skull-and-crossbones is instantly obvious, even to small children. The meaning of the schematic may take hours or days and much specialized training to decipher.

Of all graphic types, photographs generate the most reader interest. Which, for example, would you prefer to page through, a catalog of designer quilt patterns or a copy of *Life Magazine*? The photographs in *Life Magazine* satisfy our curiosity about ourselves and the world around us. Quilt patterns are, well, just quilt patterns—they tell us nothing about ourselves.

One often overlooked, but highly effective graphic is the comic strip or cartoon (see fig. 1.4). Humor can be a powerful tool for eliciting reader response. For example, think of the number of people who reach first for the comic section before reading the front page of the Sunday newspaper. However, be careful when using humor. What may seem funny to some readers can turn other readers off. Humor is a two-edged sword that can deliver your message—or kill the messenger.

Fig. 1.4

A cartoon can be an effective way to convey a message to your readers.

Picking the right graphic rarely is easy. Your choices must reflect the nature of your publication and the message you are trying to convey. Your illustrations also must be eye-catching and snappy to succeed. A well-placed graphic often means the difference between gaining or losing readers. Desktop publishing is, after all, a form of visual communication.

Making Your Layout Work

Headlines, text, and graphics are the three essential ingredients making up any layout. The way you assemble these elements determines how well your composition works. When composing pages, you must think like an artist. You have to apply the fundamental concepts of good design balance, symmetry, order, and emphasis.

Using Balance, Symmetry, and Order

Balance represents the equal and harmonious distribution of weight within an environment. Because the "weights" on pages are composed of visual elements, balance includes the attributes of shape, shade, and size. You can achieve balance, for example, by offsetting darker images with lighter images or a large shape with several smaller ones.

Symmetry affects mood. An asymmetrical arrangement, for example, can seem jarring and may put off a potential reader. A symmetrical arrangement of the same elements may look familiar and feel reassuring.

Order is an outgrowth of balance and symmetry. Order represents the natural progression of a reader's eye across the page as dictated by the placement of elements. You can force the reader's eye to travel left, right, up, or down a page. Because most readers find normal left-to-right and down-the-page flow comfortable, you should try to structure your documents accordingly.

Adding Emphasis with a Dominant Element

If your layout has balance, symmetry, and order, it should work. But you still need emphasis. One dominant element must stand out from the rest.

The dominant element is the one you want the reader to notice first. An element can be dominant because of size, shape, color, intensity, unusualness, placement, or any combination of these attributes. The trick is to emphasize or exaggerate one characteristic. For example, a large, bold headline usually stands out as the dominant element on a newspaper's front page. Dominance sometimes is created unintentionally, however, as when an excess of fine print becomes the dominant element in an intimidating legal contract.

You can have only one dominant element. To have two or more equally strong elements on the same page leads to confusion, as neither can dominate. Your readers won't know where to focus their attention, and they may give up and look elsewhere.

Proofing Your Publication

To be successful as a desktop publisher, you have to proof your work. A single typo can be disastrous. Errors, no matter how few or infrequent, can jar the reader's concentration. Typos, spelling mistakes, syntax errors, missing words, wrong homonyms, and missing or incorrect punctuation can be avoided by checking your work or having others review your documents before you print them.

Watch out especially for layout errors. Missing or poorly aligned text, meaningless captions, misplaced graphics, and other omissions or inconsistencies can be as devastating as spelling, grammar, and punctuation mistakes. A little extra care ensures that your publications always make a favorable impression.

A good way not to overlook anything is to use a checklist like the following:

1. *Read through your publication to verify content.*

   See whether each paragraph stands alone in presenting a complete thought and whether successive paragraphs follow logically to a meaningful conclusion. Make sure that you place your most important ideas up front where they are read first. Also make sure that you summarize your ideas to reinforce your message.

2. *Reread each story, checking for misspellings and typos.*

   Look specifically for punctuation errors. List any errors you find and check other stories for the same mistakes. Misspellings, typos, and punctuation errors are often habitual. Increase your awareness of habitual mistakes to prevent repeating them. Whenever in doubt about spelling, don't guess—use your dictionary.

3. *Verify proper capitalization and the spelling of proper names.*

   Almost everyone loves to see his name in print. Spell a name wrong, though, and you are not likely to be forgiven quickly. If you are preparing an ad, be sure that you include the company name, address, and phone number. Also check product descriptions and prices.

4. *Double-check all symbols, abbreviations, and acronyms.*

   Avoid using symbols, abbreviations, and acronyms unless you are sure that your readers are familiar with them. If you must use an abbreviation or acronym, make sure that you do so properly. Be sure to explain less commonly known abbreviations and acronyms the first time you use them.

5. *Verify the accuracy of all numbers.*

   Look for transpositions, misplaced decimals, and incorrect totals. One wrong digit can ruin an otherwise perfect job.

6. *Check for consistency.*

   For example, don't use "percent" and "%" interchangeably within the same story. If more than one person contributes to your publication, distribute a style sheet showing preferred uses to help eliminate confusion and make proofreading easier.

7. *Verify that headings and subheads are correct and match the text that follows.*

   Also, check that stories which continue on later pages pick up where they left off on earlier pages. Look for proper paragraph indentation and spacing and watch for unsightly word gaps in justified columns caused by improper or inadequate hyphenation. Check to make sure that you are using the correct typefaces for headings, subheads, captions, and body text.

8. *Examine your layout for symmetry.*

   Boxes and rules shouldn't crowd text and illustrations, and enough space should be inserted between elements to avoid overcrowding. Make sure that centered items are correctly centered. Do a test print and check the page margins to ensure that none of your material lies outside the printable image area.

9. *Check illustrations.*

   Captions should match illustrations, and illustrations should be in the right spots. If you use photographs, check to make sure that you include the proper credits.

10. *After making corrections, proof your publication again to make sure that all changes are recorded properly.*

Use the preceding guide as a starting point for creating a detailed checklist. Let the checklist reflect your special needs and concerns. Whether you use a checklist or not, your ultimate goal should be perfection every time you publish. Using a checklist makes attaining your goal that much easier.

Printing Your Publication

The last step of the publishing process is printing your publication. After a publication is printed, the publication is ready for distribution. You want to choose the right output device and the right print shop or service bureau to process your job.

Choosing the Right Output Device

For all but the most demanding printing tasks, the output of an ordinary laser printer is fine. Most laser printers yield a minimum 300 dpi resolution, and some offer 400 and 600 dpi.

You can do your printing on a dot-matrix printer, but the results you get are far below the quality of laser printing (see figure 1.5). With a dot-matrix printer, you cannot take advantage of the many benefits of PostScript. Most of the examples and explanations in this book assume that you are using a laser printer or one of the higher resolution Linotronic ImageSetters.

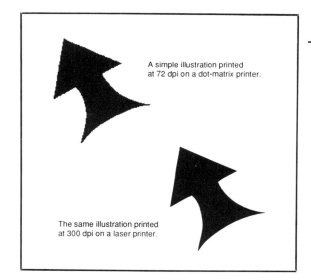

A simple illustration printed
at 72 dpi on a dot-matrix printer.

The same illustration printed
at 300 dpi on a laser printer.

Fig. 1.5

Laser-printed output is superior to output from a 72 dpi dot-matrix printer.

At times, you may prefer to use a dot-matrix printer. You can use a dot-matrix printer for preparing catalogs, informal correspondence, price lists, fliers, leaflets, and so on. Dot-matrix printers can function as proofing devices, although they do not always reflect accurately the results you get from a laser printer.

For some jobs, you may want to print color separations and take them to your printer for color reproduction. Color PostScript laser printers can be used for output, but these devices are expensive and not affordable by many users. Using a thermal-transfer or ink-jet printer, however, sometimes produces acceptable results. You also can do limited color printing on some dot-matrix printers using a multi-color ribbon and on others using separately colored ribbons for successive passes over the same page. These methods, however, are unwieldy and generally produce poor results. Color pen-plotters sometimes can be used to create quality output, especially when printing simple line art. Film recorders also offer you the ability to print high-quality color slides for presentations directly from your computer. Color copiers, available at many service bureaus, enable you to reproduce color documents in quantity.

PageMaker supports a variety of printers through A Printer Description (APD) files. These APD files are text-only documents. An APD file tells PageMaker the information needed to work with your printer. Unfortunately, many kinds of printers are not supported by APDs, and to use those printers you have to buy special connecting cables or printer driver software.

The easiest approach is to print your PageMaker documents using one of the many Aldus-supported PostScript laser printers. If you must use some other device, obtaining good quality output may be difficult or impossible, and may cost you more in time, effort, and money than the results are worth.

Choosing the Right Print Shop or Service Bureau

If you don't have ready access to a laser printer, or if your print job demands high-resolution Linotronic output, you should become acquainted with your local print service bureau. Print service bureaus usually offer laser-printer and Linotronic printing at a nominal cost. You generally pay by the sheet, but you may pay by the hour if your job is complex and takes a long time to print. Many bureaus also offer limited printing services. If your job requires more sophisticated handling, such as stripping in photos, visit a good commercial print shop. Try to find one familiar with the Macintosh and acquainted with the anomalies of desktop publishing. If you cannot find a commercial printer meeting that description, have your print service bureau operator prepare the mechanicals or film. Then, deliver the mechanicals or film to the print shop with instructions for final processing.

In most cases, you have to produce only one master copy of your publication. Duplicate copies can be made at small cost using a high-speed copier and the paper of your choice.

Be careful about making alterations late in the print cycle. Author's alterations are subject to extra premiums and often start a new and costly billing cycle. Discuss the entire printing cycle in detail with your printer and agree beforehand on what each item and each step of the process costs. Get a signed estimate before committing. When your copies are printed, they still may need to be cut, folded, and bound before they are ready for distribution. Most commercial print shops and service bureaus can handle these tasks without difficulty.

When looking for a print shop or service bureau, be sure to shop around carefully. You may find a wide variation in printing costs and work quality. Pick a shop with a reputation for meeting deadlines and satisfying customers.

Chapter Summary

In this chapter, you acquired an overview of the entire desktop publishing cycle, starting with the conceptual stage and ending with a printed document ready for distribution. You now understand the philosophy behind each step. You learned that publishing is more than assembling words and pictures on a page— you need to adhere to certain basic design principles if you want to achieve consistently good results.

You saw that every layout has three key elements—headlines, text, and graphics. You have a clear idea of how to make these elements work for you. You know how to evaluate your work and how to do those all-important reviews that make the difference between error-free and error-filled publications. You learned how stories and artwork combine to attract reader interest, and you now know what it takes to be successful, even when the competition gets tough.

Most importantly, you acquired a deeper appreciation of what desktop publishing is all about. You have taken the first step toward creating professional-looking publications. You now are ready to begin learning the mechanics of using PageMaker.

PageMaker Basics

In this chapter, you learn the basics of working with PageMaker. If you are new to the Macintosh, you may want to review Appendix B, "Installing PageMaker and Configuring Your System." This appendix helps you configure your operating environment so that PageMaker can operate at its best.

If you feel comfortable working with your Macintosh and have installed Page-Maker, you can get started. This chapter introduces you to the main components in the PageMaker environment—the pasteboard, toolbox, rulers, page icons, and page. You learn what these components do and how to use the components. You also learn how to move around your publications and view pages at different magnifications. You discover how to open and edit documents and how to save and print your work. If you get stuck at any point, PageMaker's on-line help can get you moving again.

PageMaker is a "page layout" or "page makeup" program in which you can assemble text and graphics created elsewhere. You import text and graphics and then rearrange these elements on your pages to produce finished publications. Although PageMaker has many advanced text editing and graphics refinement features rivaling those of stand-alone programs, the concept of page assembly remains unchanged. Most of your work is directed at producing attractive, functional layouts.

PageMaker combines several traditional publishing tools within the framework of one easy-to-use software program. You no longer need T-squares, compasses, triangles, X-ACTO knives, ruling pens, and other traditional implements to prepare your publications. However, you still need to assemble and review your articles, illustrations, and preliminary layout sketches before getting started.

Never skip the prepublication review process. You should begin work at PageMaker's electronic drawing table only when you have all the pieces laid out in front of you. If you open PageMaker and start importing and rearranging items on your pages, you may find that the finished document looks disorganized. Your publications also become more difficult and take longer to produce if you don't plan ahead. Planning your pages before laying out the pages is essential to producing quality work.

Opening PageMaker

You open PageMaker like any other Macintosh program—double-click the Page-Maker icon or highlight the icon and select Open from the File menu. The first display you see is PageMaker's start-up screen, which shows the Aldus logo, program version number, and copyright credits. After a few seconds, the screen changes to show the name, company, and serial number that you entered during installation (see Appendix B for installation instructions). This screen is similar to the screen displayed when you select About PageMaker from the Apple menu, except that the About PageMaker screen also tells you which operating system version you are using and how much memory you have left for other programs to use after PageMaker is loaded (see fig.2.1).

Fig. 2.1

*The About
PageMaker
display.*

The About PageMaker display also contains a Help button. Clicking this button accesses PageMaker's on-line help information. (See the section, "Getting Help," later in this chapter for details about using PageMaker's on-line Help.)

Note

Hold down the Shift key when you choose About PageMaker from the Apple menu for a slide show listing of key people who played a role in the creation of PageMaker. Hold down the Command key when you choose About PageMaker from the Apple menu to get a scrollable listing of all installed dictionaries and import and export filters.

After PageMaker is loaded, the start-up screen disappears.

Viewing the Publication Window

When you open a new or existing file, depending on which Page Setup dialog box options you select, one or more pages are displayed in PageMaker's publication window. The publication window includes the pasteboard (PageMaker's equivalent of the traditional drawing table) and the current page or pages on which you are working. Several other elements also appear: the toolbox; a set of horizontal and vertical rulers; and a row of numbered, dog-eared page icons. These elements, along with the usual menus, scroll bars, and other Macintosh fixtures, make up the primary components of PageMaker's user interface.

Using the Pasteboard

PageMaker's *pasteboard* is like the surface of a large work table. The pasteboard surrounds the pages of your publication and extends beyond the immediate window boundaries. You can adjust the page view or scroll your publication window to see more of the pasteboard area. Think of the pasteboard as a temporary holding area for storing text and graphics. You can drag items from your pages to the pasteboard and from the pasteboard onto your pages.

Tip

To quickly move a block of text, a design element, an illustration, or a photograph to a new page without cutting and pasting via the Clipboard, do the following:

1. Drag the item off the page onto the surrounding pasteboard.

2. Turn to the new page.

3. Drag the item from the pasteboard onto the new page.

This shortcut works because PageMaker's pasteboard remains constant as you switch from page to page. Items stored on the pasteboard are available no matter what page you turn to. The contents of the pasteboard also get saved with your publication; the contents are there the next time you open that publication. Items stored on the pasteboard, however, do not print.

> **Warning**
>
> Any item on the pasteboard that barely touches the edge of a page stays with that page; the item doesn't reappear on the pasteboard when you turn to another part of your publication.

You can create text and graphics directly on the pasteboard using PageMaker's various tools. You then can drag the items you create onto your pages. This capability enables you to work with a clear view uncluttered by columns, grid lines, text, or graphics. The pasteboard is a great place for creating and editing headlines, cropping and scaling graphics, customizing graphic boundaries for text wrap, and experimenting with reversals (white elements set against a dark background).

Using the Toolbox

PageMaker's toolbox contains eight tools that select and modify elements; create and edit text; draw lines, rectangles, and ovals; and crop illustrations. Figure 2.2 shows these various tools. If you do not see the toolbox, choose Toolbox from the Windows menu. The toolbox appears.

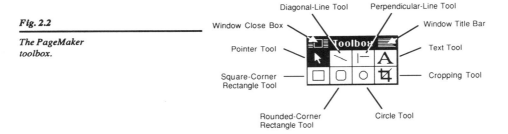

Fig. 2.2

The PageMaker toolbox.

You can hide PageMaker's toolbox whenever you want to gain an unobstructed view of your work. Choose the Toolbox command under the Windows menu or click the close box in the upper left corner of the toolbox itself. To redisplay the Toolbox, choose the Toolbox command under the Windows menu again. You can toggle the display by typing Command-6.

Using the Pointer Tool

The *pointer tool* is shaped like an arrow. In PageMaker, you use the pointer tool primarily to move and resize graphics and columns of text. To move an object, position the tip of the arrow over that object, press the mouse button, and while keeping the mouse button held down, drag the object. This technique is called *click-*

dragging. If you hold down the Shift key while you click-drag, you confine object movement to horizontal or vertical directions.

To resize an object, like a graphic or block of text, click the object with the pointer tool. Then position the tip of the arrow over any of the small black reshaping handles that appear and click-drag. This action changes the dimensions of the object.

Any tool that you use in PageMaker changes into a pointer tool whenever you move the cursor outside the publication window. This effect enables you to pull down menus, click page icons, and operate scroll bars without first selecting the pointer tool from the toolbox. You also can change any tool temporarily into a pointer tool by pressing Command-space bar. Press Command-space bar a second time to change the pointer tool back into the tool you were using.

Using Diagonal-Line and Perpendicular-Line Tools

The *diagonal-line tool* cursor looks like a crosshair. You use this tool to draw lines, or *rules*, at any angle. Click the center of the crosshair where you want the line to begin. Then hold down the mouse button and drag. Release the mouse button when the rule is the length you want. Press the Shift key as you use the diagonal-line tool to draw horizontal and vertical rules angled at multiples of 45 degrees.

Using the *perpendicular-line tool* is the same as using the diagonal-line tool while pressing the Shift key. You get horizontal and vertical rules angled at multiples of 45 degrees. Using the perpendicular-line tool is more convenient than remembering to press the Shift key as you draw with the diagonal-line tool.

With these tools, rule thickness is determined by your choice of widths from the Line menu. Eight widths are available, ranging from hairline to 12 points. Attractive multiple-line styles and an assortment of dashed lines also are available. You also can reverse any line so that the line appears white against a dark background. By making menu selections before drawing your rules, you turn your choices into default settings that apply to all new rules. If you select an existing line, or group of lines, before choosing a menu command, your menu choice affects those selections only, and the default settings remain unchanged.

Lines or rules are design elements used often in publications to partition stories, break up large chunks of material into smaller areas on the page, and generally add visual interest to your documents. To learn more about using rules, see Chapters 10 and 11.

Using the Text Tool

The *text tool* has an I-beam cursor similar to cursors used in most word processing programs. You can use the text tool to select, edit, and create text. If you position the text tool anywhere within an existing block of text and click, you can back space to delete existing text or type new text for insertion. If you click and drag the cursor, you can select text character by character. Double-clicking and dragging is a shortcut that selects text on a word-by-word basis. Another shortcut, triple-clicking, selects an entire paragraph (all text up to and including the carriage return). Triple-clicking and dragging through multiple paragraphs selects the entire range of paragraphs instantly.

Another shortcut enables you to select any range of text, even across many pages. First, you click to position the cursor at the starting point in the range of text. You then move your cursor to the end of the range, hold down the Shift key, and click. All the text between your first and last clicked positions is selected.

To create a block of text with a certain column width, choose the text tool and click-drag anywhere on the page or pasteboard away from other text. (To click-drag, position the cursor over the item and hold down the mouse button while dragging the mouse.) This technique determines the width of your column. As you drag the text tool, the tool produces a ghost outline of the enclosed area. The outline disappears when you release the mouse button, but PageMaker remembers the column width. You can start typing immediately. As you type, text wraps to fit within the column boundary.

Using the Square-Corner Rectangle, Rounded-Corner Rectangle, and Circle Tools

The square-corner rectangle, rounded-corner rectangle, and circle tools all work alike. Each cursor is shaped like a crosshair and is used to draw its representative shape by dragging with the mouse button held down. To get perfect squares and circles, press the Shift key as you drag the cursor.

The rectangles and ovals you create using PageMaker's drawing tools are all objects. You can fill these objects with shades and patterns, and you can change their border (line) thicknesses. Select the object using the pointer tool and then choose the appropriate shade or pattern using the Fill command and the appropriate line width or style using the Line command. Both commands are found under the Element menu.

When you first draw an object, the object is selected. The object remains selected until you click elsewhere to draw another object or you choose another tool from the toolbox. You then can assign different fills and borders after drawing each object.

Rectangles and ovals are design elements like the diagonal and perpendicular lines. You learn more about using rectangles and ovals throughout the remainder of this book (see also Chapters 10 and 11).

Using the Cropping Tool

The *cropping tool* enables you to crop or trim illustrations within PageMaker to improve their appearance and make the illustrations fit your layouts. Using the cropping tool, you click a graphic to select it. You then click-drag any of the reshaping handles (the small black squares) that appear. To drag a reshaping handle, place the cropping tool icon on top of the handle. The icon changes to a pair of arrows signifying the directions you can crop the image. Drag the handle inward in the direction you want to crop; outlying areas of your image disappear. Notice, however, that the graphic doesn't change size. As you trim away the edges, the overall dimensions get smaller, but the picture doesn't change. The areas you trim can be recovered by dragging the reshaping handle in the opposite (outward) direction.

You also can pan a cropped graphic within its frame. You may want to pan a graphic, for example, to center the image. To pan a cropped image, position the cropping tool above the image and press the mouse button. After a brief instant, the cropping tool changes into a hand tool. Still holding down the mouse button, move the hand tool in the direction you want to slide the image. As long as you continue to press the mouse button, you can move the image. Release the mouse button when you are satisfied with the display (see fig. 2.3).

Fig. 2.3

Cropping and centering imported graphics.

Cropping tool /   Hand tool

The scanned image in figure 2.3 is larger than the predrawn box into which the image is expected to fit. You use PageMaker's cropping tool to trim the graphic to fit within the box; the size of the image doesn't change. Finally, you use the cropping tool to adjust the display. Pan the image slightly by moving the image up and to the left to conceal the thick border lines.

Only imported graphics can be cropped. Graphics created within PageMaker are exempt from cropping. You resize and reshape graphics by using the tools with which the graphics were created.

The toolbox does not impede the use of any tool. PageMaker's palettes all "float" above the page, so that when drawing a line or box, for example, you can drag from one side of a palette to the other without moving the palette out of the way. If you want to move a palette out of the way to better view your work, click the title bar and drag the palette to another location.

Using Rulers

PageMaker has two rulers. One ruler runs vertically down the left side of the publication window. The other ruler runs horizontally across the top of the window. Dotted markers travel the lengths of each ruler to pinpoint the exact location of your cursor on the page, which enables you to position text and graphics precisely. You can hide PageMaker's rulers by unchecking the Rulers command on the Options menu.

The Preferences command under the Edit menu enables you to preset the rulers to different units of measurements. Pop-up menus enable you to choose fractional inches, decimal inches, millimeters, picas, and ciceros (a European unit of measure for determining type size). You can configure the vertical ruler independently of the horizontal ruler. Figure 2.4 shows the Preferences dialog box.

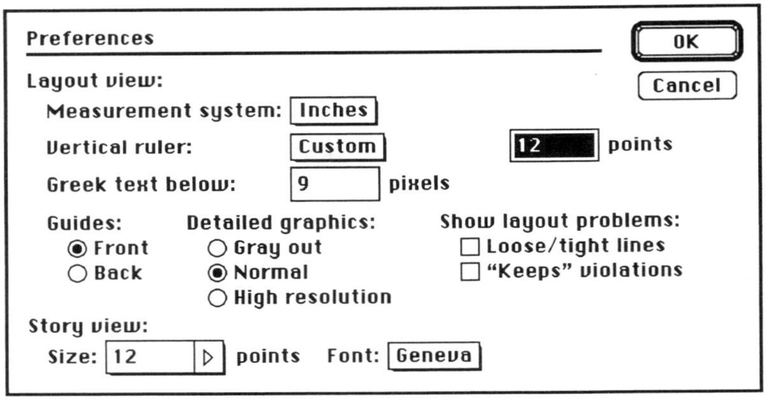

Fig. 2.4

PageMaker's Preferences dialog box.

```
Preferences                                          [  OK  ]
Layout view:                                         [ Cancel ]
   Measurement system: [ Inches ]
   Vertical ruler:      [ Custom ]         [ 12 ] points
   Greek text below:    [ 9 ] pixels
   Guides:      Detailed graphics:     Show layout problems:
   ● Front      ○ Gray out             ☐ Loose/tight lines
   ○ Back       ● Normal               ☐ "Keeps" violations
                ○ High resolution
Story view:
   Size: [ 12  ▷ ] points   Font: [ Geneva ]
```

Note

Six picas equal 1 inch, and 12 points equal 1 pica. A point is roughly 1/72 inch—equal to one display pixel on most Macintosh monitors. (*Pixels* are the tiny square black dots that make up your screen image.) As a rule of thumb, twelve pixels of horizontal or vertical spacing represent one pica when laying out your publications.

Tip

You can override the preset measurement values for any of PageMaker's dialog boxes by typing the appropriate letter designation for the kind of measurement you want to substitute. If your rulers are set for inches and you prefer picas, for example, type *p* after each value that you enter. PageMaker handles the substitution automatically. You learn more about this technique in Chapter 3.

Tip

If you choose **Custom** for the vertical ruler and type a point size of your choosing in the points field, you can force the vertical ruler divisions to correspond to a given line spacing. Then the vertical ruler divisions (tick marks) can match the line leading exactly. (You learn how to specify leading in Chapter 6.) You can use this feature to calculate the depth of a column by doing a simple line count. For this process to work, however, the assigned leading must equal the value you type in the Preferences dialog box. For example, if you type *12* in the points box, PageMaker adjusts the vertical ruler to match 12-point line leading. Counting the number of ruler increments, then, gives you the vertical line count for a column of type set with 12-point leading.

You can reset the zero markers for both of PageMaker's rulers wherever you like. Resetting the zero markers makes measuring the size or distance to any element on your page easy. Note the crossed-lines icon in the upper-left corner of the publication window at the point where the rulers intersect (see fig. 2.5). If you position your cursor over the crossed lines and click-drag, the cursor changes into a giant crosshair that spans the entire window. As you move the cursor across the page, the dotted ruler markers follow the rulers so that you can position the cursor accurately. The spot in which you release the mouse button becomes the new zero point. You can anchor the zero markers by choosing the Zero Lock command on the Options menu.

The rulers also serve as the source for PageMaker's nonprinting vertical and horizontal ruler guides. You learn more about this feature in Chapter 3.

Moving around in Your Document

Clicking the page-shaped icons at the bottom left of your publication window enables you to browse through a document quickly (see fig. 2.6). When you click

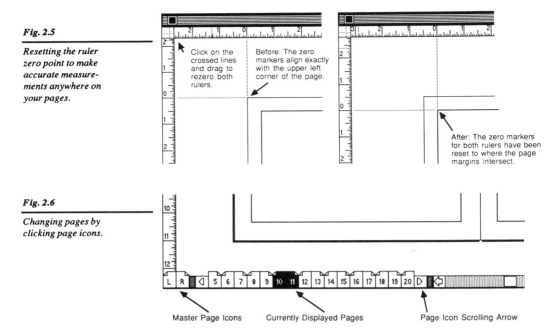

Fig. 2.5

Resetting the ruler zero point to make accurate measurements anywhere on your pages.

Click on the crossed lines and drag to rezero both rulers.

Before: The zero markers align exactly with the upper left corner of the page.

After: The zero markers for both rulers have been reset to where the page margins intersect.

Fig. 2.6

Changing pages by clicking page icons.

Master Page Icons   Currently Displayed Pages   Page Icon Scrolling Arrow

a numbered page icon, PageMaker displays the corresponding page (or facing pages). Icons for currently displayed pages are highlighted.

If your document contains more pages than the screen has room to display, small arrows appear at both ends of the row. Click these arrows to scroll through the numbered page icons one at a time. If you continue to press the mouse button after clicking an arrow, the pages begin to whiz by; release the mouse button to stop the pages. If you hold down the Command key as you click either arrow, PageMaker takes you to that end of the row instantly and displays the first or last page in your publication.

The pair of page icons at the far left of the row (one icon only may be showing if you did not set up your publication to view facing pages) represents your master pages. You use *master pages* to hold any elements that you want to repeat on every page throughout your publication. Click the master page icons to jump directly to the master pages display. To learn more about using master pages, see Chapter 3.

You can jump to any page in your publication by choosing the Go To Page command from the Page menu or pressing Command-G, an equivalent keyboard shortcut. When the Go To Page dialog box appears, type the desired page number and press Return or Enter (see fig. 2.7). (Pressing Return or Enter is the same as clicking the OK button.) To return to the page you just left, choose the Go To Page command and press Return or Enter—PageMaker remembers the last page you were on and displays that number in the dialog box. If you choose Go To Page from the Page

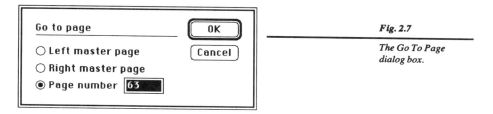

Fig. 2.7

*The Go To Page
dialog box.*

menu while pressing the Shift key, PageMaker steps through each page in slide-show sequence, starting with page one. Click the mouse button to stop on any page.

To move forward in your document one page at a time, press Command-Tab; to skip back a page, press Command-Shift-Tab. If you hold down these keys instead of just pressing and releasing the keys, you steadily move forward or backward (but slower than if you held down the mouse button after clicking a page-icon arrow).

Viewing Your Publication

PageMaker provides eight levels of magnification to zoom in and zoom out on your work. Seven levels are listed under the Page menu; the other level is somewhat obscure, but equally important. When you pull down the Page menu, you see the first seven levels listed as separate entries. In order, the seven levels of magnification are Fit in Window, 25% Size, 50% Size, 75% Size, Actual Size, 200% Size, and 400% Size. Each of these viewing commands has a keystroke equivalent, shown on the Page menu, that you can execute directly from the keyboard (see fig. 2.8).

Page	
✓Fit in window	⌘W
25% size	⌘0
50% size	⌘5
75% size	⌘7
Actual size	**⌘1**
200% size	⌘2
400% size	⌘4
Go to page...	⌘G
Insert pages...	
Remove pages...	
✓Display master items	
Copy master guides	

Fig. 2.8

The Page menu.

The Actual Size command indicates that the page display you see on-screen is the same size as when printed. If you work on a standard 8.5-by-11-inch page, for example, your page on-screen is shown at actual 8.5-by-11-inch size. With the other viewing commands, you see your pages scaled by some percentage of actual size.

Fit in Window reduces your pages, single or facing, so that the pages fit entirely within the publication window (see fig. 2.9).

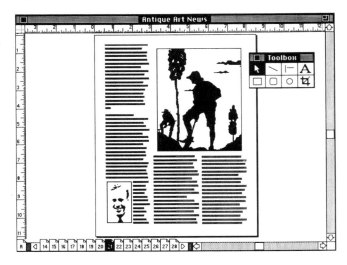

The missing level of magnification is the Fit in World size. Fit in World reduces your page and the surrounding pasteboard so that both fit entirely within the confines of the publication window (see fig. 2.10). This viewing command is accessible only from the Page menu and by choosing Fit in Window while pressing the Shift key. Fit in World enables you to easily access text and graphics stored on the surrounding pasteboard.

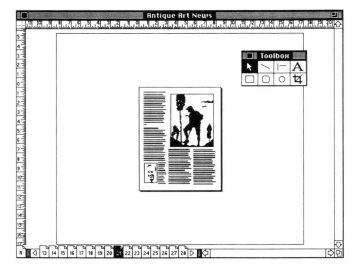

> **Tip**
>
> To view any page in the Fit in Window view, click its page icon while holding down the Shift key.

Enlarged views are indispensable for positioning elements accurately on your pages. Enlarged views are especially helpful for doing detailed work, such as aligning adjoining columns of text. Reduced views, on the other hand, enable you to examine your work with a more global perspective. Drawing a vertical column rule, for example, can be awkward unless you work using a reduced-page view. Choose a view appropriate for the task at hand so that your work goes smoothly.

In reduced views, small text usually is represented by lines of gray shading, called *Greeking*. Greeking text at small sizes (when reading is difficult) enables your computer screen to refresh more quickly than if each character has to be redrawn individually. Greeking text greatly speeds page makeup within a production environment. You can change the pixel size below which Greeking occurs by typing a new value in the Preferences dialog box.

> **Tip**
>
> To speed up screen redraws, consider changing the Greeking value to a larger number of pixels in the Preferences dialog box. PageMaker takes considerably less time to redraw pages displaying all Greeked text.

Another useful way to move about on your pages is to press the Option key and click the mouse anywhere in the publication window. No matter what tool you select, the cursor changes into a grabber hand. If you continue to press the mouse button, you can slide your pages and the pasteboard in any direction. The screen is updated when you release the mouse button.

You also can move through your document using the standard horizontal and vertical scroll bars. Most Macintosh programs have these bars, and PageMaker's scroll bars work in the usual fashion. *Scroll bars* are useful when you have to shift your page view slightly and you don't want to change your page magnification. The actual amount of movement that results when you click a scroll bar varies, depending on the page magnification. You can hide the scroll bars and page icons to see more of your publication by unchecking the Scroll Bars command under the Windows menu.

At times, you may want to work on a part of the page that lies outside the immediate viewing area. Using the scroll bars or the grabber hand to get there can be tedious. Both are too slow, and you cannot see where you are going. Fortunately, a shortcut enables you to race around your pages like a jackrabbit. You can click exactly where you want to end up and get there as fast as your screen can refresh. You don't have to fuss with scroll bars, the grabber hand, or menu commands.

If you are working on an actual-size page, for example, pressing Option-Command-Click takes you to the Fit in Window view. Pressing Option-Command-Click again takes you back to an actual-size view. The page and pasteboard are centered about the spot where you just clicked in the Fit in Window view. This shortcut gives you a speedy way to jump instantly from one spot on a page to another.

In the same way, pressing Option-Command-Shift-Click takes you to a 200% view with the page centered about the spot where you clicked. Option-Command-Shift-Click or Option-Command-Click takes you back to an actual-size view.

Holding down the Option key while choosing a page magnification from the Page menu assigns that page view to all pages in your publication, which is a quick way, for example, to reset all pages to Fit in Window size after you finish working on your layout.

Tip

Another way to get around your pages quickly is to *auto scroll*. Select the pointer tool and then click-drag the cursor to just off the screen in the opposite direction you want the window to scroll. Continue pressing the mouse button until the desired area of the page rolls into view. Your window stops scrolling the moment you release the mouse button.

Getting Help

Until you gain proficiency with PageMaker, you may forget how to do something. Looking up the solution in PageMaker's manuals or this book is the best way to learn and to refresh your memory. Occasionally, however, you may be in a hurry. PageMaker provides on-line Help, therefore, to supply quick answers to your questions.

You can access PageMaker's on-line Help in several ways. You can choose the Help command under the Windows menu; you can press the Help key on extended keyboards; you can choose the About PageMaker command under the Apple menu and then click the Help button; or you can type Command-?. This last method is a shortcut to getting specific, context-sensitive help information. Your cursor changes into a question mark. Use this question-mark cursor to choose any menu command or type a keyboard command-equivalent. PageMaker's Help dialog appears instantly. PageMaker intercepts the keyboard command and matches the command to the appropriate menu item. For example, pressing Command-? and using the question-mark cursor to choose the Type Specs command from the Type menu brings up the Help window shown in figure 2.11.

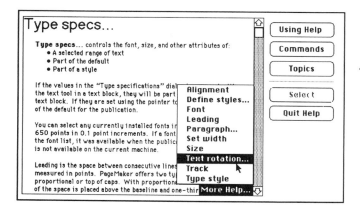

Fig. 2.11

*The Aldus on-line
Help screen.*

Warning

If you remap your keyboard using a utility such as QuicKeys from CE Software, PageMaker substitutes the contextual help information for the newly assigned commands. Suppose that you reassign the keystroke combination Command-A to execute Save As instead of Select All. When you type Command-A, PageMaker displays the help information for Save As, not Select All. To get help with Select All, you have to choose the Select All command under the Edit menu using the question-mark cursor.

The main Help screen has several options. Clicking the Using Help button displays information about navigating PageMaker's on-line Help. Clicking the Commands button displays a scrollable list of all PageMaker commands. You double-click any item listed (or select the item and click the Select button) to bring up its associated help information.

The Topics button works the same way as the Commands button, but you get a list of topics dealing with various aspects of using PageMaker. A pop-up More Help menu in the lower-right corner of the information window lists related topics. You choose a related topic from the pop-up menu to jump directly to that topic. PageMaker's Help facility is for only on-line use. You cannot copy information from Help to the Clipboard. For example, choosing Text Rotation from the pop-up More Help menu in figure 2.11 displays specific help information about rotating blocks of text.

Saving Your Work

With PageMaker, you can save documents in one of two formats as publications or as templates. You indicate your preference in the Save As dialog box. If you choose the Save command from the File menu (press Command-S as a shortcut), Page-Maker resaves your document under its current name and in the same format as when opened. To save a copy of your document under a different name or to convert the document into a different format, use the Save As command (there is no assigned keyboard shortcut for Save As). If you are working on a new publication, the Save and Save As commands bring up the Save As dialog box. You name your file, choose an appropriate format, and tell PageMaker where to store the file on disk.

Warning

With PageMaker, you can replace a publication on disk with a template of the same name; you also can replace a template with a publication of the same name. The only warning you get is the standard dialog box asking whether you want to replace the file of the same name. If you want to replace the file, fine. If you click the wrong format button in the Save As dialog box, however, you may write over your only copy of an important template.

You can prevent this loss by selecting your template in the Finder and choosing Get Info from the File menu. Click the Locked box that appears in the upper-right corner of the Get Info dialog box. After you lock the template file, you cannot save changes to the template unless you unlock the file first.

Save your work frequently. You never know when you may suffer a sudden power outage or computer malfunction. Even if you haven't saved your most recent changes, however, you still may be able to recover most of your work intact. PageMaker has a built-in automatic feature that helps prevent data loss.

When you change Page Setup specifications, add or delete pages, turn to a new page in your publication, copy, or print, PageMaker does a mini-save. This mini-save produces a complete copy of your publication as the file exists prior to any changes. You can revert to the last mini-save version of your file at any time by choosing Revert from the File menu while pressing the Shift key. To restore the last version you saved using the Save or Save As command, choose Revert without pressing the Shift key.

Tip

You can force a quick mini-save at any time with a single click of the mouse. Click the highlighted page icon at the bottom of the publication window. Because the highlighted icon represents the current page, no page turning occurs, and you can continue working uninterrupted. You benefit by protecting your most recent changes without updating or altering your last-saved version.

Tip

When you save a document by using the Save command, you retain quite a bit of excess baggage, including information about recently deleted text and graphics. PageMaker needs this data to recover the current file using its mini-save feature if a sudden power outage or computer malfunction occurs. Storing this excess data causes PageMaker files to grow quickly to huge proportions. Eventually, you may not be able to transfer a file to a floppy disk. If you use a modem to send PageMaker files to a service bureau, your telecommunications costs can soar.

To counteract this unrestrained file growth, choose Save As from the File menu instead of Save. Using the Save As command as the final step in archiving a publication deletes all excess data needed for mini-saving and shrinks the file to a fraction of its previous size.

After you save a file using Save or Save As, you don't need mini-save to recover the data. Using Save, however, doesn't delete the excess baggage.

Printing Your Publication

Chapter 9 is devoted to the subject of printing PageMaker documents. In Chapter 9, you learn about different printing options, including using alternate drivers, printing color, and using a Linotronic ImageSetter. Briefly, you print PageMaker documents by choosing the Print command from under the File menu, which brings up the Aldus Print dialog box.

The Aldus Print dialog box gives you more options than the standard Apple dialog box (see fig. 2.12). Some of these options you may want to use right away. Straightforward choices include selecting the number of copies to be printed, printing a specific page range, scaling your page output, and choosing a paper source (**Paper tray** or **Manual feed**). These options work the same as their counterparts in the standard Apple Print dialog box.

```
Print to:  LaserWriter II NTX                    [  Print  ]

Copies: [1]    □ Collate  □ Reverse order        [  Cancel ]
Page range: ⦿ All  ○ From [1]   to [51]          ·····················
Paper source: ⦿ Paper tray  ○ Manual feed        [ Options... ]
Scaling: [100] %  □ Thumbnails, [16] per page     [PostScript...]
Book: ○ Print this pub only  ○ Print entire book

Printer: [LaserWriter II NTX]        Paper: [Letter]
Size:       8.5 X 11.0   inches      Tray:  ⦿ Select
Print area: 8.0 X 10.8   inches
```

You should check one thing before you print, especially if you are on a network with more than one printer attached. The lower-left corner of the Print dialog box contains a pop-up menu labeled Printer. Make sure that the name of the correct output device shows. If the name is wrong, use the Chooser desk accessory under the Apple menu to effect a printer change. If you have questions about using Chooser, refer to the manual that came with your Macintosh.

Quitting PageMaker

To exit PageMaker, choose Quit from the File menu. You are prompted to save your work if you haven't done so already. You also can close your current publication by choosing Close from the Edit menu. PageMaker remains open so that you can open another new or existing publication to work on.

Tip

Before quitting PageMaker, save a backup copy of your publication to another disk. A backup comes in handy if you ever damage or ruin the original disk. Choose Save As from the File menu and insert a floppy disk (or select a different hard disk location using the dialog box that appears). Rename your publication to distinguish the backup from the original. You may want to append the characters BU or BAK after the file name to indicate that the file is a backup copy. Click the OK button to save the backup copy to the new location.

Chapter Summary

In this chapter, you learned how to open new and existing documents, set document size, adjust page orientation, assign page numbers, and configure margins.

You were introduced to PageMaker's publication window with its pasteboard, toolbox, rulers, and page icons. You gained familiarity with each of these items and now can move about freely in a PageMaker publication.

You also discovered that PageMaker offers an abundance of shortcuts for quickly moving about in your publications and for viewing pages. You learned how to access on-line help when needed. Finally, you learned how to save your work and how to print using PageMaker's Print dialog box.

Now that you have covered the basics of working with PageMaker, you are ready to move on to Chapter 3, in which you learn how to create documents.

Creating a Document

In this chapter, you study the most important steps to take when creating a publication. You begin by opening a new document and configuring the Page Setup dialog box. You learn how to customize PageMaker's default settings to eliminate the need to reconfigure the settings for each new document. Then you learn how to use PageMaker's master pages—a powerful, timesaving feature that enables you to place text and graphics that repeat on every page throughout your publication.

You also learn how to develop and refine layouts using non-printing guides to align text and graphics. You discover the secrets of using a grid to help structure your documents. Finally, you learn how to use PageMaker's rulers and measuring system to position elements accurately on your pages.

When you finish this chapter, you will be ready to start creating your own publications.

Opening and Setting Up a Document

To open a new document, choose New from the File menu. PageMaker's Page Setup dialog box appears (see fig. 3.1). In this dialog box, you define your publication's page size using the pop-up Page menu. You set the page orientation and page margins. You indicate whether your document is to have double-sided pages and whether you want to work with facing pages (two pages displayed side by side on-screen at the same time).

You also assign a starting page number and specify the number of pages your publication contains. Clicking the Numbers button brings up a second dialog box in which you choose a page-numbering style and table of contents and index prefix. (You learn more about creating tables of contents and indexes in Chapter 6.) After you make your selections and click the OK buttons, PageMaker displays the first page of your blank publication.

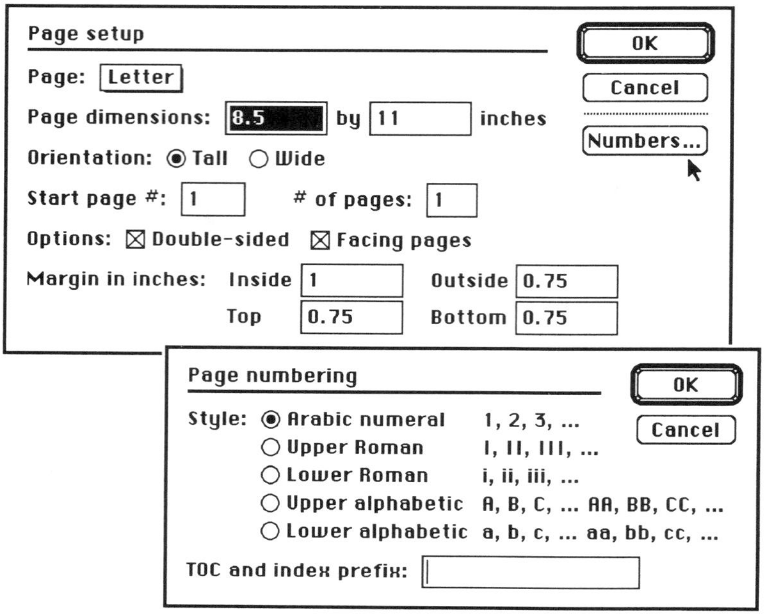

Fig. 3.1

PageMaker's Page Setup dialog box with options that determine the physical appearance of your pages.

```
Page setup                                    [    OK    ]

Page: [Letter]                                [  Cancel  ]

Page dimensions: [8.5      ] by [11      ] inches
                                              [ Numbers... ]
Orientation: ● Tall  ○ Wide

Start page #: [1    ]    # of pages: [1    ]

Options: ☒ Double-sided  ☒ Facing pages

Margin in inches:  Inside [1    ]      Outside [0.75 ]
                      Top [0.75 ]      Bottom [0.75 ]
```

```
Page numbering                                [    OK    ]

Style: ● Arabic numeral      1, 2, 3, ...     [  Cancel  ]
       ○ Upper Roman         I, II, III, ...
       ○ Lower Roman         i, ii, iii, ...
       ○ Upper alphabetic    A, B, C, ... AA, BB, CC, ...
       ○ Lower alphabetic    a, b, c, ... aa, bb, cc, ...

TOC and index prefix: [                    ]
```

When the Page Setup dialog box first appears, default settings exist for every option. You learn how to create default settings under "Setting Document Defaults," later in this chapter. You can change any page specification default in the Page Setup dialog box when you open a new document. You also can change these settings at any later time by selecting Page Setup from the File menu.

Tip

A quick way to move through any dialog box in PageMaker, instead of clicking your cursor in each field, is to use the Tab key. Every time you press Tab, a different field in the dialog box is highlighted. You can type a new value in the highlighted field and then Tab to the next field. When you reach the last field, pressing Tab cycles you back to the starting field.

Determining Page Size and Orientation

The original default settings in the Page Setup dialog box are for a standard 8.5-by-11-inch vertical page. To select legal (8.5-by-14-inch page), tabloid (11-by-17-inch page), or a custom size, choose the appropriate command from the pop-up Page menu (see fig. 3.2). The correct page dimensions appear in the fields when you make your choice. These fields follow the accepted convention of listing the page width first. Page dimensions are shown in inches unless you choose a different measurement system, such as picas or millimeters, using the Preferences command under the Edit menu.

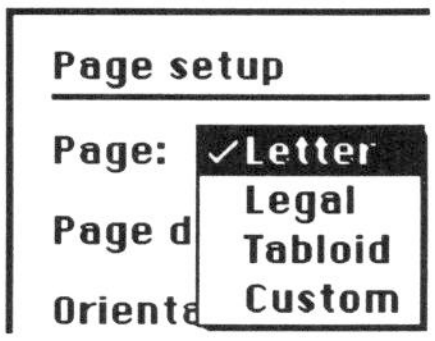

Fig. 3.2

The pop-up Page menu.

You can define custom page sizes for special jobs by typing the desired dimensions directly into the appropriate fields. When you enter a page dimension manually, the pop-up Page menu switches to display Custom as the selected size.

PageMaker can create pages up to 17 by 22 inches, but generally you select a page size no larger than what your printer can handle (consult your printer manual for page-size specifications). If you must print oversized pages, tile your output. You learn about tiling oversized pages in Chapter 9.

For the page **Orientation** option, you can pick **Tall** for a vertical (portrait) page or **Wide** for a horizontal (landscape) page. Whatever your choice, the page orientation remains constant. You cannot mix different page orientations within the same publication.

Selecting the Starting Page and Number of Pages

The **Start page #** and **# of pages** settings tell PageMaker on which page to begin numbering your publication and how many pages you initially plan to include. These choices don't have to be exact. PageMaker first creates the number of pages you indicate, but you can change that number later to accommodate new publication-length requirements.

You can change the **Start page #** setting at any time by choosing Page Setup from the File menu and typing a new value. The initial **# of pages** setting, however, is fixed, unless you manually add or delete pages using the appropriate menu commands. You learn how to add and delete pages in Chapter 6.

You can number pages sequentially from 1 to 9,999, but PageMaker limits you to 999 pages for any one publication. If you plan a publication longer than 999 pages, break the document into separate files. The **Start page #** setting in the Page Setup dialog box enables you to renumber the first page of each file so all the pages show sequential numbering when you print the pages.

For example, a 1,200-page publication must be divided into at least two files. If you make the first file 800 pages long and the second one 400 pages long, you can set **Start page #** for the second file to 801. PageMaker numbers the pages in the second file 801 through 1,200. When you print both files, the pages of your assembled publication are numbered properly from 1 to 1,200.

You learn how to set up your publication for automatic page numbering later in this chapter.

Tip

The original default setting for **# of pages** is 1 for new documents. By changing that number to a larger value whenever you open a new publication, you may find that experimenting with different layouts is easier, because you don't have to insert additional pages manually. Later, you can add or remove pages as needed to obtain the correct final page count.

Tip

Breaking lengthy publications into multiple sections having fewer than the maximum allowable pages is a good idea. If you break a 2,400-page book into three 800-page sections instead of two 999-page sections and one 402-page section, for example, you have room to expand earlier chapters to make editing changes that call for adding text or graphics.

Using the Double-Sided and Facing Pages Options

When you click **Double-sided** in the Page Setup dialog box, PageMaker configures facing pages so that their inner margins lie along the spine of your publication. Facing pages mirror one another. PageMaker displays odd-numbered facing pages on the right and even-numbered pages on the left. You click the **Facing pages** box to view facing pages on-screen. This option is available only if the **Double-sided** box is checked. Viewing facing pages makes it easier to build symmetrical layouts.

> *Tip*
>
> If you are working against a deadline and want to speed up screen redraws when changing page views, don't check the **Facing pages** box. PageMaker takes longer to redraw two pages instead of one.

Generally, you want to make the inside margin of your publication larger than the outside margin. This setting compensates for the page area lost when you bind your publication. Determine beforehand how much edge you lose and then adjust the inside margin accordingly.

Setting Margins

The **Inside** margin setting (left margin setting for single-sided pages) defines the gutter—that strip of empty vertical space, usually about an inch wide, that runs along the binding edge of each page. The **Outside** (right margin setting for single-sided pages), **Top**, and **Bottom** margin settings serve the same function. Margins help you frame the contents of your pages. However, many desktop publishers initially use PageMaker's **Top** and **Bottom** margin settings to establish upper and lower boundaries for automatically flowing columns of text. They later place headlines, page numbers, and other header or footer material above and below these margin boundaries.

Setting margins is the first step in laying out your pages. You learn more about working with margins in Chapter 6.

Changing a Document

To edit an existing publication, choose Open from the File menu. Remember that you have to close any publication you already may have open—PageMaker enables you to work within only one open file at a time.

When you choose Open, you see the Open Publication dialog box, which differs from other Macintosh Open dialog boxes in that you can open your original document or a copy of your original (see fig. 3.3). PageMaker normally opens the original file for editing. You can open a copy by clicking **Copy** before you click the OK button. That way you can experiment and make extensive editing changes without altering your original file. In any case, documents always open to the last page and page view you were working in when you closed the document.

With PageMaker, you also can create and save templates. You learn more about working with templates in Chapter 10. Whenever you open a template, PageMaker

Fig. 3.3

*In PageMaker,
you can open a
copy of your
publication to
work on and
preserve the
original.*

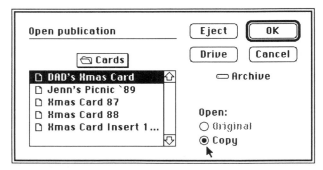

opens a copy and not the original. You can open an original template (to make formatting changes, for example) by clicking the **Original** button before you click the OK button.

Setting Document Defaults

PageMaker often is used to produce periodicals that retain the same formatting from issue to issue. If your company specializes in publishing tabloid-size newsletters, for example, you want to set up the program so that PageMaker defaults to a tabloid-size page whenever you open it. You can set up this default in two ways: you can design and use a template to create publications, or you can set the program defaults beforehand to match anticipated publishing requirements.

Templates are used best when your publication format is fixed (see Chapter 10). Setting program defaults, on the other hand, is the same as establishing a standard. The defaults serve as a basis for designing publications but don't provide a complete framework like a template does.

If your publishing requirements are varied, you may want to set separate defaults for each document you work on. If you need to create a series of sales brochures and accompanying catalogs, for example, you may choose a two-column spread for the sales brochures and a six-column spread for the catalogs. You do not convert these column specifications into program defaults, because you have to change the settings when you switch layouts. To get around this problem, you can set file defaults for each publication individually. File defaults override PageMaker's program defaults.

Default settings are nothing more than preset choices. When you open PageMaker for the first time, you find the menu choices and dialog box options already configured for general document preparation. You can revise any or all of PageMaker's program and file defaults to reflect your own publishing needs.

Changing Program Defaults

Program defaults are the global settings you expect to be in effect when you open a new document. Almost everything on-screen (and much of what you don't see immediately) is controlled by default settings and can be changed. You can preset ruler settings, the number of columns, font sizes and styles, paragraph indents, and dozens of other options as program defaults.

Setting program defaults is easy. When you first open PageMaker, press any key, select any menu item, or click the mouse button to make the start-up screen disappear. Don't choose New from the File menu yet. After a publication is opened—any changes you make apply to only that publication and not to the program.

From the PageMaker desktop, pull down the File menu and choose Page Setup. The Page Setup dialog box appears. Enter your choices for the physical characteristics of your pages and click the OK button. Do the same for the Preferences dialog box by choosing Preferences from the Edit menu. You can continue in this way for all other dialog boxes, including Column Guides (under the Options menu), Text Wrap and Rounded Corners (accessible through the Element menu), and Type Specs, Paragraph, Indents/Tabs, and Define Styles (accessible through the Type menu).

PageMaker enables you to convert most menu commands into default settings— even those menu items without dialog boxes. Pull down each menu and make your selections. You can, for example, set a specific line width and an object fill pattern as defaults (see fig. 3.4). You also can turn the Snap to Guides command on or off, hide or display the toolbox, and hide or display the scroll bars and page icons. Any menu commands you select or deselect from the desktop become program default settings.

Some menu commands are displayed in light gray type to show that they are inaccessible—you cannot change these commands. Accessible commands are displayed in normal black type and can be preset as program defaults.

You don't have to quit and restart PageMaker to change program defaults. You can close the current publication window and make changes from the PageMaker desktop before opening another document. New program defaults take effect immediately and remain active until you change the new defaults.

Changing File Defaults

File defaults are handled like program defaults, except that you set file defaults from within open publications and not from PageMaker's desktop. Generally, you choose page-setup defaults from the Page Setup dialog box that appears when you create a document. After a new document is opened, however, the page-setup

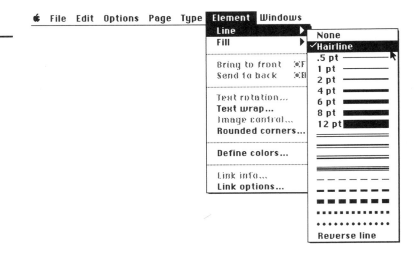

Fig. 3.4

*Selecting the Hairline
line width while in
PageMaker's desktop
view makes that line
choice a program
default.*

defaults can be revised only by choosing the Page Setup command from the File menu.

When you assign text attributes, such as font type, style, and size, as new file defaults, you must be careful not to have any text selected at the time you make the changes, or the changes affect only the selected text and not the default settings. If text is selected when you change the settings, when you deselect your text, the file defaults remain the same as before—only selected text is changed. The same holds true for graphics. Any alterations you make become file defaults only if no graphic elements are selected when you change the settings.

Contrary to what the PageMaker documentation says, you don't have to use the pointer tool to set file defaults. Any tool can be used. The tool changes to a pointer when you move the tool out of the publication window to pull down a menu. You also can leave various elements selected on your pages while changing defaults, if those elements aren't affected directly by the changes you make. It doesn't matter whether you have a graphic selected, for example, if you are changing the default setting for type size.

Default changes made to an open file are temporary until you save your publication—only then do they become a permanent part of the file.

Understanding the Magic of Master Pages

Master pages are like building blueprints. They help establish the framework of a publication. To access master pages, click the miniature master page icons at the lower left of the publication window—the icons with "L" and "R" represent the left and right master pages. You have one left master page (for all left-hand pages) and one right master page (for all right-hand or single-sided pages). Whatever you place on master pages repeats on all regular pages. Master pages can shorten the amount of time required to create lengthy documents—especially documents requiring a consistent look. If you draw repeating elements such as rules along the tops and bottoms of your master pages, for example, the rules appear along the tops and bottoms of all pages.

Master pages are different from regular pages in several important ways. You can work on master pages like you do any other page, but master pages do not print with the publication. Although everything you do on a master page shows up on its corresponding left or right regular pages, you cannot edit or change the master text or graphics that repeat on these regular pages. The only place you can change a master-page element is on a master page. Working with master pages is like working with overlays that are visible but inaccessible. Master pages remain completely isolated from your regular pages.

In addition to text and graphics, you can include columns and ruler guides on master pages (see fig. 3.5). You set the columns you want by choosing Column Guides from the Options menu and typing the appropriate number of columns in the dialog box that appears. The column guides appear on your pages. Every page must have at least one column.

To place a horizontal or vertical ruler guide on your master pages (or on any page), click the appropriate ruler, hold down the mouse button, and drag the cursor onto the page. A new ruler guide appears and follows the cursor. Release the mouse button when you have positioned the ruler guide where you want it. These column and ruler guides repeat throughout your publication.

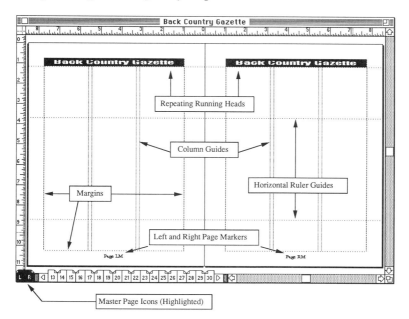

Fig. 3.5

A pair of double-sided, facing master pages showing columns, ruler guides, margins, and running heads that repeat on all pages.

Unlike master text and graphic elements, non-printing guides on any regular page can be repositioned at any time. Click on the guide, hold down the mouse button, and drag the guide to a new location. You can reposition column guides the same way.

To remove a ruler guide, drag the ruler guide out of the publication window. To remove a column guide, choose Column Guides from the Options menu. In the dialog box that appears, type a new number that is one number smaller than the old number. After you click the OK button, the page appears minus one column.

Non-printing guides are never anchored permanently, unless you intentionally lock the guides in place with the Lock Guides command from the Options menu. If you lock guides on any pages, they remain locked on all pages.

If you want PageMaker to number all the pages of your publications automatically, drag out a text box on each master page, using the text tool, and press Command-Option-p. (Make sure that the Caps Lock key is not engaged, or nothing happens when you press this key combination.) Position the master-page number markers where you want page numbers to appear on corresponding regular pages. Page-Maker uses the letter combination LM to represent the left master-page number marker and RM to represent the right master-page number marker. If you want composite numbers like Page 6 of 12, type the appropriate text on the master page, substituting Command-Option-p for the number that changes from page to page in your publication (the number 6 in this example). See fig. 3.6 for an example of a master-page number marker.

Fig. 3.6

A composite page number on a right master page of a confidential document.

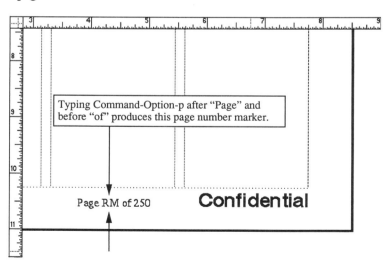

Typing Command-Option-p after "Page" and before "of" produces this page number marker.

Page RM of 250   Confidential

You have a choice of numbering styles. First, click the **Numbers** button in the Page Setup dialog box to bring up the Page Numbering dialog box. Then click one of the five buttons to choose the corresponding numbering style indicated. Your page numbers change to reflect the newly assigned style.

Note

The Roman numbering styles can be used for page numbers up to 4,999. From page 5,000 on, Roman styles revert to Arabic. Alphabetic numbering styles are good through page 52. From page 53 onward, alphabetic styles also revert to Arabic.

You can assign any font type, size, or style to the number markers on your master pages. PageMaker numbers your pages, starting with the page number specified in the Page Setup dialog box. If you later add or delete pages using the Insert Pages and Remove Pages commands on the Page menu, PageMaker updates the remaining page numbers automatically.

Note

If you don't want PageMaker to number every page in your publication, draw a text box and press Command-Option-p on just those pages where you want numbers to appear. PageMaker inserts the correct numbers and updates these numbers whenever you add or delete pages.

Include on your master pages only those elements you want to appear on every regular page. Less frequently used text and graphics can be stored on the pasteboard and copied onto your regular pages as needed.

Tip

Use repeating ruler guides to mark areas on your pages where elements you don't want to include on every page should appear. If you plan, for example, to center a boxed illustration in the same spot on only a few pages, predefine that area on the master pages using horizontal and vertical ruler guides. Then, when it's time to draw the boxes around the pictures on your regular pages, you can do so quickly and accurately. Similarly, by positioning vertical ruler guides between adjoining columns on your master pages, you later can draw the column rules exactly where you need the rules.

An organized approach to setting up your master pages is as follows:

1. Position all non-printing guides on both master pages, including column guides and horizontal and vertical ruler guides. Later, you can rearrange master column and ruler guides on any regular page without affecting other parts of your layout. If you decide to reinstate the original master guides arrangement on a page where you have moved the guides, select Copy Master Guides from the Page menu.

2. Draw any repeating rules, including rules between columns and along the tops and bottoms of pages.

3. Place repeating graphics. Position company logos or other design elements on the master pages exactly where you want the design elements to appear on all pages.

4. Add repeating text such as running heads, automatic page numbers, and classification markings.

5. Draw remaining borders and boxes.

6. To save time when creating identical master pages, do steps two through five for only one master page. Select all the elements on that page (Shift-click on each element in sequence or click-drag the pointer tool so that the marquee surrounds all the elements) and copy the elements to the Clipboard. Paste the Clipboard contents back onto your master pages. With all the pasted elements still selected, drag the elements as a unit onto the facing master page. Use ruler guides to position individual elements as necessary for perfect alignment.

To hide the master elements on just one of two regular facing pages, you normally deselect the **Facing Pages** option in the Page Setup dialog box and revert to a single-page display. You deselect this option because the Display Master Items command under the Page menu toggles both page displays simultaneously. You can get around this constraint, however. To continue working on two pages at the same time and still hide the master elements on just one page when printing, use any one of the following three methods:

1. To remove all master elements from one facing page, deselect the **Facing Pages** option in the Page Setup dialog box. Then hide the master elements on just those pages in which you don't want the master elements to print. Reselect the **Facing Pages** option and continue working on the publication with both pages showing.

   Note that the companion facing page now also has its master elements hidden. However, deselect the **Facing Pages** option again before printing your publication, and the pages print correctly with master elements hidden on the one page but not on the other. This method works because the **Facing Pages** option controls only the screen display, not your actual layout.

2. To retain some, but not all, master elements on a facing page, copy just those master elements you want to keep from the master page to the Clipboard. Paste these master elements onto the publication page while holding down the Option key. This action pastes the copied elements so that they lie exactly on top of the corresponding master elements already showing on the page. Next, deselect the Display Master Items command. The repeating master elements disappear from both facing pages, but those elements you pasted from the Clipboard remain behind. Note that these pasted elements are no longer treated as inaccessible master elements. You can work with pasted elements as with any other elements.

3. To retain some, but not all, master elements on a facing page, cover any master page items you don't want to print with "electronic whiteout." Select an appropriate tool from the toolbox and draw a line, oval, or box roughly the size needed to cover the offending element. In figure 3.7, for example, a rectangle tool was used to draw a box around the object (see parts 1 and 2). Then, the box was filled with white by choosing Paper from the Fill menu (see part 3 in fig. 3.7). Paper is always the same color as your page—in this case white. The boundary of the box was hidden by choosing None from the Line menu (see part 4 in fig. 3.7). Finally, the opaque box was dragged into position over the master element to be obliterated. Part 5 in figure 3.7 shows the final result.

Laying a Solid Foundation

The framework of every PageMaker publication is the layout. Layouts bring order to the way you place text and graphics on pages. With a little care in planning and executing layouts, your publications can look as professional as any seen on your local newsstand.

Determining the Layout Grid

You can spot a poor layout as easily as a good one—generally easier. Your layouts should follow certain basic design principles, if you want your publications to be successful. Using a layout grid often makes the difference.

In PageMaker, a *layout grid* consists of non-printing margin, column, and ruler guides. These guides help you place and align text and graphics on your pages. You can think of the layout grid as shaping the underlying structure of your publication. Whole cities are laid out, and complex roadways are built, according to predeter-

Fig. 3.7

Eliminating a master element using "electronic whiteout."

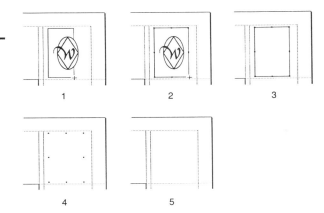

mined grids—and so it should be with your publications. The principle is the same. The larger and more complex your publication, the more important using a grid becomes.

Traditional publishers use preprinted grid sheets to lay out publications. These grid sheets provide a ruled environment for paste-up of text and graphics. The grid lines are light blue so that they do not reproduce during printing. Similarly, the non-printing guides used in PageMaker become invisible during printing. On-screen, these guides are more flexible and easier to use than a fixed grid sheet. You can drag only the ruler guides you need, for example, onto your pages and reposition each one independently. Using just a few guides on a page gives you an unobstructed view of your work. By contrast, the many crossed lines of a fixed grid sheet would clutter your screen and make viewing your pages difficult. You also would have to change the entire grid spacing each time you wanted to adjust a small part of your display.

In addition to non-printing guides, PageMaker provides an invisible grid that you can toggle on or off to help align page elements. This invisible grid corresponds to the intersections of imaginary lines drawn from horizontal and vertical ruler divisions. The spacing of these divisions, or tick marks, is a function of your display monitor and whatever units of measure are set in the Preferences dialog box. For example, a ruler setting of picas in the Fit In Window view on a two-page monitor has much wider spacing between tick marks than a ruler setting of inches or millimeters.

When you check the SnapTo Rulers command under the Options menu, PageMaker's invisible grid becomes active. When you drag text, graphics, or non-printing column and ruler guides, these elements snap to the invisible grid lines (see figs. 3.8 and 3.9).

A layout grid provides page-to-page consistency for the placement of text and graphics. Using a layout grid doesn't mean that you have to stay within its

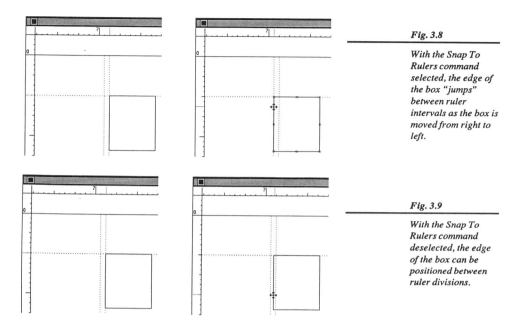

Fig. 3.8

With the Snap To Rulers command selected, the edge of the box "jumps" between ruler intervals as the box is moved from right to left.

Fig. 3.9

With the Snap To Rulers command deselected, the edge of the box can be positioned between ruler divisions.

boundaries, though. You may want to place page numbers, header and footer information, and design elements outside your page margins. Margins frame the central areas of your pages where you do most of your layout work, but you can place text and graphics anywhere on a page. The only constraint you face is the imaging area of your output device. If, for example, you print to a Linotronic, you can do bleeds (run text and graphics to the very edges of the pages), and your pages print fine (see fig. 3.10). On a LaserWriter, however, you can print only to within 1/4 inch of the sides and 1/8 inch from the tops and bottoms of your pages.

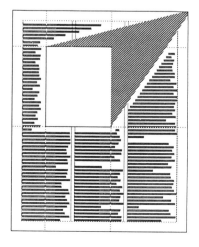

Fig. 3.10

"Bleeding" a graphic element.

Tip

You can get a full bleed on the top and bottom edges of an 8.5-by-11-inch page by printing on 8.5-by-14-inch legal paper and trimming the finished page down to 8.5-by-11 inches afterward. Cut the bleed edge of your page first.

Designing a workable layout for a publication takes thought and planning. Setting up the layout grid, however, is easy. To set up a layout grid, perform the following steps:

1. In the Page Setup dialog box, select a page size from the pop-up menu (or type a custom page size into the **Page dimensions** fields). Pick a page orientation by clicking the **Tall** or **Wide** button. If you want double-sided pages (with or without facing pages), click the appropriate options boxes. Type the number of pages (including the starting page number) into the **Start page #** and **# of pages** boxes. Finally, type the margin settings you want into the four margin fields. You can type whole or decimal numbers. The units of measure are those that you select using the Preferences command under the Edit menu (see step 2). Keep in mind that how you set the margins in this dialog box is how they appear on every page. If you want the margins wider or narrower, type new values accordingly.

2. Configure the Preferences dialog box for the units of measurement you want applied to the rulers. Remember that ruler settings directly affect how PageMaker's invisible grid behaves. (You learn more about setting up rulers later in this chapter under "Rulers and Measurements.")

   Note: Complete as many of the following steps as possible on your master pages to eliminate having to repeat these steps for each regular page.

3. If your layout calls for columns of text, choose Column Guides from the Options menu and type a whole number value for the desired number of columns into the **Number of columns** field. Type a whole or decimal value for column spacing into the **Space between columns** field. Your columns appear on the page evenly spaced. Later, you can drag individual column guides as necessary to modify the column widths.

4. Use as many horizontal and vertical ruler guides as necessary to indicate the proper placement of running heads, graphic placeholders, rules, and other design elements. Remember, you click-drag ruler guides directly

from the horizontal and vertical rulers. Try to limit the number of ruler guides used, or you may find it difficult to sort them out later. Place the most important ruler guides on master pages (to have the guides repeat on all your pages) and add any supplementary ruler guides to your regular pages later. When you are satisfied with the arrangement of guides, use the Lock Guides command under the Options menu to lock the guides in place.

5. Select or deselect the Snap To Rulers and Snap To Guides commands under the Options menu, depending on how you plan to work on your pages. Leaving the Snap To Rulers command selected, for example, makes it easy to evenly align separated blocks of text horizontally. Leaving the Snap To Guides command selected enables you to position text, graphics, and drawing tools accurately, even in greatly reduced views. Deselecting these commands enables you to position elements freely—sometimes a convenient way to work, such as when trying to center text exactly within a circle.

Changing Columns

PageMaker's Column Guides command enables you to use up to 20 equally spaced, even-width columns per page. You may think 20 is an excessive number, but many companies produce tabloid-size publications containing horizontal tabular data, such as phone lists, product catalogs, and financial data. In such cases, even 20 columns may be too few. You can make column assignments separately for double-sided facing pages by selecting **Set left and right pages separately** in the Column Guides dialog box (see fig. 3.11).

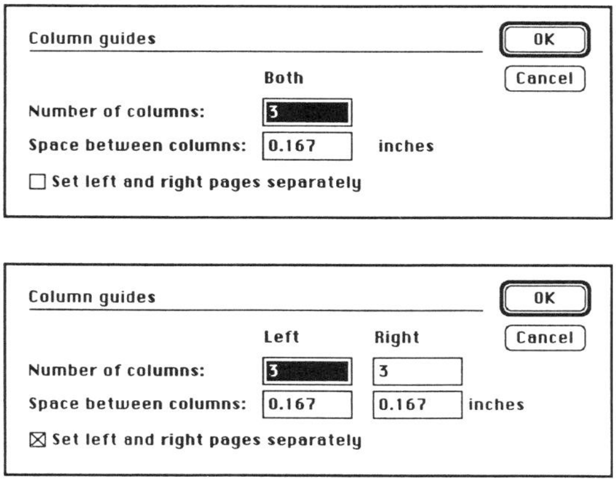

Fig. 3.11

Using the Set left and right pages separately box for double-sided facing pages.

Many layout designs call for columns of variable width. After creating the desired number of columns on the page, you can drag any column guide to change the width of that column. When you drag a column guide, the value in the **Number of columns** field in the Column Guides dialog box changes from a one-digit or two-digit number to the word Custom to show that you made alterations to the column layout. The value in the **Space between columns** field remains constant, because you did not change column spacing; you changed only the column width. PageMaker's initial default column spacing is 0.167 inch or 1 pica width, a value you can change by typing a new number in this field.

Note

You cannot change the column spacing for columns of variable width. (You create variable-width columns by dragging column guides—the word Custom appears in the **Number of columns** field.) To change the spacing for variable-width columns, choose Column Guides from the Options menu and again specify the number of columns (type a whole number to replace the word Custom) and the new column spacing you want. After you click OK, even-width columns having the desired spacing appear on your page. To re-establish the original variable-width layout, drag the appropriate column guides back to their former locations.

Warning

PageMaker arranges all newly created columns to fit evenly within existing page margins. If you change the inside or outside (left or right) margin settings in the Page Setup dialog box, every column on every page in your publication is adjusted to fit evenly between the margins. The number of columns per page doesn't change, just the column widths. If your publication contains custom columns, changing either side margin, even by the slightest amount, causes you to lose all custom, variable-width spacing. This loss occurs even if you lock the guides beforehand, using the Lock guides command under the Options menu. You can select Undo Page Setup immediately from the Edit menu to undo the damage before the change becomes permanent. The damage becomes permanent after you click your mouse anywhere in the publication window.

You cannot drag a column guide outside a margin boundary, but you can place text outside a margin. A common use of margins is to define the "live" area on the page into which you "pour" repeated columns of text. You then place other text items, like headlines and titles, outside the margins.

When you pour text into a column, your copy stays within the left and right column boundaries as the text flows down the page. Flowing text into columns gives you enormous flexibility when laying out publications, especially when you consider that you also can change column widths, the number of columns, and margin settings at any time. Only column guides restrict the flow of text. Ruler guides aid in the placement and alignment of elements.

Suppose, for example, that you want to create a travel brochure with two extra-wide columns containing promotional material spanning the upper one-third of the page. Across the bottom two-thirds of the same page, you want four columns in which you can list benefits and booking information in smaller type (see fig. 3.12). To create this brochure, do the following:

1. Pull a ruler guide down from the horizontal ruler and position the guide on the page where you want your columns to break. Make a note of the vertical placement of the ruler; you need this information later when you reset the top and bottom margins.

2. Reset the bottom margin temporarily to just above where you want the page break to occur.

3. Use the Column Guides command to set the number of columns to 2. Pour the promotional text into these two columns by clicking the text placement tool within and at the top of each column. The bottom margin limits the text flow so that the text lies above the page break.

4. Change the bottom page margin back to the original setting. Reset the top margin temporarily to just below the page break.

5. Use the Column Guides command to change the number of columns for the bottom portion of the page to 4. The text you already have poured is not affected. Pour the benefits and booking information into these four columns. The top margin now establishes the upper boundary of the second set of columns for flowing text.

Fig. 3.12

Creating a split-column publication in PageMaker.

You learn more about working with columns in Chapter 6.

Using Guides

You have seen how you can use ruler guides to help determine where to set margins to define upper and lower column boundaries. Setting margins is only one of many creative ways that non-printing guides can help make the preparation of your publications easier. Other techniques include adjusting page margins to create accurately sized working areas and changing the columns on a page to control text display. You learn more ways to work with non-printing guides in later chapters.

PageMaker imposes a limit of 40 horizontal and vertical ruler guides per page, including master-page ruler guides and any guides added to regular pages. The maximum number of columns you can have on a page is 20, which gives you 22 column guides (the two outermost column guides overlap the side margin guides).

You can have only a single set of top, bottom, and side page margins.

As long as you don't move or add ruler guides to regular pages, you can change the guides on your master pages—the regular pages are updated automatically. If you adjust even one ruler guide on a regular page, however, that page becomes independent of the master page and is no longer updated automatically. The same restriction holds for working with column guides. To update a page in your document so that the page again reflects the most recent changes to the master page, choose Copy Master Guides from the Page menu. This command copies the current guide arrangement from the master page to the displayed publication page, replacing any guides on that page.

You can lock or unlock column and ruler guides by toggling the Lock Guides command under the Options menu. Because guides are easy to move accidentally when repositioning text and graphics, locking the guides in place often helps. By choosing the Snap To Guides and Snap To Rulers commands under the Options menu, you also can align text and graphics more easily. When these commands are checked, the column, ruler, and margin guides act like magnets and exert a pull on any items placed near the guides. This feature enables you to do precision work that you could not do otherwise, except in greatly enlarged views.

Tip

When you click a column or ruler guide, the cursor changes to a double-headed arrow to show the possible directions of guide movement. Use this feature to distinguish between vertical and horizontal guides when trying to select one guide in an area where several guides intersect. If you move the wrong guide, immediately choose Undo from the Edit menu. If you click a side margin, you also get a double-headed arrow. This arrow, however, indicates a column guide that overlaps the margin, not a movable margin boundary. Remember, margins can be set only from the Page Setup dialog box. You cannot move margins by click-dragging with the mouse.

Tip

If you want to see clearly the edges of elements overlapped by non-printing guides, click the Guides Back button in the Preferences dialog box. This action sends all non-printing guides behind any elements on your pages. You gain an unobstructed view of the page.

To see what your completed pages look like when printed, hide all non-printing guides by deselecting the Guides command under the Options menu. You also can do this when working on your publication to reduce visual clutter on your pages and to get a clearer idea of how your publication is taking shape. When the guides are hidden, you no longer can snap to the guides.

Using Rulers and Measurements

PageMaker's rulers extend horizontally and vertically along the top and left sides of the publication window. Each ruler can be configured independently, and the increments depend on the selections made in the Preferences dialog box. The number of increments along each ruler varies, depending upon the size of your screen and your page magnification. Dotted track lines travel along both rulers to indicate the exact position of the cursor on the page. The track lines enable you to accurately size graphic elements; position text, graphics, and non-printing guides; and crop imported illustrations and photos to fit. You can hide the rulers by deselecting the Rulers command under the Options menu.

Tip

An important use of rulers is setting variable-width columns. Variable-width column guides must be set independently for each page. These guides cannot be copied from page to page (except through the magic of master pages). You cannot easily ensure that you have identical variable-width columns on facing pages. To get around this restriction, adjust your column widths on one facing page. Then use the rulers to mirror those same column widths on the opposite facing page.

The tick marks on PageMaker's rulers are accurate in all views to within 1/2880 or 0.0003 inch. This accuracy enables you to do precision layout work for output to a high-resolution printing device like the Linotronic.

When you first open a publication, the zero point of the rulers is aligned to either the upper left corner of the page when displaying pages one at a time or to the center of the upper edge of double-sided pages displayed as facing pages. After you open a publication, you can realign the ruler zero point to anywhere on the page. This feature makes measuring the sizes of objects or boundaries or determining the distances between two or more elements easy.

To reset the ruler zero point, do the following:

1. Unlock the zero point by deselecting the Zero Lock command under the Options menu.

2. Click the mouse button above the crossed-lines icon in the upper left corner of the publication window. This point is where the rulers intersect.

3. Press the mouse button and click-drag to the desired spot on the page. The ruler tick marks track along with the cursor so that you can position the ruler zero point accurately.

4. Release the mouse button.

5. Relock the zero point (by again selecting the Zero Lock command under the Options menu).

The units of measure set in the Preferences dialog box apply to your entire publication, including the rulers and all dialog boxes in which you enter dimensional values. You can override the measurement settings at any time, as described next, but you do not want to complicate the layout by using too many systems of measurement.

If you work in an environment in which your publication must be set up for one measurement system, but you are more comfortable working with another, you can use abbreviations when typing values into dialog box fields. The abbreviations override the current units of measure assigned in the Preferences dialog box. Suppose that your publication is set up for measurement using inches, but your background is in traditional printing, and you prefer to work with picas and points. In each dialog box you encounter, you can enter your measurements expressed as picas and points. First, you type the number of picas, followed by a small p, and then type the number of points (for example, *6p3*, as in fig. 3.13). PageMaker recognizes the override and makes the conversion to inches automatically. Note that a number always must precede the abbreviation, even if that number is zero. Table 3.1 lists abbreviations that you can use.

Table 3.1
Measurement Abbreviations

Abbreviation	Example
i for inches	3.75i (3-3/4 inches)
m for millimeters	16.2m (16.2 millimeters)

Abbreviation	Example
p for picas	12p (12 picas) (Note that the *p* follows the number.)
p for pica points	0p3 (3 points) (Note that a zero precedes the*p* that precedes the number.)
p for picas and pica points	12p3 (12 picas, 3 points) (Note that the *p* lies between the numbers.)
c for ciceros	12c (12 ciceros) (Note that the *c* follows the number.)
c for cicero points	0c3 (3 points) (Note that the zero precedes the*c* that precedes the number.)
c for ciceros and cicero points	12c3 (12 ciceros, 3 points) (Note that the *c* lies between the numbers.)

Page setup

Page: [Letter]

Page dimensions: [8.5] by [11] inches

Orientation: ⦿ Tall ◯ Wide

Start page #: [1]   # of pages: [1]

Options: ⊠ Double-sided ⊠ Facing pages

Margin in inches: Inside [9p]   Outside [6p3]

               Top [9p]   Bottom [12p]

[OK] [Cancel] [Numbers...]

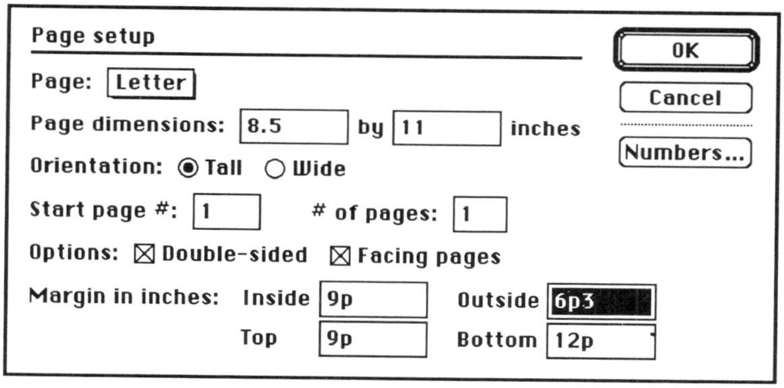

Fig. 3.13

*Pica margin values
can be typed into the
Page Setup dialog
box set for inches.*

If you use PageMaker's rulers intelligently, preparing your layouts goes more smoothly. By custom setting your vertical ruler to the same point size as your text, for example, you can use PageMaker's Snap To Rulers command to align the baselines of text in adjoining columns. By setting your measurement system to inches, you can use an ordinary household ruler to check existing hard-copy specs when re-creating existing documents. If you produce publications for clients who supply you with pica-point or metric specifications, you can configure your measurement system the same way. Then, you don't have to compute each conversion or remember to type overriding abbreviations in all of your dialog boxes.

Chapter Summary

In this chapter, you added to your knowledge of PageMaker basics. You learned how to configure the Page Setup dialog box to assign physical characteristics to your pages. You learned how to set program and file defaults and how to tap the hidden power of PageMaker's master pages. You also acquired an understanding of grids and how to use them effectively to produce professional-looking publications. You sharpened your skills by learning how to manipulate column and ruler guides, change measurements, and adjust ruler settings. You now are ready to move on to the quick start in Chapter 4, where you begin to put into practice what you have learned so far by creating a sample four-page newsletter.

Quick Start: Creating a Newsletter

In this chapter, you create a simple four-page newsletter. First, you assemble an overall layout and then design a detailed front page. This chapter reviews what you have learned so far and briefly previews several design techniques you learn about in later chapters. Try to follow along and duplicate as many of the steps as possible. Use whatever text and graphics you have handy—you don't have to reproduce exactly what you see here to benefit from the example. When you finish this section, you should have a better understanding of how to do practical desktop-publishing design and layout using PageMaker, and you can start creating your own publications.

Opening PageMaker

Your assignment is to create a four-page fictitious weekly newsletter titled *Barnyard Gossip*. The design calls for a simple, informal layout that must avoid a cosmopolitan look if the newsletter is to appeal to a target audience of farmers.

The first step is to open PageMaker and select New from the File menu. Choose the standard **Letter** page size from the pop-up Page menu. PageMaker enters the page dimensions for your selection automatically.

Next, set the margins in the Page Setup dialog box by typing the appropriate numerical values into the **Inside, Outside, Top,** and **Bottom** margin fields (see fig. 4.1). The inside margins must be set large enough to allow room for archiving the newsletter in a three-ring notebook binder. Make the top margin larger than the outside and bottom margins for a more eye-pleasing effect.

Type the number *4* into the **# of pages** field. This number tells PageMaker that your publication has four pages. Leave the **Start page #** as is. PageMaker initially enters the number 1 into this field for you. Select the **Double-sided** and **Facing pages**

Fig. 4.1

Setting new document specifications in the Page Setup dialog box.

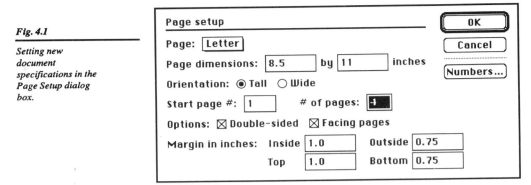

options by clicking the check boxes. These options make creating a balanced layout easier. Click the OK button to open your new publication.

Setting Up Master Pages

The next step is to set up your master pages. Click the master page icons in the lower left corner of the publication window to display your master pages. This quick start assumes that you have assembled your text and graphics, prepared a preliminary layout sketch, and have a clear idea of how you want your newsletter to look.

Fig. 4.2

The Column Guides dialog box.

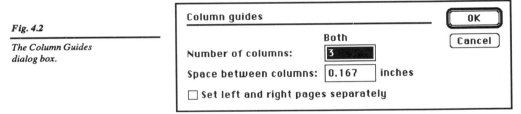

To set the desired number of columns, choose Column Guides from the Options menu and type the number *3* (see fig. 4.2). Your master pages display the familiar three-column newsletter layout (see fig. 4.3). This 3-column layout provides plenty of design flexibility and is easy to read.

If you publish a newsletter on a regular basis, you save your layout as a template for later use. With a template, you don't have to start over from scratch each time you put together a new edition. The template is the same as a regular publication, except that each time you open a new document, you get an untitled version; the template itself remains unchanged. You create a publication and then save the publication as a publication file using the Save As command on the File menu. To save your publication as a template instead, click the **Template** button in the Save As dialog box.

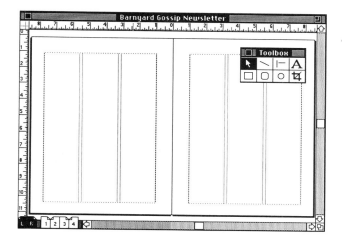

Fig. 4.3

Left and right master pages set up in a three-column format.

Positioning the Logo

A recognized trademark of your newsletter is a rooster-chasing-a-chicken logo that appears at the bottom of each page (see fig. 4.4). Although most newsletters traditionally include the logo as part of the banner, the unique graphic design of this logo enables you to use the logo in a way that encourages readers to turn your pages. On the last page, you reverse the logo to provide a gentle touch of humor and to mark the end of the newsletter.

Fig. 4.4

A birds-eye view of the newsletter layout.

The infamous Barnyard Gossip logo! Note how it's used to entice the reader to keep turning pages. On the last page its reverse orientation marks the end of the publication.

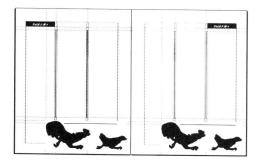

To ensure accurate logo placement, pull down one vertical and two horizontal ruler guides and position the guides on your pages (see fig. 4.5). The vertical ruler guide and intersecting lower horizontal ruler guide help you place the logo accurately. The upper horizontal ruler guide shows where columnar text directly above the logo should end. To access the ruler guides, take turns clicking within the rulers at the top and left sides of your publication window and drag into the window while holding down the mouse button. The ruler guides appear and follow your cursor. If the rulers are not visible, choose the Rulers command from the Options menu.

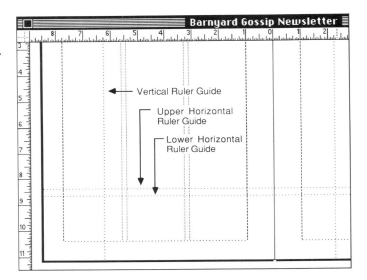

Fig. 4.5

Marking off the area for the logo with horizontal and vertical ruler guides.

You place your logo on both the left and right master pages to have the logo appear on each publication page. Note that whatever you place on your master pages appears on all subsequent pages. If you want an item not to appear on a particular page when printed, choose the Display Master Items command from the Page menu to toggle the display off. The program now hides all items you have placed on the corresponding right or left master page.

Turn now to page 4 and choose the Display Master Items command to hide the right-facing logo in preparation of placing the left-facing version. You learn how to import your logos later in this chapter under the section "Preparing and Placing Graphics."

You also can place the logo separately on each publication page. If you decide to use this approach, do not include the logo on your master pages.

Creating a Page-Number Block

You need a page number at the top of each page. To create an attractive page-number block, complete the following steps:

1. Drag down a horizontal ruler guide to the 1.5-inch tick mark on your vertical ruler.

2. Use the pointer tool to select PageMaker's square-corner rectangle tool from the toolbox. Click and drag the crosshair that appears. Draw a horizontal rectangle equal to one column's width on your left-hand master page.

3. Use the pointer tool to drag your finished rectangle into position at the top of the first column on the left master page. If you did not get the rectangle dimensions quite right on your initial try, click the pointer tool on a corner-reshaping handle and drag (while still holding down the mouse button) to resize and reshape the rectangle.

4. Click the rectangle with the pointer tool to select it. While the rectangle is still selected (the small black reshaping handles are visible), fill the rectangle with black. Choose the Fill command from the Element menu and then choose Solid from the available menu selections (see fig. 4.6).

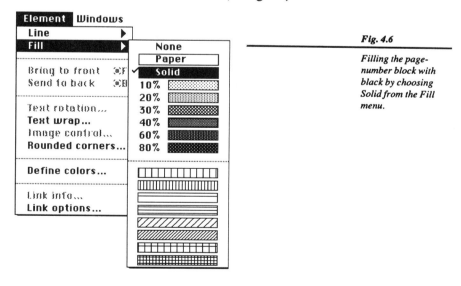

Fig. 4.6

Filling the page-number block with black by choosing Solid from the Fill menu.

5. Duplicate your rectangle by selecting the rectangle with the pointer tool and choosing Copy from the Edit menu. Choose Paste from the Edit menu. The duplicate rectangle appears. Drag this rectangle to the top of the third column on the right master page.

6. Click the text tool in PageMaker's toolbox and use the text tool to drag out a marquee exactly the width of one of your columns. The marquee disappears and the text insertion cursor appears. Type the expression *Page (Command-Option-p) of 4*. Make sure that the Caps Lock key is not engaged as you type the Command-Option-p combination keystroke. Also, press all three combination keys at the same time. The expression **Page LM of 4** or **Page RM of 4** appears, depending on which master page you typed the text. Repeat for the opposite master page.

Note

The LM and RM are page-number markers. Your page-numbering text block appears on all your regular publication pages. PageMaker substitutes the corresponding page numbers in place of the page-number markers.

---

7. Use the text tool to select your page-numbering text. Click-drag through the text to select it. Then choose the Type Style command from the Type menu and select Reverse from the available styles. This process inverts your selected text, changing the text to white (see fig. 4.7). Repeat for the second page-numbering text block.

8. Using the pointer tool, drag and center the reversed text blocks over the black rectangles (see fig. 4.8).

Fig. 4.7

Reversing selected type changes the lettering from black to white.

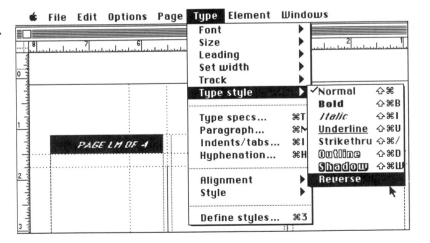

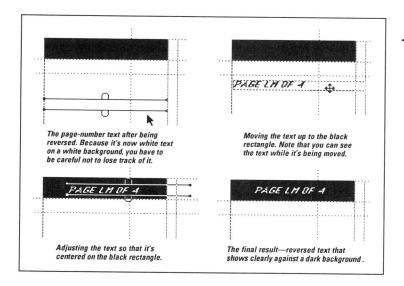

The page-number text after being reversed. Because it's now white text on a white background, you have to be careful not to lose track of it.

Moving the text up to the black rectangle. Note that you can see the text while it's being moved.

Adjusting the text so that it's centered on the black rectangle.

The final result—reversed text that shows clearly against a dark background.

Fig. 4.8

Placing reversed type on a dark background is a way of highlighting important text.

Preparing and Loading Text

You can prepare your stories in any word processor, or you can type text directly within PageMaker. In most cases, using a dedicated word processor to prepare your stories is more convenient. Dedicated word-processing programs enable you to process text more efficiently than you can in PageMaker. However, PageMaker has a built-in Story Editor that enables you to edit your stories, spell-check them, and find and change specific text based on various assigned paragraph and type styles.

You can import formatted text from several word processors into PageMaker. If you are using a word processor not supported by PageMaker, save your stories as text-only files and let PageMaker apply the formatting later. For this example, each story is prepared first in Microsoft Word (see fig. 4.9).

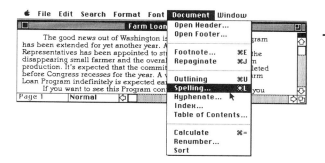

Fig. 4.9

Creating text in Microsoft Word before importing it into PageMaker.

To bring an existing story into PageMaker, choose Place from the File menu, which displays the Place Document dialog box (see fig. 4.10). Select the file you want from the listing in the document-selection window. Click the **As new story** button. When you click OK, your cursor changes into an icon that resembles a small block of text. Position the upper-left corner of this icon in the first column of your publication page and click the mouse button. PageMaker flows your text within the existing column boundaries (see fig. 4.11).

Fig. 4.10

The Place Document dialog box.

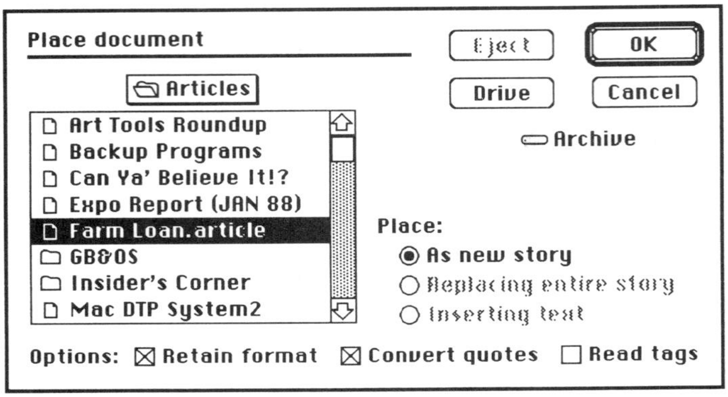

Fig. 4.11

Placing text in a PageMaker column.

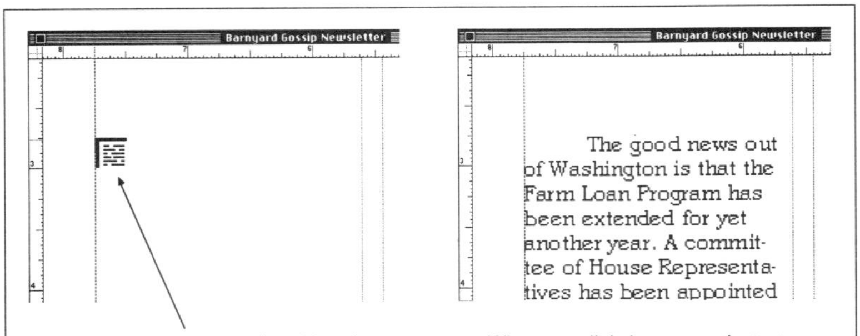

The text-placement tool positioned to place a story into PageMaker.

When you click the mouse, the text flows down between column guides.

If your story is longer than one column, click the arrow symbol in the windowshade handle to recover your text icon (see fig. 4.12). You then can click the text-placement icon anywhere in your publication to flow the remaining text. Front-page stories can continue on following pages. An empty windowshade handle indicates that you have placed all the text for that story.

Preparing and Placing Graphics

PageMaker provides a basic selection of drawing tools for creating graphic design elements like circles, boxes, and rules. To prepare detailed artwork or illustrations,

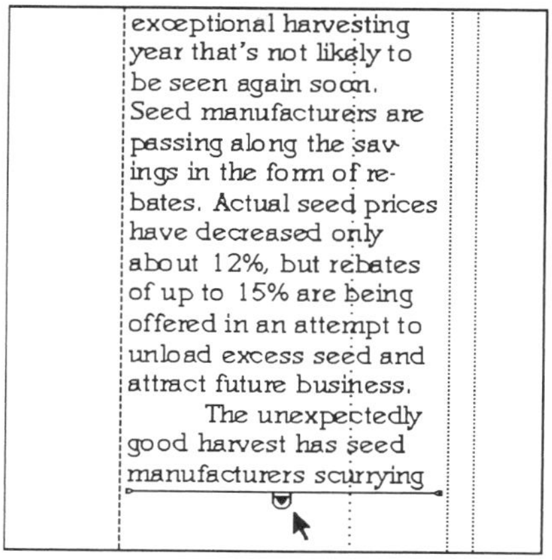

exceptional harvesting
year that's not likely to
be seen again soon.
Seed manufacturers are
passing along the sav-
ings in the form of re-
bates. Actual seed prices
have decreased only
about 12%, but rebates
of up to 15% are being
offered in an attempt to
unload excess seed and
attract future business.
   The unexpectedly
good harvest has seed
manufacturers scurrying

Fig. 4.12

The arrow in a column windowshade handle indicates that there is more text to place.

you have to use a separate drawing program. You import pictures created elsewhere using PageMaker's Place command from the File menu. Depending on the type of graphic you select, the graphic-placement cursor changes into a paintbrush (for a Paint file), a pencil (for a PICT file), a gray box (for a TIFF file), or the letters PS (for an EPS file). You also can place the Scrapbook. Your cursor changes into a tiny suitcase containing a number that indicates the number of items available for placement. Each time you click the graphic-placement cursor, you place one more item from the Scrapbook.

To import an illustration, choose Place from the File menu. In the Place Document dialog box, select the file you want from the listing in the document-selection window. Click the **As independent graphic** button. When you click OK, your cursor changes into the corresponding graphic-placement icon for the type of file selected.

Position the upper left corner of the graphic-placement icon at the spot on your page where you want the upper left corner of the illustration to appear. Click the mouse button. The entire illustration appears on the page. To resize the image, click a reshaping handle with the pointer tool and drag. If you hold down the Shift key while dragging, you scale the image proportionally.

After placing your illustrations, scale them proportionally to fit within the areas defined by your ruler guides. Click-drag the graphics using the pointer tool to move your images into final position on each page.

To wrap text around your logo, use the pointer tool to click on the logo. This action selects the logo. Choose Text Wrap from the Element menu. In the Text Wrap dialog box, click the wrap-all-sides icons for **Wrap option** and **Text flow** (see fig. 4.13). For now, leave the standoff values unchanged. (*Standoff* is a measure of the distance between the graphic and a rectangular text-wrap boundary. In this example, you adjust the boundary perimeter so that the boundary is no longer rectangular; the standoff then becomes meaningless.) Click OK.

Fig. 4.13

The Text Wrap dialog box.

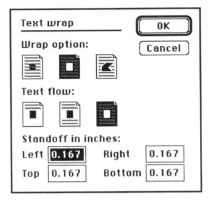

Next, click the graphic to see the text-wrap boundary. The boundary, at first, is a rectangular dotted line with diamond reshaping handles. To create more handles, click anywhere along the boundary perimeter. A new handle appears wherever you click. To adjust the boundary to fit the outline of your graphic, click-drag the individual reshaping handles. The pointer tool changes into a crosshair (see fig. 4.14).

After you finish adjusting the boundary, text wraps to follow the contour of your graphic. You learn more about text wrap in Chapter 8.

Fig. 4.14

Adjusting the text-wrap boundary by dragging a diamond reshaping handle.

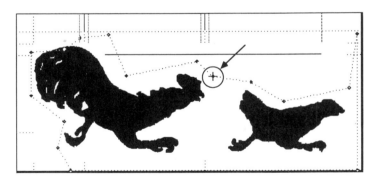

Refining the Document

Importing stories and illustrations is a first step in creating your publication. Most of your time and effort after that is spent refining your layout.

Working with Short Text

Short pieces of text, such as headlines, bylines, tables of contents, and column continuations, are best typed within PageMaker after you import your stories.

Typing these short text items in your word processor makes little sense because headlines generally have different font type, style, and size characteristics than the bodies of your stories. For this exercise, create each non-story text element within PageMaker.

To set up the formatting for your banner, pull down three horizontal ruler guides. Position the guides at the 2 5/8-, 2 7/8-, and 3 1/4-inch tick marks on the vertical ruler. These guides mark off the banner area and a 1/4-inch space below the banner to house the newsletter's subhead, issue number, and publication date. The lower guide also separates the banner from the main text.

Use the text tool to type the issue number, subhead, and publication date as separate text blocks. Afterward, use the text tool to select the text and assign an appropriate column justification. Choose Alignment from the Type menu and assign Align Left to the issue number, Align Center to the subhead, and Align Right to the publication date (see fig. 4.15). Finally, drag each text block into place using the pointer tool.

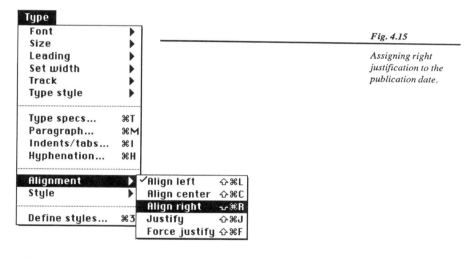

Fig. 4.15

Assigning right justification to the publication date.

Because you want to handle the banner a bit differently to make the title of your newsletter stand out, follow these steps:

1. To create your banner, type the text in MacDraw, FreeHand, Adobe Illustrator, or any other graphics program that enables you to save files in PICT or EPS format.

2. Import the PICT or EPS graphic into PageMaker and stretch or compress the graphic to fit (click-drag a corner reshaping handle). You now can adjust your banner easily to lie exactly within its designated space at the top of your page. Your banner also takes on a more striking appearance than if you typed the banner in place using the text tool. You also can add embellishments within your drawing program that scale without distortion when you reshape the graphic in PageMaker.

3. Use the pointer tool to select the banner and then choose the Links command from the File menu. In the Links dialog box, click the **Links options** button to display the Link Options dialog box (see fig. 4.16). Click all three options. Because your banner is so important to the identity of your publication, you want any changes you make to the original graphic to show up immediately in your newsletter. Selecting these options tells PageMaker to update your newsletter whenever the original graphic changes, but to alert you before making the update.

Fig. 4.16

The Link Options dialog box.

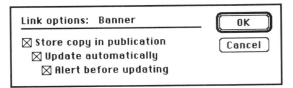

Link options: Banner

☒ Store copy in publication
☒ Update automatically
☒ Alert before updating

OK

Cancel

Note

Position the guides so that they lie behind whatever text and graphics they otherwise would overlap. You can position the guides by choosing the **Guides Back** button in the Preferences dialog box (choose Preferences under the Edit menu). This procedure reduces the chances of accidentally grabbing and moving a guide when trying to move graphic and text elements. As a further precaution, after arranging your guides, lock them in place by choosing Lock Guides from the Options menu.

You now have completed the banner area of your front page (see fig. 4.17).

Fig. 4.17

Using ruler guides enables you to position your banner and any subhead text more accurately.

Creating a Backdrop for Your Text

In this example, you reserve the center column of the front page for a table of contents. This layout helps guide the reader's eye directly from the banner at the top of the page to the logo at the bottom of the page; in effect, visually tying the two elements together and reinforcing their relationship. To strengthen this eye movement, create a light sidewalk of gray with PageMaker's square-corner rectangle tool as follows:

1. Type your table of contents listing as a text block.

2. Draw two intersecting rectangles on the page—one horizontally around the lower part of the banner and the other so that the rectangle completely surrounds the table of contents.

3. Move both rectangles behind the text. Select the rectangles and choose Send To Back from the Element menu.

4. Choose a line width of None from the Line menu (under the Element menu) to eliminate border lines.

5. Select a minimum 10% fill from the Fill menu (also under the Element menu) so that the foreground text stands out sharply from the light gray background.

A shaded path now walks the reader's eye down the page toward the logo, and the nature of the logo subtly urges the reader to turn the page and continue reading (see fig. 4.18).

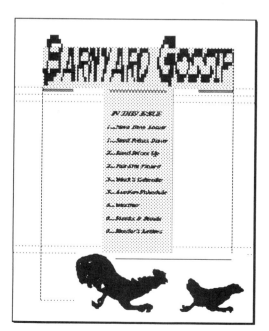

Fig. 4.18

Using background shading as a design tool helps tie together different elements on the same page.

Using Drop Caps

Drop caps are a popular design feature for marking the beginnings of stories. Creating drop caps may seem a little tricky at first, but after you create one, the rest are easy. For this example, make each drop cap a 48-point bold character using the same typeface as the body text. Use the following step-by-step procedure to create drop caps (see fig. 4.19):

1. Use the text tool to type the drop cap somewhere convenient. Choose Type Specs from the Type menu and assign the desired font type, size, and style. Select the drop cap with the pointer tool and move the drop cap into place over the existing column of 12-point text.

2. Use the pointer tool to select the underlying block of text.

3. Again using the pointer tool, click on the leftmost lower column reshaping handle and drag to resize the column. Size the column to fit within the space to the right of the drop cap. Match the number of lines of text to the height of the drop cap.

4. Delete the first letter in the text block the drop cap is replacing. In this example, delete the letter "T."

5. Click the arrow in the column windowshade handle to recover the text-placement icon.

6. Position the text-placement icon just beneath the drop cap and click the mouse button. The remaining text reflows between the original column guides.

7. Use the pointer tool to select both text blocks. Drag the upper windowshade handle of the lower text block until the handle just overlaps the lower windowshade handle of the upper text block. This technique restores the original line spacing between the two text blocks.

Selecting Fonts

In this example, Adobe System's ITC Benguiat bookface in 12-point size is used for the newsletter's body text because of its readability and whimsical styling. ITC Benguiat is a serif face that complements the informal tone of the newsletter. Serif fonts have small cross strokes at the characters' ascenders and descenders (see fig. 4.20). The typeface also conveys a clean, non-busy look to the reader.

ITC Benguiat also is used for story headlines, although using a non-serif face like Helvetica for headlines is more customary. ITC Benguiat is used here because most designers agree that you shouldn't mix more than two typeface families on the same page, and the banner is boldly set in Image Club Graphic's casual Paint Brush font.

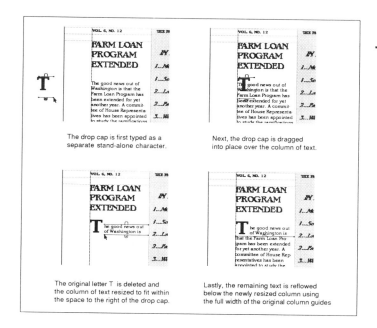

Fig. 4.19

Creating a drop cap.

The drop cap is first typed as a separate stand-alone character.

Next, the drop cap is dragged into place over the column of text.

The original letter T is deleted and the column of text resized to fit within the space to the right of the drop cap.

Lastly, the remaining text is reflowed below the newly resized column using the full width of the original column guides

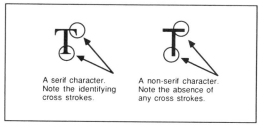

Fig. 4.20

Distinguishing between serif and non-serif type.

A serif character. Note the identifying cross strokes.

A non-serif character. Note the absence of any cross strokes.

All story headlines are 22-point bold, or slightly less than twice the size of the accompanying body text.

To make font type, size, and style assignments, choose Type Specs from the Type menu. In the Type Specifications dialog box (see fig. 4.21), choose the font type from the pop-up Font menu. Choose the type size from the pop-up Size menu or type the desired size into the **Size** field (tenth point sizes are permitted). Choose the style by clicking the appropriate **Type style** check boxes.

Because the Paint Brush font used in the banner is italicized, the table of contents beneath the banner also is italicized to avoid interrupting the reader's eye movement. The table of contents is 14-point bold and double-spaced to set the list apart from the main stories.

The issue number, banner subtitle, publication date, and story continuations are set in 10-point type. The story continuations at the bottom of each column also are italicized to set them apart from the main body text.

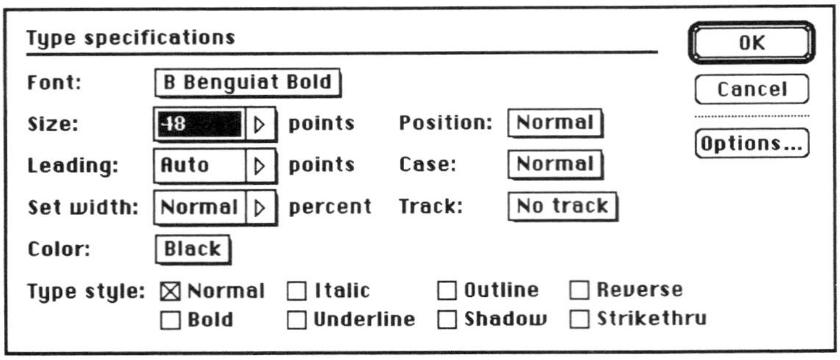

Fig. 4.21

PageMaker's Type Specifications dialog box.

```
┌─────────────────────────────────────────────────────────┐
│  Type specifications _____    ┌────────┐ │
│                                              │   OK   │ │
│  Font:      [ B Benguiat Bold ]              └────────┘ │
│                                              ┌─────────┐ │
│  Size:      [ 18    ▷] points   Position: [Normal]  │Cancel │ │
│                                              └─────────┘ │
│  Leading:   [Auto  ▷] points    Case:    [Normal]  ┌─────────┐│
│                                                     │Options...││
│  Set width: [Normal ▷] percent  Track:  [No track] └─────────┘│
│                                                          │
│  Color:     [Black]                                      │
│                                                          │
│  Type style: ⊠Normal  □Italic    □Outline  □Reverse     │
│              □Bold    □Underline  □Shadow   □Strikethru  │
└─────────────────────────────────────────────────────────┘
```

As you design your publications, you have to make many type-style choices. You make most of your selections from the submenus under PageMaker's Type menu. Others you set using the Type Specifications dialog box. Using the Type Specifications dialog box gives you more control over text formatting, and you can assign several type attributes at the same time. The 22-point size used for this newsletter's story headlines is not one of the commonly listed sizes on PageMaker's Type Size menu. You have to type this size into the Type Specifications dialog box's **Size** field.

Using Rules and Snap To Guides

To help separate your columns visually, use the straight-line tool to draw vertical rules between the column guides on both master pages. These rules repeat on all your publication pages and show up when you print your pages. These rules are graphic elements; do not confuse them with nonprinting ruler and column guides. Choose Display Master Items from the Page menu to hide the repeating vertical rules on the first page of your newsletter; the gray backdrop for the center column already provides a natural column separation.

To create perfectly placed vertical column rules, drag vertical ruler guides to the spaces between the adjoining columns on your master pages. Draw your rules along the ruler guides. Make sure that the Snap To Rulers command is selected from the Options menu. This command makes the rules lie exactly on top of the guides (see fig. 4.22). The same technique can be used to draw the horizontal rules.

Use the straight-line tool to draw a horizontal rule just above the logo on each page (except on the last page) to separate the logo from the columns of text above the logo. Leave the horizontal rule off the last page so that the text of the first two columns wraps around the reversed logo.

Editing Your Work

You can edit text easily with PageMaker's Type menu commands and text tool. To change font types, sizes, or styles, select the text to be edited and choose the appropriate menu commands. Remember that if you choose the menu commands

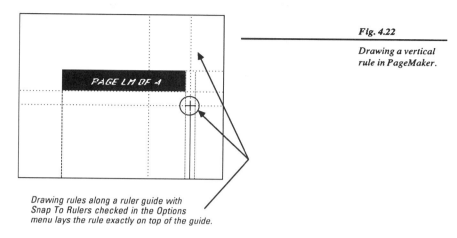

Fig. 4.22

*Drawing a vertical
rule in PageMaker.*

*Drawing rules along a ruler guide with
Snap To Rulers checked in the Options
menu lays the rule exactly on top of the guide.*

first, only newly typed text is affected. To manipulate body copy, use the text tool as you would within your favorite word processor. To insert new text into an existing story, click your text cursor at any point and start typing.

Making changes and corrections by zooming in on your documents is sometimes convenient. Zooming in on a small section of a page enables you to work on tiny details. Zooming out again enables you to see how your overall layout is shaping up. Choose the appropriate commands for the page size you want from the Page menu (Fit In Window, 25%, 50%, 75%, Actual Size, 200%, and 400%), or use the equivalent keyboard shortcuts presented in Chapter 2.

You can use PageMaker's Story Editor instead of working in the layout view. Click an insertion point in a story and then choose Edit Story from the Edit menu. Your story opens into PageMaker's built-in word processor (see fig. 4.23). You cannot view your type and style formatting in this window. The story view is mainly for processing text quickly and easily without having to wait for screen redraws in the layout view. However, PageMaker displays the names of assigned paragraph styles to the left of the paragraphs.

PageMaker's Story Editor enables you to check the spelling of your stories. You have to be in the story view for this command to be available. Choose Spelling from the Edit menu. The Spelling dialog box appears. Click the **Start** button for Page-Maker to begin searching for spelling errors. Click the appropriate button at the bottom of the dialog box to conduct a check of selected text, the currently open story, or all stories in your publication. PageMaker flags all errors the program finds and suggests corrections. In figure 4.24, for example, PageMaker suggests a correction for the misspelled word highlighted in figure 4.23. You also can type a new word into the **Change to** field. Click the **Replace** button to make the substitution.

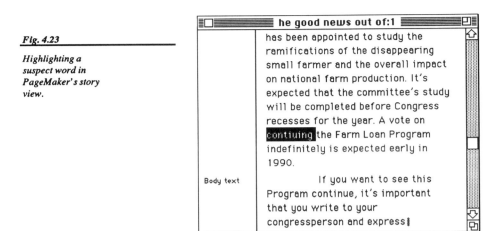

Fig. 4.23

Highlighting a suspect word in PageMaker's story view.

Fig. 4.24

PageMaker flags the suspect word when spell-checking the story in the previous illustration.

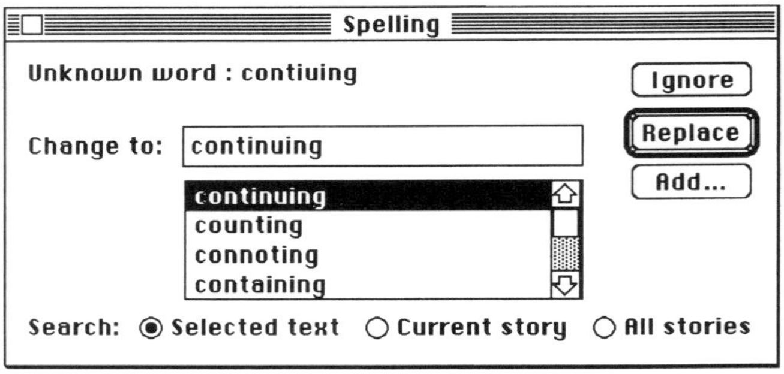

When you are working in the story view, PageMaker also enables you to find and change text. Choose Find or Change from the Edit menu. The Find or Change dialog box appears. Note that the Change dialog box is an expansion of the Find dialog box. You can use the Change command for both functions.

PageMaker enables you to search a selected range of text, the currently open story, or all stories in your publication. Type the text you want PageMaker to find into the **Find what** field. Type the text you want PageMaker to substitute into the **Change to** field. Choose the special options to exactly match the capitalization of your text (**Match case**) or to search for whole words only (**Whole word**). If you leave these options unchecked, PageMaker searches without regard for capitalization and whole words. For example, searching for the word "lend" without checking these options finds "lend," "Lending," and "blend."

In figure 4.25, PageMaker searches for every instance of the phrase "Farm Loan Program," exactly as typed, and substitutes the phrase "Farm Lending Program" for each occurrence. Click the **Change** button to make the substitution and pause momentarily. Click the **Change & find** button to make the substitution and find the next occurrence. Click the **Change all** button to change every occurrence.

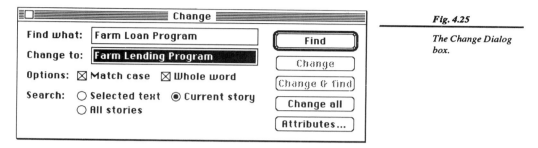

Fig. 4.25

The Change Dialog box.

Click the **Attributes** button to search and replace text by paragraph styles or type attributes. In figure 4.26, PageMaker searches for the text shown in figure 4.25, changes the text from Benguiat plain to Benguiat Bold, and makes the selection italic.

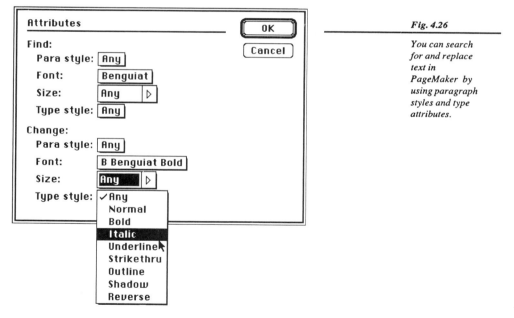

Fig. 4.26

You can search for and replace text in PageMaker by using paragraph styles and type attributes.

Saving and Backing Up

Saving your publication should not be left for last. Always save your work at regular intervals to avoid losing everything you have accomplished up to that point. PageMaker executes a mini-save (see Chapter 2) when you add or delete pages,

Fig. 4.27

The completed front
page printed on an
Apple LaserWriter.

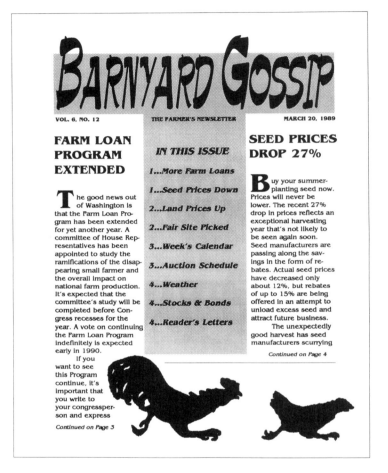

change page setup specifications, or turn to a new page in your publication. Do not count on this automatic mini-saving feature, however, to recover important work.

Assign your publication a name and save the publication to your hard disk when you set the initial specifications in the Page Setup dialog box. Choose Save from the File menu. Also, save a backup copy of your publication to a second disk by choosing Save As from the File menu. Save your work at least every 10 or 15 minutes to both locations. You lose only 10 or 15 minutes of changes if you experience a power failure, system error, or other problem. Saving and backing up this way someday may keep you from having to rebuild a publication from scratch.

Printing Your Work

To print your publication, choose Print from the File menu. The Print dialog box appears. This dialog box contains many choices. For this exercise, use the existing settings. Click the OK button to produce your final output (see fig. 4.27 on preceding page). You learn more about printing in Chapter 9.

Chapter Summary

In this chapter, you learned how to produce a sample four-page newsletter using many of the concepts and techniques covered in earlier chapters. You also gained exposure to several new features you learn more about in following chapters. If you are unclear about something you studied earlier, now is a good time to quickly review the material before going on to the next chapter.

Up to this point, you have been laying a solid foundation of basic skills upon which to build. The remainder of this book helps you acquire the more advanced skills you need to become proficient at designing and laying out your own publications.

II

Working with Text

Includes

Text Basics

Formatting Text

5

Text Basics

In this chapter, you begin working with text. You learn how to place text so that it flows throughout a publication and how to edit and manipulate your stories afterward. You learn how to use PageMaker's links to update your stories automatically. You also discover how to create additional text using PageMaker's Story Editor.

You learn how to spell check your publication, how to search for and replace text by font type, size, and style attributes, and how to format your stories using various type specifications. You learn how to export text out of PageMaker so that you can update your original word processing files or use them elsewhere.

As you explore PageMaker's text-handling capabilities, you discover how to improve the readability of your publications by kerning type and adjusting tracking. To *kern type* means to adjust the space between adjoining characters for a better fit (for example, tucking the little *o* under the overhang of the capital letter *T* in the word *To*). To *adjust tracking* is to vary the space between letters and words of selected text.

This chapter is your introduction to the detailed mechanics of using PageMaker. You begin to master the fundamental hands-on skills needed to produce professional-looking publications on your own. As with earlier chapters, you should follow along at your computer. Learning by doing is the best and quickest way to gain proficiency.

Bringing Text into PageMaker

Most of the time, you want to create and format your text using one of the many popular Macintosh word processors. A dedicated word processor enables you to do the kind of power editing that a page-layout program is not designed to do. Word processors generally come with many built-in keyboard shortcuts and other convenience features that make preparing stories easier and faster. A good stand-alone word processor is your best choice to prepare text quickly for your publications.

You can bring text into PageMaker using the Place command from the File menu or the Import command from the Story menu (when working in Story Editor). You also can copy and paste text into your publications via the Clipboard.

When you bring text into PageMaker, not all the original formatting always comes through intact. The formatting retained depends greatly on the kind of word processor you use. However, except for a few special characteristics like double underlining, headers, footers, and hidden text, PageMaker fully supports most popular word processor file formats via special import and export filters. These filters serve as translators to enable PageMaker to correctly interpret formatted files created with other programs. One filter enables you to import fully formatted stories directly from other PageMaker documents.

When you first install PageMaker on your hard disk, you pick the filters you want to include. Filter files are compressed to save disk space. PageMaker's Installer utility creates an Aldus Filters folder, decompresses the selected filters, and places them inside the folder. If you later decide to add a new filter, PageMaker's Installer utility makes installing new filters easy. To install a new filter, double-click on the filter. The installer decompresses the file and enables you to designate a folder in which to install the filter.

You also can import data from any word processor, spreadsheet, or database that enables you to save documents in text-only (ASCII) format. *Text-only* means that a file carries no assigned style or formatting attributes beyond simple carriage returns, spaces, and tabs. PageMaker comes with a Smart ASCII filter that handles importing and exporting text-only documents. PageMaker applies current default type specifications to imported text-only files.

After you install the filters you need, you can forget about them. Filters work in the background to interpret and place the files you select using the Place Document dialog box.

Tip

If you prepare your documents as text-only files, you can use a much wider range of utilities, such as grammar checkers, that otherwise may not be able to decipher your word processor's proprietary file structures. Use these utilities to check your stories before importing them into PageMaker.

Preparing Formatted Text for Importing

Importing text into PageMaker is fairly straightforward. Problems may occur, however, if your documents contain formatting that PageMaker doesn't recognize or handle well. Because PageMaker doesn't have as many sophisticated editing features as most of today's advanced word processors, you occasionally may encounter some minor incompatibilities when importing text into PageMaker. However, if you import stories directly from other PageMaker files, you experience none of these incompatibilities.

PageMaker handles most character type specifications without difficulty, including font types, styles, and sizes. PageMaker recognizes most fonts as whole-point sizes only, however, rounding any half-point sizes up to the next whole-point size. An exception to this rule is that PageMaker recognizes half-point font sizes when importing MacWrite II files.

PageMaker also supports most superscripting, subscripting, single underlines, and strikethroughs. PageMaker sometimes recognizes a particular format but modifies the format slightly, as when importing super- and subscripted text. Other unique formatting, such as double underlines, hidden text, and formulas, however, always fails to import properly. You can change type specifications after importing using the Type menu commands and Type Specifications dialog box (choose Type Specs from the Type menu).

PageMaker preserves most paragraph formatting when importing text, including tabs, indents, line and paragraph spacing, and left, right, or center justification. PageMaker does not preserve columns, auto page numbers, headers and footers, or widow and orphan control settings. PageMaker also cannot reconstruct right margins. PageMaker does preserve footnotes (with all numbering intact) but groups the footnotes together at the end of your story.

Note

PageMaker sometimes has difficulty handling first-line indents. Regular indents (indented normally to the right) and hanging indents (extended to the left away from the body of a paragraph) sometimes produce unpredictable results. Problems occur if the imported indent is wider than the column into which you place the text.

For example, an overly wide, regular first-line indent may cause the first word of your indented paragraph to be squashed against the right column guide. The squashed type you see displayed on-screen prints the same way on your laser printer (see fig. 5.1).

Make sure that your first-line indents are narrower than the columns into which you place them. If you run into this problem, you can reset the first-line indent marker without reflowing the text. You learn how to handle indents in Chapter 6.

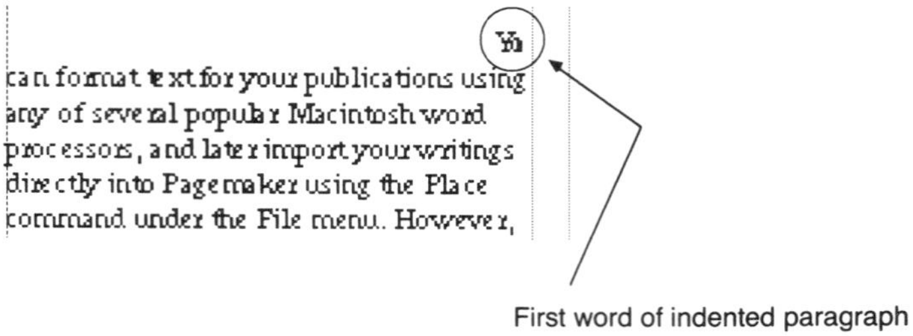

Fig. 5.1

The result of importing a paragraph with a first-line indent set wider than the column.

can format text for your publications using any of several popular Macintosh word processors, and later import your writings directly into Pagemaker using the Place command under the File menu. However,

First word of indented paragraph

PageMaker does a good job of importing left, right, center, leader, and decimal tabs. You can use tabs in your word processor to create complex tables that retain their formatting when imported into PageMaker. As with indents, however, you must be careful to set tab spacing to fit within your columns. After importing your files, you can reset the tabs using PageMaker's Indents/Tabs command from the Type menu.

You also can use PageMaker's Table Editor to create custom tables for use in PageMaker documents. When you use the Table Editor, you avoid many of the problems that may occur with imported word processor files. You learn more about using the Table Editor in Chapter 6.

PageMaker imports styles (preconfigured text formatting) directly from some word processors, most notably Microsoft Word. The amount of formatting that carries over is determined by the import filter and the degree of compatibility the filter allows with PageMaker's own style sheets. To copy styles into PageMaker, be sure the **Retain format** button is checked in the Place Document dialog box. (You learn to import style sheets in Chapter 6 under "Using Style Sheets.")

When importing table-of-contents or index entries, condensed or expanded character spacings, or page-breaks-before-paragraph settings from Microsoft Word 4.0, press the Shift key as you click the OK button in the Place Document dialog box to bring up a Microsoft Word 4.0 Import Filter dialog box. You then can configure the settings appropriate to the file you are importing (see fig. 5.2).

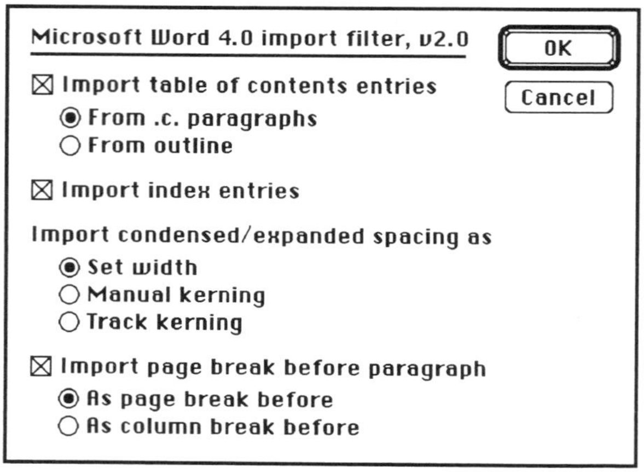

Fig. 5.2

You get the Microsoft Word 4.0 Import Filter dialog box by holding down the Shift key when clicking OK in PageMaker's Place Document dialog box.

Microsoft Word 4.0 import filter, v2.0   [OK]

[Cancel]

☒ Import table of contents entries
  ◉ From .c. paragraphs
  ○ From outline

☒ Import index entries

Import condensed/expanded spacing as
  ◉ Set width
  ○ Manual kerning
  ○ Track kerning

☒ Import page break before paragraph
  ◉ As page break before
  ○ As column break before

PageMaker can import inline (embedded) graphics along with your word processed documents. After the graphics are in PageMaker, you can treat them like any other text. You can adjust tracking, do pair-kerning, and assign new leading values.

You also can manipulate inline graphics as you do other graphics by resizing and cropping them and assigning colors. If the inline graphics are TIFF or Paint images, you can apply PageMaker's full range of image-control editing capabilities. However, you cannot drag an inline graphic left or right but only up or down to adjust its baseline. To convert an inline graphic to an independent graphic, select the graphic using the pointer tool, cut or copy the graphic to the Clipboard, and then paste the graphic back onto your page. You learn more about working with inline graphics in Chapter 8.

Tip

When you save spreadsheet data as text-only files, most spreadsheet applications use carriage returns to delineate columns containing tabs and rows. Similarly, most database applications use tabs to separate fields. This formatting is retained when text-only saved files are imported into PageMaker. For spreadsheet and database applications that use commas instead of tabs, use your word processor to search for the commas and replace them with tabs. After you import the newly formatted documents into PageMaker, you can adjust the tab spacing using the Indents/Tabs command from the Type menu.

Importing Text

The first step before importing text, of course, is to prepare your layout. Set up your columns before you begin and identify how you want your text arranged. Use ruler guides to mark where you want major blocks of text to appear. Don't begin placing text until you complete these initial steps, or you may waste time later readjusting your layout to make everything fit.

You can import text into PageMaker in three ways. You can use the Place command from the File menu to bring in a whole text file at the same time. You can use the Import command on PageMaker's Story menu to display the text in Story view for editing before placing the text. You also can cut and paste selected text via the Clipboard. Whichever method you choose, PageMaker enables you to control fully the final placement of text on your pages.

Using the Place Command To Import Text

The easiest way to import text is to use PageMaker's Place command to flow an entire story at the same time. When you choose Place from the File menu, a Place

Document dialog box appears. The dialog box lists by name the types of documents PageMaker recognizes. Because the Place command is used to import text and graphics files, both kinds of files are listed in the scrollable window of the Place Document dialog box.

Tip

If in doubt about whether a particular file is a story or an illustration, click the file name in the Place Document dialog box. The placement option at the right reads **As new story** or **As new graphic,** depending on the nature of the file.

All stories and headlines that you are importing as text should be housed in separate text blocks for easy handling. A *text block* is an invisible boundary that defines where text sits on a page. A text block can contain as little as one character or as much as a full page of text. The boundaries of the text block become visible when you do one of the following:

❑ Click the text block with the pointer tool.

❑ Draw a selection marquee around the block with the pointer tool.

❑ Choose the Select All command from the Edit menu.

Text blocks can be any size and shape. When you import a lengthy story into PageMaker, many separate text blocks may be required to hold all the text. You can thread text invisibly throughout multiple text blocks to provide story continuity. Additions or deletions made to text anywhere in a threaded text block produce a ripple effect through all the remaining threaded text blocks.

Tip

To locate quickly all text blocks that contain a particular story, no matter where they reside in your publication, click the text tool within one of the text blocks known to contain part of the story. Choose the Select All command from the Edit menu. All the threaded text in all the related text blocks is highlighted.

Using Text Placement Options

The placement options in the Place Document dialog box enable you to import a file as a new story and thread the text independently throughout your publication. You also can use the placement options to replace an existing story or text selection or to insert new text within an existing story (see fig. 5.3). Click the title of the document you want to import from the Place Document dialog box and then click the appropriate button for the option you want to use.

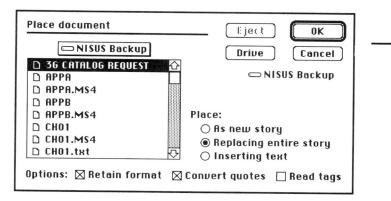

Fig. 5.3

Use PageMaker's Place Document dialog box to place text directly into your publication.

To place a new story, make sure that the **As new story** button is highlighted before you click OK. After the arrow cursor changes to the text-placement icon, click the page where you want to begin flowing the imported text. If you click in a column, PageMaker flows the text to lie entirely within the column boundaries.

To define a new text block on the page or pasteboard to hold imported text, continue holding down the mouse button after you click and drag out a rectangular boundary to the desired size and shape (see fig. 5.4).

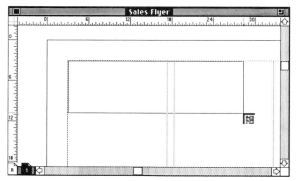

Fig. 5.4

Dragging a text block across column boundaries with the text-placement icon.

When you release the mouse button, PageMaker fills the block with the imported text. If the whole story does not fit, a downward-pointing arrow appears in the windowshade handle at the bottom of the column to indicate that more text remains to be placed (see fig. 5.5).

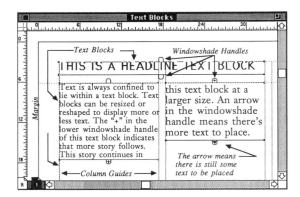

Fig. 5.5

Text blocks can be different sizes and shapes and can stand alone or be invisibly threaded for story continuity.

Tip

To reflow a text block that you have just placed, close the windowshades and then click the top windowshade handle. You get the text placement icon again, ready to reflow the text. This trick can be used to adjust a column's width and reflow the text from the original column to fit the new dimensions. The trick also works with the first text block in a story no matter when the block was placed. Click the top, empty windowshade handle after closing up the text block to recover the text-placement icon.

Note

An empty bottom windowshade handle means no more threaded text follows that text block. An empty upper windowshade handle means no threaded text precedes that text block. Conversely, a plus sign in the bottom windowshade handle means that more threaded text follows that text block. A plus sign in the upper windowshade handle means that threaded text precedes that text block.

To replace an existing story with a new one, click the text tool anywhere in the existing story before choosing Place from the File menu. In the Place Document dialog box, click the **Replacing entire story** button before clicking OK. PageMaker deletes the original story and replaces it with the new one. The arrangement of the text blocks remains the same, but replacing a long story with a short one deletes any excess blocks. Similarly, replacing a short story with a long one extends the last text block down the page to hold the extra text. (If **Autoflow** is selected on the Options menu, text blocks and pages are added as necessary until the entire story is placed.)

> ***Note***
>
> PageMaker has a self-imposed limit of 64K when using the **Replacing entire story** or **Replacing selected text** button. This limit restricts the amount of text you can place at one time. Files larger than 64K must be broken into smaller files before placing them. This size limit does not apply to files placed as new stories.

To insert text into an existing story, first create an insertion point by clicking the text tool at the desired location. You also can highlight any range of text you want replaced. Create the insertion point or highlight the text before choosing Place from the File menu. In the Place Document dialog box, click the **Inserting text** button and then click OK. PageMaker threads the new text starting at the insertion point. If you select a range of text, PageMaker replaces the highlighted text.

Along the bottom of the Place Document dialog box are three options buttons: **Retain format, Convert quotes,** and **Read tags.** The **Retain format** button keeps intact the original formatting of the files you import. This button also enables you to import any style sheets. If you don't use the **Retain format** button, PageMaker assigns the default type specifications to the placed text.

The **Convert quotes** option changes straight quotation marks (") and straight apostrophes (') into curly ones (")('). Use this option with care. If your document formatting isn't perfect, you easily can end up with a backward quotation mark or apostrophe.

The **Read tags** option tells PageMaker to read embedded style tags and use them to format paragraphs. (You learn more about using style tags in Chapter 6.)

Using the Story Importer To Place Text

If you select in the Place Document dialog window an existing PageMaker file from which you want to import a story into your current publication, you get a special PageMaker Story Importer dialog box. Its document selection window shows the first few words of each story in the selected document. Remember, stories can be as short as a headline or caption or many pages in length. You type a number into the **List only stories over xx characters long** field to tell PageMaker the minimum number of characters a story must contain to be eligible for selection (see fig. 5.6).

Because you may have difficulty finding the story you want based on the few beginning words shown, the Story Importer dialog box includes a **View** button. Click this button to get a scrollable viewing window. The viewing window displays the contents of the story you selected (see fig. 5.7). This window feature makes correctly identifying the story you want to place easy.

Fig. 5.6

The Story Importer dialog box enables you to import stories directly from other PageMaker documents.

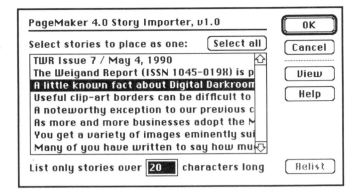

Tip

You can use the Story Importer viewing window to copy selected text from a story in another PageMaker publication to the Clipboard for pasting into your current publication. Use this procedure to include some of the text but not the entire story.

Note

You cannot edit the text displayed in the Story Importer viewing window.

Fig. 5.7

You can preview the contents of PageMaker stories before importing.

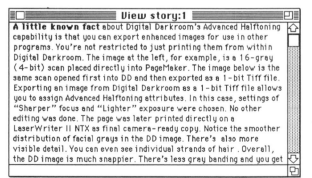

Using Text Flow Options

When you place text into PageMaker, you have three placement choices: manual, automatic, and semiautomatic text flow (see fig. 5.8). The advantages and disadvantages of each method are covered in the following sections.

Fig. 5.8

The text-placement icons for manual, automatic, and semiautomatic text flow.

Manual Flow

Manual flow is the easiest type of document placement to control. When you import a file using the Place command, the manual text-placement icon is the one you already are familiar with: the icon looks like a miniature page of text. When you click to place the story, the imported text flows down existing column guides until the text reaches the bottom of the page. To continue flowing the remaining text, click the downward-pointing arrow in the windowshade handle at the bottom of the column (see the first part of fig. 5.9). This procedure gives you another text-placement icon that you can click elsewhere to continue your story. Continue this process to place the entire story.

In the second part of figure 5.9, the continuation text has flowed into the adjoining column. Note the "+" in the upper windowshade handle, which tells you that threaded text precedes this text block. An arrow in a lower windowshade handle similarly indicates that more threaded text follows that text block. When the windowshade handle is blank, no text remains to be placed.

You can start placing a story on one page of your publication and continue the story on another page. You also can define specific column widths in which to flow text during story placement by holding down the mouse button as you drag out a desired column width. When you release the mouse button, the text flows within the defined boundaries.

Automatic Flow

You can use PageMaker's Autoflow command to flow text from page to page. The Autoflow command is especially useful when importing lengthy stories for books, catalogs, and other long documents.

To use PageMaker's Autoflow feature, choose Autoflow from the Options menu. Then select the story to be placed using the Place command. Notice that when you use Autoflow, the text-placement icon changes to an arrow with a snaked tail. This icon reminds you that the text flows down one column and then immediately down the next. After you click the icon where you want to start flowing text, PageMaker continues filling successive columns, adding pages as necessary, until you have no more text to place (or until the 999-page limit is reached).

Fig. 5.9

*When you place a
story in PageMaker,
each text block
becomes a separate
thread in a
continuous chain.*

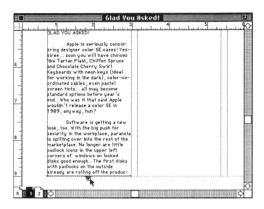

Tip

If your computer has enough memory, you manually can place several stories
at the same time and have PageMaker keep track of the unplaced text as you
work. Suppose that you have several articles that you want to thread
throughout a lengthy newsletter, and all the articles start on the front page.
Instead of working your way through the publication several times to place
each story separately, start all your stories together at the same time. Use the
Place command repeatedly to flow text from each story file into text blocks
on the first page. Proceed through the remainder of your newsletter, page by
page, to place the remaining text for each story. Each time you click a column
windowshade arrow, PageMaker picks up where it left off with that story so
that you can continue placing text. If you use this approach, you have to work
your way through a publication only once to place all your stories.

Autoflow works on publication and master pages but not on the pasteboard. If you click the autoflow text-placement icon on the pasteboard, one column of text forms, and you have to click the windowshade arrow to continue flowing text elsewhere.

You can stop autoflowing at any time by clicking the **Cancel** button in the Composing Text dialog box. To resume autoflowing, click the windowshade arrow. The text-placement icon reappears. Click the text-placement icon on the page to start autoflowing text again.

When PageMaker autoflows text, the text runs over, skips over, or wraps around any graphics. The way in which the text wraps depends on how you configure each graphic using the Text Wrap command from the Element menu. If PageMaker encounters a graphic that completely fills a column, and Text Wrap is set so that the story skips over the image, PageMaker places an empty text block at the top of the column as a placeholder. (The empty text block has upper and lower windowshades pressed together—no text can fit in the empty text block until the block expands.) If you later move or resize the graphic, the empty text block expands downward to fill the open space. You learn how to configure graphics for text wrap in Chapter 8.

When PageMaker runs into another block of text while autoflowing, the text being flowed starts at the top of the next open column instead of jumping over the existing text. The usefulness of autoflow, therefore, is limited in documents where multiple blocks of text are scattered about on your pages. To overcome this limitation, you can flow text semiautomatically, a process discussed in the following section.

Figure 5.10 shows how PageMaker flows text automatically in some typical situations. Part A of the figure shows the screen as you get ready to autoflow a story onto a page with a graphic at the top of the second column and a stray text block overlapping the first column.

Part B of the figure shows that as the story flows down the first column, the stray text block forces text flow to jump to the top of the second column. However, because that column is filled with a graphic, PageMaker places an empty text block above the graphic and then skips to the top of the third column to continue flowing text. After filling the third column, the program continues autoflowing text throughout your publication, adding new pages as needed until the entire story is placed.

Part C of the figure shows that by deleting the stray text block (select the block with the pointer tool and press the Del key) and pulling down the lower windowshade handle of the preceding text block, text flows down the remainder of the first column.

Part D of the figure shows that cropping the graphic to conceal the uppermost image causes the empty text block above the graphic to expand downward. (You learn about cropping graphics in Chapter 7.) Text flows into the empty space.

Fig. 5.10

Autoflowing text in a typical publication layout.

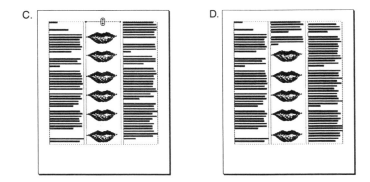

Semiautomatic Flow

Semiautomatic flow works much like manual flow in that text stops at the bottom of each column. Unlike manual flow, however, you don't have to click the windowshade arrow to recover the text-placement icon. When flow stops in one column, the text-placement icon reappears, ready to continue placing text in another column. This feature gives you more control over text placement than you have with autoflow. You can continue flowing stories past other text blocks in the same column, for example, without skipping to the top of the next open column. Flowing text semiautomatically is slower than autoflowing but less tedious than placing your stories manually.

Changing Text-Flow Modes

You can switch quickly between text-flow modes at any time during story placement using special combination keystrokes. The only way to flow text semiautomatically is to hold down the Shift key when clicking a text-placement icon. Pressing the Shift key changes the autoflow and manual flow icons into the semiautomatic flow icon. The semiautomatic flow icon looks similar to the autoflow icon, except that the curved tail of the arrow is a dashed instead of a solid line.

You can change text-flow from automatic to manual by holding the Command key when clicking the text-placement icon.

Tip

If you already have clicked OK in the Place Document dialog box but decide not to flow the text, click the pointer tool in the toolbox to cancel the operation.

Using the Clipboard To Import Text

When you import text using the Clipboard, you get different results depending on where the text originates. If you copy text from another application, the text is assigned PageMaker's default type specifications when you paste the text into PageMaker. Whether you copy and paste text from another PageMaker document or from your current PageMaker publication, the text retains the existing type specifications, even if the text is pasted into the middle of a block formatted with styles.

If you highlight a selection with the text tool and copy the text to the Clipboard, the text wraps to fit within column boundaries when pasted back into the document. If you use PageMaker's pointer tool to select and copy a block of text, the block of text retains its original dimensions when pasted back onto your pages. If you click the text tool in an existing block of text to create an insertion point before pasting, the text you paste threads itself into that story.

Linking Your Stories

PageMaker can track the text and graphics you place into your publications. Pagemaker can update your publications each time the original files change by building an independent link to each source file. These links tell PageMaker the name of the file, where the file is stored, what kind of file it is (text, EPS graphic, TIFF image, etc.), the size of the file, when you placed the file in your publication, and when you last modified the file. PageMaker also tracks any internal modifications you make. You can decide whether to let PageMaker update the file.

Tip

You can use the Clipboard to create composite text from multiple text blocks. If you first click the text tool in a story to create an insertion point before pasting, or if you click-drag to define a column boundary, the separate text blocks reappear as one continuous block of text. If, however, you select a group of text blocks, copy them together as a unit to the Clipboard, and then paste them back into PageMaker, they reappear as separate text blocks.

Use this technique to meld multiple text blocks into one or to thread them into an existing block of text. When you combine multiple text blocks this way, the composite text reads in sequential order if you first click each text block and choose Bring To Front from the Element menu. This process stacks the blocks so that they are in the correct order when you copy or cut them to the Clipboard. The pasted text reads sequentially starting with the first block you brought to the front to the contents of the last. The pasted text also retains its style specifications.

The primary control center for managing links is the Links dialog box, which shows the current status of all linked files (see fig. 5.11). Choose the Links command from the File menu to display the Links dialog box.

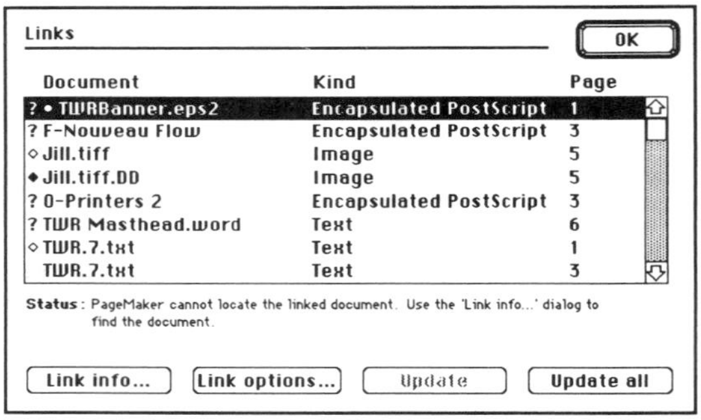

Fig. 5.11

The Links dialog box.

Links			OK
Document	**Kind**	**Page**	
? • TWRBanner.eps2	Encapsulated PostScript	1	
? F-Nouveau Flow	Encapsulated PostScript	3	
◇ Jill.tiff	Image	5	
◆ Jill.tiff.DD	Image	5	
? 0-Printers 2	Encapsulated PostScript	3	
? TWR Masthead.word	Text	6	
◇ TWR.7.txt	Text	1	
TWR.7.txt	Text	3	

Status : PageMaker cannot locate the linked document. Use the 'Link info...' dialog to find the document.

[Link info...] [Link options...] [Update] [Update all]

To display more detailed link data for any particular source file, click the **Link info** button or select the element in your publication and choose Link Info from the Element menu. This procedure brings up the Link Info dialog box (see fig. 5.12).

The symbols to the left of the file names in the Links dialog box show the status of the link for each file. If no indicator appears, the link is current or no link is established for that file. A question mark indicates that PageMaker cannot find the file. Click the **Link info** button to help PageMaker locate the file.

A black diamond symbol in the Links dialog box indicates that modifications have been made to the file. PageMaker updates the internal version the next time you open

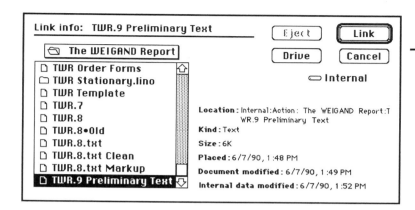

Fig. 5.12

The Link Info dialog box gives a complete status report of each linked file.

your publication. A hollow diamond is the same as a black diamond, except that PageMaker does not update your publication automatically. A hollow triangle indicates that modifications exist for the external linked file and the internal version. If you update, you lose all changes made to the internal version.

The Links dialog box also shows on which page you placed text or graphics. Other page indicators include **LM** and **RM** for left and right master pages, **PB** for the pasteboard, **X** for an open story that you have not yet placed, **OV** for a linked text element that is overset but not completely placed, and **Page #?** for a linked inline graphic within a story that has not been placed.

PageMaker builds links for all stories you import using the Place and Import commands. To link stories you create using PageMaker's Story Editor, you can export your stories using the Export command from the File menu (you learn how to export stories later in this chapter). PageMaker builds a link to each exported story file.

You can instruct PageMaker to update stories automatically or to alert you before updating (see fig. 5.13). You should check the **Alert before updating** box in the Link Options dialog box. Otherwise, you may find that PageMaker updates your files with altered versions that completely disrupt your page layout. For example, after you have assigned kerning, changed tracking, adjusted spacing, or applied some other type or style modifications to a story, updating that story causes you to lose all your newly assigned formatting. PageMaker warns you about this possibility (see fig. 5.14).

Text files should be as complete as possible when you first place them into your publications so that you don't have to worry about recomposing your layouts because of revisions to the source files. When you work with text, spec your copy before placing it and then do any last-minute editing using PageMaker's Story Editor. However, if you prefer to do all your formatting using a compatible word processor (like Microsoft Word), and if you generally save final layout and

Fig. 5.13

*You can configure
PageMaker to warn
you before it updates
a linked element.*

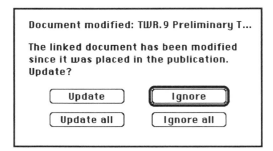

Fig. 5.14

*Updating a linked
element causes you to
lose all modifications
done within
PageMaker.*

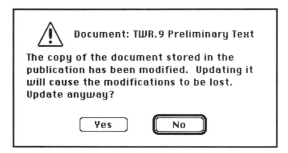

formatting changes until just before printing, using PageMaker's links to update your stories can greatly streamline the publishing process.

PageMaker searches for links when opening a publication and while printing a publication. If PageMaker cannot find a link, you are given a chance to cancel printing (see fig. 5.15).

Fig. 5.15

*PageMaker verifies
the status of each link
when printing a
publication.*

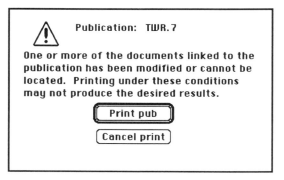

If you move an external linked file to a new location on your hard disk, change its file name, change the name of your hard disk, or change the names of any of the folders in which the file is nested, you break the link. You can re-establish a link between an element and its source file by clicking the **Link** button in the Link Info dialog box or the **Update** or **Update all** button in the Links dialog box.

Linking is a powerful feature that can make preparing complex publications easy, particularly when working within a shared workgroup environment where text editing changes and file updates must be tracked carefully throughout each revision stage. Unfortunately, updating stories via links also can lead to unexpected difficulties if not approached with care. PageMaker's linking features are best used for managing and updating graphics files. You learn more about linking graphics in Chapter 7.

Creating and Editing Text

You can use PageMaker's text tool to type new text or edit old text in the layout view. Select the text tool from the toolbox and click anywhere on your page to get started.

If you click within an existing text block, the text you type becomes part of that story and takes on the same formatting as the surrounding text. Text that comes after the insertion point is pushed forward to accommodate the new material. The text blocks don't change size or shape, except for the last text block in the story, which expands to handle any overflow.

If you click the text tool outside an existing text block, anything you type takes on PageMaker's default type specifications. The new block assumes different shapes, depending on where you click. Click anywhere within a column, and the insertion point appears at that column's left-column guide. As you type, text wraps at the right-column guide to fit within the column.

If you click the text tool in a page margin or on the pasteboard, whatever text you type wraps within a column width equal to the distance between your document's left and right margin settings. Click and drag to specify a column width, and your words wrap to lie within that defined column width, even if that area starts between, or extends across, existing column boundaries.

Tip

The click-drag technique is a powerful way to control the placement of text. Use this technique to create large text blocks to hold items like headlines and pull quotes that span multiple columns. Also, click-drag to create small text blocks for holding narrow items like picture captions and page numbers.

To create text blocks having an exact width, drag two vertical ruler guides onto your page. Use your ruler tick marks to set these guides exactly where you want them. Then click-drag the text tool or text-placement icon between the guides. Make sure that the Snap To Guides command in the Options menu is toggled on.

As you continue typing within a column, the text extends down the page. Text blocks lengthen as necessary to hold whatever text you type into them. However, if the bottom of a text block bumps into a non-wrapping graphic, touches the lower edge of the page, or reaches the edge of the pasteboard, the computer beeps. If you try to type more characters, you get an error message telling you that PageMaker no longer can show the insertion point (see fig. 5.16). If you receive this message, drag a corner handle to resize your text block and resume typing. You also can click the windowshade arrow and create a text block to hold any text overflow.

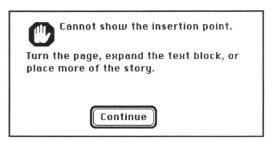

Fig. 5.16

PageMaker must display the text cursor when you enter new text.

Tip

If you click instead of click-dragging the cursor before typing, pasting, or placing text in a page margin or on the pasteboard, the width of the column becomes the same as the distance between your publication's left and right page margins. This distance sometimes can be quite large. When you later drag the text block onto your pages, the text block may overlap other columns and block the automatic flow of newly placed text. You may not notice this overlap at first, because the boundary of the text block remains invisible until you select the block with the pointer tool. Your text block also may overlap other elements in the same vicinity, such as captions, lines, ruler guides, and graphics. The overlap makes selecting these elements with the pointer tool difficult.

The easiest way to control the size of a text block is to click-drag using the text tool or text-placement tool to define a specific column width. Define a specific column width before typing or pasting or when you place text. In any case, you always can adjust the width of a too-long text block later. Select the block with the pointer tool to highlight the invisible boundary and then drag a corner handle.

To edit existing text, click the text tool to create an insertion point, backspace to delete individual characters, and type any replacement text. You also can replace a range of text by dragging across the selection with the text tool and typing new text to effect the replacement. The familiar Macintosh Cut, Copy, Paste, and Clear commands on the Edit menu also can be used to effect changes to selected text (for details on how these commands work, consult the manual that came with your Macintosh).

Tip

To select a particularly lengthy passage of text for editing, create an insertion point at the start of your selection and then hold down the Shift key while clicking to mark the end of your selection. Everything lying between the clicks is highlighted for editing. This technique works anywhere in the same story, even if the start and the end of your selection lie on different pages.

With PageMaker, you can use the keyboard cursor-movement (arrow) keys as a shortcut to move a text insertion point up, down, left, or right, one character or line at a time. If you hold down these keys, the movement is repeated. You also can use the numeric keypad to do the same thing. The 8, 2, 4, and 6 number keys on the numeric keypad correspond respectively to the up, down, left, and right cursor-movement keys. If you hold down the Shift key while pressing these keys, all the intervening text is selected.

Using the Story Editor

The Story Editor is a built-in word processor that displays your story as a text file for straightforward editing. You don't have to deal with the constant screen refreshes you get in the layout view each time you make an editing change. With the Story Editor, you can create new stories, import stories from other applications for editing before placement, and edit stories already in your publication. You also can view special characters like tabs and carriage returns by choosing Display from the Options menu (see fig. 5.17).

The Story Editor is strictly for processing text. When you are finished, you place (or replace) your story into your publication. You do any necessary layout and copy-fitting that has to be done in the layout view.

Opening Your Stories

To open the Story Editor, triple-click using the pointer tool on any text block containing part of your story. Your story opens with the text centered roughly at the spot in the story where you clicked. You also can type an insertion point in your story using the text tool and then choose Edit Story from the Edit window. Your story opens with the insertion point in the same place where you clicked. To use the Story Editor to create a story or to import a story created elsewhere, choose Edit Story from the Edit window. Make sure that no text block is selected and no insertion point is placed in any story.

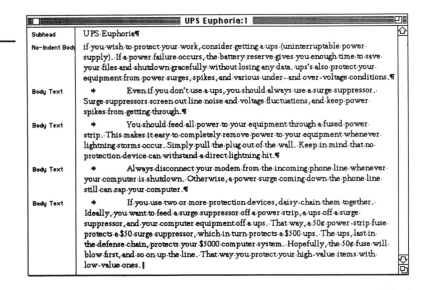

Fig. 5.17

*The Story view with
Display selected.*

Note

When you open the Story Editor, the PageMaker menu bar changes to reflect
the new working environment. The Page and Element menus disappear, and
a new Story menu appears. Also, the contents of the Edit and Options menus
change. Commands on the Edit menu that pertain only to the Layout view
dim, and entries that pertain only to the Story view become active. Commands
on the Options menu that pertain only to the Layout view disappear and two
new menu commands that pertain only to the Story view appear (see fig. 5.18).

Fig. 5.18

*The Main menu bar
changes when you
switch from Layout to
Story view.*

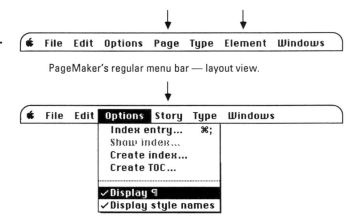

PageMaker's regular menu bar — layout view.

PageMaker's shortened menu bar — story view.

You can have several Story windows open at the same time. Each Story window contains one story. This feature makes copying, cutting, and pasting text between different articles easy. To open more than one Story window, choose New Story from the Story menu or return to the Layout view without closing the currently open story and open another story. To return to the Layout view, click anywhere on your publication pages or choose your publication's title from the Windows menu.

The Windows menu lists your publication's title and all stories open in the Story Editor. The Windows menu identifies stories by showing the first few words of each story. Choose the appropriate menu listing to jump quickly between Story views and your layout.

When you open a story in the Story Editor, the corresponding text blocks in your publication are grayed out. When you close a Story window, the text reflows back into your publication. You also can choose the Replace command from the File menu to reflow an existing story. This menu command changes from Replace to Place when you work on a new story or on a newly imported story in the Story Editor. Choose the Place command to place the new story into your publication. The text-placement icon you get is the same one you see when placing a story from the Place Document dialog box.

To cancel placing a story from the Story Editor, click the pointer tool in PageMaker's tool box. PageMaker returns you to the Story view so that you can continue editing. If you close a Story window or your publication without placing a story open in the Story Editor, you get a dialog box with three choices: **Place, Discard,** and **Cancel** (see fig. 5.19). You can place, discard, or leave your story open for further editing. If you save changes (using PageMaker's Save or Save As commands) and close your publication, the next time you open your publication the unplaced stories reopen so that you can continue editing where you left off.

Fig. 5.19

PageMaker warns you if you close a story in Story view without first placing it in your publication layout.

The Story Editor displays stories in whatever font type and size you specify in the Preferences dialog box (choose Preferences from the Edit menu). You can assign various type styles (except for Reverse) and view them in the Story window. You also can assign paragraph styles, but you cannot see them until you return to the Layout view. Paragraph styles, however, are listed by name in a sidebar to the left of the Story window. You can toggle this display on or off using the Display Style Names command from the Story Editor Options menu.

> **Tip**
>
> Clicking a paragraph style name selects the entire paragraph for editing in the Story window.

Because the Story Editor is intended only for processing text, the Story Editor does not display story formatting. To examine character and word spacing, line breaks, hyphenation, pair-kerning, and so on, you have to be in the layout view.

Remember that Story Editor enables you to view special characters like carriage returns, tabs, and space markers. This feature enables you to check basic formatting without switching back to the layout view. Select the Display command from the Story Editor Options menu to toggle between the two different displays.

The Story Editor displays special markers in your text to show the positions of inline graphics, page number markers, and index entries (see fig. 5.20). You cannot manipulate these markers (to resize an inline graphic for example), but you can cut, copy, paste, and delete them, and the changes show up in your publication when you place your stories. You also can import and paste pictures directly into the Story Editor where they appear as inline-graphics markers. The actual graphics appear in your layout after you place the story.

Fig. 5.20

The Story Editor uses special markers as placeholders for index entries, page numbers, and inline graphics.

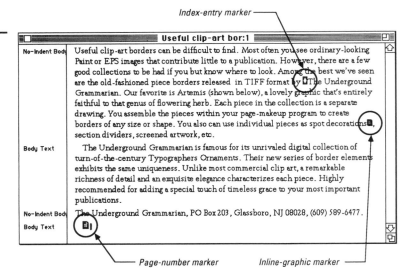

The Underground Grammarian is famous for its unrivaled digital collection of turn-of-the-century Typographers Ornaments. Their new series of border elements exhibits the same uniqueness. Unlike most commercial clip art, a remarkable richness of detail and an exquisite elegance characterizes each piece. Highly recommended for adding a special touch of timeless grace to your most important publications.

Spell Checking Your Stories

PageMaker includes a 100,000-word spell checker accessible through the Story Editor. You can install a number of language dictionaries (available from Aldus), but you can use only one at a time. Choose a language dictionary from the pop-up Dictionary menu in the Paragraph Specifications dialog box (choose Paragraph from the Type menu).

Choose the Spelling command from the Story view Edit menu to display the Spelling dialog box (see fig. 5.21). When spell checking, you can instruct PageMaker to check a selected range of text, the current story, or all stories. Click the appropriate button for the type of search you want PageMaker to do.

When confronted with an unknown word, PageMaker displays that word in the **Change to** field. You can ignore the word if it is correct (click the **Ignore** button or press the Return or Enter key). You also can edit the word and click the **Replace** button to effect the change. If you prefer, you can select a replacement word from the scrollable list of possible substitutions. Click the **Replace** button to effect the change.

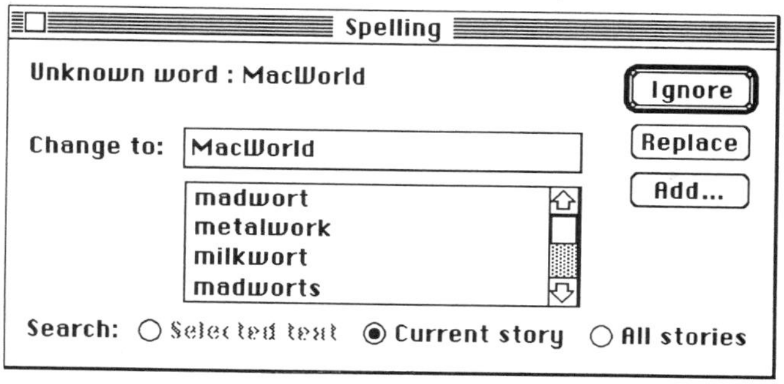

Fig. 5.21

PageMaker uses a 100,000-word dictionary to check your stories for correct spelling.

If you want PageMaker to learn a word, click the **Add** button. PageMaker displays an Add Word to User Dictionary dialog box (see fig. 5.22). The word from the **Change to** field of the Spelling dialog box is shown in the **Word** field, complete with suggested hyphenation breaks (PageMaker uses the same dictionaries to check spelling and hyphenate text). The number of hyphens between syllables indicates the ranking of hyphenation choices (the fewer the hyphens, the higher the ranking). You can edit the word and the hyphenation breaks. Click the appropriate **Add** button to add the word to your dictionary exactly as the word appears or in all lowercase letters. Click the OK button to effect the update.

Tip

While spell checking your publications, you can leave the Spelling dialog box without closing it to open desk accessories or other programs (if running under MultiFinder). This feature enables you to verify the correct spelling of proper names or any other words you may want to add to the user dictionary.

When adding words to the dictionary, make sure that you enter them correctly. PageMaker does not enable you to view words stored in the user dictionary.

You can remove any word you have added to the user dictionary. To delete a word, type the word to be removed into the **Word** field and then click the **Remove** button.

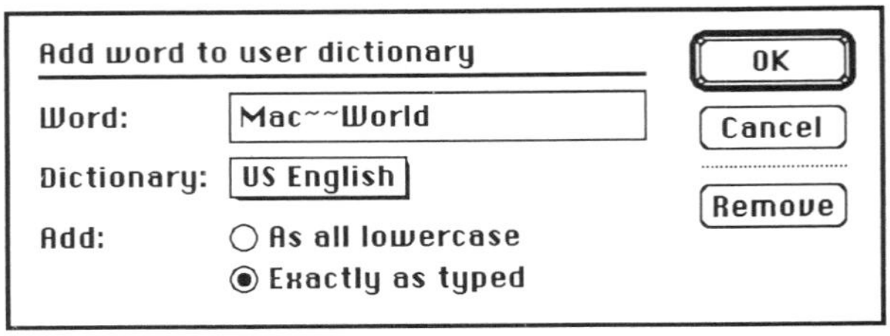

Fig. 5.22

You can add new words, including hyphenation breaks, to PageMaker's user dictionary.

Add word to user dictionary

OK

Word: Mac~~World

Dictionary: US English

Cancel

Remove

Add: ○ As all lowercase
          ◉ Exactly as typed

Finding and Changing Text

The Story Editor enables you to find and change text using the Find, Find Next, and Change commands on the Edit menu. You can search for specific text or search by paragraph styles and text attributes such as font types, styles, and sizes (see fig. 5.23). You also can search for special nonprinting characters like tabs and carriage returns. PageMaker even supports wild-card searches. Type the expression ^? for each missing character in the **Find what** field of the Find or Change dialog boxes. For example, to find all occurrences of Smyth and Smith in a directory publication, you type *Sm^?th* in the **Find what** field. To narrow a search, select the **Match case** and **Whole word** options as appropriate. For example, searching for the whole word "m^?^?n" finds "moon" and "mien" but not "moonbeam" (see fig. 5.24). If you also select the **Match case** option, PageMaker finds "moon" but not "Moon."

As with PageMaker's spell checker, you can search a selected range of text, the current story, or all stories in a publication. When you search all stories using the Find command, PageMaker stops each time that a match occurs. To continue searching, click the **Find Next** button, use the Find Next command on the Edit menu, or press the keyboard shortcut Command-, (comma). If you search all stories using the Change command and click the **Change All** button to effect all changes at the same time, PageMaker opens and closes each Story window until the entire publication has been searched and all changes have been made.

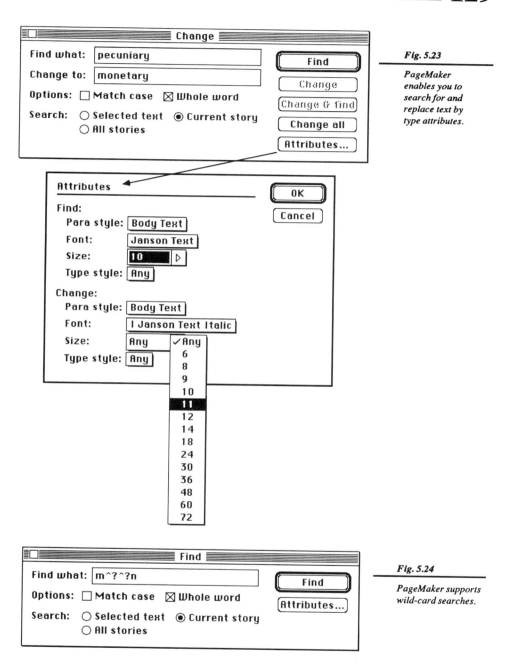

Fig. 5.23

PageMaker enables you to search for and replace text by type attributes.

Fig. 5.24

PageMaker supports wild-card searches.

> **Tip**
>
> Use PageMaker's capability to search for and change text based on attributes to make global formatting changes (for example, changing all subheads from 12-point Times Roman bold to 11-point Helvetica bold-italic) throughout your publication. Making global formatting changes often is more convenient than updating or changing style sheets or applying styles individually to selected paragraphs. (You learn about using style sheets in Chapter 6.)

Fonts and Type Styles

A *typeface* consists of a family of fonts. Each *font* is a distinct style variation on the basic typeface. For example, Times and Helvetica are typefaces, but Times 12-point italic and Helvetica 24-point bold are fonts. Typefaces may be proportional or non-proportional. Proportional faces, like Times and Helvetica, use variable character spacing to produce a more pleasing typeset appearance. Non-proportional or monospaced typefaces, like Courier, closely resemble typewritten text, with each character equally spaced. Monospaced typefaces give text a slightly uneven appearance. Non-proportional type is used rarely today unless needed to simulate the informal look of typewritten copy (see fig. 5.25).

Fig. 5.25

These typefaces are the same size and style, but they look completely different because of their character spacing.

This is Times. It's a proportional, serif face. Each of its characters enjoys a slightly different spacing for a better fit with its neighbors. This gives Times an almost typeset, business look.

This is Courier. It's a non-proportional, serif face. Each of its characters is equally spaced. This gives Courier an informal "typewritten" look.

One common mistake beginning desktop publishers make is using the wrong kinds of fonts in their publications. You may be tempted to use monospaced fonts like Courier because you're comfortable with the look of typewritten copy. This font is okay if your readers expect a casual-looking publication, but not if they expect one that appears professionally typeset. At other times, you may mistakenly use for body text the more difficult-to-read sans serif decorative faces. Instead, stick to serif bookfaces for body copy. Serif type has proven itself satisfactory for a wide variety of publishing tasks. Most readers now expect the documents they read to be set using a traditional serif face.

For headlines, avoid small serif fonts that nearly are indistinguishable from the text of your stories. Don't mix multiple typefaces such as bold, outlined, shadowed, and italic styles on the same page. Although PageMaker enables you to use a wide variety of font types, sizes, and styles in your documents, remember that using all this typesetting power for every publishing task is not necessary.

Setting Type Attributes

In PageMaker, you choose the fonts and type styles you want to apply to selected text from the Type menu or Type Specifications dialog box (select Type Specs from the Type menu). You also can preset font and type style choices as program and file defaults. The right-pointing arrowheads under the Type menu indicate that the submenus pop up to the right of the main menu. Drag the pointer into a submenu to assign a particular font attribute to selected text or to set a program or file default.

PageMaker's Type menu contains six hierarchical submenus used specifically for assigning type attributes to text. The Font submenu lists your system's installed fonts, and the Size and Type Style submenus offer a generous selection of popular font sizes and styles. The Leading submenu enables you to vary the space between successive lines of type. (Although you can assign leading to selected text using the Type menu and Type Specifications dialog box, leading often is considered a paragraph or story specification. You learn more about leading in Chapter 6.) The Track submenu you learn about later in this chapter.

Another submenu, Set Width, enables you to vary character widths without altering letter or word spacing. This command is the same as the **Set width** option in the Type Specifications dialog box. To scale character widths horizontally, choose one of the fixed percentages listed in the submenu or choose Other to enter any scaling value between 0.1% and 250%. You can change horizontal character scaling in 0.1% increments. This capability is useful especially for adjusting the sometimes squashed look of small caps. Horizontal character scaling also serves as an effective design tool for manipulating display type.

PageMaker's Type submenus list the most popular font attributes. A wider selection of choices is available using the Type Specifications dialog box (see fig. 5.26). The primary advantage of using the Type Specifications dialog box (choose Type Specs from the Type menu) is that you can set several attributes at the same time. When you use the hierarchical Type submenus, you have to pull down the menus repeatedly and set each type attribute separately.

The Type Specifications dialog box also uses pop-up submenus. The submenus are displayed when you click a font attribute. Make your selections by dragging the pointer tool through the menus, just as you do when using a normal drop-down menu.

Fig. 5.26

*PageMaker's Type
Specifications dialog
box.*

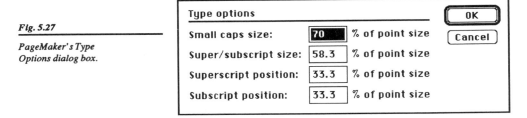

Using the Type Specifications dialog box, you gain access to two pop-up submenus not available from the Type menu. These menus are Case (with the options **Normal, All caps,** and **Small caps**) and Position (with the options **Normal, Superscript,** and **Subscript**). A pop-up color menu also enables you to assign colors to selected text. Click the **Options** button to get the Type Options dialog box in which you can adjust the percentage size and position values PageMaker assigns to small caps and super- and subscripted text (see fig. 5.27). The percentages are based on currently selected type sizes.

Fig. 5.27

*PageMaker's Type
Options dialog box.*

The Type Specifications dialog box enables you to assign more precise type attributes than you can select from the individual Type submenus.

Tip

Many of PageMaker's dialog boxes contain buttons that open additional dialog boxes. To quickly exit a series of nested dialog boxes, press the Option key as you click the OK or Cancel button or as you press the Return or Enter key. These procedures close all open dialog boxes and return you to your publication's Layout or Story view.

Font Types

PageMaker normally lists in the Font menu and Type Specifications dialog box the fonts installed currently in your system. If you open a PageMaker document created using fonts not installed in your system, however, PageMaker also displays the names of those fonts but grays out the names to indicate that they are not installed. You cannot select a grayed-out menu listing.

Tip

To find out the fonts, sizes, and style attributes used in a document created on someone else's system, select some of the text in question and choose Type Specs from the Type menu to bring up the Type Specifications dialog box. The correct type specifications for that text are displayed, even when those fonts are missing from your system (the names of all the missing fonts used in the document are shown grayed out in the pop-up Font menus). After you identify the missing fonts, install the fonts in your system before printing the document.

Font Sizes

PageMaker's hierarchical Type Size menu enables you to apply a limited selection of fixed point sizes (6, 8, 9, 10, 12, 14, 18, 24, 30, 36, 48, 60, and 72 points) to your text. If you need a size other than those listed, choose **Other** and enter the desired value into the dialog box that appears or use the Type Specifications dialog box and enter a value into the **Size** field. You can assign any type size between 4 and 650 points in 1/10th-point increments.

Tip

A quick way to change font sizes without accessing a menu or dialog box is to use the keyboard shortcuts Option-Command-Shift-> and Option-Command-Shift-<. Each time you press one of these combinations, the highlighted text becomes one point-size larger or smaller, respectively. If you press Command-Shift-> or Command-Shift-<, your text increases or decreases incrementally according to the point sizes listed in the Type Size menu.

> ### Tip
>
> The largest font size that PageMaker can produce is 650 points. To create and use larger font sizes, you must type the text in a program that enables you to save files in PICT or EPS format. You then import these files into PageMaker as graphic images. Because the text is a graphic image, you can stretch the text to any desired size. The oversized text still prints smoothly.
>
> You can achieve the same results by copying a block of text using the pointer tool (remember that a block of text can contain only one character) and pasting the block of text to the Scrapbook. Use PageMaker's Place command to place the Scrapbook. The text block pastes into your publication as a graphic that you can resize.

Type Styles

You can assign type styles individually using the Type Styles menu or collectively by selecting options in the Type Specifications dialog box. A type style consists of attributes, such as bold, italic, or underlined, that you assign to a selection of text to differentiate it from surrounding text. You can combine multiple type styles for a given text selection. A common example is a headline assigned bold and italic styles at the same time. PageMaker provides the following type styles from which you can choose:

> Normal
> Bold
> Italic
> Underline
> Strikethrough
> Outline
> Shadow
> Reverse

Type styles are best applied sparingly. Outline, shadow, and reverse (white type that can be viewed only if set against a dark background) should be used strictly for special effect. Underlined type should be used rarely—bold or italic styles are more effective for adding emphasis (underlining is a holdover from early typewriter days when bold and italic were not available as options).

Position and Case

The Position menu in the Type Specifications dialog box gives you three choices for arranging text: **Normal, Superscript,** and **Subscript.** You usually work with normal text: text positioned directly on the character baseline. Superscripted and subscripted text is smaller than normal text and raised above or below the baseline. Superscripts and subscripts generally are used for typesetting mathematical formulas, scientific notation, footnote markers, and special characters, including trademark, registration, and copyright symbols.

PageMaker's Case menu in the Type Specifications dialog box also provides three choices: **Normal case**, **All caps**, and **Small caps**. When you choose **Normal case**, your text looks just as you originally typed it, generally a mixture of upper- and lowercase letters. When you choose **All caps**, however, selected text is converted to all uppercase characters. The **Small caps** option affects lowercase letters, changing them to small caps (at whatever percent of full size you assign in the Type Options dialog box). Use the **All Caps** and **Small Caps** options sparingly. Text consisting of all caps, even a mixture of full-size and small caps, is more difficult to read than text consisting of uppercase and lowercase letters.

Tip

The Case and Position menu options have keyboard equivalents that you can use to make type style assignments without bringing up the Type Specifications dialog box. The keyboard shortcuts are listed in the following chart:

Option	*Keyboard shortcut*
Small caps	Command-Shift-H
All caps	Command-Shift-K
Subscript	Command-Shift- - (minus)
Superscript	Command-Shift- + (plus)

To undo these assignments, press the same key combinations again.

Typing Special Characters

Almost all fonts come with a complement of built-in special characters, including curly quotation marks and apostrophes, trademark and copyright symbols, bullets, paragraph markers, and so on. You can use the Apple Key Caps desk accessory supplied with your system software to identify the locations of these characters on your keyboard (refer to your Macintosh user's manual for details on using the Apple Key Caps desk accessory).

PageMaker provides additional special characters that are useful for formatting text. The most important of these characters are the page-number marker (Command-Option-p), which you learned about in Chapter 3, four nonbreaking spaces, and a nonbreaking hyphen.

Nonbreaking spaces are inserted between words or characters to ensure that adjoining text stays together on the line. PageMaker's four nonbreaking spaces are as follows:

Em space (Command-Shift-M) equal to the selected point size

En space (Command-Shift-N) equal to 1/2 the selected point size

Thin space (Command-Shift-T) equal to 1/4 the selected point size

Fixed space (Option-spacebar) varies according to the selected font type

---

Tip

Because the fixed space is font dependent, the space may not be available. If you find that you cannot type a fixed space in one font, select another font of the same type size from the Type menu. Type the fixed space using that font and then select the original font to continue typing. Remember that a fixed space is roughly the same size as a thin space, and you may be able to use one in place of the other.

You can type a *nonbreaking hyphen* by pressing Command-Option-- (hyphen). The nonbreaking hyphen enables you to keep hyphenated text, including numbers with minus signs in front of them, together on the same line (see fig. 5.28).

Fig. 5.28

Use a nonbreaking hyphen to keep a hyphenated word from breaking at the end of a line.

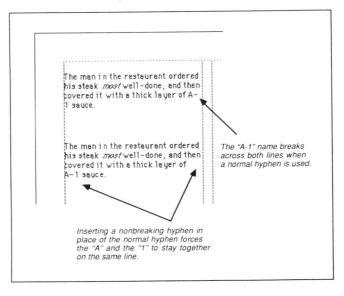

The man in the restaurant ordered his steak *most* well-done, and then covered it with a thick layer of A-1 sauce.

The man in the restaurant ordered his steak *most* well-done, and then covered it with a thick layer of A-1 sauce.

The "A-1" name breaks across both lines when a normal hyphen is used.

Inserting a nonbreaking hyphen in place of the normal hyphen forces the "A" and the "1" to stay together on the same line.

Another special character worthy of mention is the *discretionary hyphen*. The discretionary hyphen is a hyphen inserted manually to tell PageMaker where to break a word at the end of a line if PageMaker does not list that word in its hyphenation dictionary. To add a discretionary hyphen, press Command-- (hyphen) at the point where you want the word to break at the end of a line. You don't see the discretionary hyphen until hyphenation occurs. (You learn more about discretionary hyphenation in Chapter 6.)

Kerning Type

To *kern type* is to adjust the space between adjoining characters to obtain a more pleasing fit. Kerning has little noticeable effect on small type sizes: most type is designed to look good at 12 points or less. However, kerning becomes important when you are typesetting headlines and other large text. At larger point sizes, unequal spacing between adjoining characters quickly becomes noticeable.

To eliminate unsightly gaps, you can let PageMaker kern your text. PageMaker uses the pair-kerning information built into each installed font. (PageMaker pair-kerns type based on specific character pair information. For example, the character pair consisting of a capital *T* and a lowercase *o* is stored in the installed fonts.) You can refine automatically kerned type further by kerning manually.

Automatic Kerning

To have PageMaker kern your type, choose the Paragraph command from the Type menu to display the Paragraph Specifications dialog box. Click the **Spacing** button to bring up the Spacing Attributes dialog box (see fig. 5.29). Click the **Pair kerning Auto** button and type a point size above which you want type to be kerned. Be sure that you set a point size large enough so that only headlines and other text you want kerned are affected. PageMaker does not kern type smaller than the value you specify.

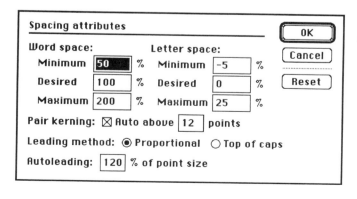

Fig. 5.29

PageMaker's Spacing Attributes dialog box.

Because automatic pair-kerning causes your screen display to refresh slowly, the less type you kern, the quicker you can work. To help speed production, wait to apply pair-kerning until your publication is nearly complete.

To kern an unkerned paragraph, insert the cursor anywhere in the paragraph before turning on pair-kerning. To auto-kern a group of unkerned paragraphs, select them first with the text tool. PageMaker auto-kerns whole paragraphs, even if only parts of the paragraph are highlighted. If you later delete one character of a kerned pair, the other character reverts to its normal spacing without affecting other kerned pairs. If you turn off automatic pair-kerning for a paragraph, the paragraph text reverts to its normal unkerned spacing.

Automatic kerning works only with fonts having built-in pair-kerning information. You cannot tell by looking at a font, however, what built-in kerning information the font has, but you can see the effects of kerning on-screen when using large type sizes. If pair-kerning doesn't work satisfactorily for a particular font, you still can kern the type manually. You also can kern type manually that has been kerned automatically. The effects are cumulative.

Manual Kerning

Kerning type manually gives you the most control over the final appearance of your text. Although the built-in spacing of many fonts is satisfactory, some jobs call for more refined character spacing. For example, headlines generally call for tighter spacing so that they are compact and easy-to-read. At times, you may want to widen the space between selected characters for heightened visual emphasis. PageMaker's manual kerning enables you to add or subtract space easily over a range of text or between individual character pairs.

To kern type manually, do the following:

1. Using the text tool, click-drag to select the range of text or place the insertion point between any two characters you want to kern. Don't double-click to select a whole word unless you also want to kern the space following the word.

2. Press Command-Delete or Command-(left arrow) to tighten character spacing in increments equal to 1/25th of an em space. Press Option-Delete or Command-Shift-(left arrow) to tighten character spacing in increments equal to 1/100th of an em space.

3. Press Command-Shift-Delete or Command-(right arrow) to widen character spacing in increments equal to 1/25th of an em space. Press Option-Shift-Delete or Command-Shift-(right arrow) to widen character spacing in increments equal to 1/100th of an em space.

Press the appropriate keys for each bit of space you want to add or remove. An em space has the same dimensions as the selected point size. Fine-kerning 48-point headline type, for example, adds or removes space in increments of 48/100ths of an em space, or approximately 1/2 a point. The larger the type, the larger the increment of change. Figure 5.30 shows the process of kerning type manually.

To remove applied kerning from a selected range of text, press Command-Option-k or Command-Option-Shift-Delete.

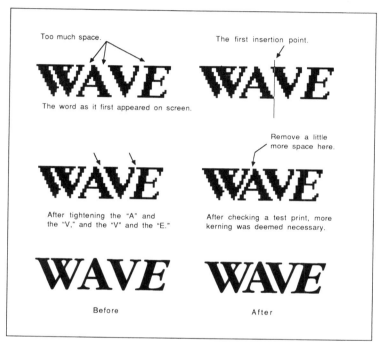

Fig. 5.30

Manual kerning can greatly improve the appearance of headline type.

When you kern type smaller than 25 points or fine-kern type smaller than 100 points, the kerning increments always are less than one point in size. Because the pixels that make up your screen display also are generally one point in size, you may not be able to see the effects of kerning smaller type, especially if you work in PageMaker's Actual Size page view. To better evaluate the effects of kerning, manually kern your type only when working in an enlarged page view.

Tracking

PageMaker's Track command on the Type menu and the **Track** option in the Type Specifications dialog box give you a choice of six options you can use to kern globally or adjust the spacing between letters and words over a selected range of text. If no text is selected, your menu choice applies to all text you subsequently type.

If you find the choices **No track** and **Normal** confusing, remember that **No track** means what it says: track-kerning is not applied to your text. **Normal** means that slight adjustments in track-kerning are applied as text changes in size. (You get tighter overall kerning at sizes larger than 12 points and looser overall kerning at sizes smaller than 12 points.) If your work calls for much looser or tighter-looking text, choose one of the other four available track options (see fig. 5.31).

Fig. 5.31

PageMaker enables you to adjust track-kerning to improve the appearance of selected text.

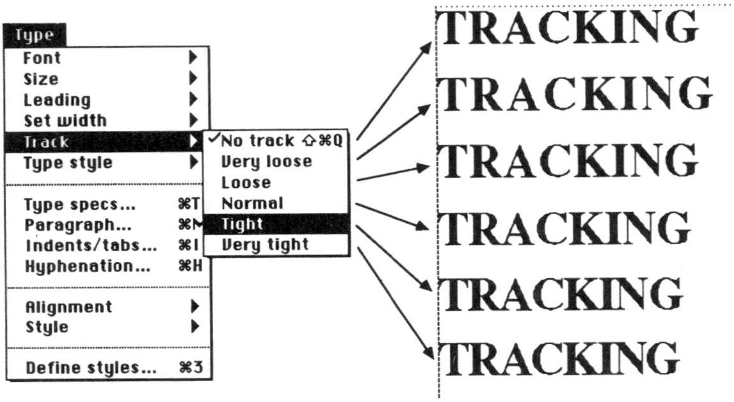

Type	
Font	▶
Size	▶
Leading	▶
Set width	▶
Track	▶
Type style	▶
Type specs...	⌘T
Paragraph...	⌘M
Indents/tabs...	⌘I
Hyphenation...	⌘H
Alignment	▶
Style	▶
Define styles...	⌘3

Track submenu:
✓No track ⇧⌘Q
Very loose
Loose
Normal
Tight
Very tight

TRACKING
TRACKING
TRACKING
TRACKING
TRACKING
TRACKING

Exporting Text

An exciting PageMaker feature is its capability to export text back out of your publications to update your original word-processed documents. You can create stories externally using your favorite word processor, import them into PageMaker, make any necessary corrections or editing changes, and update the original files without ever leaving PageMaker. You also can save exported text as separate files to use elsewhere, preserving your original documents unaltered.

Export filters, similar to the import filters PageMaker uses to import formatted text, enable you to export formatted text back to your word processors. The only limitation is that PageMaker cannot export formatting attributes that your word processor doesn't support.

PageMaker enables you to export selected (highlighted) text or complete stories. Unthreaded text blocks must be exported separately. To set up text for exporting, click an insertion point in a threaded text block or select a specific range of text and choose Export from the File menu. In the Export dialog box, click the appropriate **Export** button (**Entire story** or **Selected text only**), pick the appropriate **File format**, and assign a name to the exported file (see fig. 5.32). To update an original file, type that file name and choose the same storage location as the original file.

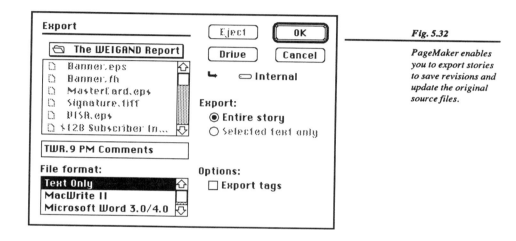

Fig. 5.32

PageMaker enables you to export stories to save revisions and update the original source files.

Chapter Summary

In this chapter you learned many of the basic skills needed to work with text in PageMaker. You saw how to bring text into your publications and how to export text back out of PageMaker. You discovered that in most instances you can preserve much of the original formatting when importing or exporting. You learned how to control the flow of text onto your pages and how to create text. You also learned how you can have PageMaker update your stories when you revise the original source documents.

You learned how to edit text, change type specifications, and kern type to improve the content and appearance of your pages. You also learned how to do word processing in PageMaker's Story Editor. You learned how to spell check your stories and find and replace text by type attributes. Now, you're ready to move on to Chapter 6, where you acquire more text-handling skills.

Formatting Text

In this chapter, you continue to explore PageMaker's text-handling capabilities. You start with simple layout tasks, such as adjusting guides and reshaping text blocks, and then move on to more complex formatting chores using indents and tabs, leading, and hyphenation. You learn how to align text, and you discover how paragraph formatting interacts with word spacing to help control the general appearance of your pages.

Later in this chapter, you learn how to apply style sheets to your work to save production time and speed document preparation. You also explore PageMaker's advanced book editing features, including how to generate tables of contents and indexes. You may never use these features if you don't publish lengthy manuals, books, or end-of-year indexes to periodicals, for example. But PageMaker provides the right tools if you ever need these types of documents.

Finally, you learn about PageMaker's Table Editor, a utility that enables you to prepare tables quickly and easily for placement into your publications.

Performing Simple Layout Tasks

When you create a publication, you generally go through several layout revisions. Along the way, you may want to experiment with different column formats, add or delete whole pages, resize or reshape text blocks, or use guides to help position text and graphics accurately. You also may want to store items on the pasteboard so that the items are accessible when you need them. All these layout tasks are easy to do in PageMaker.

Creating Columns

PageMaker's columns are made up of nonprinting guides that help you define text placement. Choose Column Guides from the Options menu to specify the number of columns you want displayed on a page. The columns PageMaker creates have equally spaced left and right guides. You can move these column guides to vary column widths, but the spacing between the columns themselves remains fixed, unless you enter a new value in the Column Guides dialog box. You can move the far left and right column guides (that overlap the page-margin boundaries) independently; all other column guides move together in fixed pairs. You click-drag any column guide to move the guide.

Note

You can lock column guides in place using the Lock Guides command from the Options menu. Note that this command affects your entire publication, not just the page you are working on.

Tip

Although you can vary column widths, you cannot adjust the spacing between columns on the same page. If this restriction limits your layouts, create more columns than you need. Let the extra column guides on your pages act as spacers between the main columns. Then skip over these extra "spacer" columns as you pour your text.

Column guides determine your column line widths as you place your text. As you place text into a column, the text wraps to fit within the left and right column boundaries as the text flows down the page. Each line is broken at the right column boundary, regardless of the original margin settings of the word processor used to create the text. However, PageMaker retains other paragraph formatting you may have set in your word processor (such as indents and tabs).

After you place your text, you can move the column guides and use them elsewhere on the page without affecting text blocks already on the page. Similarly, you can change the number of columns on a page using the Column Guides command without affecting the arrangement of existing text on the page. In this way, you can create different column layouts for different parts of the same page.

PageMaker enables you to have from 1 to 20 columns per page. If you use many columns on a single page, your page margins and column spacing must be set narrow enough to allow a column width of at least one pica (1/6th of an inch). You specify the spacing between columns, the number of columns per page, and the page-margin boundaries between which the columns lie. But you do not specify the column widths—PageMaker determines column widths from the other settings you provide.

The only way PageMaker can set exact column widths is if you pre-calculate them and then enter the appropriate variables for PageMaker to use. Adjusting column guides afterward, however, is easy. After you create the number of columns you want, use PageMaker's horizontal ruler to reposition each column-guide pair accurately.

If you plan to use the same column structure throughout a publication, set the column guides on your master pages so that the guides repeat on all regular pages. You later can adjust any column guide on any regular page by click-dragging the guide with the pointer tool. When you work with double-sided pages, the Column Guides dialog box enables you to specify the number of columns and column spacing separately for each facing page (see fig. 6.1).

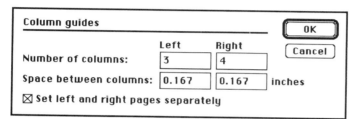

Fig. 6.1

Configuring columns separately for facing pages.

Inserting and Removing Pages

After you type the desired number of pages for your new publication into the Page Setup dialog box and click the OK button, you cannot go back and change that number. You can add or remove pages later, however, by choosing Insert Pages or Remove Pages from the Page menu (see fig. 6.2). The only restriction is that you cannot exceed PageMaker's 999-page limit for a publication.

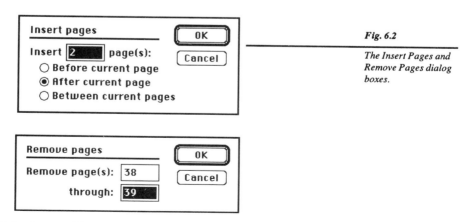

Fig. 6.2

The Insert Pages and Remove Pages dialog boxes.

The Insert Pages dialog box enables you to add new pages to your publication. You tell PageMaker how many pages to add and where to insert them—before the current page, after the current page, or between current pages. *Current page* means the page (or pair of facing pages) you are viewing at the time of menu selection. The **Between current pages** option applies only to facing pages.

Each page you add later is configured according to existing Page Setup dialog box settings. PageMaker renumbers all pages that come after any newly inserted pages. New pages also display master page elements. When you insert new pages between pages that contain threaded text blocks, the stories in those text blocks remain threaded.

Warning

Inserting an odd number of pages into a double-sided, facing-pages publication forces PageMaker to rearrange all following pages. Not only do previously facing pages no longer face one another, but if your publication's inner and outer margins differ, PageMaker repositions text and graphics to lie within the newly adjusted margin boundaries. This repositioning can destroy a carefully composed layout, and PageMaker gives you no warning on-screen.

Using the Remove Pages command, you can remove existing pages from a publication. You tell PageMaker which pages to delete by specifying the beginning and ending page numbers (to remove a page, make both numbers the same). PageMaker discards those pages and any pages that lie between. PageMaker also discards all text and graphics on removed pages. To save text or graphics, you must transfer them to other pages or drag them onto the pasteboard for safekeeping.

Note

The same warning about inserting an odd number of pages into a double-sided, facing-pages publication also applies when removing pages.

Be careful not to remove pages containing text from the middle of a story. Text blocks on earlier and later pages remain threaded, but any text on deleted pages is lost. The only way to recover the missing text is to place your story again. To prevent losing text, use the column windowshade handles to close up all the text blocks on those pages you plan to delete. Click-dragging the top and bottom windowshade handles of a threaded text block together forces the text to flow out of that text block and into any follow-on text blocks.

If you make a mistake while adding or deleting pages, immediately choose Undo from the Edit menu to restore your publication.

Rearranging Text Elements

PageMaker enables you to grab text blocks with the pointer tool and click-drag to move the blocks anywhere on your pages, much as you would pick up a newspaper clipping and move the clipping to another spot on your desk.

When you click a text or graphic block and continue pressing the mouse button, your pointer tool changes into a four-headed cursor arrow. If you begin dragging immediately after clicking, you see a solid box surrounding the boundaries of your block. Because this outline follows the movement of your cursor, you can use the outline as a guide to position your text block. The original text or graphic remains behind until you release the mouse button. Only then does the text jump to its new location on the page.

If you wait a couple of seconds before dragging a text block, you see the text surrounded by a dotted marquee. Click-dragging with the text visible enables you to position the block more accurately. After you have moved the block to its new location, release the mouse button. The text or graphic redraws. If you are not satisfied with its placement, choose Undo from the Edit menu or click-drag the block again.

Using this method, you can move text blocks to different areas of your page and drag them onto the pasteboard for temporary storage. Column and ruler guides help with alignment on your pages (you cannot use guides on the pasteboard). If you choose the Snap To Guides command from the Options menu before you start dragging, your text blocks are attracted to nearby guides like metal shavings to a magnet. If you also choose the Snap To Rulers command, your text blocks jump in small increments equal in distance to the intervals between adjoining ruler tick marks.

Adjusting Guides

Margin, ruler, and column guides are nonprinting visual elements that you use to help structure your pages. PageMaker normally places guides in the foreground where they lie in front of text and graphics. This placement sometimes proves problematic, because the guides tend to get in the way of whatever lies behind them. You can move the guides behind other elements by clicking the **Back guides** option in the Preferences dialog box (choose Preferences from the Edit menu). Moving the guides to the back makes selecting text and graphics easier and prevents you from accidentally grabbing and moving a guide.

After you have all your guides arranged the way you want them, lock them in place to prevent further movement by choosing Lock Guides from the Options menu.

Tip

If you are using several guides and rearranging them frequently, leave the guides in the foreground so that they are easy to get at. If you move the guides to the rear, you may not be able to select them if they are covered by text or graphics. If you try to select an element in the background, and you snag an overlapping guide instead, hold down the Command key and click again. This technique enables you to select whatever lies beneath the guide.

Occasionally, you may want to adjust your page margins to meet changing layout requirements. Enter the new margin values in the Page Setup dialog box (choose Page Setup from the File menu) and click OK. PageMaker displays the new margins on all pages (see fig. 6.3). PageMaker also rearranges all column guides throughout your publication (but not the text within the column guides) to fit equally within the new margin boundaries. If you have any variable-width columns on any of your pages, that column formatting is lost.

Fig. 6.3

Adjusting page margins has no effect on existing text blocks.

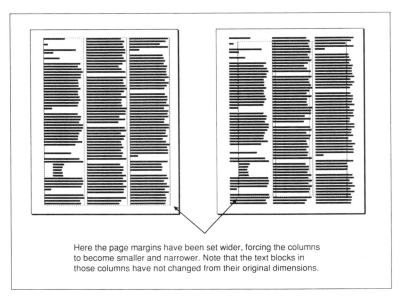

Here the page margins have been set wider, forcing the columns to become smaller and narrower. Note that the text blocks in those columns have not changed from their original dimensions.

Column and ruler guides placed on master pages repeat on all regular pages. Unlike other master-page elements on regular pages, however, you can rearrange the guides to meet changing layout requirements. To move a column or ruler guide, click-drag the column or ruler guide with the pointer tool. Your pointer tool changes to a two-headed arrow to show the possible directions of movement. As you drag the guide, a dotted marker follows along in the corresponding ruler to indicate the exact position of the guide on the page.

If you need additional ruler guides, click the appropriate ruler (the horizontal ruler for horizontal guides and the vertical ruler for vertical guides) and drag the guides one at a time onto your pages. To remove a ruler guide, drag the guide off the page onto the pasteboard or entirely out of the publication window.

To change the number of columns on a page, choose Column Guides from the Options menu. You cannot drag column guides on or off your pages. Column guides can exist only within the page margins.

To see how your pages look when printed, deselect the Guides command from the Options menu. This action conceals all margin, column, and ruler guides temporarily. To view the guides again, reselect the Guides command.

Resizing Text Blocks

You can resize and reshape text blocks to meet changing layout requirements. Suppose, for example, that you want to place a graphic in a bottom corner of a page where a column of text already sits. You need to resize the text block that already fills this space to make room for the graphic. You have two ways to resize the text block.

The first method is to drag the bottom windowshade handle up far enough to make enough room for the graphic. Click the loop of the windowshade handle with the pointer tool, press the mouse button, and drag in an upward direction (see fig. 6.4). The text block shortens, and any threaded text is pushed into follow-on text blocks. If no follow-on text blocks exist to hold the overflow, an arrow appears in the windowshade handle to indicate that more of the story needs placing.

Note

If you lengthen a text block by dragging downward on its bottom windowshade handle, threaded text flows backward into that block from follow-on text blocks. The text fills the newly expanded space. If there is no follow-on text, an empty windowshade handle marks the end of the story.

Fig. 6.4

You can resize a text block within a column by dragging a windowshade handle.

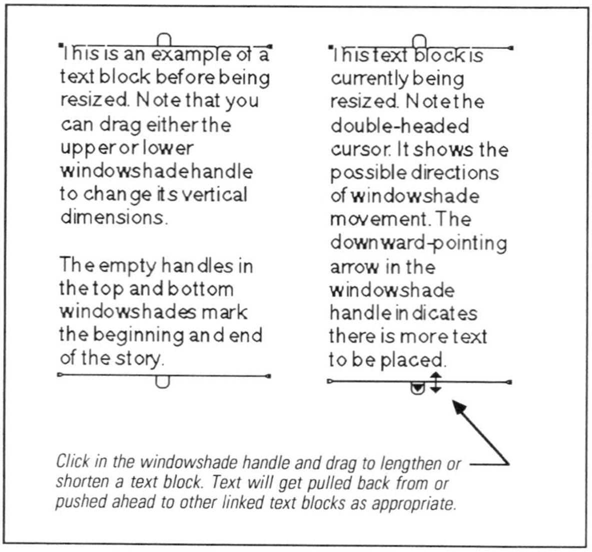

This is an example of a text block before being resized. Note that you can drag either the upper or lower windowshade handle to change its vertical dimensions.

The empty handles in the top and bottom windowshades mark the beginning and end of the story.

This text block is currently being resized. Note the double-headed cursor. It shows the possible directions of windowshade movement. The downward-pointing arrow in the windowshade handle indicates there is more text to be placed.

Click in the windowshade handle and drag to lengthen or shorten a text block. Text will get pulled back from or pushed ahead to other linked text blocks as appropriate.

Tip

To determine at a glance which text blocks contain threads of a story, insert the cursor anywhere in the story and choose the Select All command from the Edit menu. PageMaker highlights the text in all threaded text blocks.

The second way to resize a selected text block is to drag a corner reshaping handle (see fig. 6.5). Dragging a corner handle enables you to reshape a text block without regard for column boundaries. You can reshape the block to span multiple columns, bleed across facing pages, or fill an arbitrarily shaped area. The text rewraps to fit within the new column boundaries.

Fig. 6.5

You can reshape a text block by dragging a corner handle.

This text block is currently being reshaped. Note the double-headed arrow. The trick here is to grab a corner reshaping handle and drag it with the mouse button held down.

You can reshape a text block to any dimensions not to exceed the size needed to completely hold its enclosed text.

As you drag, you see a solid-line bounding box. Use this box as a guide to final positioning.

When you release the mouse button, your text block refills and rewraps to fit within the area you dragged out with the bounding box.

This text block is currently being reshaped. Note the double-headed arrow. The trick here is to grab a corner reshaping handle and drag it with the mouse button held down.

You can reshape a text block to any dimensions not to exceed the size needed to completely hold its enclosed text.

As you drag, you see a solid-line bounding box. Use this box as a guide to final positioning.

When you release the mouse button, your text block refills and rewraps to fit within the area you dragged out with the bounding box.

Note that making this block larger pulled back these additional words from a follow-on block of text (to which it was invisibly linked).

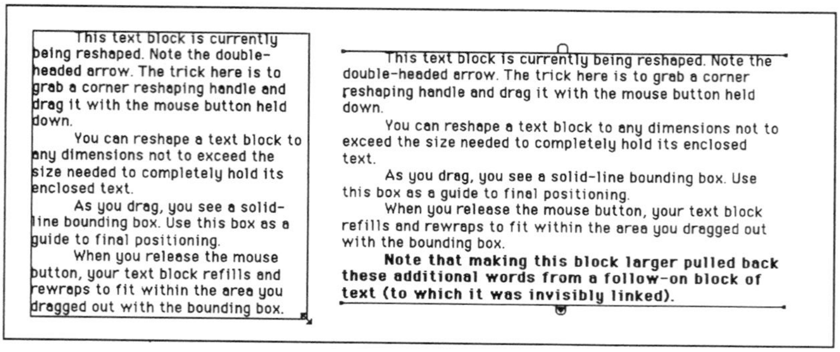

> **Tip**
>
> Column and ruler guides help you shape text blocks accurately to lie within designated areas. If you outline each area beforehand using horizontal and vertical ruler guides and then choose the Snap To Guides command from the Options menu, the edges of your text-blocks snap to the guides for perfect alignment.

Isolating Text Blocks

Resizing or reshaping a threaded text block produces an immediate ripple effect throughout the remaining text blocks of a story. This ripple effect can undo much of your formatting, as threaded text pushes forward into follow-on blocks or pulls backward into a resized block. To get around this problem, you can isolate text blocks from one another.

To isolate a threaded text block, select the block with the pointer tool and cut the block to the Clipboard using the Cut command from the Edit menu. Paste the block back onto your page. The text in the block looks as it did before, except that the text block now is disconnected from the rest of your story. Changes you make to other threaded text blocks do not affect the isolated text block. To rethread the text into your story, cut the now unthreaded block to the Clipboard, use the text tool to create an insertion point at the end of the previous text block (or at the beginning of the next), and repaste. The text rethreads itself into your story starting at the insertion point.

> **Warning**
>
> When you isolate a text block, the invisible threading of your story still exists for any remaining text blocks. If you make editing or formatting changes to your story, your text pushes forward or pulls backward through the chain, skipping over the isolated block, and eventually knocking your text out of sequence. To keep this from happening, isolate all text blocks anytime you isolate one text block.

To break a text block into several smaller text blocks, click-drag a windowshade to shorten the original block and then click the plus symbol in the windowshade handle. Flow the continuation text into a new block (click-drag the text-placement tool to create a block). Repeat as many times as necessary. Each time you create a block this way, you push the threaded text ahead as you compress the copy and then pull the text backward to fill the newly created block. Your text threads through all the new text blocks.

To consolidate two or more text blocks into one, completely close up one of the blocks by dragging the windowshade handles together (see fig. 6.6). Text pushes ahead, and the empty block disappears when you click elsewhere on the page. Next, enlarge the preceding or following text block so that the text block occupies the open space. The text you pushed ahead flows backward and fills the expanded block.

Fig. 6.6

To consolidate multiple text blocks, drag the windowshade handles to close up the extra blocks.

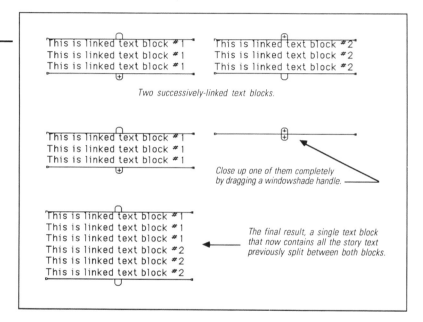

This is linked text block #1
This is linked text block #1
This is linked text block #1

This is linked text block #2
This is linked text block #2
This is linked text block #2

Two successively-linked text blocks.

This is linked text block #1
This is linked text block #1
This is linked text block #1

Close up one of them completely by dragging a windowshade handle.

This is linked text block #1
This is linked text block #1
This is linked text block #1
This is linked text block #2
This is linked text block #2
This is linked text block #2

The final result, a single text block that now contains all the story text previously split between both blocks.

To delete a text block permanently, select the block with the pointer tool and press the Delete key or choose Clear from the Edit menu.

Note

Just as clicking in the bottom windowshade handle of a selected text block enables you to continue flowing text into a new, follow-on text block, clicking in the top windowshade handle enables you to reflow text into a new, preceding text block.

Tip

To stack two isolated text blocks vertically so that the text they contain reads continuously and has the same line spacing where the blocks touch, use the following procedure:

1. Align both text blocks vertically using a vertical ruler guide (see fig. 6.7). Position the top block in its final position. This block is the anchor block. The other text block is the move block.

2. Select both blocks with the pointer tool so that their windowshade handles show.

3. Select the upper reshaping handle of the move block and drag the handle so that the adjoining windowshades overlap. Even though you have selected both text blocks, you still can reshape just one text block.

4. Delete any extra blank lines within the text blocks at the point where they touch. Your text is aligned and spaced evenly.

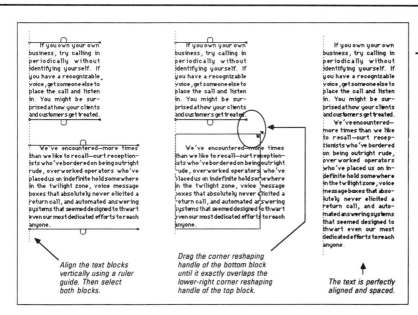

Fig. 6.7

You can align isolated text blocks easily without having to rethread the text the text blocks contain.

Rotating Text Blocks

With PageMaker, you can rotate unthreaded text blocks in 90-degree increments. This rotation enables you to position credits vertically alongside photos and artwork, for example, or create a vertical headline. Whatever your design intent, rotated text, used sparingly, can give your pages a distinctive look.

To rotate a block of text, click the text with the pointer tool and choose Text rotation from the Element menu. You get a dialog box with the character "A" shown rotated to four 90-degree orientations (see fig. 6.8). Click an icon, and your text block rotates to the corresponding angle. You can rotate only one text block at a time, and the block must contain only fully placed text. You cannot rotate text blocks containing inline graphics.

If you decide later that you need to edit a block of rotated text, triple-click the block to open the story editor. Edit the text in the Story view. If you prefer to edit the text in the Layout view, rotate the Block back to zero degrees. You then can edit the text normally in the layout view.

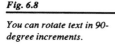

Fig. 6.8

You can rotate text in 90-degree increments.

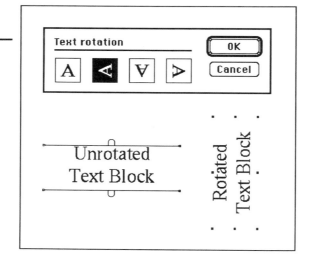

Using the Pasteboard

The pasteboard is like an artist's work table. The pasteboard provides a convenient storage area that completely surrounds your page display (see fig. 6.9). You can view the whole pasteboard by holding down the Shift key as you choose Fit In Window from the Page menu. The pasteboard is a handy place for creating custom text blocks for things like headlines and picture captions. You later can drag finished blocks into place on your layout. The pasteboard also serves as a temporary holding area for text and graphics that you intend to use later in your publication.

You can drag any element onto the pasteboard, and whatever you store on the pasteboard you can drag or copy and paste back onto your pages. Because the pasteboard remains constantly present as you turn pages, items you store on the pasteboard always are available for use. Be sure, however, that no part of an element

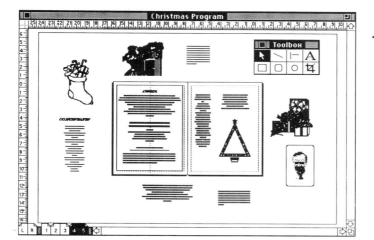

Fig. 6.9

*Using the pasteboard
to store text and
graphics.*

you store on the pasteboard touches any part of a page. Otherwise, that element remains behind with that page. When you turn to a new page, the element does not appear on the surrounding pasteboard.

If you store an item on the pasteboard and quit PageMaker, the item still is on the pasteboard the next time you open your publication. Any items you store on the pasteboard do not print with your publication.

You can use the pasteboard as a working area to store text and graphics temporarily as you experiment with different layouts. The pasteboard also is a good place to store rules, boxes, and other design elements. That way you don't have to worry about copying design elements from one page to another.

Tip

If you don't have enough identically formatted text to warrant creating a separate style sheet (see "Using Style Sheets" later in this chapter), prepare a text placeholder and store the holder on the pasteboard. A placeholder is a block of pre-formatted text. When you want to use this format, copy and paste the placeholder onto your pages. Then, using the text tool, select the sample text and replace the sample text by typing new text. The newly typed text assumes the placeholder's assigned formatting.

Working with Paragraphs

In PageMaker, as with most word processors, a paragraph is a string of text that ends with a carriage return. A paragraph, however, is not the same as a text block. A text block can contain part of a paragraph, or many paragraphs. A paragraph can run the full length of a publication, or be as short as one typed character.

You can format paragraphs independently of one another. The formatting style of one paragraph also can be saved and later applied to other paragraphs. PageMaker gives you complete control over how your paragraphs look when printed.

Paragraph formatting includes left, right, center, and full justification (how the text fits between the left and right column guides), leading (pronounced ledd-ing), indents, and tabs (to help structure your text), spaces before and after the paragraph, widow and orphan control, and so on.

Assigning Paragraph Specifications

The Paragraph Specifications dialog box is the starting place for most paragraph formatting (see fig. 6.10). You can set left, right, and first line indents from the Paragraph Specifications dialog box. You can choose paragraph alignments (text justification) and specify any blank space you want PageMaker to insert before and after paragraphs. Several additional options enable you to manage line and page breaks. The **Rules** and **Spacing** buttons open additional dialog boxes that contain other paragraph formatting options.

Fig. 6.10

The Paragraph Specifications dialog box.

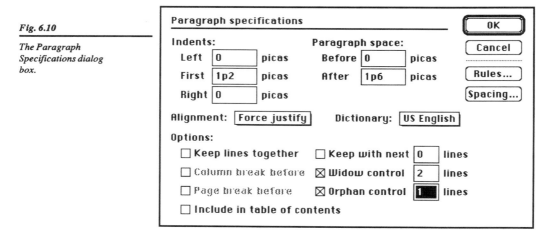

Understanding Leading

Although not strictly a paragraph attribute, the most important leading controls are in the Spacing Attributes dialog box (click the **Spacing** button in the Paragraph Specifications dialog box). Leading refers to the vertical spacing between successive lines of text (see fig. 6.11). This spacing is measured in points and can be set manually in increments as small as 1/10th of a point. You also can instruct

PageMaker to assign leading values based on a specified percentage of the current type size.

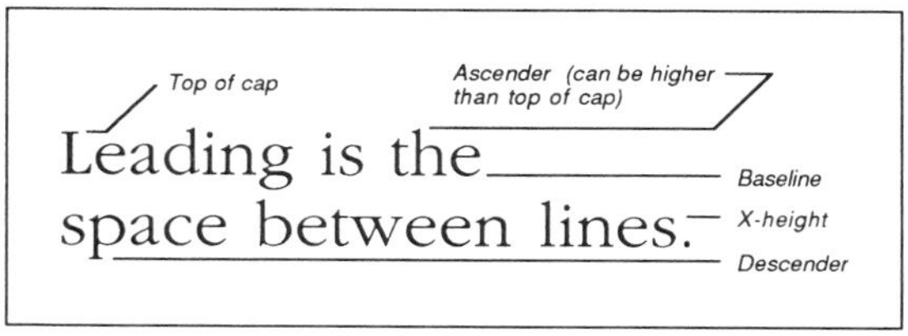

Fig. 6.11

Leading determines the space between lines of text.

Although you can assign arbitrary leading values for successive lines of text, using different leading values generally yields uneven line spacing and detracts from the readability of your pages. You normally apply a particular leading value only to whole paragraphs or entire stories.

Your goal should be to format your documents so that the text is easy to read and understand. Often, legibility can be improved by changing the assigned leading to add or remove space between lines of type. If your leading is too tight, your text looks cramped and may be difficult to read. If the leading is too loose, your reader may have difficulty finding the beginning of the next line. In both cases, legibility suffers, and reader comprehension decreases. If your pages are too difficult to read, your readers may give up altogether.

If you allow PageMaker to compute leading automatically, you get a default leading equal to 120 percent of current type size. For example, PageMaker spaces 10-point type using 12 points of leading. This default is the same as inserting two points of empty space between successive lines of type. To assign other leading values, do the following:

1. Select the text you want changed and pick a point size from the Leading submenu accessed from the Type menu. PageMaker displays a list of values close to the current type size. If no text is selected, PageMaker displays a set of commonly used leading values to pick from. You also can choose the Other command on the Leading submenu and type into the dialog box that appears a value anywhere from 0 to 1,300 points in 1/10th of a point increments.

2. Choose Type Specs from the Type menu to display the Type Specifications dialog box. Pick a point size from the pop-up menu or type a new value into the **Leading** field.

3. To change the percentage that PageMaker uses to compute auto-leading values, choose Paragraph from the Type menu and click the **Spacing** button in the Paragraph Specifications dialog box. In the Spacing Attributes dialog box, type a revised value into the **Auto**

leading percent field. PageMaker assigns leading (when auto-leading is in effect) based upon the percentage you specify.

Tip

If you increase the point size of even one character and Auto Leading is in effect, the leading for that entire line of type changes. This leading change can cause irregular vertical line spacing. To avoid this condition, choose a fixed leading value for the entire paragraph or story. If you always assign leading manually, your vertical line spacing always remains constant, even if you increase the point size of a character or word in a line.

PageMaker enables you to choose between **Proportional** and **Top of caps** leading. You make this selection in the Spacing Attributes dialog box. PageMaker views each line of text as framed by a horizontal bar called a *slug*. When you select a character, word, or line of text, the area highlighted in black is the slug (see fig. 6.12). The height of the slug is equal to the assigned leading. The characters that lie within the slug sit on a common reference line that allows for precise horizontal character alignment. This reference line is called the *baseline*. The type of leading you use tells PageMaker where to place the baseline within the slug, which determines how successive lines of text relate to one another.

Fig. 6.12

PageMaker places each line of text within a slug. The slug is equal in height to the assigned leading.

With proportional leading, for example, two thirds of the assigned line spacing lies above the baseline, and one third lies below the baseline. In this case, PageMaker places 16 points of 24-point proportional leading above the baseline and 8 points below the baseline. Proportional leading enables you to mix disparate font types on the same baseline and still keep overall vertical line spacing uniform, because every character sits on a baseline that is always the same distance from the top of the slug.

Top of caps leading uses the height of the tallest font ascender to position the baseline. The distance of the baseline from the top of the slug equals the height of the tallest font ascender, whether that character is present or not. The characters sit on a baseline that "floats" up or down in successive line slugs, depending on your font selection. Consequently, your lines of type may look unevenly spaced.

The best rule is always to use **Proportional** leading. The one time you may want to use the **Top of caps** method, however, is when you design pages that call for special type effects, such as when preparing creative advertising layouts.

Tip

To start a paragraph with an oversized capital letter without disrupting subsequent line spacing, assign the capital the same leading value as the rest of the paragraph. Make sure that you also have chosen **Proportional** leading in the Spacing Attributes dialog box.

Tip

If you regularly use an odd type size and leading combination, for example, 10-point type over 11.5 leading, set your vertical ruler divisions in the Preferences dialog box to match the assigned leading, in this case 11.5 points. Make sure that you have turned on the Snap To Rulers command on the Options menu. You now can align adjoining text blocks or other page elements to a given baseline much easier. You also can lay out tables quickly within PageMaker, using data from multiple text blocks, without having to exit PageMaker and build your tables in the Table Editor.

Setting Paragraph Spacing

When you specify the exact spacing between paragraphs, it is unnecessary to double-space with carriage returns to insert extra space between paragraphs. You can have PageMaker insert space before or after a paragraph. Paragraph spacing is cumulative with line leading. PageMaker inserts the combined amount of blank space each time you press the Return key.

To assign extra paragraph spacing, select the paragraphs you want to configure and then choose the Paragraph command from the Type menu to display the Paragraph Specifications dialog box. Enter a new value in the **Paragraph space: Before** or **Paragraph space: After** field. (You rarely have reason to enter values in both fields.) The paragraph spacing is updated after you click the OK button.

Note

The **Paragraph space: Before** value is ignored if a paragraph begins a text block. Similarly, the **Paragraph space: After** value is ignored if a paragraph ends a text block.

Tip

Always set paragraph spacing using the Paragraph Specifications dialog box. Inserting extra carriage returns to introduce extra spacing sometimes creates alignment problems, especially if the returns carry a type style assignment that is different from that of the surrounding text. Carriage returns are characters in themselves, which means that you can assign style attributes to them. However, carriage returns also are normally invisible on-screen (you can view carriage returns, however, while in the Story view by choosing Display ¶ from the Options menu), which makes them easy to overlook when assigning or changing type style attributes.

You can have PageMaker keep paragraphs intact so that they do not split across columns or pages. Select the paragraph or paragraphs you want to keep whole and choose the **Keep lines together** option in the Paragraph Specifications dialog box. PageMaker keeps your paragraphs together. Note that your columns may become uneven in length, because some paragraphs no longer break where the columns normally end on the page.

You also can have PageMaker start a new column or page with a chosen paragraph. Select the paragraph and choose the **Column break before** or **Page break before** option in the Paragraph Specifications dialog box. PageMaker moves the paragraph to the appropriate location.

Controlling Widows and Orphans

Aldus defines *widows* as finishing lines at the bottom of an earlier paragraph that somehow end up leading off at the top of a new column or page. They are "widowed" from their husband paragraphs. Similarly, Aldus defines *orphans* as lines that really should lead off a new column or page, but somehow get tacked onto the tail end of a preceding column or page. In both instances, widows and orphans are lines of type that end up separated from the paragraphs to which they belong. They sort of dangle at the tops and bottoms of columns, looking a little lost.

Several respected reference publications, including some well-known dictionaries, define widows and orphans differently. No two authorities, it seems, can agree fully on which definition goes with what description. What is important, however, is that PageMaker enables you to control the unsightly effects widows and orphans produce by specifying in advance how many lines constitute each. You tell PageMaker the minimum number of lines you want to have end or begin a column (any whole number from 0-3), and PageMaker does the rest. Note that, as with keeping paragraphs together, your columns sometimes become uneven in length, because not all paragraphs continue to break where they would normally.

A related feature is the **Keep with next xx lines** option. The number you type into this field (again, any whole number from 0-3) tells PageMaker to keep the last line of the paragraph with however many lines you specify belonging to the next paragraph. You use this option to have PageMaker tie headlines and subheads to the paragraphs that immediately follow. You don't have column breaks separating your headlines and subheads from the paragraphs to which they apply.

Sometimes PageMaker overrides the choices you make. This happens when PageMaker faces especially complex or difficult formatting. To correct any widow and orphan problems PageMaker overlooks, you first have to locate them. Choose the **Keeps violations** option in the Preferences dialog box, and PageMaker highlights any text in your publication that violates the assigned widow, orphan, and **Keep with next xx lines** controls. You then can make any necessary corrections.

Using Paragraph Rules

Paragraph rules are horizontal lines you use to subdivide columns into vertical segments. You normally use paragraph rules to mark the beginnings and endings of articles in publications such as newsletters, magazines, and other periodicals.

When you let PageMaker manage your paragraph rules, the rules remain in place relative to the surrounding text, even when you edit stories so that the text flows forward or backward through your document. Click the **Rules** button in the Paragraph Specifications dialog box to get the Paragraph Rules dialog box (see fig. 6.13). From the Paragraph Rules dialog box, you specify the kind of rules that you want to insert above or below selected paragraphs. You have the same choices for styling rules as you do for styling lines, except that you cannot apply Reverse styling. You also have complete control over the length and placement of paragraph rules.

You start by setting the length of the rule so that the length matches the width of text or the width of the column. Note that if a paragraph begins with a first line indent, the length of a rule above the paragraph matches the indented text if you choose the **Width of text** option. You can further indent the rule by specifying precise inset distances from the left and right sides of the column. PageMaker accepts negative values for rules that you want to protrude beyond column boundaries.

Next, you click the **Options** button in the Paragraph Rules dialog box to get the Paragraph Rule Options dialog box. Here you specify the distance above or below the baseline where you want PageMaker to draw the rule. If you use PageMaker's default value of **Auto**, PageMaker draws the rule exactly along the top or bottom edge of the slug (depending on whether the rule is above or below the paragraph) and does not change the size of the slug. Most of the time, though, you want PageMaker to draw the rule some specified distance above or below the baseline. PageMaker shifts the rule up or down according to the values you type and stretches the slug vertically to accommodate the rule.

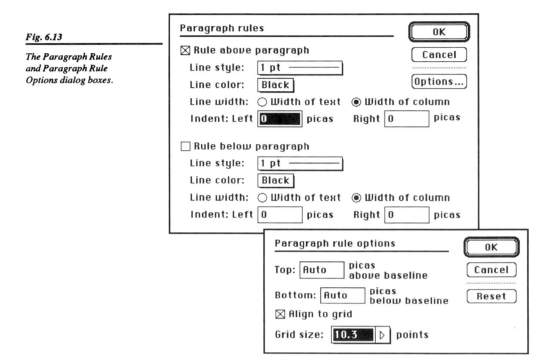

Fig. 6.13

*The Paragraph Rules
and Paragraph Rule
Options dialog boxes.*

You may have to experiment to get the feel of how automatic placement of paragraph rules works, particularly if you use thick or multiple line styles. After you understand how to configure rules, they help make your layouts easier to manage. The **Reset** button restores the paragraph rule options to PageMaker's default settings.

Aligning Text Horizontally

Historically, the most difficult of layout tasks has been obtaining consistent horizontal text alignment. Frequently, you use different sizes of type and assign different leading values for headlines, subheads, captions, and pull quotes. You also may use different spacings before and after paragraphs, paragraph rules, and so on, which can throw off vertical spacing so that baselines in adjoining columns of text no longer align evenly with one another. With PageMaker, you can make sure that text baselines align properly no matter how many size or spacing variations you introduce within your text.

The trick is using the **Align to grid** and **Grid size** options—two features nested three dialog boxes deep in the Paragraph Rule Options dialog box. Although well concealed from ordinary viewing, you may use these options often enough that you may want a shortcut to access the options quickly. You can use a macro utility like Tempo II to whisk you there with only a keystroke combination (see the discussion about Tempo II in "Additional Tips and Techniques" at the back of the book).

When you check the **Align to grid** box, PageMaker begins each new paragraph so that the paragraph aligns perfectly with the leading grid. PageMaker aligns the paragraph by inserting extra space as needed after the preceding paragraph to compensate for any vertical offset. This alignment also works with inline graphics that you configure as separate paragraphs.

To ensure that baselines across adjoining columns align properly, type the current leading value into the **Grid size** field. This process works predictably whenever you use proportional leading and assign fixed leading values to your text.

Tip

To get absolutely consistent text placement when laying out pages, set your vertical ruler spacing and the leading value in the **Grid size** field the same. Then, reposition the ruler zero point to align exactly with the upper edge of the first slug on the page. Choose Snap To Rulers from the Options menu. You then can drag elements quickly into place with full assurance that text baselines will snap into perfect alignment every time.

Setting Indents and Tabs

Indents and tabs enable you to control the internal formatting of your paragraphs. Understanding how indents and tabs work makes assembling and formatting complex documents much easier.

Setting Indents

PageMaker's left and right indents determine how far your text sits in from the left and right page margins or the left and right column guides. You also can use nested indents to create paragraphs set in from the main body of text. To set left and right indents, select the paragraphs to which you want the indents to apply and then choose the Paragraph command from the Type menu to access the Paragraph Specifications dialog box. Type the desired values into the **Indents Left** and **Indents Right** fields.

You may find choosing Indents/Tabs from the Type menu is quicker and easier. Indents/Tabs gives you a visual display that makes setting indents a snap (see fig. 6.14). On the ruler, the left indent is represented by the small lower triangle at the left end of the scale; the right indent is represented by the large triangle at the right end of the scale. You can move these indent markers to any position along the ruler by click-dragging the markers with your pointer tool.

You also can drag the ruler window to any position on the page and scroll the ruler left or right, using the small hollow arrows at either end of the ruler. This technique helps you align the tick marks for more accurate indent and tab placement. The zero tick mark on the ruler indicates the left page margin or column guide, not the left edge of the page. When the Indents/tabs ruler first appears on the page, the zero tick mark is aligned with the left column guide of the column in which you clicked the insertion point. If no insertion point exists, the ruler centers itself on the page.

Fig. 6.14

The Indents/Tabs ruler showing proper settings for regular and hanging indents.

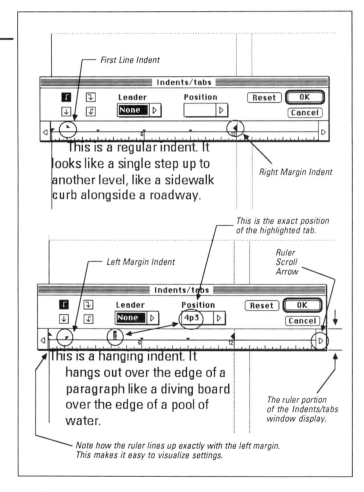

PageMaker's first-line indent determines how far the first line of text in a paragraph is indented. Indentation set in toward the right is called a normal or regular indent. Indentation set out toward the left (away from the body of a paragraph) is called a hanging indent. As with PageMaker's left and right indents, you can set a first-line indent value in the Paragraph Specifications dialog box or with the Indents/Tabs ruler. On the ruler, the first line indent is represented by the small upper triangle at the left end of the ruler. Drag the triangle to any spot along the ruler to set the first line indent.

To set a hanging indent, enter a negative value in the **Indents First** field in the Paragraph Specifications dialog box (type a minus sign before the value you enter). Be sure to enter a larger positive value for **Indents Left,** or PageMaker does not accept your numbers. You need enough room for the hanging indent to exist within the left page margin or column boundary.

To set a hanging indent using the Indents/Tabs ruler, drag the left indent marker to the right to make room for the hanging indent. The first-line indent moves with the left indent to hold its position with respect to the left edge of the paragraph. When you have enough room, move the first-line indent marker back to the left to create the hanging indent.

When you drag an indent or tab marker along the ruler, you see a corresponding value displayed in the **Position** field. This number gives the exact position of the marker along the ruler in the units of measure you specify in the Preferences dialog box. Use this positional value as a guide to precise marker placement.

Tip

If you are working in a 400% Size page view and your publication's units of measure are set to picas, the Indents/Tabs ruler displays ruler tick marks at exactly one-point intervals. These divisions make setting indents and tabs in one-point increments easy. Use the value shown in the **Position** field to check your work.

You can set indents only within existing page margins or column guides, and any settings you make apply to only the selected paragraphs. Unless you make a change, when you create a paragraph, PageMaker assigns the paragraph the same indents as in the preceding paragraph.

Tip

If you discover that your text wraps short of the right column boundary when placing a story, make sure that you did not set a right indent in your word processor. If you did, remove the right indent in your original document and reflow the text or select the text within PageMaker and reset the right indent using the Indents/Tabs ruler.

Setting Tabs

PageMaker enables you to use several kinds of tabs and tab leaders in your documents. Tabbed text is easy to set up. But certain key steps must be performed in strict sequence if you want consistent results. Unlike indents that apply to only whole paragraphs, tabs can be set for a selected range of text within a given paragraph. You can insert up to 40 tab stops on any one line.

You can assign four kinds of tabs—left, right, center, and decimal. Think of tab stops as invisible wires running down the page. The left tab aligns the left edge of your text to this invisible wire. The right tab aligns the right edge of your text to the wire. The center tab causes each line of text to be split equally—half on the left side of the wire and half on the right. The decimal tab stacks columns of numbers, aligning each decimal point vertically along the wire.

Tip

Use tabs instead of spaces to format tables and lists of data. Most fonts are proportional, and the space surrounding individual characters varies. If you space data using the space bar, the alignment comes out uneven when you print your document, even if the text looks good on-screen. If you use tabs, the alignment is exact.

Each tab marker is shaped like an arrow. The left-tab marker has a bent tail that points to the right toward its aligned text. The right-tab marker has a bent tail that points to the left toward its aligned text. The center-tab marker has a straight tail to indicate that its text is split evenly. The decimal-tab marker has a small decimal point next to a straight tail to indicate that its text aligns exactly on the decimals, wherever they fall (see fig. 6.15).

When you set tabs in PageMaker, you also can set accompanying tab leaders. Tab leaders are repeating characters—usually dots, dashes, or lines, that precede indented text.

To set your tab stops and leader styles, use the following procedure:

1. Select the text to which you want to apply the tabs. Do not select any text if you intend to set a publication or program default.

2. Choose the Indents/Tabs command from the Type menu.

3. Unless you want to use the existing tabs as displayed, click the **Reset** button to remove the existing tabs from the ruler. Otherwise, adjust the tabs individually by click-dragging. You also can remove the tabs (see step 9).

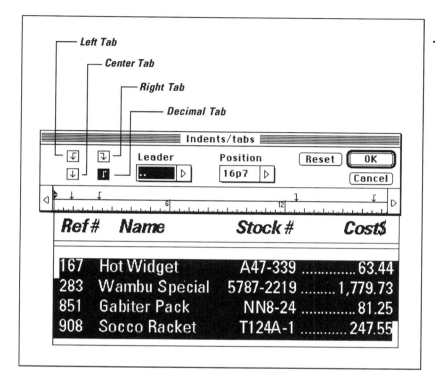

Fig. 6.15

The highlighted text is tabbed according to the placement of tab markers along the Indents/Tabs ruler.

4. Choose the kind of tab you want (left, right, center, or decimal) by clicking its corresponding icon.

5. Choose the kind of leader style you want from the pop-up Leader menu. The menu choices are dots, dashes, solid line, Custom, or none. If you want to create your own tab leader, choose Custom and type one or two repeating characters into the **Leader** field. PageMaker assigns the same font attributes as the preceding text.

Tip

To create a tab leader composed of dots less tightly spaced than in the style provided, type a period followed by a space into the **Leader** field.

Tip

To edit a tab leader so that the tab leader uses a different font than that which precedes the tab, click an insertion point just before the tab leader. Assign the new font specifications, and, without moving the insertion point, type a space. The tab leader changes to the new font (see fig. 6.16).

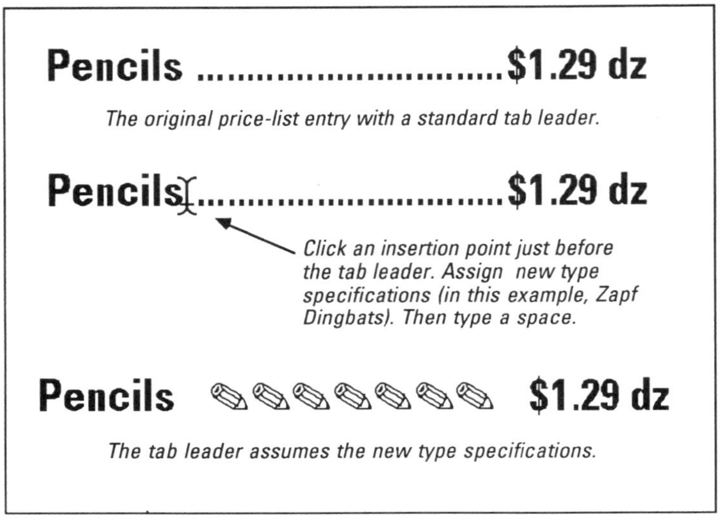

Fig. 6.16

Changing the type specifications for a tab leader.

Pencils ....**$1.29 dz**

The original price-list entry with a standard tab leader.

Pencils..............................**$1.29 dz**

Click an insertion point just before the tab leader. Assign new type specifications (in this example, Zapf Dingbats). Then type a space.

Pencils ✎✎✎✎✎✎✎ **$1.29 dz**

The tab leader assumes the new type specifications.

6. Click the ruler (not the ruler window) to make the tab marker appear. The tab takes on the current leader style.

7. Drag the marker to the desired location along the ruler. Each tab marker aligns to a ruler tick mark. You can drag any marker over any other. Use the value shown in the **Position** field to check placement accuracy.

Note

You can use the pop-up Position menu to add a new tab or move a highlighted tab to the exact position indicated in the **Position** field. You also can delete a highlighted tab (or whatever tab occupies the indicated position). To create tabs that repeat at certain intervals, select a tab and type the desired spacing into the **Position** field. Choose Repeat Tab from the pop-up menu. The tabs repeat across the ruler at the specified intervals.

---

8. If you assign a tab leader that you later want to change, click the tab marker to which that leader is assigned. Use the **Leader** field to assign a new tab leader.

9. To change a tab marker, select the tab marker and click the icon for the type of tab marker you want. To remove a tab marker, drag the marker off the ruler.

Warning

If you assign several tabs and later clear all tab markers from the ruler and start over, PageMaker defaults to setting invisible tabs every half inch. All your tab-formatted text reorganizes itself on your page to conform to PageMaker's invisible default settings. This can turn formatted text and tables into screen garbage. Any new tabs that you add eliminate the invisible half-inch default markers to the left of those tabs so that you get proper spacing when you press the Tab key. However, PageMaker's invisible tabs still exist to the right of the last tab marker placed.

If you remove one tab marker, the text aligned with that marker shifts to the left and aligns with the preceding tab stop. If you have no preceding tab stops, your text aligns with the left indent, first-line indent, or column guide. If you remove the last tab marker from the ruler, your text aligns itself with the next invisible default tab stop to the left.

To use tabs that you create when typing new text, press the Tab key to move your text insertion point to the next tab stop. If the tab has an associated tab leader, the leader appears when you type the first character. To tab existing text, create an insertion point and press the Tab key. Your text reformats at the next tab stop according to the type alignment specified. If your tab has an associated tab leader, you see the leader after you press the Tab key.

When you import a document, PageMaker normally assigns tabs and indents to match the formatting created in your word processor.

The tick marks on the Indents/Tabs ruler change their spacing as you switch between different page views and assign different units of measure using the Preferences dialog box. Because each indent and tab marker must align exactly with a ruler tick mark, you may want to try different window views and units of measure when assigning indents and tabs. Generally, assigning indent and tab markers accurately is easier when you work in an enlarged page view.

Hyphenating

PageMaker hyphenates text so that the text wraps evenly within your columns. If a word at the end of a line is too long to fit within the column boundaries, and PageMaker cannot hyphenate the word, the word moves to the beginning of the next line. This can leave unsightly gaps of white space at the ends of lines that detract from the appearance of your publication. To overcome this deficiency, you can hyphenate your text manually. PageMaker uses the same dictionaries for hyphenating text as for spell-checking.

To display the Hyphenation dialog box (see fig. 6.17), choose the Hyphenation command from the Type menu. Hyphenation can be turned on or off. If turned on, PageMaker hyphenates your stories according to the options you select.

You can limit PageMaker to manual hyphenation only. In this case, PageMaker hyphenates words only where you have inserted discretionary hyphens (Command-hyphen) previously. Discretionary hyphens remain invisible until PageMaker uses them to break words at the ends of lines.

You also can tell PageMaker to use the dictionary. PageMaker hyphenates words according to the ranking of the hyphenation breaks the program finds in the dictionary and at any discretionary hyphens that you insert.

Finally, you also can instruct PageMaker to use its special built-in dictionary algorithm. This last method gives PageMaker the most flexibility when hyphenating your text. When you choose this option, PageMaker hyphenates words using manual hyphenation and the dictionary. Additionally, the program applies, as needed, a sophisticated hyphenation algorithm that is based on the structure of the language in use. (PageMaker knows which language because of which dictionary is installed.) The algorithm enables PageMaker to hyphenate words not in the dictionary.

The manner in which PageMaker sets hyphenation breaks at the ends of unjustified column lines affects how your layouts look. You can tell PageMaker exactly how

Fig. 6.17

You can limit the number of consecutive hyphens using PageMaker's Hyphenation dialog box.

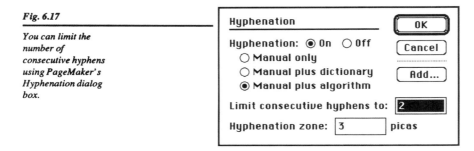

much space at the end of an unjustified line to use for hyphenation. Hyphenation occurs only within the area you designate. To specify a hyphenation zone, type the desired size interval into the **Hyphenation zone** field. Unjustified text shows either a more or less ragged right margin, depending on how large or small an area you specify. Fully justified and force justified text remain unaffected by this setting, because their column line widths are constant.

PageMaker sometimes hyphenates consecutive lines of type. This happens most often in narrow columns and produces a ladder effect that detracts from the appearance of your text. Typing a whole number between 1-255 into the **Limit consecutive hyphens to** field tells PageMaker not to insert any more than that number of consecutive hyphens into your text. Type the phrase *no limit* if you do not want to place a limit on the number of consecutive hyphens PageMaker inserts. Generally, you want to limit consecutive hyphens to no more than two.

Automatic Hyphenation

To turn on automatic hyphenation, choose the Hyphenation command from the Type menu and select the **Manual plus algorithm** option. PageMaker hyphenates all newly typed or imported text and any text selected at the time auto-hyphenation is turned on. Normally, you want to leave auto-hyphenation turned on as you work. PageMaker re-hyphenates your stories as you resize or reshape text blocks, or insert or remove text.

Manual Hyphenation

If you want the most control over PageMaker's hyphenation, choose the **Manual only** option in the Hyphenation dialog box. This option enables you to copy-fit your text with greater accuracy than when hyphenating automatically. Manually hyphenating text sometimes is tedious, but you do not have to find and fix any bad hyphenation that PageMaker applies using its built-in dictionary algorithm. Algorithms, after all, are not perfect—they are only best-guess approximations.

The supplementary user dictionary enables you to add or delete discretionary hyphens to suit your preferences. You access the user dictionary by clicking the **Add** button in the Hyphenation dialog box or by choosing the Spelling command from the Edit menu when in Story view (see Chapter 5). You can add proper names, technical jargon, and other words you use frequently that are not contained in PageMaker's built-in dictionary. You also can insert discretionary hyphenation breaks, complete with rankings. Just type one, two, or three tilde (~) symbols. One tilde indicates the highest priority hyphenation break; two the next highest; and three tildes, the lowest priority break. If you don't want a particular word ever to be hyphenated, add that word without hyphens, but place a tilde just before the word (see fig. 6.18). PageMaker does not hyphenate words that are preceded with a discretionary hyphen.

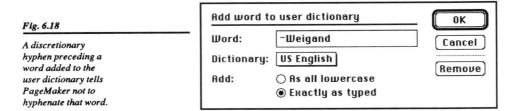

Fig. 6.18

A discretionary hyphen preceding a word added to the user dictionary tells PageMaker not to hyphenate that word.

Discretionary Hyphenation

Inserting discretionary hyphens tells PageMaker how you want the program to hyphenate those words. Unlike ordinary hyphens, you don't see discretionary hyphens until PageMaker uses them to break words at the ends of lines. Discretionary hyphens that you insert into your stories apply only within your current publication. Discretionary hyphens you add to the user dictionary apply to all stories in all your publications.

To insert a discretionary hyphen into a word in your text, press the Command key and type a hyphen at the exact spot you want the word to be divided. Use this procedure for words that already are hyphenated, if you want to change the hyphenation for a better column fit. For example, entering a discretionary hyphen within the first word of a line breaks that word and moves part of the word up to fill a gap, if one exists, at the end of the preceding line. Entering a discretionary hyphen at the beginning of the last word in a line, even if PageMaker already has hyphenated the word, moves the whole word down to the beginning of the next line.

To remove a discretionary hyphen from a word at the end of a line of type, insert the cursor immediately after the hyphen and backspace over the hyphen. To remove a discretionary hyphen from a word in the middle of a line of type (where the hyphen isn't displayed), select and replace the word by retyping.

Tip

Always use discretionary (soft) hyphens instead of regular (hard) hyphens. When you reformat your layout by resizing or reshaping text blocks, discretionary hyphens disappear if the words move to the middle of a column. However, a regular hyphen within a word that later shifts to the middle of a column does not disappear. You still see the hyphen.

Aligning Text

PageMaker's Alignment command on the Type menu (also the pop-up menu in the Paragraph Specifications dialog box) gives you several choices for aligning text within columns (see fig. 6.19). You can align text evenly along the left edge (Align Left), its right edge (Align Right), left and right edges (Justify), and left and right edges regardless of line length (Force Justify). You also can center your text (Align Center). These commands should not be confused with tab stops. Tab stops apply to only tabbed text; the alignment commands apply to columnar text. For example, if you choose Align Right, the selected text reformats so that the right edges of each line lie flush against the right column guide.

This is an example of left justification. Note how the text is even down the left side of the column, and ragged down the right side.	This is an example of right justification. Note how the text is even down the right side of the column, and ragged down the left side.	This is an example of center justifica-tion. Note how the text is balanced evenly across the center of the column, but remains ragged along both edges.	This is an example of full justification. Note how the text is even on both sides of the column. There are no ragged edges.	This is an example of forced justification. Note how the last line of text spreads out to fill the entire column w i d t h .
↑	↑	↑	↖	↗
Left-Aligned	*Right-Aligned*	*Center-Aligned*	*Left & Right-Aligned*	

Fig. 6.19

In PageMaker, you can left-align, right-align, center-align, fully justify, and force-justify text.

Text often is left-aligned (sometimes called ragged-right justification), because this kind of layout is the easiest to read. The next easiest-to-read alignment is fully justified text, also called left-right justified. PageMaker's Justify command formats text so that most column lines are equal in length, often to the detriment of overall word or letter spacing.

Right-aligned or right-justified text generally is used in only special instances, such as when preparing a list of items confined to the right side of a page. Right-justified text is difficult to read, unless limited to narrow columns.

Center-aligned (center-justified) text often is used for design emphasis or to focus reader attention. Because long, center-justified passages can be difficult to read, use this kind of formatting sparingly.

Forced justification tells PageMaker to stretch the last line of text in a paragraph so the text fits fully across the column. Note that forced justification can be used to stretch headlines to fit text blocks of any width, but without regard for the aesthetics of letter and word spacing.

Tip

Justifying columns can create uneven spacing between bullets (Option-8) and the text following the bullets. To ensure even spacing, insert a tab to mark the beginning of the text. Tab over to the text after typing each bullet. You also can enter a fixed Space (Option-spacebar) if the fixed-space character is supported by the current font.

After you have aligned your text within your columns, check the vertical alignment of multiple text blocks. To align text blocks vertically, place a vertical ruler guide alongside where you want to stack the text blocks. Choose the Snap To Rulers command from the Options menu and drag each text block so that the block lies snugly against the ruler guide.

Adjusting Word and Letter Spacing

When PageMaker justifies text, the program sacrifices word and letter spacing to achieve equal line lengths. This process sometimes produces unsightly "rivers" of white space that snake down a column. To compensate for this white space, you can use PageMaker's Spacing command to specify better spacing for words and letters. You also can set an acceptable range of maximum and minimum spacing values. You type these values into the Spacing Attributes dialog box (see fig. 6.20). Click the **Spacing** button in the Paragraph Specifications dialog box to display the Spacing Attributes dialog box. Spacing Attributes apply to entire paragraphs, not just to selected text.

Fig. 6.20

The Spacing Attributes dialog box.

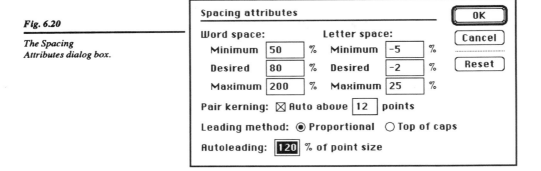

Although adjusting word and letter spacing often improves the appearance of a publication, applying these attributes to justified text requires a mixture of skill and patience. Many variables, including the vagaries of auto-hyphenation and your choices of column widths, come into play. You may go through much trial-and-error before you approach ideal formatting results. However, don't be discouraged. PageMaker generally does a credible job of justifying text, and you can improve overall spacing with little extra effort.

To adjust word or letter spacing, enter an insertion point in your paragraph, then open the Spacing Attributes dialog box. The values you enter for **Word space** and **Letter space** take effect immediately after you click the OK button. To add more space between words and letters, increase the range values by entering a smaller number in the **Minimum** field and a larger number in the **Maximum** field. (Do just the opposite to subtract space.) Keep in mind that increased range values tend to create more rivers in your columns; decreased range values help eliminate rivers.

The allowable range of values you can enter for **Word space** is 0 to 500 percent. For **Letter space**, you can enter -200 to 0 percent for **Minimum** and 0 to 200 percent for **Maximum**. However, all you really need to know is that if you enter 100 percent for **Word space Desired** and 0 percent for **Letter space Desired**, PageMaker uses the selected font's built-in spacing.

You can adjust the **Maximum** and **Minimum** field percentages as necessary to achieve optimal column justification (make sure that you also have hyphenation turned on to get the best results). Values greater than 100 percent entered into the **Word space** fields expand the space between words; values less than 100 percent condense the space between words. Similarly, values greater than 0 percent entered into the **Letter space** fields expand the space between letters; values less than 0 percent condense the space between letters.

Sometimes a combination of fonts, column justification, and assigned hyphenation causes PageMaker to override the values you enter for word and letter spacing. Check the **Loose/tight lines** option in the Preferences dialog box to have PageMaker indicate spacing problems. PageMaker highlights any text that falls outside the ranges you specify. After you identify the problems, you can make any corrections or editing changes you think necessary.

Tip

Most fonts benefit from slightly tighter word and letter spacing. Tighter spacing gives your publications a more finished appearance and makes them easier to read (see fig. 6.21). Tighter spacing can be more difficult to edit on-screen, however. Wait until you finish editing before you set spacing to a lesser value. Depending on the font and size you use, you get different results for different assigned values. Try reducing the desired word spacing by 20 to 30 percent and the desired letter spacing by 2 to 5 percent. Set the minimum letter spacing only slightly less than or equal to the desired letter spacing for best results when using justified columns.

This text is set in 12-point Times. The word and letter spacing are those assigned by the font designer.

This is the same font, but the word and letter spacing have been tightened 20% and 3% respectively.

Fig. 6.21

Improve the appearance of your text by tightening word and letter spacing.

Tip

Use PageMaker's Spacing command to refine the word and letter spacing of your headlines. PageMaker considers headlines complete paragraphs if they reside in their own text blocks.

Tighter word and letter spacing applied to justified columns, especially narrow ones, helps to eliminate unsightly gaps. However, tighter spacing also increases the amount of hyphenation required. You should adjust the spacing attributes to limit the number of consecutively hyphenated lines.

Use the Hyphenation dialog box to specify the size of the hyphenation zone. If the hyphenation zone is too wide, unjustified columns may appear excessively ragged.

Tip

You cannot always see the full effects of adjusting word and letter spacing on-screen. Most screen resolutions are limited to 72 dots per inch. When you assign new spacing attributes to your text, do a test print to evaluate the results.

Inserting Line Breaks

Sometimes you may want to type a carriage return to begin a new line, as when preparing a table or listing of items, but you don't want to start a whole new paragraph. A preceding paragraph may be styled to have a first line indent, or a large amount of blank space above it, and you don't want to carry those special style characteristics over to the next "paragraph." To circumvent this problem in PageMaker, all you have to do is type a line break.

A line break functions the same as a carriage return, but, as far as PageMaker is concerned, does not actually begin a new paragraph. To insert a line break, type Shift-Return or Shift-Enter. If your current paragraph style calls for a first line indent, or space before or after the paragraph, typing Shift-Return or Shift-Enter makes it appear as if you have begun a new paragraph, but without assigning those special paragraph attributes you want to avoid.

> ### *Tip*
>
> Using a line break to begin a new "paragraph" while working within a fully justified column has the same effect as applying forced justification to the preceding paragraph.

Using Style Sheets

Style sheets are sets of predefined paragraph specifications called styles (not to be confused with everyday type styles like bold and italic). You use styles to make global formatting changes to your publications. Each PageMaker publication has a style sheet that can contain any number of different styles.

Suppose that you create a style and use that style to set all your subheads to 12-point Helvetica bold type. You then decide that 14-point bold italic type is more appropriate. You can call up the style named "subhead" from your style sheet and make the necessary editing changes using the Type Specifications dialog box. When you click OK, PageMaker updates every subhead throughout your entire publication.

Style sheets are great time-savers and bring a look of consistency to your publications. Style sheets, however, can be tricky to work with at times. The problem stems from making ordinary menu style changes (by using PageMaker's menus and Type Specifications dialog box choices) within paragraphs that have style-sheet formatting applied. If you later change the style that was used, or another style upon which that one was based, or apply a new style to those same paragraphs, you may lose ordinary style changes you have made.

Use caution when working with style sheets. Start by formatting just one or two items. As you gain experience, gradually work up to applying styles throughout your publications. After you master the basics, you discover many exciting ways to use style sheets.

Style sheets enable you to assign type, paragraph, indent/tab, hyphenation, and even color specifications globally to selected paragraphs (remember that a paragraph is defined as a range of text that ends with a carriage return). Applying styles is a fast way to do extensive formatting. You can select a group of paragraphs or a whole story, and, with one click, completely change the way your text looks.

Style sheets are publication-dependent. When you create a style, the style sheet is saved with your publication (or template). If you send that file out for printing, the built-in styles accompany the file. Each new PageMaker publication opens with a default set of built-in styles that you can modify to match your own formatting needs.

Tip

Create a Master Styles publication template. After that, when you begin a new publication, start by opening a copy of the template. All your styles are available so that you don't have to import the style attributes selectively from other publications.

You can add styles to your publications by creating styles, basing styles on pre-existing styles, copying styles from other PageMaker publications, or importing styles along with your word-processed documents. Currently available styles are listed as follows:

- The Style palette (choose Style Palette from the Windows menu).
- The Style submenu (choose the Style command from the Type menu).
- The Define Styles dialog box (choose the Define Styles command from the Type menu).

Generally, you want to set up different styles for different paragraphs in a publication—headings, subheads, picture captions, credit lines, footnotes, body text, and so on.

Defining and Editing Styles

To define a new style, choose the Define Styles command from the Type menu to display the Define Styles dialog box (see fig. 6.22). Click the **New** button. In the Edit Style dialog box that appears, type the name of your new style. If you are basing your new style on an existing style, choose the name of that style from the Based on pop-up menu. To edit an existing style, click the style name in the scrolling window, and then click the **Edit** button.

Note that the **New** and **Edit** buttons both bring up the same Edit Style dialog box. The only difference is that the name of the style you are editing appears in the **Name** field when you select **Edit**.

Tip

A shortcut to displaying the Edit Style dialog box is to hold down the Command key as you click on a style name in the Style palette. You can edit that style directly. Choose No Style from the Based on pop-up menu to create a style. When you edit a style, your changes apply to every paragraph assigned that style previously.

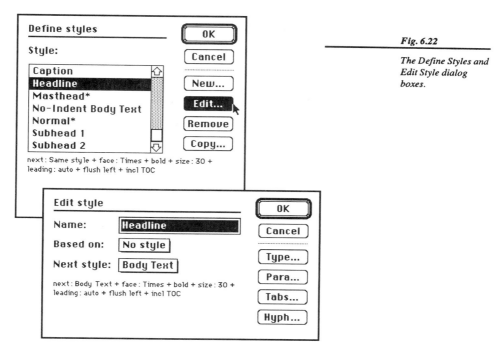

Fig. 6.22

The Define Styles and Edit Style dialog boxes.

In the Edit Style dialog box, you click the **Type** (Type specifications), **Para** (Paragraph), **Tabs** (Indents/tabs), and **Hyph** (Hyphenation) buttons one at a time. Each button brings up its associated dialog boxes in which you make your formatting choices.

Tip

If you click a style name in the Style palette before opening the Define Styles dialog box and clicking the **New** button, that style name appears in the Based on and Next style pop-up menus accessed from the Edit Style dialog box; you don't have to enter the name each time.

You also can create a style based directly on existing text that you have formatted using menu commands. Select the text you want to base your style on or click an insertion point anywhere within the text. You see the style attributes for that text listed in the lower part of the Define Styles dialog box. Open the Edit Style dialog box to make further modifications.

When you are finished, click OK to apply your style and save your style to your publication's style sheet.

> ***Note***
>
> If you base new styles on existing styles, they become threaded permanently into a style chain. If you later edit any style upon which other styles are based, all the other styles update to reflect the changes made. All the paragraphs throughout your publication to which those styles have been applied also update automatically.

To copy styles from another PageMaker publication, click the **Copy** button in the Define Styles dialog box. Choose the publication containing the styles you want to copy. When you click OK, PageMaker copies that publication's styles (all of them) into your current document. If some styles have the same name, PageMaker alerts you, asking whether you want to copy over the existing styles (see fig. 6.23). Click OK to continue. The styles copy into your open publication. You then can modify any of these styles to meet current layout requirements.

Fig. 6.23

PageMaker alerts you if the styles you try to import from other PageMaker publications have names the same as those in your current style sheet.

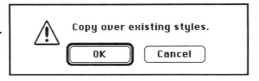

To remove a style from a style sheet, select the style name from the Define Styles dialog box and click **Remove**. This option does not remove any formatting applied previously using that style. Click the Cancel button if you remove a style by mistake.

Importing Styles

To import styles created by your word processor, the styles must be assigned to the document you import using PageMaker's Place command. When you place these documents, make sure that you select the **Retain format** option in the Place Document dialog box. The assigned styles come through unaltered (when the styles are compatible with PageMaker), and PageMaker adds the assigned styles to your publication's style sheet. These imported styles show up in both the Style palette and Styles menu and are followed by an asterisk to distinguish the imported styles from styles you define within PageMaker. If any imported styles have names that match the names in PageMaker's style sheet, PageMaker uses its own styles instead.

PageMaker also can read word processor style tags. Each style tag must be set at the beginning of the paragraph to which the tag applies. The tag also must be enclosed in angle brackets, such as <caption>. However, no tags are needed for a paragraph that is formatted the same as the preceding paragraph. PageMaker applies the appropriate style for each tag with a corresponding style name. To import style tags, make sure that you check the **Read tags** option in the Place Document dialog box.

If, for example, you import the style tag <caption>, and a style of that name already exists in your publication style sheet, PageMaker applies that style to the text. If PageMaker doesn't find a matching style name in its style sheet, the program creates a new style having the same name as the tag. You then edit the new style and assign whatever formatting you like.

After applying the appropriate styles, PageMaker deletes the style tags from the text.

Assigning Styles

To assign a style, first use the text tool to select a paragraph or range of paragraphs. Click the name of the style you want to apply. The style names are listed in the Style palette and the Style submenu. Your choice takes effect immediately. You also can choose a style from the Define Styles dialog box. Click OK to apply the style attributes to your text.

If you want a particular style to always follow another style (body text after a headline, for example), select the lead style and open the Edit Style dialog box. Choose the follow-on style by selecting the follow-on style from the Next Style pop-up menu. After that, any new paragraphs you type after a lead-style paragraph assume the follow-on style. You can assign a whole chain of successive paragraph styles in this way.

Warning

Exercise caution when applying styles. You cannot use the Edit menu's Undo command to undo the changes you make. The only way to recover original paragraph formatting is to choose Revert from the File menu (which restores the last-saved version of your publication) or apply another style having the same formatting specifications as your original paragraphs.

Overriding Styles

You can apply new type attributes to text within paragraphs having a prescribed style. For example, after assigning a style based on italic type to a paragraph, you can select a word or phrase and make that selection bold for additional visual emphasis. When you modify an applied style this way, a plus sign (+) is placed after that style's name in the Style palette and Style menu to indicate that the style has been overridden.

You can create permanent or temporary overrides. Permanent overrides apply conventional type style attributes, like bold or italic, to your text. They are considered permanent, because they are the kind of changes you generally want to be permanent. If you later apply a new style to a paragraph that contains a permanent override, the override itself remains unaffected.

The only exception to permanent overrides is when a new style applies the same attribute used to create the override in the first place. Under those circumstances, the override toggles to maintain its distinguishing characteristics. If, for example, you apply a style using bold type to a paragraph containing words or phrases already set in bold, those words or phrases change back to normal type. The contrast in type styles is what makes the words stand out from the rest of the paragraph. PageMaker preserves this contrast in styles.

Temporary overrides are created by applying other type attributes to your styled text, including point size, hyphenation, leading, tabs, and indents. These overrides are called temporary because, if you later apply a new style having the same attributes, you can wipe out all your changes. For example, if you change a selected range of text to 12-point to make the text stand out within a paragraph made up of all 10-point text and later apply a new 12-point style to that paragraph, your 12-point formatting no longer stands out. The entire paragraph is now set in 12-point type.

Deciding whether to apply a new style or to use menu commands as overrides sometimes is difficult. If you use many different type attributes interchangeably, your list of styles may become unmanageable. You may prefer to use menu commands as overrides. If your layouts are complex, however, and you inadvertently apply a new style to a paragraph containing overrides, you can lose all your carefully planned formatting. The best approach is to use the power of style-sheet formatting to streamline your work, but keep a list of overrides handy to double-check your work, before your publication goes to press.

Tip

To keep temporary overrides intact while you apply a new style, hold down the Shift key and click the style name in the Style palette or choose the style from the Style submenu. Your paragraphs update to reflect the new attributes, and your temporary overrides remain unchanged.

Generating Tables of Contents

Tables of contents are outlines that briefly introduce the organization and content of book-length publications. To assemble book-length publications using Page-Maker, you create and maintain a book publication list via the Book command from the File menu (see fig. 6.24). PageMaker combines and prints those publications you designate as being part of your book.

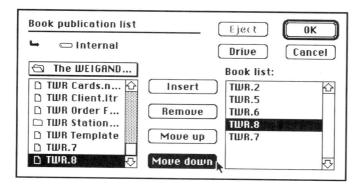

Fig. 6.24

*You can build a
sequential book
publication list using
the Book Publication
List dialog box.*

For example, you can create individually the many chapters making up a technical manual and save the chapters as separate publications. You list those publications in sequential order in your book publication list. The **Insert, Remove, Move up,** and **Move down** buttons enable you to combine and arrange publications in final order. PageMaker uses your list to assemble the book.

Note

You have to assign the starting page numbers independently for each publication in your book list so that PageMaker prints your publications with sequential page numbering.

The next step, of course, is to have PageMaker prepare a table of contents (TOC) for your book. First, however, you must tell PageMaker just what to use as TOC material by tagging paragraphs as table-of-contents entries. Click an insertion point in each paragraph (or select a range of paragraphs) and activate the **Include in table of contents** option in the Paragraph Specifications dialog box.

Choose the Create TOC command from the Options menu to get the Create Table of Contents dialog box (see fig. 6.25). Configure the appropriate options and click OK. A text-placement tool appears. Use the text-placement tool to flow your table of contents like any other story.

Fig. 6.25

*The Create Table of
Contents dialog box.*

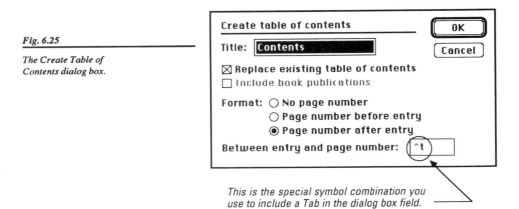

This is the special symbol combination you
use to include a Tab in the dialog box field.

Tip

Normally, you have to wade through your publications to tag all the headlines
or subheads you want to include in your TOC listing. To save time, prepare
a new paragraph style with the **Include in table of contents** option in the
Paragraph Specifications dialog box checked. After that, you need only click
that style in the Style palette to apply that style to TOC-destined paragraphs.
PageMaker lists TOC styles in the Style palette prefixed with the letters TOC
for easy identification.

One of the options in the Create Table of Contents dialog box enables you to update
and replace earlier TOC versions. You also can insert page numbers before or after
TOC entries, place special characters like tabs between TOC entries, and include
TOC entries extracted from other publications in your book list.

You can type a series of up to 16 characters in the **TOC and index prefix** field in
the Page Numbering dialog box (click the **Numbers** button in the Page Setup dialog
box), which enables you to assign a volume number or other identifying prefix to
your TOC page numbers (see fig. 6.26). PageMaker adds the specified prefix to
produce the required composite page numbers.

Fig. 6.26

*Typing a TOC and
index prefix into the
Page Numbering
dialog box.*

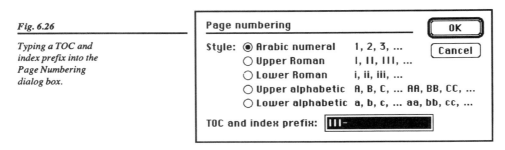

After placing your table of contents, you can edit and reformat the table of contents like any other text, using PageMaker's full range of text-editing and formatting tools.

Indexing Your Publications

One of the most difficult tasks when creating book-length publications is indexing those publications. PageMaker does not relieve you of the burden of deciding what goes into an index. You must choose each index entry beforehand. After you have completed that step, however, PageMaker takes over and compiles finished indexes, complete with formatting and page numbers.

Creating Index Entries

To create an index entry, select the text in your publication you want to include as a topic. Choose the Index Entry command from the Options menu or type the Command-semicolon keyboard shortcut. The Create Index Entry dialog box appears with the selected word displayed in the first **Topic** field ready for editing (see fig. 6.27). Alternatively, you can click an insertion point at the first occurrence of the topic in your text and then open the Create Index Entry dialog box. Type your topic entry into the first **Topic** field.

Tip

When you decide to include a particular topic as an index entry, let PageMaker help you conduct a search for every occurrence of that topic. Choose the Find command from the Edit menu while in Story view. Instruct PageMaker to search all stories. PageMaker stops on each find so that you can index each occurrence appropriately.

You can enter additional related, primary topics in the second and third **Topic** fields. For example, if your first index entry is the word *newsletter*, you also can type the words *periodical* and *journal* in the fields following that entry. These related topics help your readers find the appropriate information in your publication, regardless of which descriptive word springs to mind.

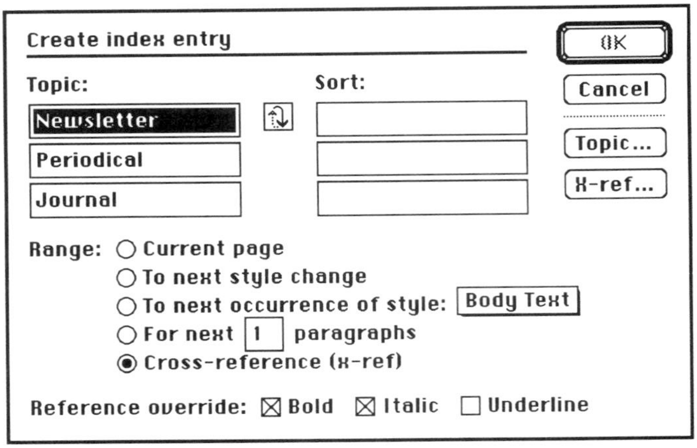

Fig. 6.27

*Creating multiple
primary entries
for one topic in
the Create Index
Entry dialog box.*

```
Create index entry                    [   OK   ]

Topic:                    Sort:         [ Cancel ]
[Newsletter      ]  [↻]  [          ]
[Periodical      ]       [          ]   [ Topic... ]
[Journal         ]       [          ]   [ X-ref... ]

Range:  ○ Current page
        ○ To next style change
        ○ To next occurrence of style: [ Body Text ]
        ○ For next [1]  paragraphs
        ● Cross-reference (x-ref)

Reference override: ☒ Bold  ☒ Italic  ☐ Underline
```

Note

You can click the promote/demote button (the circling-arrows button) in the
Create Index Entry dialog box to step index entries in cyclic fashion through
the **Topic** and **Sort** fields. This promote/demote feature enables you to
change instantly the order of topic priority by promoting or demoting a given
topic entry.

Assigning Index Parameters

The **Sort** fields to the right of the **Topic** fields enable PageMaker to sort indexed
entries logically, without regard to actual spelling. For example, if you enter *2-Year
Warranty* into a **Topic** field at the left, you can type *Two-Year Warranty* into its
corresponding **Sort** field at the right. Your entry then would appear in the index
sorted alphabetically under the T's but displayed with the numeral 2 as a prefix (just
as you entered the entry in the **Topic** field). If you leave a corresponding sort field
empty, PageMaker sorts the Topic entry by its current spelling.

The Create Index Entry dialog box contains several range options. The **Current page
range** option tells PageMaker that the topic entry appears only on the page in which
you selected the text or clicked an insertion point. The range options **To next style
change** and **To next occurrence of style xxx** (select the appropriate style from the
pop-up menu) tell PageMaker to assign a page range that extends only until the next
style change occurs. You also can type a whole number into the **For next xx
paragraphs** field to tell PageMaker how many successive paragraphs your index
entry spans. PageMaker assigns the corresponding page ranges to your topic entries.

To avoid repeating index entries in slightly different ways, and thus producing an index burdened with similar entries all describing the same topic, use PageMaker's Select Topic list (see fig. 6.28). This menu enables you to duplicate entries exactly and avoid misspellings or typos. This menu also serves as a reminder if you have difficulty remembering whether you already have indexed a topic.

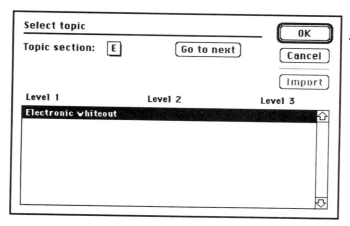

Fig. 6.28

Choose repeating topics from the Select Topic menu to avoid misspellings and typos when creating index entries.

You open the Select Topic dialog box by clicking the **Topic** button in the Create Index Entry dialog box. Current index entries are shown. Select the appropriate index entry from the list to have that entry added to your index. The tiny Index section pop-up menu at the top of the dialog box enables you to access topic listings alphabetically by groups. You can step through alphabetical groups by clicking the **Go to next** button.

Selecting a reference override enables you to change the type attributes of a given index entry to make that entry stand out noticeably from other entries.

To make a simple index entry quickly, do the following:

1. Select the text in your publication that you want to appear as an index entry. Each entry can contain up to 50 characters (including spaces).

2. Open the Create Index Entry dialog box (use the Command-semicolon key combination to save selecting the menu command). Your text is displayed in the first **Topic** field.

3. If you are adding the entry to an existing topic, click the promote/demote button to cycle the entry to the second or third field. Open the Select Topic dialog box and locate the topic. Select the topic and hold down the Command key as you click the Return button (or double-click the topic while holding down the Command key). The Create Index Entry dialog box displays the topic in the first **Topic** field without deleting your entry. If you forget to hold down the Command

key, retype your entry into the second or third **Topic** field as appropriate.

4. Enter any special spellings for sorting into the corresponding sort fields. Also, indicate the appropriate **Range** choice and choose any reference overrides you may want to assign.

5. Click OK. Your index entry is complete.

Note

You can assign an endless number of secondary (and tertiary) entries to a given topic. Each time you make a new, related entry, be sure that your primary topic appears in the first **Topic** field in the Create Index Entry dialog box. PageMaker indexes the many secondary and tertiary entries you create under that topic heading.

To better visualize how this works, think of your primary entry as your main topic. Each secondary entry then becomes a subtopic. Each subtopic, in turn, can have sub-subtopics. Thus, you have three possible levels for indexing entries: the main topic, subtopics, and sub-subtopics. You can include many separate entries in each of these levels.

Under the main topic "Life," for example, you can include the secondary entries "Childhood," "Adolescence," "Early Adulthood," "Middle Age," and "Old Age." Under "Old Age," you can include the tertiary entries "The Golden Years," "Planning for Retirement," "Developing New Interests," and "Coping with Disease and Illness." When creating the secondary topics for Life, you enter the topic "Life" each time as your primary entry in the Create Index Entry dialog box. When creating the tertiary topics for Old Age, you enter the topic "Life" each time as your primary entry and the topic "Old Age" as your secondary entry.

Cross-Referencing and Formatting Entries

PageMaker helps you create cross-references to other index topics. Cross-references can apply within a given publication and across multiple publications. Cross-references do not include page numbers; they only identify related topics that the reader may want to look up for additional information.

To import a cross-reference topic, click the **X-ref** button in the Create Index Entry dialog box. This action brings up the Select Cross-Reference Topic dialog box. Choose a topic from the list displayed and then click the **Import** button. PageMaker adds the cross-reference topic to your index listing.

After you complete preparing the index, choose the Show Index command from the Options menu to review your entries (see fig. 6.29). You can edit any entry to make corrections, to add new cross-references, or to remove duplicate items. The Show Index command displays the index for your entire book list. To review just the entries for your currently open publication, press the Command key as you choose the Show Index command.

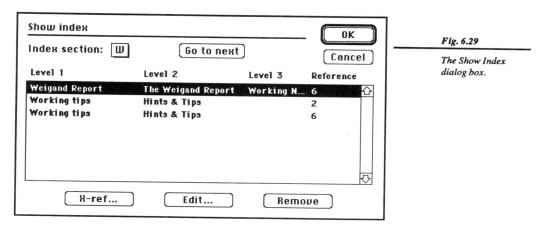

The final step in preparing your index is to format the index using the Index Format dialog box (see fig. 6.30). Click the **Format** button in the Create Index dialog box to get to the Index Format dialog box. Here you tell PageMaker whether entries should be nested (PageMaker formats all entries for a given topic as separate paragraphs) or run-in (all entries for a given topic lie within the same paragraph). You assign special font characters to index entries, mark the start and end of page ranges, introduce cross-reference entries, and so on. The active display at the bottom of the dialog box removes guesswork by showing you exactly how PageMaker handles each of the formatting attributes you assign.

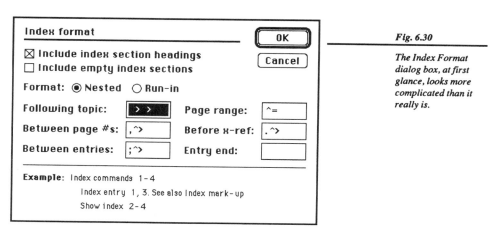

Even if you fully understand all of PageMaker's many indexing features, you may have to rework your indexes several times before getting the indexes just right. Slight variations in formatting can produce drastic layout changes. Also, doing even a little editing to one part of your publication can throw off your page numbering for index entries in other parts of your publication. You always should do a final re-index of your publications prior to printing.

Using the Table Editor

PageMaker comes with a separate Table Editor application for creating tables and other lists of tabular data quickly. The Table Editor is straightforward and easy to use. The Table Editor enables you to import data from databases and spreadsheets, build rows and columns of information, and then export completed tables as PICT graphics for placement into PageMaker. You can resize these PICT tables easily within your publications so that they fit your layouts exactly. You also can export tables from the Table Editor as tab-delimited text for later reformatting within PageMaker. You can export a whole table or a selected range of cells.

To prepare a table using the Table Editor, specify the overall table size and the number of rows and columns using the Table Setup dialog box (see fig. 6.31). Note that the gutter dimensions determine the vertical and horizontal spacing between cells. You can change any of these values later by choosing the Table Setup command from the File menu. When you click OK, an empty table grid appears on-screen (see fig. 6.32).

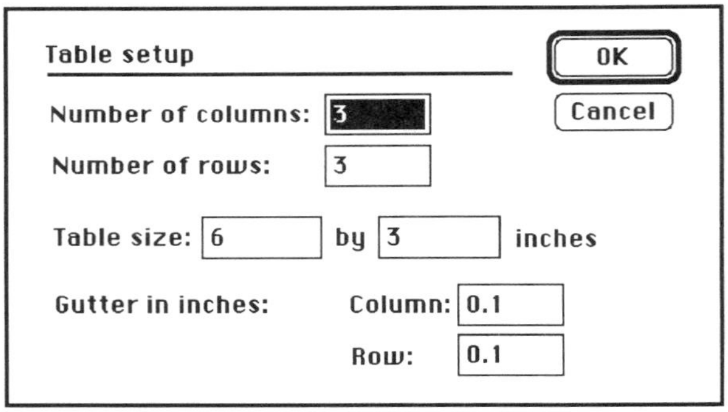

Fig. 6.31

The Table Setup dialog box.

Table setup	OK
Number of columns: 3	Cancel
Number of rows: 3	
Table size: 6 by 3 inches	
Gutter in inches: Column: 0.1	
Row: 0.1	

Tip

If you copy to the Clipboard a box drawn with PageMaker's square-corner rectangle tool and then open the Table Editor, the box dimensions appear in the Table Setup dialog box's **Table size** fields. The **Table size** fields enable you to create tables to fit your layouts exactly.

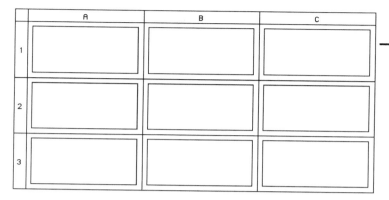

Fig. 6.32

After you configure the Table Setup dialog box, an empty table grid appears ready for you to enter data.

Choose Import from the File menu to import tab- or comma-delimited text from other programs. The Define Flow command from the Edit menu enables you to control the manner in which the data fills a selected range of cells. To enter data manually into a cell, click an insertion point and start typing. Your text wraps to fit within the cell. To move to another cell in the same column, press the Return key. To move to another cell in the same row, press the Tab key.

To resize a row or column, click-drag the appropriate row or column boundaries, or choose the Row Height or Column Width commands from the Cell menu. Adjoining rows and columns adjust to accommodate the changes you make. If you prefer that the entire table resize to preserve existing row and column dimensions, press the Option key as you click-drag a row or column boundary. Choose Insert or Delete from the Cell menu to insert or delete rows and columns.

You can use multiple font types, styles, and sizes within a given table, but you can assign only one font type, size, or style combination per individual cell. You also can apply various shadings to cells and assign different line widths and styles to cell boundaries. For creating flexible table layouts, you can format each side of a selected cell boundary independently of its remaining three sides. Choose the Borders command from the Cell menu to display the Borders dialog box (see fig. 6.33). Then click the appropriate boxes to make your formatting choices.

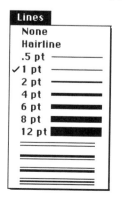

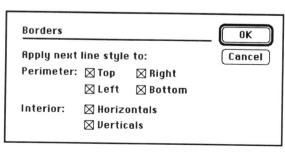

Fig. 6.33

You can assign any of several line widths and styles to cell boundaries in the Table Editor.

> *Tip*
>
> Applying shading to individual cells or alternating rows and columns helps readers quickly assimilate the information you present in your tables. However, if you print your publications on a 300 dpi laser printer, do not use a background shading darker than 10% gray. Darker shadings tend to obscure whatever text lies over the shading. The one exception is when you place reverse (white) text over an all black background. In this case, your type stands out well. Don't overdo alternate shading, however, or your tables may begin to look like checkerboards.

To make global changes, select whole rows and columns by clicking the individual row and column labels. Hold down the Shift key and click repeatedly to select multiple rows and columns. To highlight an entire table, click the upper left corner of the table grid. You can click-drag through cells to select the cells as a group. To combine a selected range of cells into one large cell, choose the Group command from the Cell menu. You can produce good-looking tables quickly, with very little effort (see fig. 6.34).

Fig. 6.34

Using the Table Editor makes creating professional-looking tables a snap.

#		TWR's Top Ten Utilities
1	QuicKeys & Tempo II CE Software & Affinity Microsystems	The ultimate productivity tools, and a tie for First Place in our listings. QuicKeys is superb at executing quick and dirty keyboard and menu customizations. It's particularly useful for anyone using an extended keyboard. Tempo II, on the other hand, is a powerful and sophisticated macro generator that's remarkably easy to use. Tempo II lets you readily simplify even the most complex routines, and is ideal for automating tedious or repetitive tasks.
2	SuitCase II Fifth Generation Systems	The one indispensable DA that belongs under every Apple menu. SuitCase II lets you quickly access and use a variety of fonts and DAs without first having to install them into your System file. Master Juggler from Alsoft works just as well, but not nearly so elegantly.
3	Adobe Type Manager Adobe Systems	Need we say more? The type you see is the type you get, both on screen and off. ATM works only with Adobe Type 1 fonts, a limitation that soon may be overcome with the release of third-party utilities designed to convert non-Adobe faces into Type 1 format.
4	DiskTop CE Software	All the functionality of the Finder rolled into one easy-to-use desk accessory. No matter what you're doing, DiskTop lets you control your system . . . instead of it controlling you!
5	Boomerang 2.0 Hiro Yamamoto — Shareware	Boomerang installs a convenient pop-up menu in Open and Save dialog boxes that gives you direct access to your most frequently used files and folders. You can create new folders on the fly while the dialog window is open, also switch instantly between daisy-chained hard disks. Boomerang AUTOMATICALLY remembers your most recent selections, also their individual scroll-bar positions within the dialog windows. A real timesaver.
6	Smart Alarms Jam Software	Pop-up reminders that can be scheduled minutes, hours, days, weeks, months… even years in advance. Reminders also can be made to repeat at regular intervals. Smart Alarms works silently in the background to keep you from missing important meetings, anniversaries and birthdays, favorite TV shows, etc. Comes with Appointment Diary, a capable calendar-planning DA that lets you create Smart Alarms reminders from daily calendar entries.
7	Smart Art & Type Align Adobe Systems	Two companion desk accessories designed especially to work with ATM. Smart Art lets you create special effects for text and graphics. Type Align lets you bind text to curves and fit the results to existing layouts. Both tools are indispensable to desktop publishers.
8	SmartScrap Solutions International	A versatile replacement for Apple's standard Scrapbook desk accessory. SmartScrap switches between multiple Scrapbook files, searches for images by name, and lets you select and copy any portion of any Scrapbook page. Comes with Clipper, a handy DA that lets you scale items on the Clipboard to exact size before pasting.
9	SuperClock II Steve Christensen — Freeware	SuperClock II is the only menu clock that's never caused us any problems. It displays in the upper right corner of our screen where it gives a continuous digital readout of the time. SuperClock II can be preset to alarm at any time, chime every hour on the hour, and function as an automatic timer.
10	Møire John Lim — ShareWare	An absolutely splendid screen saver that produces a stunning display of moving geometric shapes. If you prefer "cuteness," try Pyro 4.0 or After Dark. Both are excellent products, and both offer a varied selection of custom screen displays. However, if you want simple, uncluttered, reliable performance, Møire is your best choice.

Some features in the Table Editor work like similar features in PageMaker. A few are identical, like the horizontal and vertical rulers and the Snap To Rulers command. Others are slightly different, like the toolbox, which contains only a pointer tool and a text tool, and the View, Lines, and Shades menus. A few of the built-in shortcuts also are the same. If you are comfortable working in PageMaker, you feel right at home using the Table Editor.

Chapter Summary

In this chapter, you learned how to manage text to format your layouts and structure your documents. You saw how to vary the number of columns on a page and adjust the number of pages in a publication. You discovered that you can rearrange and align text blocks accurately with other page elements, and that you can resize and reshape text blocks to create more interesting layouts. You found that PageMaker's pasteboard serves conveniently as a supplemental work area.

You learned how to use indents and tabs and assign variable leading. You deciphered the mysteries of hyphenation and learned how to control hyphenation to improve column fit. You acquired new insights into word and letter spacing, and you saw how subtle changes in both can affect dramatically the appearance of your pages.

Finally, you gained an appreciation for the hidden power of style sheets, and you learned how to apply style sheets to manage complex publishing tasks. You explored PageMaker's book editing tools and found that using the Table Editor can streamline the table creation process.

In Chapter 7, you learn about PageMaker's graphics-handling and printing capabilities.

III

Graphics and Printing Techniques

Includes

Graphics Basics

Formatting and Enhancing Graphics

Printing Techniques

7

Graphics Basics

With PageMaker, you can import, resize, reshape, and crop many different kinds of graphics, ranging from simple bit-mapped pictures to highly refined Encapsulated PostScript (EPS) drawings. PageMaker also provides several basic drawing tools for enhancing your pages with visually appealing graphic design elements. Because PageMaker is a page-layout program, however, its focus is on page assembly, not the creation of original artwork. Most of the pictures and illustrations you use are created in separate drawing programs and later imported into PageMaker.

In this chapter, you get to know each of the different graphic formats PageMaker supports. You learn how to import, modify, and even export illustrations. You discover that PageMaker provides links between the graphics you import and the originals, and you learn how to update your publications when you modify the originals. You also learn how to use PageMaker's own drawing tools to produce simple design elements such as rules, boxes, and circles.

Graphics Supported by PageMaker

PageMaker supports four kinds of graphic formats when importing images from other programs: Paint for bit-mapped illustrations; PICT and PICT2 for object-oriented drawings; EPS for high-resolution EPS images; and TIFF (black-and-white, gray-scale, and color) for scanned line art and photographs. Each of these formats is described in the following sections.

Using Paint Images

Paint images are *bit-mapped* images composed of dots, or pixels (72 pixels per inch). The Paint format became popular shortly after Apple introduced the Macintosh. In those days, Apple bundled MacPaint, a primitive bit-mapped graphics program, with every Macintosh sold. The popularity of the Macintosh led to MacPaint's file format becoming a standard for the interchange of bit-mapped graphics. Today, nearly all Macintosh software that handles bit-mapped graphics supports this format.

The dots that make up Paint images are the same size as Macintosh screen pixels. Because pixels are square instead of round, Paint images tend to look ragged around the edges. This raggedness restricts the usefulness of Paint images to applications in which high-resolution printing isn't critical (see fig. 7.1). Dots always print as dots, and 72-dpi images always look slightly jagged, even with the **Smooth** option applied (a LaserWriter option in the Print dialog box). This jaggedness is present no matter how high the resolution of the output device.

Fig. 7.1

The more you enlarge a Paint image, the more apparent the raggedness becomes.

Paint graphics can be unusually rich in detail. The tools found in most Paint programs closely simulate traditional artist's tools, and the ability to edit an image down to the single-pixel level gives the electronic artist complete control over the final appearance of a bit-mapped image. Although you cannot edit Paint images in PageMaker, you can modify them by changing their brightness and contrast and by applying different screen patterns. You learn more about modifying images in Chapter 8, "Formatting and Enhancing Graphics."

Using PICT Images

Draw-type graphics are *object-oriented*, with each object outline, or shape, described by mathematical vector notation. Objects can float above and overlap one another as if stacked in layers. This approach to handling graphics enables you to rearrange and stack images to produce composite groupings. You also can change the line widths and fill patterns of objects easily. Because of their geometric nature, draw graphics are ideally suited for precision work, such as engineering or architectural drawings.

In a Paint program, each pixel represents a unique data point, and its individual page coordinates are stored separately in memory. When you draw a shape using a Paint tool, the shape consists of hundreds of independent pixels.

Describing a shape, or object, in a drawing program, however, requires much less data. A rectangle, for example, requires only enough information to identify the object type (a rectangle), the location of the object on the page (the coordinates of a single corner point), and the object's size and orientation (the angle and length of an invisible diagonal from the corner point to the opposite corner of the rectangle). The advantage of this method is that changing the dimensions of an object, in this case the rectangle, requires only that you change its mathematical representation. Because objects are described mathematically, they can be printed at any size or resolution without distortion.

Apple's MacDraw was the first object-oriented drawing program for the Macintosh. With this program, you can save drawings as MacDraw files (a proprietary format) or as PICT files (now a standard for transferring object-oriented files between applications). Since MacDraw was released, the original PICT format has been modified somewhat to accommodate new features and special effects, such as rotated text and graduated shading, preferred by some of the newer drawing programs. The expanded PICT format is PICT2. PageMaker can import files saved in the original PICT format and later PICT2 variations.

Using EPS Images

The EPS file format is a graphic file-interchange standard based on Adobe Systems' high-level PostScript page-description language. EPS drawing programs, such as Adobe Illustrator and Aldus Freehand, give you exceptional control over the creative drawing process and enable you to assign to your artwork an enormous range of special graphics effects, including curved and filled text, graduated shadings, and various shape transformations. EPS files have a distinct advantage over their draw counterparts in that their line widths can be scaled for finer output on high-resolution printers and Imagesetters (see fig. 7.2).

The Adobe PostScript interpreter built into most Macintosh-compatible laser printers converts EPS files directly into printed copy. The output print resolution is limited only by the printer itself. For this reason, EPS graphics often are referred to as device-independent. Most laser printers reproduce images at 300 dpi. Some can handle 400 dpi or 600 dpi, and a few can print at 1,000 dpi on plain paper. A high-resolution Imagesetter like the Linotronic L300, for example, outputs images at 2,540 dpi (resolutions above a range of 1,100 to 1,200 dpi are considered magazine-quality printing). No matter which device you use to print an EPS image, the image prints at the maximum resolution of that device.

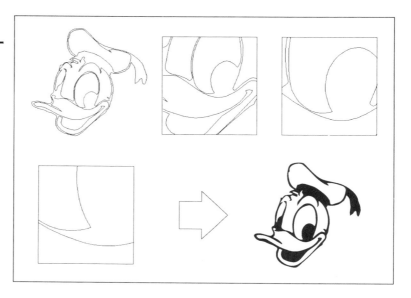

PostScript images are stored as text files. If you know how to program in the PostScript language, you can create or edit PostScript files by using an ordinary word processor and import the files into PageMaker for printing. You also can code PostScript text files in PageMaker, add the appropriate header information, export them as text files, and then import them back into PageMaker for placing on your pages.

EPS files differ from ordinary PostScript files because EPS files enable a PICT image to be attached to the pure PostScript code. In PageMaker, such EPS files provide screen representations that you can use to adjust image size, shape, and position on the page.

Although many graphics and special effects drawing programs fully support the EPS format, a few still fail to take advantage of the screen-display capabilities of EPS files. When you import files produced by such programs into PageMaker, you see only a gray box. This box is used to control image placement. You can resize, reshape, and move the box like any ordinary graphic, but you must print a test sheet to gauge accurately the effects of your work.

Using Scanned Images

Scanners digitize artwork and photographs for use in your publications. You can edit and manipulate scanned images by using a variety of drawing and image-enhancement programs and later import your images directly into PageMaker.

Scanning black-and-white line art produces high-density bit-mapped pictures ranging in resolution from 75 dpi to 300 dpi. Such bit-mapped images are excellent for use as general-purpose illustrations and can be edited using almost any Paint program.

Scanning photographs is much more complex. To understand how to reproduce a typical glossy photograph as an electronically scanned, digitized image, you first should know something about how photographs normally are handled by commercial printers.

Black-and-white photographs are continuous-tone images consisting of varying shades of gray. To reproduce the gray tones on traditional printing presses requires that images first be broken into a series of discontinuous, or discrete, halftone dots. This image then is transferred chemically to metal printing plates. Printing presses apply ink to printing plates wherever the dots appear. If the images were made up of continuous tones instead of discrete dots, the application of ink also would be continuous, and shades of gray would appear as solid black when printed (much the same thing can be seen when trying to photocopy a glossy photograph on an office copier machine—all subtle gray shading is lost).

To divide photographs into dots, commercial printers first recopy the image using a camera and a halftone screen. A halftone screen is actually a piece of film made up of a fine array of opaque dots. When a halftone screen is laid over the film in the camera, the tiny dots break up the exposed image coming in through the camera lens. The result on the film is a pattern of dots that vary in size, depending on the intensity of the light reflected from the photograph. The finer the screen used, the more dots produced per inch, and the higher the quality of the final print.

When an offset printing plate is prepared from the exposed negative, instead of a continuous image being formed, a pattern of evenly spaced halftone dots of varying sizes is produced. The ink from the press is applied to each individual dot, and the composite collection of dots creates an image that then transfers back onto the paper. Because the dots are different sizes, they effectively simulate the original grays in the photograph. Smaller dots that appear more widely spaced yield a lighter shade of gray; larger dots that look closer together produce a darker shade of gray. Take a magnifying glass and examine any photograph in any newspaper or magazine— the photograph is composed of nothing but thousands of tiny halftone dots.

Scanning photographs and outputting them directly to a laser printer effectively bypasses this whole traditional printing cycle. Although electronic reproduction of photos is adequate for many desktop publishing endeavors, scanned images generally yield softer, fuzzier output than images a commercial printer strips in by hand—even when you use a Linotronic imagesetter to generate output directly to film. The time it takes to print finely digitized images on a Linotronic also can be excessive, resulting in increased production costs.

Most scanners produce digital halftones or gray-scale images. Digital halftones are normal bit-mapped images with the dots arranged in pseudo-random patterns to simulate the distribution of gray tones. These halftone simulations are produced during the scan itself, and their quality depends greatly on the scanning software used. Because the resultant images are bit maps, with each dot having the same fixed size, scaling or reshaping digital halftones usually causes distortion.

Gray-scale scanners, on the other hand, assign varying levels of gray to each area of the interpreted image but leave the halftone simulation to the output device. Because the printer handles the final halftone conversion, output quality is improved greatly. Most importantly, this approach enables you to resize and reshape gray-scale images without distortion.

To reproduce gray-scale images, your laser printer builds halftone cells, or matrices, to hold the gray-scale information. A 4 by 4 cell, for example, can display 16 different gray values, plus white. With all the dots in the cell filled in, the cell is black. With none of the dots filled in, the cell is white. That leaves 15 in-between gray values that can be simulated by turning on different numbers of dots. In the same fashion, a 16 by 16 cell can display up to 256 gray shades. Note, however, that the larger the cell's dimensions, the fewer cells you can crowd into a given area. Different combinations of settings, therefore, entail significant printing trade-offs. The issue is one of numbers of gray values versus lines-per-inch (cells per inch) resolution (see fig. 7.3). You learn more about these trade-offs in Chapter 9, "Printing Techniques."

Because the standard Paint format is fixed at 72 dpi and cannot handle gray-scale or color information, another file format is needed for photographs. This format is known as TIFF, or Tag Image File Format, and is used to store scanned data and transfer the data between applications. PageMaker recognizes black-and-white, gray-scale, and color TIFF files.

Importing Graphics

You can import graphics directly into PageMaker by using the File menu's Place command or indirectly through the Clipboard by using the Edit menu's Paste command. The Place command gives you more control over image placement, but using the Clipboard is sometimes more convenient, especially when working in MultiFinder (to learn more about using MultiFinder, consult the manual that came with your Macintosh).

Using the Place Command

To place a graphic in a document using the Place command on the File menu, choose the name of the image file from the scrollable list in the Place Document dialog box. Select the **As independent graphic**, **Replacing entire graphic**, or **As inline graphic** option, and then click OK.

If you choose the **As independent graphic** option, PageMaker displays a graphic-placement cursor in the shape of the type of graphic being imported: Paint, PICT, TIFF, EPS, or Scrapbook PICT (see fig. 7.4). Click the upper left corner of the graphic-placement cursor on the page exactly where you want the upper left corner

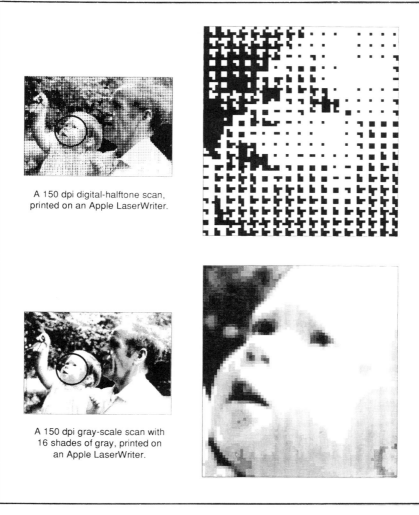

A 150 dpi digital-halftone scan, printed on an Apple LaserWriter.

A 150 dpi gray-scale scan with 16 shades of gray, printed on an Apple LaserWriter.

Fig. 7.3

Viewing an enlarged detail shows the differences between digital-halftone and gray-scale scans.

of the graphic to appear. PageMaker imports and displays the graphic at its original size. If you want the graphic to fit within a specific area, drag the graphic-placement cursor to define the area boundaries. When you release the mouse button, Page-Maker draws the graphic resized to fit within that boundary.

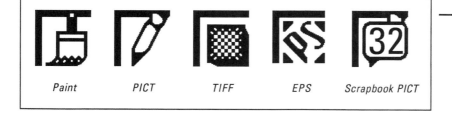

Paint   PICT   TIFF   EPS   Scrapbook PICT

Fig. 7.4

PageMaker's graphic-placement icons.

When you select the Scrapbook using the Place Document dialog box, the graphic-placement cursor initially shows the total number of Scrapbook images available for placement. You can import all the images at one time by repeatedly clicking the mouse. Each time you click to place an image, PageMaker subtracts one number from the remaining total. You have to click repeatedly, placing images consecutively, until you get to the one you want. To cancel placing additional Scrapbook images, click on the pointer tool in the toolbox. To delete from your pages any items you don't want, select them with the pointer tool and press the Delete key or choose Clear on the Edit menu.

Tip

If you frequently use an assortment of graphics when preparing your publications, store the graphics in separate, custom Scrapbooks. Load a selection of graphics into your main Scrapbook and rename it to identify the kind of images you store there (select the Scrapbook icon in the Finder and type a new name). If you store a bunch of design elements, for example, you may rename your Scrapbook *Great Design Stuff*. Create as many supplementary Scrapbooks as you like and tuck them away in a folder somewhere on your hard disk. Later, when you need a particular collection of images, open the appropriate Scrapbook, using PageMaker's Place command.

Tip

You can create text in another application and save the text as a PICT or EPS file. When you import one of these files into PageMaker, you can stretch and shape the image like any other graphic and still have the text print at the same high resolution as the original text. To fit your *graphic text* exactly within a predefined area on your page, drag the graphic-placement icon during placement. Use this technique to create giant headlines or prominent advertising copy.

If you choose the **Replacing entire graphic** option, PageMaker substitutes the imported graphic in place of the selected graphic, without regard to format. The newly imported graphic occupies the same bounding-box area as the old. If, after placement, you want to restore the new graphic to its original proportions, select the graphic with the pointer tool, hold down the Shift key, and click on any reshaping handle.

If the graphic you replace has text-wrap attributes assigned, the new graphic assumes the same attributes, even if those attributes include a customized standoff boundary (you learn about PageMaker's Text Wrap command in Chapter 8). Using the **Replacing entire graphic** option enables you to replace graphics you have imported and graphics you have created in PageMaker. You, therefore, can create a publication template using graphic placeholders (shaded boxes) to mark where illustrations should go and later substitute the final artwork or photographs as replacements (see fig. 7.5).

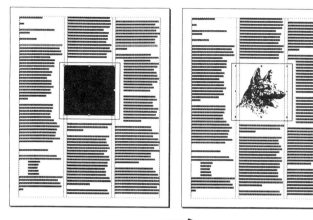

If you choose the **As inline graphic** option, PageMaker inserts the imported graphic into your text at the insertion point. Note that you must have an insertion point (blinking text cursor), or a range of text selected, to import a graphic and place it as an inline graphic.

Using the Clipboard

The Clipboard is a common communications bridge between applications. You can copy a graphic to the Clipboard when working in one program and later paste the graphic into another program. Each time you copy something to the Clipboard, the new image replaces what was there previously.

You can use the Clipboard to copy and paste Paint and PICT graphics into PageMaker without difficulty. The Clipboard is limited, however, in its capability to handle more complex graphic formats. If you try to copy and paste a TIFF or EPS image from outside PageMaker, the image comes through as a low-resolution bit map and prints that way. For this reason, TIFF and EPS files always should be imported by using the Place command.

Tip

If you import a PICT image by using the Place command, the image generally comes into PageMaker as an opaque object, obscuring anything in the background. The same image copied to the Clipboard and pasted into PageMaker may come in as a transparent object instead (background objects show through any surrounding empty space). With Paint images, just the opposite is true: the Place command brings Paint images in as transparent objects; the Paste command (via the Clipboard) brings them in as opaque objects. For the type of file being imported, experiment to find the method that best satisfies your particular design requirements.

Using Inline Graphics

You can add graphics to your stories so that they become an integral part of your text. These inline graphics *float* along with your text as you edit your layouts. PageMaker anchors the graphics within the paragraphs to which they belong. The graphics stay with the text as the text moves through your threaded text blocks. This feature can be especially important when you must make revisions to your publications. Dotted lines, keyboard icons, mathematical formulae, and other essential graphics remain adjacent to their surrounding text (see fig. 7.6).

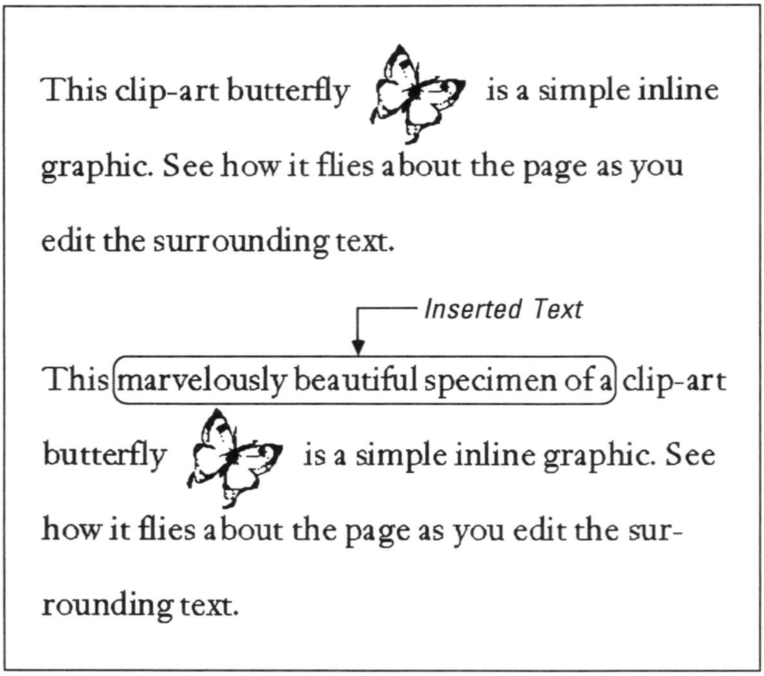

Fig. 7.6

The butterfly, an inline graphic, moves to the following line with its surrounding text as you insert new text into the paragraph.

This clip-art butterfly is a simple inline graphic. See how it flies about the page as you edit the surrounding text.

———— Inserted Text

This marvelously beautiful specimen of a clip-art butterfly is a simple inline graphic. See how it flies about the page as you edit the surrounding text.

To add an inline graphic to your publication, first click the text tool to create an insertion point. Next, paste or place the graphic. If you use the Place command, PageMaker selects the **As inline graphic** option for you. Click on the **As independent graphic** button only if you decide to place the graphic as a separate element (when you click OK, PageMaker displays the normal graphic-placement cursor).

Note

PageMaker recognizes inline graphics you import as part of compatible word-processor files.

Tip

Add an inline graphic as a separate paragraph within PageMaker to have the graphic stand apart from the surrounding text, yet still move with the text as you make editing changes to your story. To center precisely the inline graphic within your column, select the graphic with the text tool and choose the Align Center command on the Alignment submenu (accessed from the Type menu), or Center on the pop-up Alignment menu in the Paragraph Specifications dialog box.

After you have an inline graphic, you no longer can treat it as a normal graphic. You handle inline graphics, for the most part, as text characters. You can assign tracking, kerning, leading, and other paragraph-based attributes, but you cannot assign normal type-size and style attributes (bold, italic, and outline, for example). To assign text attributes to inline graphics, use the text cursor to select the graphic.

You can adjust the baseline of an inline graphic by using the pointer tool to drag the graphic up or down (you cannot assign sub- and super-scripting). This repositioning capability enables you to make positioning adjustments for special inline graphics, such as mathematical symbols. You cannot drag an inline graphic to the left or right. To do that, you have to kern the graphic, or insert blank spaces next to it.

Inline graphics are, in some ways, much like other graphics. You can resize and reshape them by dragging a reshaping handle. You also can crop them. In the case of Paint and TIFF graphics, you can vary their contrast and brightness by using the Image Control command on the Element menu. You can even assign colors. (You learn how to apply image-control and color settings in Chapter 8.)

To import inline graphics when working in the Story Editor, you use the Import command on the Story menu. PageMaker represents inline graphics in Story view by an inline graphics marker. You do not see the actual graphic until you return to the Layout view.

Linking Graphics

You can save the graphics you import into your publications as part of those publications. Text and graphics combine to form one integrated, page-layout file. If you have PageMaker store graphics internally, however, your publications may grow to gargantuan proportions. Many graphics, particularly color TIFF images, take up tremendous amounts of disk space. If a graphic is more than 256K in size, PageMaker suggests that you store it outside your publication (see fig. 7.7). You don't have to take the hint, but it is a good idea to do so. Your files become smaller and more manageable. PageMaker links the screen representations of your imported graphics with their corresponding externally stored source files.

Fig. 7.7

PageMaker warns you if you try to store within your publications graphics larger than 256K in size.

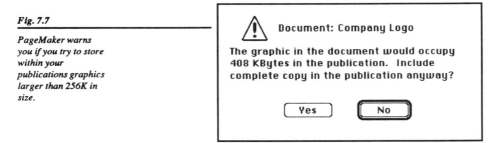

PageMaker can store all graphics externally, including even the smallest ones. To have PageMaker do this, deselect the **Store copy in publication** option in the Link Options dialog box. To access the Link Options dialog box, choose the Links command on the File menu and then click on the **Link Options** button in the Links dialog box.

If you select a graphic beforehand, you get an abbreviated Link Options dialog box that applies only to that image (see fig. 7.8). If you do not select a graphic beforehand, you get the full Link Options dialog box, which applies to text and graphics. You use this latter version of the Link Options dialog box to set publication and program defaults.

Viewing Linked Graphics

In the Preferences dialog box are three viewing options to choose among for displaying graphics (these options apply to an entire publication, not to individually selected graphics). The options are **Gray out, Normal,** and **High resolution** (see fig. 7.9).

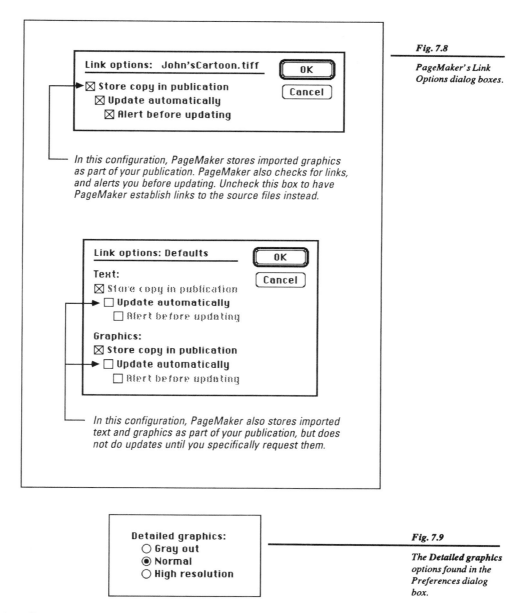

Fig. 7.8

*PageMaker's Link
Options dialog boxes.*

Fig. 7.9

*The **Detailed graphics**
options found in the
Preferences dialog
box.*

If you select **Gray out,** PageMaker displays simple bounding boxes or graphic
placeholders to mark where detailed images reside on your pages. This feature
greatly speeds up production work, for example, when you edit complex layouts;
you don't have to deal with constant, slow screen refreshes. You can change this
option at any time so that you can view your graphics.

If you choose **Normal,** PageMaker displays low-resolution bit-mapped images in place of the actual imported graphics. It does not matter whether the graphics are stored externally or within PageMaker. Unless you decide otherwise, you see only these low-resolution images while working on your pages.

If you select **High resolution,** you see the actual graphics displayed at the best resolution your screen can produce. You do not want to choose this option, however, except for those few occasions when you truly need to preview your pages as they will look when printed. Otherwise, numerous, slow screen redraws may impede production, particularly if any large gray-scale or color TIFF images are on your pages.

Tip

To view a low-resolution screen image at high resolution momentarily, hold down the Ctrl (Control) key as you force the graphic to redraw. You can force a redraw in several ways, including moving the graphic slightly, scrolling it off screen and back on again, and changing page views (you also can type the appropriate keyboard shortcut for the page view in which you are currently working). Press the Ctrl key at the same time you force a redraw, and PageMaker redraws your graphic at full resolution. This method has the same result as choosing the **High resolution** viewing option in the Preferences dialog box, except that the temporary high-resolution display lasts only until the next screen redraw.

To view half the image at low resolution and half at high resolution, scroll one half of the image out of the window. Next, scroll that half of the image back into the window while holding down the Ctrl key.

Managing Linked Graphics

Links enable PageMaker to use the source files for printing, even though all you see on-screen are low-resolution reproductions of those files. When printing your publications, PageMaker checks for links, locates any linked files, and downloads to your printer the original graphics instead of the low-resolution screen images. Any changes you make to the screen images (resizing, reshaping, cropping, and so on), however, appear also in your printouts.

PageMaker always searches for linked files when you open a publication. If the source files are not in the same folder they were in the last time you opened that publication, PageMaker asks for help in locating them (see fig. 7.10). After you locate a file, click on the **Link** button to re-establish the link. After you save changes, PageMaker remembers the new storage locations for the linked files. If you do not need to re-establish links (for example, when doing preliminary layout work or editing a story), click on the **Ignore all** button. PageMaker opens the publication without updating the links.

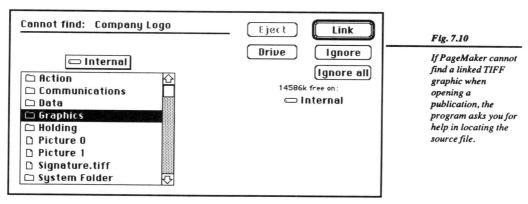

Fig. 7.10

If PageMaker cannot find a linked TIFF graphic when opening a publication, the program asks you for help in locating the source file.

PageMaker's links enable you to replace old publication graphics with new ones without the need to completely re-edit your layout. Use the Link Options dialog box to tell PageMaker to update your graphics whenever the source files change. After issuing that command, each time you open a publication, PageMaker checks the links. If you have made any changes to the source files, PageMaker updates your pages. If you asked PageMaker to alert you first, the program displays a Document Modified dialog box that tells you that the source file has been modified (see fig. 7.11). Click on the **Update** button to complete the update process. You immediately see the new or revised screen images when your publication opens.

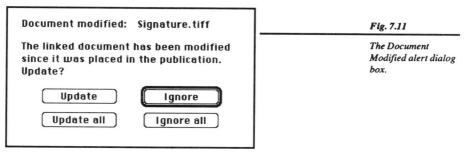

Fig. 7.11

The Document Modified alert dialog box.

PageMaker builds links by file names and folder locations. Change these names or locations, and you break the links. For this reason, you should make it a habit always to save at least one copy of each source file you work on under its original filename and to the same disk location. Otherwise, one of the following two things happens:

- PageMaker continues to use your outdated source files, if they still have the same names and still exist in the original folders.

- You end up constantly having to re-establish links as PageMaker searches for renamed and relocated source files.

The problem most often arises when you make editing changes you are not sure about. You use the Save As command in your drawing program to save your file modifications under another name and to a different folder, thus preserving your originals in case you want to re-use them later. You may delete the original file, however, after deciding the changes you made were satisfactory.

In the first case, PageMaker does not know that you have made any modifications because you did not save over the original version. If you print your publication, PageMaker downloads the unaltered file. Later, if you delete the original file, PageMaker loses the link. You must manually re-establish the link to the new source file.

Tip

Automatic updating of graphics through linking means that you can quickly revise recurring publications such as catalogs, shopper's guides, and year-books without having to do extensive editing for each new issue. If you set up an orderly system for naming your files, managing the substitution is easy, even for large publications. The trick is to give the new graphics files the same names as the old ones. Store all the original files in one folder. When you prepare the new graphics, drag them into the same folder. Click OK when asked whether you want to replace items having the same name. The next time you open your publication, PageMaker replaces your old graphics with the new ones.

Tip

When you send your publications to a service bureau for printing, be sure to include the source files for your linked graphics. If you transfer a document and its source files on a set of floppy disks, open your document at least once to re-establish the file links. Be sure to save changes. PageMaker locates and prints your graphics correctly without the service bureau operator having to guess which file goes with what graphic.

Tracking Link Status

PageMaker tracks the status of all links in a publication and displays that status in the Links dialog box (choose the Links command from the File menu). You first encountered PageMaker's Links dialog box in Chapter 5 in connection with linked text files. The same dialog box and symbols are used for tracking the link status of your graphics files (see fig. 7.12).

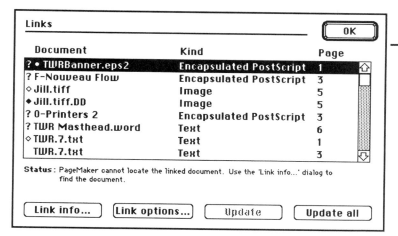

Fig. 7.12

The Links dialog box.

To get more current information about the link status of a selected graphic, click on the **Link info** button. Clicking this button brings up the Link Info dialog box. Here you can verify the file name and disk location of the original source file, what kind of image the graphic is (Paint, PICT, TIFF, EPS), the size of the graphic file, when you placed the graphic into your publication, when you last modified the source file, and when you last modified the internal version (see fig. 7.13). You can use this information to make intelligent decisions about linking source files to graphics or updating existing links.

To update any selected graphic, choose a replacement file in the Link Info dialog box and then click the **Link** button. PageMaker updates your old image, replacing it with the new one. Note that you can replace existing graphics this way and completely avoid using the Place Document dialog box. This capability represents yet another way to quickly and easily update publication templates in which you mark the positions of final detailed graphics by using simple placeholder graphics.

Note

If a graphic link is broken because you rename or relocate its source file, PageMaker cannot display a high-resolution screen image unless you first re-establish the link.

Fig. 7.13

PageMaker's Link Info dialog box provides current link status information for any selected file.

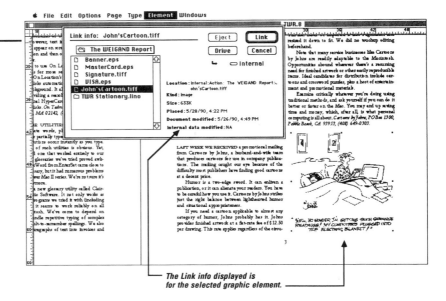

The Link info displayed is for the selected graphic element.

Note

Graphics from other programs pasted into your publications via the Clipboard cannot be tracked by PageMaker and, therefore, cannot have links to external files. Graphics you copy and paste from one PageMaker document to another, however, bring with them any previously assigned links. You also can store linked graphics in the Scrapbook, and the graphics retain their link information.

Using PageMaker's Drawing Tools

PageMaker's toolbox contains a minimum assortment of drawing tools that you can use to create rules, boxes, circles, and rounded-corner rectangles. Although the tools are few, you can use them in combination in many different ways to enhance your publications. See Chapter 2, "PageMaker Basics," for more details about what each tool does.

To use any drawing tool, click the tool in the toolbox and move the cursor over the page. The tool changes into a crosshair. Drag the crosshair to create a graphic element. The center of the crosshair is the point from which all lines and shapes are drawn.

For precise work, set PageMaker's rulers to the required dimensions and drag ruler guides onto your pages to mark drawing boundaries. Turn on the Snap To Guides and Snap To Rulers commands on the Options menu so that object edges and corners align easily. Choose an enlarged page view for detailed work but choose a reduced page view for drawing large objects. If you work in a reduced page view, continue to use the guides and snap-to commands to improve drawing accuracy.

Tip

PageMaker includes a set of keyboard shortcuts for users of extended keyboards that enable you to select any tool quickly. These shortcuts are handy if you work with a large-screen monitor, and the toolbox is some distance away from where you are drawing. The shortcuts also are handy if the toolbox is hidden (you don't have to choose Toolbox from the Windows menu before selecting another tool). The keyboard shortcuts are Shift-F1 through Shift-F8. To remember which function key goes with which tool, count each row of tools from left to right. Table 7.1 lists the keyboard shortcuts.

Table 7.1
Keyboard Shortcuts

Key Combination	Toolbox Selection
Shift-F1	Pointer tool
Shift-F2	Diagonal-line tool
Shift-F3	Perpendicular-line tool
Shift-F4	Text tool
Shift-F5	Square-corner rectangle tool
Shift-F6	Rounded-corner rectangle tool
Shift-F7	Circle tool
Shift-F8	Cropping tool

Drawing Lines

PageMaker's toolbox contains two types of line tools: a diagonal-line tool and a perpendicular-line tool. You can draw straight lines in any direction with the diagonal-line tool; you can draw straight lines horizontally, vertically, and at other multiples of 45 degrees with the perpendicular-line tool. You can constrain the diagonal-line tool to move the same as the perpendicular-line tool by holding down the Shift key while drawing.

Any time you draw a horizontal or vertical line using one of these tools, you can adjust the line to lie on either side of the crosshair by dragging slightly across the drawing axis with the cursor. The line flips from one side of the axis to the other. This capability is especially useful when drawing thick lines that you want to line up on a particular side of a nonprinting guide.

To adjust the length or angle of a line, drag one of the reshaping handles. The other end of the line remains anchored. To move the entire line without changing its length or orientation, click anywhere between the handles and drag.

Warning

A line drawn with the perpendicular-line tool *forgets* which tool you used to create the line. If you later drag a reshaping handle to change its length, the line may shift slightly off center and no longer be perfectly aligned along its original axis. To prevent the line from shifting, hold down the Shift key as you drag.

You can assign different line widths and styles to selected lines and to the outlines of selected objects. The Line menu (choose Line from the Element menu) contains eight line thicknesses, ranging from hairline (0.25 point) to 12-point. The Line menu also contains four double-line and triple-line patterns (for creating frames and borders) and five dashed-line patterns (see fig. 7.14). You can make only one menu selection at a time.

Fig. 7.14

PageMaker's Line menu.

Tip

To draw a line with a thickness different from those few line choices PageMaker offers in its Line menu, use the square-corner rectangle tool. You can use the rectangle tool to draw *lines* of any thickness. By also using the rulers, ruler guides, and Snap To Rulers command with the rectangle tool, you can create the exact line widths you need.

The Line menu also has a None command that is useful for creating objects with fill patterns but no borders, and a Reverse Line command that assigns the color Paper to lines. (Paper normally is set to white, but can be assigned a different color by using the Define Colors command on the Element menu.) The Reverse Line command is a powerful design tool that can be used in combination with any of the other Line-menu choices to produce special graphic effects. You also can use the Reverse Line command as *electronic whiteout* to touch up imported graphics.

Drawing Boxes and Circles

PageMaker's toolbox contains three types of tools for drawing boxes and circles. The square-corner and rounded-corner rectangle tools enable you to draw rectangles of varying dimensions. To produce perfect squares, hold down the Shift key while drawing with these tools. Choose Rounded Corners on the Element menu to assign any of six different corner shapes to selected boxes. Click on the appropriate icon to assign the corresponding shape.

You draw ovals with the circle tool. Hold down the Shift key while drawing to produce perfect circles.

To reshape existing rectangles and circles, drag a side or corner reshaping handle. Dragging a side handle changes object dimensions in one of two directions—horizontally or vertically. Dragging a corner handle enables you to change object dimensions in both directions at the same time.

Press the Shift key at the same time that you click-drag a handle to make the objects reshape proportionally.

Applying Shades and Patterns

PageMaker's Fill menu enables you to apply an assortment of commonly used shades and fill patterns to objects but not to lines. Figure 7.15 shows the shades and fill patterns available. You can choose from nine shades, ranging from None (0% or transparent) to Solid (100% or black). The Paper shade is the color of your paper, usually white. You also can choose from eight fill patterns made up of vertical, horizontal, diagonal, and crosshatched lines. The patterns print without distortion when you resize the objects.

Fig. 7.15

PageMaker's Shades menu.

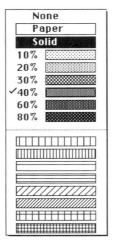

To apply a shade or pattern to an object, first select the object by clicking it with the pointer tool, then choose your desired fill from the Shades menu. To select an object filled with the None shade, click on its boundary. The object has no assigned fill, so clicking within the boundary is the same as clicking on the empty page—you select nothing.

The printed quality of shades and patterns depends entirely on the resolution of your output device. You get much finer output from a Linotronic imagesetter, for example, than from a 300-dpi laser printer.

Figure 7.16 shows an image created with PageMaker in just minutes using the line, rectangle, and oval tools. Two ovals were drawn, one on top of the other, and filled with 20% and 40% fill shades. The bottom half was covered with a rectangle filled with a shade of Paper and assigned a line width of None. The 6-point radial lines were created using the diagonal line tool. All lines were reversed after being drawn in place. A small oval filled with a shade of Paper and assigned a line width of None was used to cover the area where the lines intersect. *Fly East* was typed in MacDraw, saved as a PICT file, and imported into PageMaker as a graphic, where it was resized to fit. The phrase *And Meet The Orient* was typed in PageMaker. This example shows the imaginative and powerful uses to which PageMaker's deceptively simple tools can be put.

Modifying Graphics

With PageMaker, you can modify graphics by resizing, reshaping, and cropping them. You also can move them to different locations in your documents. As you resize

Fig. 7.16

An example of what can be done in PageMaker using the line, rectangle, and oval drawing tools.

images, you can scale them proportionally or nonproportionally. If you distort them by too much stretching or compressing, you can return them to their original proportions with a click of the mouse. You can eliminate any excess image area by cropping.

You can adjust the contrast and brightness of Paint and TIFF files for improved printing, and you can apply different halftone screens to them to create special visual effects. You also can adjust the individual gray levels of gray-scale TIFF files. (You learn to make these adjustments in Chapter 8.)

Resizing and Reshaping Images

As you enlarge or stretch Paint images in PageMaker, the number of dots in the image remains the same, but each dot expands in size. Stretching a Paint image increases overall image coarseness. On the other hand, shrinking a Paint image doesn't shrink the dots. Instead, shrinking produces less-detailed images that become muddy-looking as individual pixels squeeze together and begin to drop out. To resize or reshape a Paint image, drag any bounding-box handle. To keep the original proportions of the image, hold down the Shift key as you drag.

Tip

When you drag a corner or side reshaping handle of a selected graphic, you normally see only changes in the dimensions of the image's bounding box. The graphic itself remains unaffected until you release the mouse button; the image then redraws to its new size and shape. If you pause while dragging, however, PageMaker redraws the graphic at the interim size so that you can gauge the effect of your work. If you like what you see, release the mouse button to preserve the display. If not, continue dragging.

Some image distortion may result if you resize a complex Paint graphic to an inexact multiple of its original dimensions. This distortion occurs because fractional pixels cannot substitute for whole pixels to preserve image integrity. This image distortion produces undesirable patterns in your shading when you resize bit-mapped images inaccurately. With PageMaker, you can compensate for this distortion by resizing bit-mapped graphics in discrete steps to match the output resolution of your printer (see fig. 7.17).

Fig. 7.17

Incrementally resizing a TIFF graphic in PageMaker to prevent the introduction of Moire patterns.

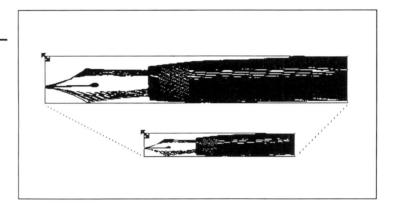

To use PageMaker's resizing feature, hold down the Command key when you resize or reshape a Paint image. The on-screen object bounding box resizes incrementally according to the optimum sizes PageMaker calculates. The graphic dimensions change visually in discrete steps as you drag any reshaping handle. If you later change printers, select the new Printer type description (APD file) from the pop-up menu in the Print dialog box. Again use the Command key to resize the image. The increments change to match that printer's output resolution. PageMaker can calculate more incremental sizes for higher resolution printers. Hold down the Shift key at the same time you drag to resize your images proportionally.

Note

For Command-key resizing to work, the graphic must be imported by using the Place command. If you import a graphic via the Clipboard by using the Paste command, the Command key has no effect when resizing, and you cannot precisely adjust the graphic to match the output resolution of your printer.

Often you can improve the appearance of bit-mapped Paint images by printing them with PageMaker's **Smooth** option turned on in the Print dialog box. The **Smooth** option applies rounding calculations to help reduce raggedness. Sometimes smoothing can detract from the flavor of your images, however, especially when you are trying to capture a pixelated look for special visual effect.

All the comments made here about Paint graphics apply equally to black-and-white TIFF graphics. A black-and-white TIFF graphic is a Paint graphic with finer resolution. TIFF and Paint graphics are composed of fixed dots. You encounter less-pronounced distortion when modifying TIFF files only because the larger number of smaller dots means that the adverse effects of scaling are less apparent. PICT and EPS graphics, on the other hand, you always can scale without distortion.

Any graphic you scale nonproportionally you can restore to its original aspect ratio. Click on any reshaping handle with the pointer tool while holding down the Shift key (see fig. 7.18). Hold down the mouse button momentarily while PageMaker does the required calculations. The graphic boundaries reshape themselves. Hold down the Command key with the Shift key as you drag at the same time to adjust the graphic's size for optimal printing.

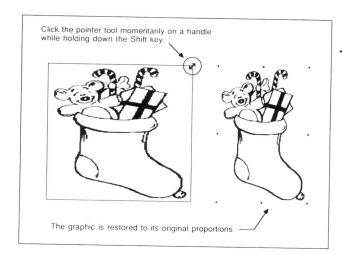

Click the pointer tool momentarily on a handle while holding down the Shift key.

The graphic is restored to its original proportions.

Fig. 7.18

Restoring a distorted graphic to its original proportions.

Cropping Images

You can trim any imported graphic (except those you create in PageMaker) by using PageMaker's cropping tool. Cropping is just like using an X-ACTO knife. You cut off the part of the graphic you want to remove. You can crop an image horizontally, vertically, or in both directions at the same time. Select the image with the cropping tool and drag a side or corner reshaping handle. The part of the image you crop disappears from view. Unlike trimming a picture with an X-ACTO knife, however, the missing part of the image is still there, hidden temporarily out of sight.

When you finish cropping your graphic, click on the image area with the cropping tool and hold down the mouse button. The cursor changes into a grabber hand that you can use to move the image within the newly sized window. The part of the image you cropped you can bring back into view. In this way, you can first crop an image to a specific size and then reposition the image for the best possible display. (To review the basics of using PageMaker's cropping tool, see Chapter 2.)

Tip

To eliminate any possible image distortion when using Paint or black-and-white TIFF graphics, crop them to fit instead of scaling them. Unlike scaling, cropping affects neither print resolution nor image quality.

Warning

If you crop and later scale a graphic up in size, PageMaker may not be able to pan the image within the cropped boundaries using the grabber hand. If you see a message warning you of this problem, scale the graphic down in size to make the necessary adjustments and then scale it back up in size.

Moving Images

To move a graphic from one page location to another, drag the graphic using the pointer tool. If you accidentally move something other than what you intended, immediately select Undo from the Edit menu.

If you start dragging immediately after clicking, a bounding box moves along with your cursor. This box serves as a visual aid to image placement. If you pause momentarily after clicking, however, and still continue to press the mouse button, the graphic changes into a transparent ghost image. The ghost image moves along with your cursor so that you can precisely position the graphic in its new location.

To move more than one graphic at a time, drag the pointer tool to form a selection rectangle around all the elements you want to move. Next, click any selected image and drag the elements as a group. You can add graphic images to the group by Shift-clicking on them. Use the Select All command on the Edit menu to select all the elements on a page. To deselect any element, click on it while holding down the Shift key.

These techniques can be used to select and move any combination of text and graphic elements. If you use a selection rectangle to select text along with graphics, be sure to drag out a large enough area to include any outlying text block handles (see fig. 7.19).

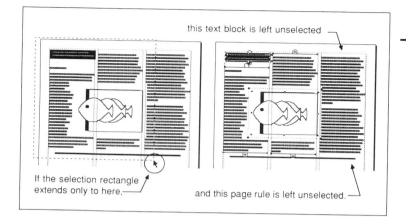

this text block is left unselected

If the selection rectangle extends only to here,

and this page rule is left unselected.

Fig. 7.19

Dragging a selection rectangle around a group of elements selects just the elements that lie completely within the dotted boundary.

To select an image buried beneath other elements, hold down the Command key as you click with the pointer tool on the spot where you think the image is located. Repeated clicking cycles you through the stack of layered elements, selecting each element in turn. When you reach the element you want, you can move or modify the image without changing its order in the stack, or you can use PageMaker's Bring To Front command on the Element menu to move the image to the top of the stack (use Send To Back to move the image to the bottom of the stack).

To move any graphic to another page in your publication, cut or copy the graphic to the Clipboard, turn to the new page, and paste the graphic onto the page. Drag the graphic to its new location. If you hold down the Option key while pasting, your graphic pastes to the same coordinates as on the old page. You also can drag the graphic onto the pasteboard, turn to the new page, and then drag the graphic back onto the new page.

To remove a graphic permanently from your publication, select the graphic and choose Clear from the Edit menu or press the Delete key.

Tip

To position graphic elements along any axis so that they are offset by equal distances, select and copy the element (or group of elements). Paste while holding down the Option key. Drag the pasted element to the first offset position and then paste again repeatedly, each time holding down the Option key. PageMaker pastes the elements onto the page so that they are offset from one another by identical amounts (see fig. 7.20).

Fig. 7.20

*Option-pasting
elements to obtain
precise offsets.*

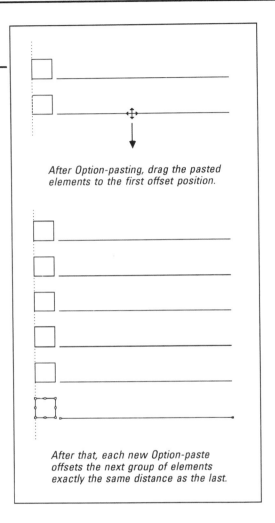

*After Option-pasting, drag the pasted
elements to the first offset position.*

*After that, each new Option-paste
offsets the next group of elements
exactly the same distance as the last.*

Tip

To group together various graphic elements, select and copy them as a unit to the Clipboard. Paste the contents of the Clipboard into your Scrapbook. Next, use the Place command to place the Scrapbook. PageMaker places the elements as one graphic that you can manipulate. If you need to get at an individual element within the group, copy the group from the Scrapbook and paste back into your publication. The group reappears as separate, discrete elements.

Exporting Graphics

To export graphics from PageMaker to another application, select and copy them to the Clipboard using the Edit menu's Cut or Copy command. The Cut command completely removes a graphic from your publication, but the Copy command leaves the original behind and places a copy on the Clipboard. Open the receiving application and paste the contents of the Clipboard into the new document. Original design elements created in PageMaker can be exported this way for use elsewhere.

Note

The standard Apple Clipboard and many programs not intended as page-makeup applications do not fully support all existing graphic formats. If you try to copy an EPS graphic from PageMaker and paste it into a simple word-processed document, for example, you get a low-resolution image. Copying the same EPS graphic between two PageMaker files, however, works fine, because PageMaker uses its own Clipboard.

Chapter Summary

In this chapter, you learned how to work with several different kinds of graphic formats. You learned how to import, export, and link your graphics and how to resize, reshape, and crop them to meet varying layout requirements. You found that although PageMaker isn't designed to create detailed, original artwork, you can use many kinds of artwork created elsewhere. You also saw how PageMaker's complement of easy-to-use drawing tools enables you to create simple design elements to dress up your publications. You are now ready to move on to Chapter 8, which introduces you to PageMaker's advanced graphics-handling capabilities.

8

Formatting and Enhancing Graphics

PageMaker's advanced graphics-handling capabilities are exceptional. In addition to importing and manipulating a variety of graphics formats, PageMaker enables you to modify the flow of text to wrap stories around accompanying illustrations. You also can customize wrap boundaries to conform to any shapes you like. With PageMaker, you can vary the contrast and brightness of Paint and TIFF images and apply custom halftone screens for special visual effect. If you import scanned gray-scale TIFF photos into your layouts, you can adjust their gray levels and vary image contrast and brightness. You even can apply spot color to text and graphics to enhance the look of your publications.

In this chapter, you explore PageMaker's advanced graphics-handling capabilities. You learn how to wrap text around irregularly shaped graphics, modify scanned images, and add color to your pages. You discover, as with so much else in PageMaker, that these tasks are easy and fun to do.

Flowing Text around Graphics

Illustrations and photographs are important visual elements that help explain the content of a publication and heighten interest in what you read. Text and graphics must work together if they are to communicate effectively. Combining both kinds of elements on your pages, however, is sometimes difficult. Some layouts are dominated by text, others by graphics. If your text and graphics don't complement one another, you may end up with large, unsightly patches of white space. PageMaker's capacity to flow text around graphics helps fill these holes and give your pages a more polished look.

Warning

Flowing text around graphics is a powerful design technique, but one that you can overuse easily. Like any other design technique, overuse reduces effectiveness.

Using Text Flow and Wrap Options

PageMaker provides several options for flowing text around and over selected graphics. To select the kind of wrap you want, click representative icons in PageMaker's Text Wrap dialog box (see fig. 8.1). You can choose from three wrap options and three text-flow options. You also can enter standoff-boundary values directly from the keyboard (standoff boundaries determine the amount of white space between a graphic and the text that flows around the graphic).

Fig. 8.1

The Text Wrap dialog box.

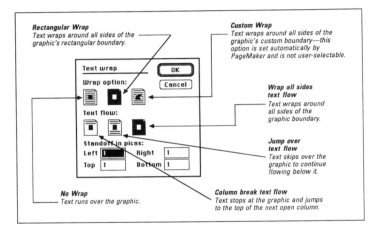

PageMaker's text-wrap options work with its text-flow options to determine the type of graphics wrap-around. To assign text-wrap attributes to a graphic, first select the graphic with the pointer tool and then choose Text Wrap from the Element menu. In the Text Wrap dialog box that appears, click the appropriate **Wrap option** and **Text flow** icons for the kind of text wrap you want. The following is a list of available choices:

❑ Clicking the No Wrap icon tells PageMaker to ignore the graphic. Choosing this option disables (grays out) all the text flow icons. As text flows down a column, the text runs over the graphic as if the graphic was not there.

❑ Clicking the Rectangular Wrap icon tells PageMaker to wrap text around the graphic. Choosing this option enables all three text flow icons.

If you click the Column Break Text Flow icon, PageMaker stops flowing text when the program encounters the graphic and jumps to the top of the next open column to continue flowing text. If you click the Jump Over Text Flow icon, PageMaker stops flowing text when it encounters the graphic, skips over the graphic, and resumes flowing text on the other side. If you click the Wrap All Sides Text Flow icon, PageMaker wraps text around all sides of the graphic.

❑ The Custom Wrap icon cannot be selected by clicking. The icon is selected by PageMaker when you customize the wrap boundary in your layout.

If the text already is in place, choosing different text-wrap options for your graphics rearranges the text to conform to the new settings. PageMaker retains any existing text formatting, including indents and tabs. If you change the text-wrap attributes of a graphic in the Text Wrap dialog box from No Wrap (the text runs over the graphic) to Wrap All Sides (the text runs around both sides of the graphic), when you click OK the text rearranges itself accordingly. Similarly, if you drag or paste a graphic with text-wrap attributes into an existing column of text, the text in the column reflows and wraps itself around the graphic (see fig. 8.2).

The selected graphic showing its custom text-wrap boundary.

Dragging the graphic into place on the page.

Fig. 8.2

Text flows around a graphic after text-wrap attributes are assigned.

Surrounding text automatically reflows itself around the graphic.

The final page after enlarging and repositioning the graphic.

PageMaker's original default setting is No Wrap, which causes the text to overrun any graphics the program encounters on the page. You may want to change this setting. You can assign your preferred text-wrap settings as publication or program defaults. Choose Text Wrap from within your open publication with no graphics selected, or choose from PageMaker's desktop before opening your publication.

Note

If you assign text-wrap attributes to graphics on your master pages, those graphics also interact with text on your regular pages. If the master-page graphics appear on your regular pages, any text you pour onto those pages wraps around those graphics. You can use this feature to mark off whole sections of pages, including columns, in which you do not want PageMaker to place text during autoflow. Just create a blank graphic on your master page, assign the graphic a Paper fill and a line width of None, and set the desired text-wrap boundary.

Tip

You can use PageMaker's No Wrap option to place a large, lightly shaded graphic behind your text to create a subliminal effect for sales fliers, announcements, and other kinds of ad copy. Use a Paint or TIFF graphic and adjust the shading (using PageMaker's image controls) until the graphic is light enough that the foreground text stands out clearly. (You learn how to use PageMaker's image controls later in this chapter.)

Specifying a Text-Wrap Standoff

PageMaker wraps text, using a *standoff boundary* to mark the separation between text and graphic. This standoff boundary initially surrounds the entire graphic. You adjust the standoff boundary to determine the amount of white space, or standoff, between the graphic and text. You can change the standoff at any time by click-dragging the standoff boundary. You also can type new values into the **Standoff** fields in the Text Wrap dialog box.

PageMaker creates this non-printing boundary around your selected graphic when you first click the Rectangular Wrap icon in the Text Wrap dialog box. This standoff boundary shows on-screen as a dotted line with diamond-shaped reshaping handles. PageMaker assigns default standoff values of 0.167 inches, or 1 pica, to each side of the graphic. You can change these values individually and even assign negative values to force text to fill space normally occupied by the graphic. To assign a negative value, type a minus sign before the number.

Tip

Set text-wrap as a program default and PageMaker assigns a text-wrap boundary to all new graphics.

Text forces itself into the space between the left column guide and the standoff boundary.

Dragging the left side of the boundary enlarges it without altering the image.

Text is blocked from flowing between the graphic and the edge of the page. The dark floor-line is extended to create the illusion of entering a tunnel.

Fig. 8.3

Dragging one side of a standoff boundary to block the flow of text on that side.

To change a standoff-boundary dimension using the pointer tool, click anywhere along the boundary and hold down the mouse button. The pointer tool changes into a double-headed arrow. Drag to adjust that leg of the boundary (see fig. 8.3). PageMaker updates the **Standoff** fields in the Text Wrap dialog box to show the revised standoff boundary dimensions.

If you drag a square graphic-boundary handle (not a diamond-shaped standoff-boundary handle) to resize or reshape the graphic, the standoff boundary shifts so that the standoff dimensions surrounding the graphic remain constant.

Tip

To keep text from wrapping around only one side of a graphic, increase the standoff on that side so that the standoff boundary touches a column guide.

Tip

If you place a caption next to a graphic to which you apply text-wrap attributes, the text wraps like any other text and pushes the caption away from its assigned location. To avoid moving the caption, increase the standoff value on the caption side of the graphic. Move the standoff boundary far enough away from the graphic so that the caption lies entirely within the boundary. Make sure that the text-block handles don't extend beyond the boundary perimeter. As long as your text block lies completely within the standoff boundary, the caption does not wrap.

Each **Text flow** option selected from the Text Wrap dialog box interacts differently with the standoff boundary. Because the Column Break Text Flow option forms a column break and continues text flow at the top of the next open column, only the upper perimeter of the standoff boundary affects text wrap. The Jump Over Text Flow option jumps text over the graphic, so that both the upper and lower perimeters affect text wrap. The Wrap All Sides Text Flow option flows text around the graphic completely, so that all legs of the perimeter affect the way text looks when the text wraps around the graphic.

Creating a Custom Boundary

You easily can modify a graphic's standoff boundary to make text flow smoothly around an irregular shape. Drag any corner handle of the standoff boundary to adjust the perimeter or click with the pointer tool anywhere along the boundary to create a new reshaping handle. You can create as many reshaping handles as you need to make the perimeter conform to the outline of the graphic, no matter how complex the shape. In effect, you convert the original standoff rectangle into a multisided standoff polygon (see fig. 8.4). The first time you move a corner reshaping handle or create a reshaping handle, PageMaker selects and highlights the Custom Wrap icon in the Text Wrap dialog box.

Tip

Use ruler guides to affect precise placement of reshaping handles when adjusting a custom standoff boundary. If the Snap To Guides command is checked on the Options menu, dragging the reshaping handles to their new locations causes them to snap to the guides in perfect alignment. Hold down the Shift key at the same time you drag to constrain handle movement to the horizontal and vertical directions.

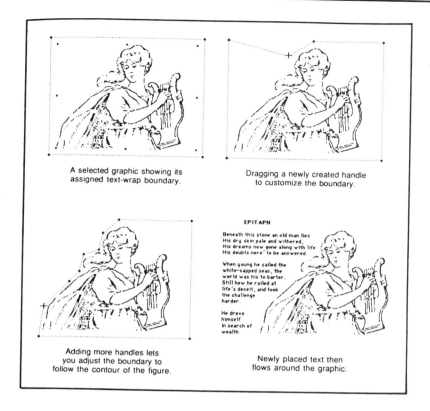

A selected graphic showing its
assigned text-wrap boundary.

Dragging a newly created handle
to customize the boundary.

Adding more handles lets
you adjust the boundary to
follow the contour of the figure.

Newly placed text then
flows around the graphic.

Fig. 8.4

*Creating a custom
text-wrap boundary.*

Custom wrap standoff boundaries require a minimum of three handles. You can add as many new handles as you like but try to limit the number. Each new handle requires additional calculations that slow screen redraws. To make several quick adjustments to a custom standoff boundary without redrawing the text each time you move a reshaping handle, hold down the space bar as you make modifications. Release the space bar when you are done. The text reflows to wrap around the new boundary. You can remove excess handles by dragging them onto adjoining handles.

After you define a graphic's text-wrap boundary, that boundary stays with your graphic no matter where you move the boundary in your layout. The boundary also stays with the graphic even if you copy the graphic to another publication. To remove a custom standoff boundary, click the Rectangular Wrap icon in the Text Wrap dialog box. PageMaker resets the text-wrap attributes to Rectangular Wrap and the standoff values to their default settings.

Tip

When creating custom standoff boundaries around irregularly shaped graphics, drag the graphics off the page onto the pasteboard. You don't have to worry about holding down the space bar to stop repeated screen redraws when the image is on the pasteboard, and you can work on several graphics at the same time. When you are done creating customized boundaries, drag the graphics back onto your pages. Your text rewraps around the graphics according to the adjustments made. Drag multiple selected graphics as a group to preserve their overall positioning.

Tip

Wrapping one column of text around both sides of an irregularly shaped graphic generally makes the text difficult to read. The reader's eye has to jump back and forth across the graphic to complete each line. A better way to use full text wrap and still keep your stories readable is to center the graphic across two columns. With the graphic set squarely between, the text in the column on the left wraps around the left side of the image, and the text in the column on the right wraps around the right side of the image. The reader's eye now travels down each column in turn, without interruption.

Tip

To wrap text inside a custom text-wrap boundary, do the following:

1. Use any of PageMaker's drawing tools to create a shape. Assign the fill shade Paper (to make the shape invisible, but still easy to select) and a line width of None. Create a standoff boundary for the shape by clicking the Wrap All Sides Text Flow icon.

2. Select one reshaping handle and click-drag the handle completely across an opposite boundary leg. This reshaping handle now lies outside the original boundary perimeter.

3. Click-drag the remaining reshaping handles and boundary legs across one another—in effect, turning the entire perimeter inside out.

4. Adjust the shape of this "inside out" boundary to hold your text. Add new reshaping handles as needed. Be as creative as you want.

5. Drag the text block into position over the reshaped perimeter. Your text now wraps inside the text-wrap boundary instead of outside (see fig. 8.5).

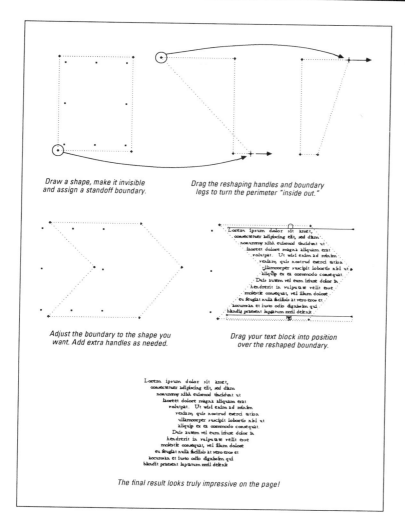

Fig. 8.5

Wrapping text within a custom text-wrap boundary.

Wrapping Text Manually

To wrap text manually around graphics, break your text up into multiple text blocks and resize each block to fit the space surrounding the graphic. To keep line leading consistent, use a ruler guide as an aid to overlapping windowshade handles. Wrapping text manually is a tedious process and generally is not worth the effort.

You have little reason to wrap text manually. Manually wrapping text is a hold-over from earlier versions of PageMaker, when automatic text wrap did not exist, and is effective only with rectangular run-arounds. Minor adjustments to the standoff boundary can be made much more easily using automatic text wrap than with manual text wrap. If you make dimensional changes to graphics, manual text wrap must be done over again—manually. With automatic text wrap, updates occur automatically. In general, stay away from manual text wrap, unless you have a rare case in which you cannot achieve desired results using automatic text wrap.

Tip

To wrap regular text around display text for special effect, draw a shape around the display text using one of PageMaker's tools. Customize the shape's text-wrap boundary and use PageMaker's Send To Back command to place the graphic behind the display text. Then assign the graphic a shade of None and a line width of None. Regular text then wraps around the invisible graphic and the display text in front of the graphic. Use this technique to wrap regular text around a drop cap, headline, callout, or pull quote. By arranging two or more invisible graphics in a pattern on your page, you can flow regular text between and around the graphics to create interesting visual effects.

Working with Scanned Images

Scanned graphics include line art and photographs saved as Paint or TIFF files. You can edit these graphics, using any of several popular drawing and image-enhancement programs, before bringing the graphics into PageMaker. After you bring scanned images into your publications, you can resize, reshape, and crop them like any other graphics. PageMaker also enables you to adjust the contrast and brightness to alter the gray-level distribution, and apply to a variety of line screens for special effect.

Detailed line art is best scanned at the resolution of your printer. If you use a 300-dpi laser printer, for example, scan your images at 300 dpi. If your line art is composed mostly of straight lines and simple curves, however, try a lower resolution. The print results are usually just as good, but your files are smaller in size and easier to edit.

Scanning images at the size you want to print them is best. Resizing Paint and TIFF files often produces image distortion (remember, they both are bitmaps). Selectively combining different scanning resolutions with known scaling percentages, however, can result in graphics of the desired size that also reproduce well.

The trick is to plan ahead. If, for example, you know that you must reduce the size of a scanned image by roughly 50% after placing the image in PageMaker, scan the image initially at half the required resolution. Halving the size later in PageMaker effectively doubles the resolution of the image for printing. Similarly, if you plan to enlarge a scanned image by 50%, scan the image initially at twice the acceptable resolution.

Note

The exception to the above rule is when scanning low-resolution images. If you start with a low-resolution original, scan the image at the highest resolution possible. Then when you reduce or enlarge the image in Page-Maker, you get good quality printouts.

Some scanners produce digital halftones when scanning photographs. Digital halftones are nothing more than sophisticated Paint files with resolutions typically varying from 75 dpi to 300 dpi, depending on the scanner, software, and settings used. The higher the resolution of your scanned image, the larger the TIFF file. Large TIFF files can take a long time to print, especially on a Linotronic; longer printing times increase production time and printing costs. Because many photos look good when scanned at 150 dpi or less, you don't always have to use the highest settings. Instead, assign the minimum resolution that produces acceptable results.

Gray-scale scans, even when scanned at low resolutions, also produce large files. Unlike digital halftones, however, gray-scale scans reproduce well when scaled. If you do a gray-scale scan of a photograph at 75 dpi, you usually get acceptable results when printing the photo on a 300-dpi laser printer. If you plan to enlarge the image before printing, increase the scanning resolution to 100 dpi, or even 150 dpi, to retain image quality. Otherwise, scan at higher resolutions only if you plan to print your pages on a Linotronic or other high-resolution output device.

Controlling Images

Scanned images, particularly photographs, frequently require slight modifications to produce acceptable output. PageMaker enables you to make adjustments to contrast, brightness, and gray levels. You can apply these changes to your screen image (as you work) to gauge their approximate effect.

You also can change the number of lines per inch (lpi), or screen frequency, to produce a higher halftone screen resolution. You also can vary screen angle to change the orientation of your line screens. Screen frequency and screen angle affect the number of grays your printer can produce.

For example, a 53-lpi halftone screen set at 45 degrees (the default for the Apple LaserWriter) can produce 32 shades of gray. If you want a finer halftone resolution, you have to sacrifice some gray shades. A 71-lpi halftone screen set at 45 degrees on the

Apple LaserWriter, for example, can produce only 18 shades of gray. Only a few combinations of screen frequency and angle are mathematically possible. Generally, a screen angle of 45 degrees produces the most acceptable results on a 300-dpi laser printer.

Note

Lines per inch (lpi) and dots per inch (dpi) are two different things. Lines per inch describes halftone resolution; that is, the number of halftone cells per inch. Dots per inch, however, represents the actual resolution of your printer. You can avoid becoming confused if you remember that the printer dots (dpi) combine to form the cells that determine halftone image resolution, expressed in lines per inch (lpi).

If you plan to print your publications on a 300-dpi laser printer, you need only an inexpensive four-bit gray-scale scanner—one that scans photos at 16 shades of gray. Six-bit gray-scale scanners that scan at 64 levels of gray and eight-bit gray-scale scanners that scan at 256 levels of gray represent overkill, unless you plan to print your publications on a Linotronic or other high-resolution output device.

On a Linotronic L300 at 2540 dpi, you can print up to 256 shades of gray using a 150-lpi halftone screen. 133 lpi at 256 shades of gray is considered magazine-quality printing, and 85 lpi at 64 shades of gray is considered newspaper-quality printing. The disadvantage, though, is greatly extended print times—the more gray shades and the higher the image resolution, the longer your pages take to print.

With PageMaker, you can choose between a dot-pattern or line-pattern halftone screen. For normal photo reproduction, you normally use a dot-pattern screen, but you may want to try a line-pattern screen. These options, combined with various settings for screen frequency and orientation, can produce some striking visual effects. This is especially true if you set screen frequency to a low enough number to generate noticeably large halftone dots or widely spaced lines. If you also set the screen angle to an odd orientation (screen angle varies between 0 and 360 degrees, measured clockwise from the horizontal axis), you can create some interesting output.

Modifying TIFF Files

PageMaker's Image Control dialog box (choose Image Control from the Element menu) may look intimidating, but the options are easy to use (see fig. 8.6). You can choose from three modes: **Black and white, Screened,** and **Gray.** All three modes can be applied to TIFF files. The following is a description of each mode.

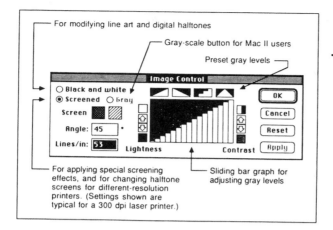

For modifying line art and digital halftones

Gray-scale button for Mac II users

Preset gray levels

Image Control

○ Black and white
◉ Screened ○ Gray

Screen

Angle: 45

Lines/in: 53   Lightness   Contrast

OK
Cancel
Reset
Apply

For applying special screening effects, and for changing halftone screens for different-resolution printers. (Settings shown are typical for a 300 dpi laser printer.)

Sliding bar graph for adjusting gray levels

Fig. 8.6

PageMaker's Image Control dialog box.

❑ **Black and white** mode generally applies to simple line art. However, this mode also can be used with gray-scale scans to convert them into high-contrast, black-and-white images.

❑ **Screened** mode enables you to set the desired lines-per-inch and angle settings for your halftone screens. This mode also enables you to choose between dot-screen or line-screen patterns.

❑ **Gray** mode (for Mac II series users) enables you to adjust gray-scale images and view the effects of your work on-screen.

In the center of the Image Control dialog box is a dynamic vertical-bar graph. This graph displays two wide bars (one black and one white) when you choose the **Black and white** option, or 16 narrow bars when you choose the **Gray** option. The bars can be adjusted vertically by click-dragging to vary the individual gray levels of gray-scale images.

When you first open the Image Control dialog box with a gray-scale TIFF image selected, the gray-level bars are arranged in an ascending pattern from left to right. This pattern is PageMaker's normal default gray-level distribution. Each bar represents one of 16 gray levels in a four-bit gray scan, with the lightest grays to the left and the darkest grays to the right. If you use a six- or eight-bit scanner to create your images, each bar represents multiple levels of gray (4 gray levels for an image scanned at 64 shades of gray and 16 gray levels for an image scanned at 256 shades of gray). Multiple gray levels are weighted proportionally within each bar to preserve the integrity of the image as you make adjustments.

Four icons at the top of the graph represent PageMaker's four preset gray levels. From left to right, the first is the normal preset, which represents a normal gray-level distribution. The second is the negative preset, which gives you a negative, or inverse, of your original image (like the film negative from which a photograph is made). The third and fourth icons are posterize and solarize. Posterizing an image reduces the smoothness of its gray-scale graduations to heighten tonal contrast dramatically. Posterizing is used entirely for special effect. Solarization, another special effect, gives your images a surrealistic look by emphasizing their middle grays. Figure 8.7 shows the effect of each of these icons. You can click any of these icons to apply its attributes to your selected image. The bar graph updates to show the new gray-level distribution.

Fig. 8.7

PageMaker's preset gray levels.

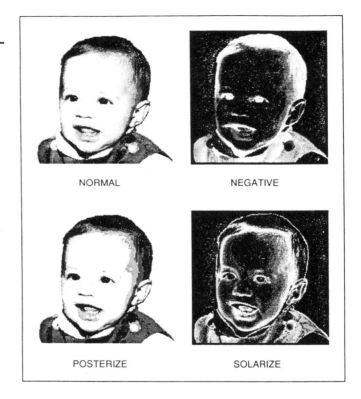

NORMAL   NEGATIVE

POSTERIZE   SOLARIZE

You can adjust the height of any gray-level bar by clicking anywhere within the bar or along its axis. The bar height moves to the spot where you click. If you click-drag your cursor horizontally across the entire graph, all the bar heights adjust to the points where the cursor passed through their axes. To change the overall image brightness (lightness) or contrast, click the Lightness or Contrast scroll-bar arrows (or the icons at each end of the scroll-bars). The bar heights move up or down as a group.

To increase overall image brightness, for example, scroll the bar heights up as a group. This action maintains the bar heights' individual variances. Scroll the bar heights all the way up and your image becomes all white. Scroll the bar heights to the other extreme, and your image becomes all black. The trick is to find an ideal middle range for good print quality.

Note

All settings in the Image Control dialog box affect the entire image. You cannot selectively adjust only part of an image.

Tip

If you have a strong photographic background and spend much production time in a darkroom, examine your scanned photos as negative images in PageMaker. You may be able to pick up shading subtleties not apparent in the normal view.

Clicking the **Apply** button in the Image Control dialog box applies to your graphic the changes you have made so that you can view the changes on-screen without leaving the Image Control dialog box. Drag the dialog box off to one side to get a better view of your image, if necessary. The **Reset** button restores the selected image to its original parameters, undoing any changes made and giving you a way to start over gracefully if the special effects you assign fail to turn out well.

Figure 8.8 shows several different variations of an image and the Image Control dialog boxes used to create each effect.

Modifying Paint Files

You can use the Image Control dialog box to apply special effects to your Paint graphics. You can convert black-and-white images to a lighter shade of gray, for example. You also can create many combinations of dot and line-pattern screens, screen frequencies, and screen orientations, which enables you to produce unusually vivid and striking illustrations. Anything you can do to a black-and-white TIFF image using PageMaker's image controls can be done to a Paint image (see fig. 8.9).

Tip

If your TIFF scan or Paint image is simple line art, the Image Control dialog box opens in **Black and white** mode. To assign an overall image shade other than black, click the **Screened** mode button and click within the solid half of the bar graph. You now can vary the gray-level assignment. You then can assign an image an ultra-light gray shade before placing the image behind any foreground text. This technique gives you a great way to screen a company logo, for example, for inclusion in the background on an award certificate.

Fig. 8.8

Different halftone frequency and angle settings produce different visual effects.

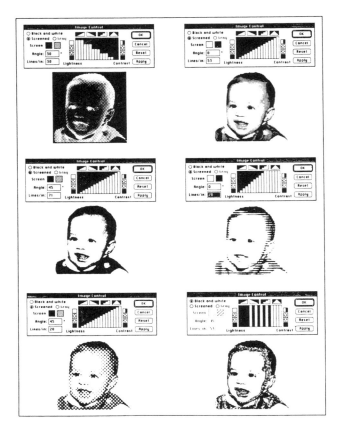

Reducing TIFF Files

PageMaker enables you to compress and decompress TIFF files to reduce the size of your publications and to save disk space. TIFF files typically are quite large. Storing compressed TIFF files in your publications keeps those publications small and easily manageable.

To save disk space for TIFF files stored outside your publications, PageMaker links the compressed versions of externally stored TIFF files instead of the originals. You can delete the original files safely.

To compress a TIFF file, choose the Place command from the File menu. In the Place Document dialog box, click the name of the file you want to compress. Press Command-Option-Shift and click the OK button. Continue pressing this key combination for at least two seconds after clicking OK. PageMaker compresses the file and assigns the file an identifying suffix. PageMaker appends the letter "L" in parentheses to black-and-white and palette-assigned color TIFF files and the characters "LD2" to gray-scale and other externally colored TIFF files.

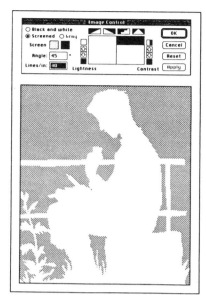

Fig. 8.9

A bit-mapped Paint silhouette screened using PageMaker's Image Control dialog box.

Note

You also can moderately compress a TIFF file by pressing just the Command and Option keys while clicking OK. PageMaker appends the letter "P" in parentheses to black-and-white and palette-assigned color TIFF files and the letters "LD" to gray-scale and other externally colored TIFF files. However, there is no advantage to reducing file size only partially. You always should fully compress your TIFF files if you want to save publication file size or disk space.

To decompress a PageMaker-compressed TIFF file, hold down the Command key as you click OK in the Place Document dialog box. PageMaker appends the letter "U" in parentheses to identify the decompressed version.

Note

When compressing or decompressing a file, PageMaker first makes a copy of the file and then compresses or decompresses the copy. Afterward, Page-Maker appends the appropriate identifying suffix. PageMaker never alters your original files.

Warning

If you delete an original TIFF file after PageMaker creates a compressed version, you may not be able to use the compressed version elsewhere. Many programs do not recognize PageMaker's TIFF compression algorithms. To bring a PageMaker-compressed TIFF file into one of these programs, decompress the file first within PageMaker to recover a usable version.

Working with Color

With PageMaker, you can apply spot color and process color, including PANTONE colors, to text and graphics to accent your publications. Spot color is not the same as process color. Spot color is more like a bunch of brightly colored balloons, with each balloon assigned a separate, solid color. Process color is similar to what you get with a color photograph—a wide variety of different colors blended into a single, composite image.

PageMaker applies spot color to graphics you select with the pointer tool and to text you select with the text tool. PageMaker assigns only one spot color per item, although you can choose any color you like from the more than 700 colors available in the PANTONE Color library. Click the **PANTONE** button in the Edit Color dialog box to display the PANTONE Color dialog box. You select colors directly from the scrolling list of colors or type the corresponding number of the PANTONE color you want into the **PANTONE** field. If you enter a PANTONE color number, PageMaker scrolls the list to that color so that you can verify your choice.

When you assign spot colors to elements on your pages, PageMaker produces a separate spot-color overlay for every color you use. If you use six colors (including black) on one page, for example, you need six spot-color overlays to reproduce all those colors.

You also can define your own colors using any of the following three color models:

❑ HLS—Hue, Lightness, Saturation. This model is similar to the HSB (Hue, Saturation, Brightness) model used by your Macintosh II system software. *Hue* represents a particular color and is defined by its angular position around the color wheel. *Lightness* (or brightness) defines a tonal value between totally bright (white) and totally dark (black). *Saturation* defines color intensity, or purity, which can be seen easily on the color wheel where saturation values increase as you move from the center toward the outer rim. HLS generally is your best choice for spot-color separations.

❏ CMYK—Cyan, Magenta, Yellow, and Black. This model separates colors into their primary subtractive components cyan (blue), magenta (red), and yellow. Primary subtractive colors are overlaid and subtract from one another to produce a composite color when light reflects off them. The CMYK model also includes black as an additional component to heighten color contrast. The CMYK model describes colors in terms of reflected light and is the kind of color you see on printed paper. Use this model to create separation overlays for full, or four-color, process printing.

❏ RGB—Red, Green, Blue. This model is based on the primary additive colors (red, green, and blue) and describes color in terms of transmitted light. Primary additive colors are mixed, or added together, to produce a composite color. You see this kind of color on your color video monitor.

If you use a black-and-white video monitor, you cannot see the colors you assign to elements on your pages, but PageMaker still generates the spot-color separations correctly (you learn more about color separations in Chapter 9).

Note

Although you can import full-color illustrations (including 24-bit color TIFF and EPS graphics) into your publications and display them in color on a color monitor, PageMaker cannot print the four-color separations needed to reproduce the illustrations properly. Four-color process printing requires four separate, precisely aligned color overlays per page to reflect accurately the exhaustive range of possible graduated colors. To do color separations, you have to separate your pages using a color-separation utility such as Aldus PrePrint.

Tip

If you print a full-color illustration in PageMaker on a black-and-white laser printer, PageMaker uses grays to approximate the coloration of the original image. However, the grays rarely replicate the original shadings faithfully. If you plan to print your pages using a black-and-white printer, try to use black-and-white or gray-scale illustrations. You get much better-looking output.

Defining Colors

PageMaker's Define Colors command in the Element menu enables you to define and edit colors in the same way you define and edit styles, with many of the same benefits and advantages. The Define Colors dialog box lists currently defined colors in a scrollable window. **New, Edit, Copy,** and **Remove** buttons to the right of the list work much like their Define Style dialog box counterparts.

To define a new color, open the Define Colors dialog box and click the **New** button. An Edit Color dialog box appears. In this box, you can assign a name to your color. Choose one of the three color models (**RGB, HLS,** or **CMYK**) and adjust color percentages, using sliding scroll bars to create the color of your choice.

Tip

After you define a color using one of the indicated color models, you can click the other **Model** buttons in PageMaker's Edit Colors dialog box to see the corresponding color values for those models.

To edit a color, select the color from the color palette (choose Color Palette from the Windows menu) while holding down the Command key. This action brings up the Edit color dialog box. You also can select a color from the list in the Define Colors dialog box. Then click the **Edit** button to edit that color.

In the Edit Color dialog box, enter the values for the new color if you know the values or adjust the component scroll bars until you see the color you want. The original color is displayed in the bottom half of the color-guide box at the right; your edited color appears in the upper half of the color-guide box. Click the original color in the color-guide box at any time to cancel any editing changes you make. Click the **PANTONE** button to assign a specific PANTONE color to a selected element (see fig. 8.10).

Note

When you assign a PANTONE color as a spot color, PageMaker prints the number of your selection in the margin of the overlay (just outside the crop marks) as a guide to the pressman for making the correct ink selection.

When you finish editing a color, click OK. You return to the Define Color dialog box. Your edited color appears in the color list. To save your changes, click OK. To discard your changes, click the Cancel button. To apply your new color, click its name in the color palette after selecting the element to which you want to apply that color.

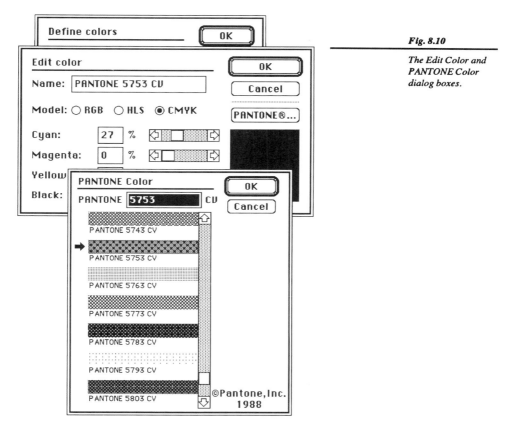

Fig. 8.10

The Edit Color and PANTONE Color dialog boxes.

If you have a Macintosh II series computer and a color monitor, you can use the Apple Color Picker to adjust HLS colors. Hold down the Shift key as you click the **Edit** button in the Define Colors dialog box (or hold down the Command and Shift keys together as you click a color name in the color palette). This brings up the Apple Color Picker. You type HSB or RGB values into the appropriate fields according to Apple's numerical notation or use scroll arrows to set the numbers. You also can use the color wheel exclusively by clicking the color of your choice.

To change color brightness (lightness) in the Color Picker, drag the scroll bar at the right up or down. To scroll through a variety of possible color choices, click-drag the pointer tool around the Color Picker wheel. Moving toward or away from the center of the wheel changes the color saturation. Moving around the circle changes the color hue. View your changes as they occur in the color-guide box at the left. To learn more about the Apple Color Picker, consult the manual that came with your Macintosh.

If you change the composition, or makeup, of a color, PageMaker updates all items in your publication to which you have assigned that color. The same thing happens if you change the name of one color to the name of another color. You are given the chance to cancel this change if you assign a matching name in error (see fig. 8.11). These two features enable you to make global color changes to your publications without having to edit each colored element separately.

Fig. 8.11

PageMaker warns you if you assign the same name to two colors.

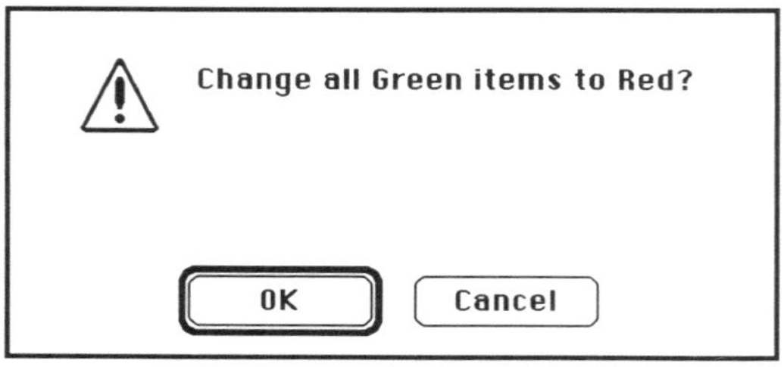

⚠ Change all Green items to Red?

[OK]   [Cancel]

To remove a color, choose its name in the Define Colors dialog box and click **Remove**. Elements in your publication assigned that color are reassigned the color black.

To copy colors from another publication, click the **Copy** button in the Define Colors dialog box. The Copy Colors dialog box appears, from which you can select another PageMaker publication and copy its color palette. Click OK to copy the new color palette into your current publication. New colors are added to the current color palette; colors having the same name replace existing colors. Use this technique to make quick updates to your current color assignments.

Three colors are always present in the color palette: **Paper, Black,** and **Registration. Paper** is the color of your page (usually white), but you can assign new color values using the Edit Color dialog box. Changing this color is useful if you plan to print your publication on color paper. You can better visualize the color combinations for text and graphics that you print on that paper. **Registration**, which applies to PageMaker's printing aids, including crop marks and registration marks, is always black. You cannot change the color assignment for **Registration** or for **Black**.

Assigning Colors

PageMaker applies colors only to areas of an image that normally are black. For example, text normally is black and can be assigned new colors. Similarly, object outlines, fill shades, and patterns normally are black and can be assigned new colors. Surrounding areas that normally are white cannot be assigned any color other than the color Paper.

To apply color to a graphic element, select the element using the pointer tool and then click the desired color in the color palette. Alternatively, choose a color from the Define Colors dialog box. The element takes on the assigned color. If the graphic is a PICT, EPS, or color TIFF graphic, your color assignment does not show on-screen. Note that when you save Paint or black-and-white TIFF images to the Scrapbook, the images are converted into PICT format. The images no longer show their color assignments on-screen.

You also can assign colors to objects you create using PageMaker's drawing tools. The assigned color applies to the object outline and its fill pattern. If you assign a shade of None to an element, the color you assign applies only to the object border. If you assign a line width of None, the color you assign applies only to the fill pattern. Reverse lines and reverse text always take on the currently assigned Paper color.

Tip

PageMaker's Fill menu contains a limited number of gray shades. If, for example, you need a 5 percent or a 50 percent fill for one-color laser printing, you won't find either gray shade listed as a possible menu choice. You can get around this, however. You can be as precise as you like when assigning gray fills. The trick is to create a gray shade "color" for the percent fill you need.

To create a 50 percent gray shade, for example, in the Define Colors dialog box, set all **CMYK** colors, except black, to 0 percent. Set the color black to 50 percent. Assign your new color a name you can easily recognize—50 percent Gray, for example—and click OK to save the color to the Color palette. After that, when you need to apply a 50 percent gray fill to an object, select the object and click **50% Gray** in the color palette.

You also can apply these gray-shade colors to lines (PageMaker does not enable you to assign shades to lines using the Fill menu) and to text you select with the text tool.

Tip

Displaying your pages in color slows screen redraws and increases the time you spend putting together a publication. To speed things up, work with your color monitor set to black and white (you change monitor settings in the Control Panel). If possible, assign colors when you near layout completion.

To apply color to text, select a range of text using the text tool and then click the desired color in the color palette. The text takes on the assigned color. Alternatively, you can pick a color in the Define Colors dialog box and click OK to make the assignment. You can assign a color text attribute to a style by choosing the color from the pop-up menu in the Type Specifications dialog box (click the **Type** button from the Edit Style dialog box). The color choice you make is saved as part of the style.

Colored text often is used to highlight critical paragraphs in a document. You may want to assign the color red to a selected range of text, for example, to highlight the information and make the information stand out. Another popular use for colored text is on letterhead stationery. The uses for colored text are limited only by your imagination.

Tip

If you misplace some colored text, use the Select All command from the Edit menu to locate the missing text block. Check to see that you haven't assigned the color Paper to the text block. If that is the case, click-drag the text tool through the invisible text to select the text and reassign a visible color.

Tip

It is easy to lose reversed text, especially if you move the text block off to one side momentarily while creating a contrasting background. The text disappears because reversing the text makes the text the same color as your page, and therefore, invisible on-screen. To avoid this possibility, type an extra character, such as a bullet, • , in front of the text. Then reverse everything but the bullet. You can find the reversed text block by looking for the stray bullet. After you have the text block positioned properly on the page, delete the bullet.

Chapter Summary

In this chapter, you learned how to work with PageMaker's advanced graphics-handling capabilities, including the Text Wrap, Image Control, and Define Colors dialog boxes. You found that you can polish your layouts by wrapping text around irregularly shaped graphics, and that PageMaker can do most of the preliminary work. You also saw how PageMaker's image-control features enable you to apply special visual effects to Paint and TIFF graphics.

You learned how to adjust the brightness, contrast, and halftone screens of scanned photographs to enhance their printing. You discovered that you can heighten interest in your publications by including color on your pages. You also learned how to apply color to text and graphics.

Now that you know how to assemble finished layouts in PageMaker, you are ready to move on to Chapter 9, in which you learn how to print your publications successfully.

9

Printing Techniques

In preceding chapters, you focused on how to work with text and graphics to prepare layouts in PageMaker. Now you are ready to print your publications. Printing, however, is the area where users most often encounter difficulties.

This chapter teaches you what you need to know to print your publications successfully every time. You learn how to adjust print options to set up, proof, and print your pages using various output devices. You also discover the secrets to using downloadable fonts. You learn when to favor traditional printing methods over laser-generated output, and when and how to use professional-caliber laser equipment such as a Linotronic ImageSetter (found in many print shops) for better-looking results. You also explore the basics of color printing, and you discover how different paper selections can change the look and feel of your documents.

As you work through the material in this chapter, keep in mind that without printing you don't have a publication, no matter how good your pages look on-screen.

Getting Ready To Print

The place to begin is with PageMaker's Page Setup dialog box, because this box is displayed when you open a new publication. Verify the existing settings; don't immediately click OK. In Chapter 2, you learn what each Page Setup option does, and in Chapter 3, you learn how to make those options into program defaults. If you always use the same settings for your publications, you can make those settings into program defaults to save time. To avoid having to make changes later that could disrupt your layout, always verify your settings before you begin working.

Before verifying your page setup, go to the Apple menu and select the Chooser desk accessory. In the dialog box that appears, select the output device you will use to print your publication. PageMaker uses this information to help match your publication's requirements to the characteristics of that printer. Selecting the output device also serves as a reminder to set your publication's page size and margins so that the text and graphics lie within the correct imaging area for that output device.

The icons in Chooser represent the various printer drivers installed in your System folder. The names listed to the right of the icons identify the printers actually connected to your system (see fig. 9.1). If you have more questions about using Chooser, consult the operating manual that came with your Macintosh.

Fig. 9.1

The Apple Chooser desk accessory dialog box.

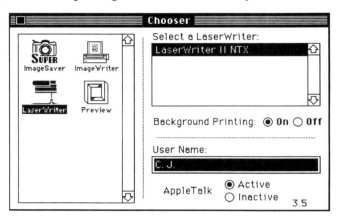

As you set up your publications for printing, you may discover that different output devices produce different size imaging (printing) areas for a given set of page dimensions. At any Linotronic print resolution, for example, you can cover a full 8 1/2-inch-by-11-inch page area (and more) with text and graphics. Printing the same letter-size document on a 300-dpi laser printer, however, constrains the image to lie within a smaller page area; on all sides of the paper, an approximately 1/4-inch margin exists where nothing is printed.

The size of the imaging area depends primarily on your printer's physical construction. Imaging area also can vary with output resolution because of the computational demands made upon your printer's memory.

Take into consideration your printer's imaging area, especially if you proof documents using an output device that is different from the one on which you plan to print your final pages. Consult the operating manual that came with your printer to determine the maximum imaging area under different printing conditions. The Apple LaserWriter, for example, enables you to select from two different size print areas for a given page size. The larger imaging area allocates less printer memory for downloadable fonts but enables you to include more text and graphics on each page.

> *Tip*
>
> If your pages are too large to print properly, reduce them with the **Scaling** option in PageMaker's Print dialog box. Type a new, smaller percentage value into the **Scaling** field to reduce your page image. PageMaker shrinks all page dimensions proportionally and centers the final output. Scaling is an easy way to reduce a legal-size layout to fit a letter-size page.

> *Note*
>
> Because you can change printers and printing specifications at any time, you can print a copy of a publication on one printer and then immediately print a second copy on another printer. This feature comes in handy, for example, when you want to proof your work on a laser printer before downloading to a Linotronic.

Using the Print Options

Choose Print from the File menu to display the Print To dialog box (see fig. 9.2). At the top of the dialog box, you see the name of the currently selected printer. To change the printer assignment before printing, click Cancel and open the Chooser to make a new printer selection.

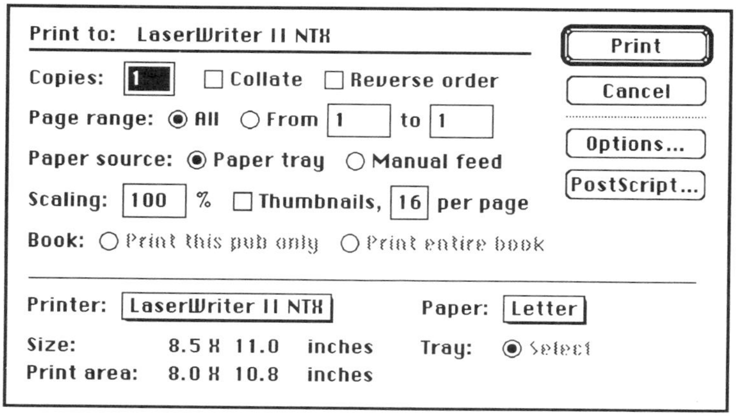

Fig. 9.2

The PageMaker Print To dialog box.

The PageMaker Print To dialog box contains many options normally not available in the standard Apple Page Setup and Print dialog boxes. To use Apple's print driver when printing a PageMaker document, however, hold down the Option key as you select Print from the File menu. (Unlike the Aldus print driver, the Apple driver supports background printing under MultiFinder and also seems to handle printing of complex PICT images better than the Aldus driver.)

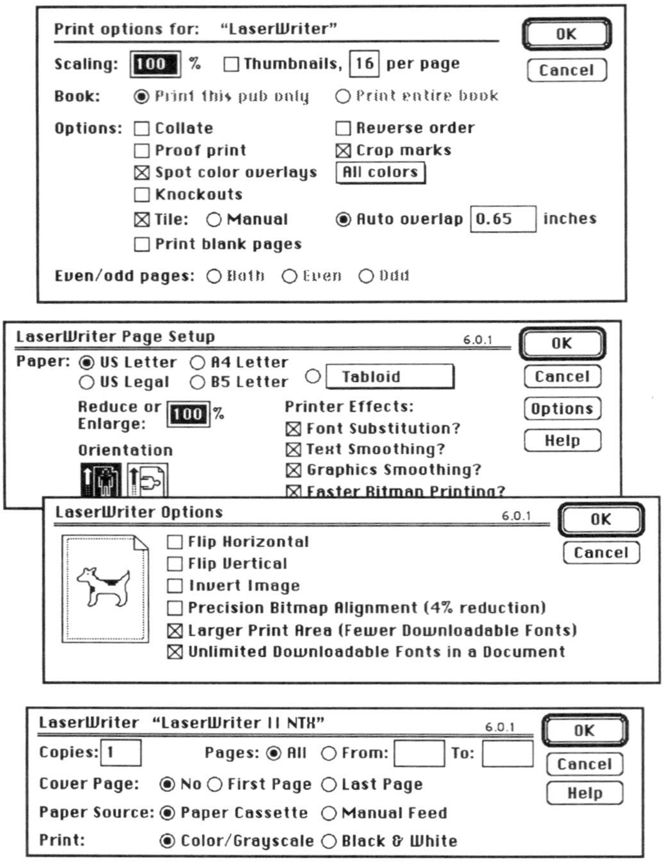

Fig. 9.3

Using Apple's page-setup features when printing from within PageMaker.

Print options for: "LaserWriter"   [OK]

Scaling: [100] %   ☐ Thumbnails, [16] per page   [Cancel]

Book: ◉ Print this pub only   ○ Print entire book

Options: ☐ Collate   ☐ Reverse order
            ☐ Proof print   ☒ Crop marks
            ☒ Spot color overlays   [All colors]
            ☐ Knockouts
            ☒ Tile: ○ Manual   ◉ Auto overlap [0.65] inches
            ☐ Print blank pages

Even/odd pages: ○ Both ○ Even ○ Odd

LaserWriter Page Setup   6.0.1   [OK]

Paper: ◉ US Letter ○ A4 Letter   [Cancel]
          ○ US Legal ○ B5 Letter ○ [Tabloid]
Reduce or [100]%   **Printer Effects:**   [Options]
Enlarge: ☒ Font Substitution?
                          ☒ Text Smoothing?   [Help]
Orientation   ☒ Graphics Smoothing?
                          ☒ Faster Bitmap Printing?

LaserWriter Options   6.0.1   [OK]

            ☐ Flip Horizontal   [Cancel]
            ☐ Flip Vertical
            ☐ Invert Image
            ☐ Precision Bitmap Alignment (4% reduction)
            ☒ Larger Print Area (Fewer Downloadable Fonts)
            ☒ Unlimited Downloadable Fonts in a Document

LaserWriter "LaserWriter II NTX"   6.0.1   [OK]

Copies: [1]   **Pages:** ◉ All ○ From: [ ] To: [ ]   [Cancel]
Cover Page: ◉ No ○ First Page ○ Last Page   [Help]
Paper Source: ◉ Paper Cassette ○ Manual Feed
Print: ◉ Color/Grayscale ○ Black & White

You see a series of three main dialog boxes. The first dialog box is a modified version of the PageMaker Print To dialog box that contains options specific to PageMaker that the Apple driver can handle. After you click OK, you see an Apple dialog box in which you choose the **Page Setup** options you want. Clicking the **Options** button at the right brings up a dialog box full of special printer options. Finally, after clicking OK again, you see the standard Apple Print dialog box in which you specify the page range and number of copies you want to print (see fig. 9.3). Make your choices, click OK, and your publication prints using the Apple printer driver.

Creating Multiple Copies

You can use the Print To dialog box to print up to 100 copies of your publication at one time and to collate pages during printing. PageMaker usually prints all copies of one page before starting the next. If you choose to collate pages by clicking the **Collate** box, PageMaker prints the entire publication once in proper page order and then repeats the cycle as many times as necessary to produce all remaining copies.

If you choose to collate pages, your publication may take longer to print because PageMaker must download each page as many times as the number of copies to be printed. Several dissimilar pages take longer to print than multiple copies of the same page.

On most laser printers, PageMaker usually prints so that the first page lies on top of the stack of output pages (last page printed first). To reverse the output so that the first page lies on the bottom of the stack (first page printed first), choose **Reverse Order** from the Print dialog box before printing. LaserWriter II printers stack your pages face-up if you open the face-up tray. This operation reverses the output stacking order.

Specify the desired page range in the **Page range** fields. If you want to print your entire publication, leave the **All** button selected.

You can print from your printer's paper tray, or you can feed each sheet manually into your printer. To feed sheets by hand (most laser printers require that you manually feed paper heavier than 24-pound), click the **Manual feed** button in the Print To dialog box.

Tip

With a LaserWriter NT or NTX, you do not need to click the **Manual feed** button in the Print To dialog box each time you want to feed an envelope or sheet of paper manually. Insert the blank piece of paper into the sliding guides (on top of the paper cassette tray) and click OK to print. The LaserWriter NT and NTX take their input from the manual-feed slot first and then from the paper tray, regardless of which button you click in the Print To dialog box.

Printing Book-Length Publications

If your current publication contains a book list, the **Print this pub only** and **Print entire book** options become active in the Print To dialog box. Click the **Print entire book** button to print all publications in the book list. PageMaker uses the currently assigned print settings unless you press the Option key when you click the **Print** button. If you press the Option key, PageMaker prints each publication in the list using the print settings saved with that publication.

Making Reductions, Enlargements, and Thumbnails

The Print To dialog box enables you to reduce your page prints to as little as 25 percent of the original size. You also can enlarge them to as much as 1,000 percent of the original size. If you choose to print enlargements, you should *tile* your pages (print them so that the images overlap one another). Be sure that you include cut marks as an aid to trimming your pages later for final assembly and paste-up. You learn more about tiling later in this chapter.

To assess the overall look of your layout before going to press, print a set of *thumbnails* (see fig. 9.4). Thumbnails are miniaturized publication pages. Each page is complete and contains the same fonts and graphics as its full-size counterpart. Viewing miniaturized pages side-by-side on one sheet enables you to see how different sections of your publication tie together.

Fig. 9.4

Thumbnails enable you to evaluate an entire layout at a glance.

Click **Thumbnails** in the Print To dialog box and type a number from 1 to 64 to generate that number of thumbnails on one sheet of paper. The size of each thumbnail depends on how many thumbnails you assign per page and the size of the paper you use for printing. Facing pages print as thumbnail pairs.

Tip

Limit the number of thumbnails to 16 per page if you want to see layout details clearly.

Note

Because thumbnails are complete pages, they take at least as long to print as normal-size pages and usually longer because of the scaling involved.

Creating Proof Prints

Proof prints are complete pages printed without imported graphics. Viewing proof prints enables you to verify your text and layouts quickly without having to wait for complex graphics to print. In place of the imported graphics, PageMaker substitutes *placeholders*, which are boxes containing Xs (see fig. 9.5). Any graphic elements you create using PageMaker's drawing tools print normally.

Fig. 9.5

A proof print of the front page of the Barnyard Gossip newsletter (see Chapter 4).

Because graphic placeholders mark the outer boundaries of the graphics they replace, placeholders may overlap other page elements on your proof sheets. Any text that normally wraps around an imported graphic still wraps on the page exactly as if the graphic was visible.

To generate a quick set of proof prints, click the **Options** button in the Print To dialog box. In the resulting Aldus Print Options dialog box (see fig. 9.6), check **Proof print** and click OK.

Fig. 9.6

The Aldus Print Options dialog box.

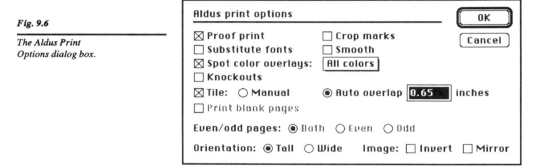

> ### Note
>
> Any headline or display text that you import into PageMaker as a PICT file does not show when you generate proof prints. PageMaker replaces PICT files with a graphic placeholder when you generate a set of proof prints. PageMaker considers text converted to PICT format to be a graphic, even though the text prints as text.

Changing Printer Specifications

You can change printer specifications at any time by choosing a different Aldus Printer description (APD) file in the Print To dialog box. Click the pop-up Printer menu to make your selection.

For each printer, you also can pick a different paper size from the pop-up Paper menu and designate an alternate paper tray. (The possible choices are printer-specific and depend on whether your printer has multiple paper trays.) These menu entries differ depending on the type of printer you select. Note that PageMaker displays a digital read-out of the paper **Size** and **Print area** dimensions in the lower part of the Print To dialog box. These dimensions are given in the units of measure you set in the Preferences dialog box.

Selecting Print Options

In the Aldus Print Options dialog box, you can choose between **Tall** and **Wide** page orientations for printing your pages vertically (portrait) or horizontally (landscape). Your selection must match that in the Page Setup dialog box, or you will print only part of your page. You can choose to **Mirror** or **Invert** images for special printing requirements, such as outputting pages directly to film on a Linotronic. **Mirror** prints a mirror image of each page; **Invert** prints a negative image.

To even out the jaggies along the edges of Paint graphics, click the **Smooth** option before printing your documents. Normally you do not want to select this option because smoothing can turn otherwise crisp-looking bitmaps into chunky-looking pictures. Smoothing also extends the print time for those graphics.

Clicking the **Substitute fonts** option in the Aldus Print Options dialog box tells PageMaker to substitute the laser fonts Courier, Helvetica, and Times for bit-mapped Monaco, Geneva, and New York screen fonts. You should avoid this option because your carefully composed layouts disintegrate when PageMaker substitutes printer fonts. Line, column, and page breaks no longer exactly match those in your original document, and your letter and word spacing may come out completely different. Use appropriate laser screen fonts, instead, to prepare your layouts.

To print blank pages in your publication, check the **Print blank pages** option. Otherwise PageMaker prints only pages with text or graphics on them. The **Print blank pages** option is not available when you print spot-color overlays.

To print just the odd or even pages in preparation for double-sided printing, choose the appropriate **Even/odd pages** option. The **Both** option, which prints odd and even pages, is the only option available when you print thumbnails or spot-color overlays.

Other options (discussed later in this chapter) enable you to tile oversized pages automatically or manually, print spot-color overlays (with or without knockouts), and add crop marks to your pages for accurate trimming.

Tip

As each page prints, PageMaker highlights the corresponding page icon at the bottom of the publication window. Watch the page icons to determine where your document is in the print cycle.

> ***Note***
>
> If you want PageMaker to remember revised print settings, save your publication before closing the file.

Tiling Oversized Pages

When you assign a scaling value in the Print To dialog box that is larger than the available image area of the current paper size, you end up with oversized pages. You generally have to break enlarged pages into sections (called *tiles*) and print them on separate sheets. This process is *tiling*. PageMaker enables you to create tiles automatically or manually. This feature enables you to create large documents like posters and signs.

To tile a document automatically, click the **Auto overlap** button in the **Tile** field of the Aldus Print Options dialog box. Type a value into the **Auto overlap** field equal to the amount of overlap you want between tiles. Because most laser printers don't print fully to the edges of the paper, some image overlap is necessary to ensure a proper fit when you later paste up the page sections (see fig. 9.7). Make sure that the overlap is larger than the gap your printer leaves between the image area and the edge of the paper. A half-inch overlap usually is adequate. You then must trim along the pages' overlapping edges and assemble the individual tiles into a composite whole.

Manual tiling is useful when you want to avoid having tiled page sections split text or graphics. Trying later to paste up two or more page sections containing parts of the same story or illustration is difficult. Getting the text and graphics to match exactly is difficult. To tile your documents manually, click the **Manual** button. This option enables you to control precisely what is included in each tile block. Reposition the ruler zero point to a new spot on the page between each print cycle. Each tile block then prints with its upper-left corner at that spot. You still cut and paste together the pages afterward, but you do not have to worry about precisely matching pieces of text and illustrations.

You print only one manually tiled block at a time. Before printing, check to see that the ruler zero point is anchored on the page where you want the next tile block to start. After each page section prints, relocate the zero point for the start of the next tile block and print again. Continue printing tiles this way until you reproduce the entire page.

Fig. 9.7

A tiled document ready for paste-up. Note how each segment overlaps the others.

Photo courtesy of Jeff Evans and The Norwich Bulletin.

Tip

If your output device cannot print to the edge of the paper, manual tiling is an effective way to produce *page bleeds* (text or graphics that run off the page). Leave **Scaling** set to 100% in the Print To dialog box and manually tile your pages to include fully any bleed areas. Be sure to use crop marks to help determine where to trim each sheet afterward. After you assemble the page sections, trim the composite pages down to normal size. Trim the bleed edges first.

Understanding Downloadable Fonts

Most PostScript laser printers contain several resident, scalable outline printer fonts for printing text at high resolution. To use these built-in fonts, create your documents using the corresponding bit-mapped screen fonts. When PageMaker prints your publications, the built-in printer fonts are substituted for the screen fonts.

To use PostScript fonts other than those already built into your printer, you must *download* them separately to your printer's memory. You can download fonts permanently by using any of several commercial or public-domain PostScript downloading utilities, or you can have PageMaker download them temporarily as you print each page.

Permanently downloaded fonts remain in your printer's memory, available for use until you reset your printer. Temporarily downloaded fonts are stored in your printer's memory only while being used. Then the fonts are purged to make room for new fonts and to free printer memory for other tasks. The only advantage to downloading fonts permanently is that you save time if you print many different documents containing the same fonts or if you collate pages. Otherwise, have PageMaker download the printer fonts as needed.

For each outline printer font you use, you must install a corresponding bit-mapped screen font in your System. You need to install only one size of a particular screen font as a minimum. If you assign other sizes to your text, your fonts look jagged on-screen, but they print smoothly. Installing separate screen fonts for each size you use greatly improves on-screen accuracy for such tasks as manually kerning type. For the best on-screen type appearance, use Adobe Type Manager (ATM), a utility that helps type appear smooth on-screen regardless of font size.

For a downloadable font to print properly, you generally must store the printer version in your System folder. If your output device cannot locate the printer version, the bit-mapped screen version is printed instead. Bit-mapped fonts take longer to print than printer fonts, and the bit maps lack the high resolution you expect from a laser printer.

Using Printer Drivers and APD Files

Your printer driver is the software that handles two-way communications between your computer and its printer. To print your publications, you must have the correct printer driver installed in your System folder. To print on PostScript devices, you also must have the appropriate laser prep file installed. The laser prep file contains a set of PostScript commands used by the printer driver. Your Macintosh System software comes with a LaserWriter printer driver and a laser prep file. Aldus supplies its own laser prep software, Aldus Prep, designed for use with PageMaker's built-in printer driver.

The built-in Aldus printer driver has several advantages over the Apple driver. The Aldus driver provides faster printing and improved output resolution for reduced bit-mapped graphics. The Aldus driver also handles fonts more efficiently, shuttling them in and out of your printer as needed so that you can use any number of fonts in one publication.

The Aldus printer driver also uses separately stored APD (Aldus Printer Description) files. These text files contain descriptive information about different printers and their features, including available paper sizes and imaging areas for different page options, a compilation of printer-error alerts and warnings, a list of resident printer fonts, and other pertinent data PageMaker needs to process your documents properly. For PageMaker to work with a new printer or a new version of an old printer, install a new or updated APD file into the Aldus folder within your System folder. Select the appropriate printer from the Chooser desk accessory and the appropriate APD file for that printer from the pop-up Printer menu in the Print To dialog box. PageMaker accesses the necessary information automatically.

Tip

You can examine an APD file's contents by opening the file from within any word processor (see fig. 9.8). Be careful, however, not to make or save any changes unless you know what you're doing.

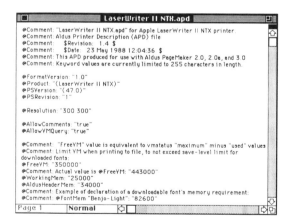

Fig. 9.8

Examining the text of a PageMaker APD file in Microsoft Word.

Apple's printer driver has the advantage of enabling you to batch-print documents when operating under MultiFinder. The built-in Aldus printer driver does not support MultiFinder's background-printing capability. To print PageMaker files as you continue working, use third-party spooler software that intercepts printed files and processes them in the background or print your publications using Apple's printer driver. Apple's driver also provides better support for some complex PICT graphics and should be used when imported PICT images don't print properly with the Aldus driver. To use the Apple printer driver, hold down the Option key as you choose Print from the File menu.

Smoothing Graphics

If your laser printer supports smoothing, choose **Smooth** in the Aldus Print Options dialog box to improve bit-mapped graphics processing. Smoothing can enhance the look of a printed image by eliminating some of the raggedness, but smoothing also can degrade some images by darkening and filling in details. You can partly offset unwanted darkening of a smoothed image, however, by adjusting **Lightness** and **Contrast** using PageMaker's Image Control dialog box. For the best reproduction of scanned images, always leave **Smooth** turned off.

Tip

Smooth is an option that applies to your entire print job. To assign smoothing to only a few pages, print those pages separately from the rest of your publication.

Printing in Color

PageMaker makes adding color to your publications easy. Nevertheless, you need to know several things to get the colors you see on-screen onto your final printed pages.

Preparing Color Overlays

When you click **Spot color overlays** in the Aldus Print Options dialog box, Page-Maker produces separate overlays for each color you use on your pages (including black). The one exception is the color **Paper**, which is used only to visualize the color of your paper on-screen (see Chapter 8 for more information about using the color **Paper**). Each color element is printed on its overlay in the same position that the color element appears on the page.

If your pages are smaller than the selected paper size and you choose the **Crop marks** option in the Aldus Print Options dialog box, PageMaker places registration marks, color labels, and corresponding page numbers in the margin of each color overlay you print; otherwise, you must add these items manually. To add registration marks to your overlays, draw the marks anywhere on your master pages using PageMaker's drawing tools. A small circle centered on a crosshair makes a good registration mark. Use at least three registration marks per page to ensure proper alignment of your overlays. Assign each mark the color **Registration** to have the marks appear on all overlays. If you want registration marks to print on the overlays of certain pages only, you can add registration marks to those pages individually.

Tip

If you assign colors to your text and graphics so that no black remains, proof your text carefully before printing. If you miss assigning color to just one space or carriage return, PageMaker prints an extra overlay sheet for that page because the program thinks a black overlay is needed for any characters to which no color has been assigned. The overlay prints blank, however, because the characters that PageMaker sees normally are invisible.

Overlooking hidden text can increase printing costs greatly, especially when you print lengthy publications on a Linotronic. To avoid this problem, create an insertion point in each story and choose Select All from the Edit menu. Then reassign the desired colors to your text. This process applies those colors to any overlooked or hidden characters.

Tip

You can include registration marks, color labels, and corresponding page numbers on all your overlays in two ways. First, you can scale down your pages slightly so that enough room is left on each printout for PageMaker to include the information. Generally a 15 percent reduction (set **Scaling** to 85% in the Print To dialog box) works well and even may improve the appearance of your pages. The second way is to print your normal-sized pages on oversized paper and to trim the paper afterward. If you use this approach, include crop marks to help determine where to trim the pages.

Using Knockouts

PageMaker enables you to prepare knockout overlays for color images that overlap. *Knockouts* are blank areas within a spot-color overlay that exactly match the shapes of overlapping images in the next overlay (see fig. 9.9). With standard overlays, each colored image is printed in its entirety. If you offset print your pages to produce composite colors, the areas where one color prints on top of another turn out muddy-looking (some colors just do not mix well).

With knockouts, each colored image is printed in a way that, if all the overlays are stacked atop one another, the overlapping images fit together neatly like pieces of a jigsaw puzzle. Each printed color remains pure and does not become contaminated by other colors as the sheets make additional passes through the presses. To print knockout overlays, click **Spot color overlays** and **Knockouts** in the Aldus Print Options dialog box.

Fig. 9.9

Spot-color overlay cutouts.

Tip

If you produce overhead transparencies on your laser printer, you may find that the toner tends to smear or flake off the smooth acetate surface. You can prevent smearing and flaking and simultaneously improve overall image contrast by applying a non-glossy spray fixative to your prints. Use the same kind of spray that artists use to seal charcoal, pastel, and pencil sketches. Cans of matte spray fixative can be found in any graphic arts supply store. Don't spray too heavily, however, or your toner will streak.

Tip

You can use PageMaker to create presentation overlays without having to duplicate the images and then edit each page. You generate the overlays you need by assigning one color to all the elements that make up an overlay. When you click **Spot color overlays** in the Aldus Print Options dialog box, Page-Maker prints a separate page for each assigned color. Stack the resulting transparencies in the desired order, make sure that they're properly aligned, and tape the edges of the sheets together. By flipping them over one at a time during your presentation, you can show a visual progression of information. Be sure to use transparencies specifically designed to withstand the heat of machine copiers and laser printers.

When you use knockout overlays, alignment problems can occur if your registration isn't perfect. When different colors from adjoining areas abut one another, you may see thin white lines along area boundaries where no ink is placed during offset printing. These alignment problems usually occur because the feed transport system of a printing press isn't precise enough to ensure an exact paper feed every time or because the mounted offset plate isn't adjusted properly. Even the slightest shift can lead to improper registration.

To eliminate the gaps that result, commercial printers usually expand area boundaries by a fractional percentage so that adjoining colors overlap slightly. This process is called *trapping*. Because PageMaker doesn't provide a way to trap, check with your printer before using knockouts to determine whether the printer can produce satisfactory color registration.

Note

PageMaker's knockouts don't work with all colored elements. If you can see an element displayed in color on your color monitor, that element prints as a cutout. If an element does not display in color (some imported graphics don't), the element does not print as a knockout. If you have a monochrome display, you have to experiment to find out what works and what doesn't.

Using Commercial Printers

The best way to produce color pages in quantity and ensure consistent results is to use a commercial printer. You and your printer should agree beforehand on the number and type of colors to be printed and the kind of paper you want to use. Find out whether you need to deliver camera-ready copy, or whether the print shop can produce the required separations directly from your disk files. Ask how your printer wants to handle scanned color photographs and complex color TIFF illustrations. Some print shops may refuse to download slow-printing graphics to their Linotronics, and you may be asked instead to deliver photo originals from which quality halftones can be made and later stripped onto camera-ready paste-ups or *mechanicals* (pasted-up camera-ready copy).

Although you can produce spot-color separations easily with PageMaker, several variables still exist that (if left to chance) can ruin an otherwise perfect layout. The colors you see on-screen, for example, always differ greatly from the colors that show up in your final prints. Colors produced by transmitted light (as from a television screen or video monitor) look different than similar colors produced by reflected light (as from the pages of a printed publication). Much depends on the skill of the commercial printer in mixing and applying the required inks.

In most cases, you tell your print shop which colors to use and where the colors appear on the pages. Specify PANTONE Matching System (PMS) colors for best results. PageMaker supports PMS colors, and your print shop also can supply a PMS color guide from which you can choose colors and compare them with what you see on-screen. Beyond that, you have little control over the color-printing process.

If you use a direct-color printer of some kind, such as a dot-matrix, ink jet, PostScript, or thermal-transfer printer, you can adjust your color choices to match the capabilities of that printer. Such printers are limited to producing a narrow range of colors, however, and the colors produced by one device may be matched only marginally by another device. Using color printers to produce multiple copies is very slow, and the printing cost per page is generally high. Using a direct-color printer may prove worthwhile only if you produce your publication in limited quantities.

Tip

Instead of tying up a Linotronic to print complex TIFF graphics (and incurring large production costs at the same time), you can produce printouts of your graphics on a laser printer and then have the print shop reduce them for paste-up. Reducing your printouts on-camera improves the resolution by the amount of the reduction. Reducing a 300-dpi TIFF graphic by 50 percent, for example, increases its resolution to 600 dpi.

Using the Linotronic

If your publications call for typeset-quality printing, output your files to a Linotronic ImageSetter. You can find Linotronics in many print shops and service bureaus across the country. The L300, for example, produces documents with resolutions up to 2,540 dpi—enough to satisfy the most demanding publishing requirements. Linotronic output, however, is much more expensive than output from a normal 300-dpi laser printer. Because a Linotronic occasionally refuses to process jobs that print readily on a regular laser printer, knowing how to prepare your documents ahead of time pays off.

Proofing before Printing

Before downloading your files to a Linotronic ImageSetter, always print a complete proof of your publication on a PostScript laser printer and check the text and graphics carefully. The Linotronic also uses PostScript as its page-description language. Documents printed on both devices should appear similar.

Check for typos, layout inconsistencies, and other errors. Then make sure that your publication is set up for Linotronic output. (Select the Linotronic APD file in the Print to dialog box.) Choose the **Mirror** and **Invert** options from the Aldus Print Options dialog box if you plan to print directly to film.

Tip

The Linotronic prints fully to the edge of a page, which makes the Linotronic ideal for doing bleeds. However, checking bleeds on laser-printed proofs is difficult because laser printers typically leave a small margin around the paper edges where nothing prints. To check pages with bleeds, run proof copies of them at reduced size. Scaling your pages to 85% and including crop marks enables you to verify that your bleeds are placed properly.

To avoid wasting time and money, use laser-printed thumbnails to check your publication's layout before printing on a Linotronic. Thumbnails help you spot any global errors or inconsistencies that you may have overlooked when examining the full-size page proofs.

Printed output from a laser printer and a Linotronic can be different. Hairline rules, for example, print thicker on a 300-dpi laser printer (where the dots are bigger) than on a Linotronic (where the dots are smaller).

On a laser printer, gray shades at the low end of the spectrum always turn out darker than when printed on a Linotronic. A 10-percent gray, for example, makes a good background shade when printed on a 300-dpi laser printer, but fades into nothingness when printed on a Linotronic. Similarly, gray shades at the high end of the spectrum always turn out lighter on a laser printer than on a Linotronic. If the grays look just right on a 300-dpi laser printer, the tones probably will be off on your final Linotronic prints. Make the necessary adjustments ahead of time by checking comparative gray-scale charts at your commercial printer.

Tip

When printing gray-scale images such as scanned photos on the Linotronic, use PageMaker's Image Control dialog box to lighten the images about 10 percent before downloading. Scanned photos typically print darker on the Linotronic than on a 300-dpi laser printer, and adjustment is necessary to replicate the originals accurately. Also, increase the **Lines/in** setting in the Image Control dialog box to at least 90 lines per inch to take advantage of the Linotronic's finer output resolution.

Outputting Directly to Film

The main advantage of printing positives (normal-looking pages) from a Linotronic is that the output can be treated as traditional high-quality, camera-ready art. Preparing mechanicals is therefore easier. The output also can be used on a high-speed copier.

Printing directly to film on a Linotronic, however, has the advantage of completely bypassing the camera. Going directly to film retains the clarity of the original (especially with ultra-fine screens) and produces an output resolution that the camera cannot equal. Shooting mechanicals with a camera to produce plate negatives introduces one more step in the production process, which increases the potential for problems. When you reproduce camera-ready copy using a camera, the image quality is degraded slightly.

Tip

When you print directly to film using a Linotronic, you must select the **Invert** and **Mirror** options in the Aldus Print Options dialog box. The **Invert** option produces the negative of the image on film; the **Mirror** option flips the image so that it comes out correctly after flipping the film. Flipping the film after it exits the Linotronic is essential to place the emulsion side against the printing plate during exposure. Placing the emulsion side down prevents light diffusion (caused by light passing through the celluloid thickness after striking the emulsion) from defocusing the image. Because the image is trapped in the emulsion and the emulsion is pressed tightly against the printing plate, the tiny dots produced by the Linotronic reproduce sharply.

Avoiding Linotronic Hang-Ups

PICT files occasionally cause printing problems, especially if your PICT images contain many smoothed polygons (multisided objects that have been converted mathematically into curves). Redrawing these images sometimes requires so many computations that the printer's memory can be overtaxed.

All objects are seen in their entirety by the Linotronic, even though you may conceal parts of some objects by overlapping them with others. The Linotronic incrementally redraws the objects in layers. This process places additional burdens on printer memory.

Several other factors can retard Linotronic print times and sometimes cause a print job to fail. These factors include using too many detailed bit maps (text or graphics) in your publications; excessively scaling or reshaping bit-mapped images; mixing large numbers of font types and styles on a page; and using an excessive number of different shades, patterns, and line styles on one page. To compensate for printing slowdowns, the print shop may charge you for the actual time used to generate your pages instead of the usual flat-rate fee.

To get a recalcitrant file to print, you can try printing fewer pages at a time. Print your publication in sections by setting the sequential page ranges in the Print To dialog box. You also can try to reduce the size of your publication. Use Save As instead of Save to archive final document versions. Save As compresses your files by eliminating the extra information PageMaker stores in case a mini-save recovery is required. You also can try removing complex graphics one at a time until your publication prints. Go back to your drawing program and simplify the graphic before re-importing into PageMaker.

As a last resort, try using the Apple printer driver instead of the Aldus version to print your publication. Press the Option key as you choose Print from the File menu to access the Apple Print dialog boxes.

Tip

If you include Paint or TIFF bit-mapped graphics in your publications, set them up to print the best resolution before you download them to the Linotronic. Select the **Linotronic APD** file from the Printer pop-up menu in the Print To dialog box. Tune each graphic separately by Shift-click-dragging one of its reshaping handles while holding down the Command key. The image boundaries adjust to match the specific printing resolution of the Linotronic.

> ### *Tip*
>
> Unlike an ordinary laser printer, the Linotronic looks at all the text in a publication, including any text residing on the pasteboard. Although text on the pasteboard does not print, the Linotronic still processes the text. The extra text can clog the printer's limited memory. If your job fails to print, delete any leftover text on the pasteboard before you print again.

If a publication you send to a service bureau comes back with the page formatting mysteriously altered, check for one of the following possible causes:

❑ You and your service bureau used different versions of the same screen fonts. For example, Apple's and Adobe's versions of Times Roman are quite different, even though both use the same outline printer font built into the LaserWriter. For any given type size, Apple's version produces tighter all-around character, word, and line spacing. Consequently, Apple's version yields denser-looking text with less frequent line breaks. If you print the same document using Adobe's version of Times, you dramatically change the look of your pages. With Adobe's version, the spacing is generally wider.

❑ You and your service bureau used different System software. If you create and print documents using different versions of the System, you can expect to see anomalies in character and word spacing. Differences occur because older versions of the System cannot handle built-in font metric information with the same degree of sophistication that newer System software can.

❑ You had the wrong printer driver selected when you created your publication. For example, leaving your ImageWriter driver selected in Chooser may adversely affect the page setup characteristics of your program for laser printing and ultimately your final output pages. The printable page area for most laser printers (except the Linotronic) is noticeably less than that of the ImageWriter.

❑ You used the bit-mapped fonts New York, Monaco, or Geneva in your publication and allowed the printer driver to substitute Times, Courier, or Helvetica. The former are bit-mapped fonts intended for use only with dot-matrix printers; their built-in font metrics differ substantially from Times, Courier, and Helvetica. Times, Courier, and Helvetica are intended for use with PostScript laser printers. When you allow substitutions to occur automatically, you sacrifice control over page formatting. The converted line breaks never exactly match the original line breaks.

Creating PostScript Files

When you send a publication to a commercial printer, you can avoid certain printing problems by sending the publication as a pure PostScript file. If you send your publication as a PostScript file, your print shop doesn't need a copy of PageMaker or the particular laser fonts you used. All the data required to print is included in the PostScript file.

To create a PostScript file from your publication, choose Print from the File menu and configure the desired print options. Select the APD file appropriate to the destination printer from the pop-up menu in the Print To dialog box. Next, click the PostScript button to bring up the PostScript Print Options dialog box (see fig. 9.10). Click **Print PostScript to disk** and **Normal** (the **Normal** button allows printing of publications containing multiple pages) and set any other preferred options. Name your file and tell PageMaker where to store the file (click **File name**), and click OK. A PostScript file containing your publication is printed to disk.

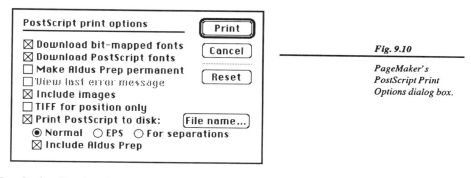

Fig. 9.10

PageMaker's PostScript Print Options dialog box.

When creating PostScript files in this manner, keep the following things in mind:

❑ Aldus Prep is needed to process your publication properly. If your commercial printer doesn't have PageMaker, click **Include Aldus Prep** in the PostScript Print Options dialog box to make Aldus Prep part of your PostScript file. If your print shop has PageMaker, tell your printer to download Aldus Prep to the printer and then save file space by not including Aldus Prep when you create your PostScript file. Make sure that you and your commercial printer use the same versions of the Aldus Prep file.

❑ If you plan to print several publications in a row, create a separate PostScript file containing only Aldus Prep. Open a publication, leave it blank, and save the publication as a PostScript file. Click **Include Aldus Prep** and **Make Aldus Prep permanent**. This file can be used to download Aldus Prep to the printer. Aldus Prep remains in memory and is used to print each publication.

❏ If the laser fonts used in your publication are not available on the destination printer, click **Download PostScript fonts** in the PostScript Print Options dialog box. The PostScript versions of each font used are added to your PostScript publication file. Click this option only if you are sure that the fonts are not available. If the fonts already are installed in the printer and you download them again, your publication may not print because the duplicate fonts clog the Linotronic's remaining memory.

Tip

If you are not sure which fonts are built into a particular laser printer, examine the laser printer's APD file using your word processor.

If you plan to print directly to film, select the **Mirror** and **Invert** options in the Aldus Print Options dialog box. Select **Download bit-map fonts** from the PostScript Print Options dialog box to use bit-mapped fonts in your publication (this option is PageMaker's normal default). Deselect **Download bit-map fonts** if you want PageMaker to substitute Courier instead. Choose the **Download PostScript fonts** option when you want to download third-party laser fonts to your printer (this option is PageMaker's normal default). If you do not select **Download PostScript fonts**, PageMaker uses Courier. You should deselect **Download PostScript fonts** only when creating a PostScript version of a publication that uses identical fonts to those resident in the destination printer.

If you are printing to a color PostScript printer, or if you are printing gray-scale TIFF files, choose **Include images**. If you are preparing your publication as a PostScript file for eventual color separation, leave **Include images** unchecked. If you are printing TIFF images as placeholders, choose the **TIFF for position only** option. PageMaker prints the low-resolution screen versions of your TIFF files instead of downloading the originals.

Select **View last error message** to see printer error messages when they occur. Selecting this option prevents you from using your Macintosh until after your document prints (normally your Macintosh is available immediately after a file has been downloaded).

Choose the **Make Aldus Prep permanent** option if you want Aldus Prep to remain in your printer's memory until you reset the printer (this option is PageMaker's normal default). Leave this option unchecked only if you want Aldus Prep to be removed from your printer's memory as soon as your publication prints. Not selecting this option frees printer memory for other uses.

Each time you print, you must reselect these options from the PostScript Print Options dialog box. PageMaker forgets your choices after each print job and reverts to its default settings.

Saving Pages as EPS Graphics

If you click the **Print PostScript to disk** and EPS buttons in the PostScript Print Options dialog box, you can create EPS graphics from individual publication pages. You later can import these EPS pages into PageMaker using the Place command from the File menu. You then can resize, reshape, and assign text-wrap boundaries to EPS pages the same as any other graphic. These PageMaker EPS files include a low-resolution PICT screen image with the PostScript code so that you can view the images on-screen.

The trick to saving pages as EPS files is to select only one page at a time in the Print To dialog box (type the same page number in the **From** and **to** fields). You also must have **Scaling** set to 100%, and the **Thumbnails** option in the Print To dialog box must not be selected. You also cannot choose the **Proof print, Spot color overlays, Tile,** or **Crop marks** options in the Aldus Print Options dialog box or the **EPS** button remains dimmed.

Tip

PageMaker's EPS graphics have the same dimensions as the pages from which PageMaker creates them. Assign smaller page dimensions in the Page Setup dialog box before printing to produce smaller graphics.

Printing Process Color Separations

PageMaker cannot print process color (four-color) separations. To print process color separations, you need to use Aldus PrePrint or another color-separation utility. You can, however, prepare your publications for separation by printing them to disk as PostScript files. Make sure that you check the **For separations** option in the PostScript Print Options dialog box. This option enables the color-separation utility to process your publication and produce full-color separations of your pages, including EPS graphics and color TIFF images.

Using Offset Printing

Small jobs cost less when run on high-speed copiers, but large jobs are cheaper when offset. *Offset printing* uses a printing press and plate to transfer an image to paper repeatedly. Choose offset when you must produce pages in large quantities or in color. You also should choose offset to include photos if you don't have a scanner, if you want the superior resolution of half-toned photos instead of the marginal quality scanning sometimes produces, or if you want to print your publications using special paper sizes or weights that high-speed copiers cannot handle. Choose offset when you and your commercial printer conclude that offset is the best and most cost-effective way to produce your documents.

You generally save the most time and money by using PageMaker to do publication design and layout. However, after producing camera-ready copy, having your commercial printer finish the job often proves more cost-effective.

Tip

You can get superior offset-quality print resolution from ordinary 300-dpi laser output and save several hundreds of dollars that you may otherwise spend on costly Linotronic output. The easiest way to improve printed resolution is to output your final copy twice the normal size and halve it on the camera for offset printing. This process effectively doubles the resolution from 300 to 600 dpi. However, this method works well only for small documents. What if you want to improve the look of full-size 8 1/2-inch-by-11-inch pages? To get near-Linotronic quality results using a 300-dpi laser printer, do the following:

❑ Set your laser printer's density dial to produce the lightest copy possible without having delicate serifs or thin, angled stems show breaks in continuity. You also want areas of black to remain solid and not look washed out. Run a series of test prints to determine the optimum setting for your printer.

❑ Print your publications using only high-resolution, bright-white laser paper designed specifically for generating camera-ready originals. Above all, don't compromise on paper quality; it really does make a difference.

❑ Overexpose slightly on the camera. Slight overexposure causes black areas on the negative (corresponding to white areas on the page) to become even blacker and heavier. As the exposure time increases, the black begins to encroach on the white areas of the negative (the text and graphics). The expanding black areas eat away at the edges of type and line art. This reduces 300-dpi jaggies, smooths line edges, and thins character strokes. In essence, overexposure counteracts the natural tendency of the camera to add weight. You get nice, crisp-looking offset copy.

Experiment to determine the optimum exposure setting for your commercial printer's particular camera and press. As a general rule, a 15 to 20 percent overexposure works well and adds about three seconds to a typical 14-second camera shot for each page. Under casual examination, the final printed results look identical to those obtained when Linotronic negatives are used to prepare the plates.

Overexposure also can improve slightly the look of a low-resolution halftone by heightening its contrast. However, for truly high-quality halftones, output your images on a high-resolution L300 or equivalent ImageSetter.

Using Paper Plates

If your commercial printer can produce paper printing plates directly from the camera, you can save quite a bit of money. Cameras normally yield negatives, which must be stripped (attached to a special masking paper) by hand before metal plates can be made. This multistep process takes time, which dramatically increases the cost of producing a job. Metal plates also cost considerably more than paper ones. Yet you get nearly the same results by using high-quality Silver Master or Black Onyx paper plates. Avoid the electrostatic variety, because their output quality is poor.

The main disadvantage of paper plates is that they are not as durable as metal plates. Metal plates can be used repeatedly and are a better choice for high-volume production work. Also, metal plates are best for jobs where precise registration is necessary (paper plates often stretch slightly during use). However, you generally can get about 10,000 acceptable copies from a good paper printing plate.

Choosing the Right Paper

Your choice of paper not only determines how good your final publication looks but also how much the publication costs to produce. Keep in mind that paper costs usually make up half or more of the expense of most print jobs.

Although you have many weights, finishes, grades, and colors to choose from, ordinary office or copier bond paper works well for laser-printed output. High-gloss and textured finishes, however, yield poor reproductions. High-gloss paper doesn't hold toner well; the toner sometimes smears, occasionally chips, and frequently heat-spatters during application. Textured paper doesn't accept toner evenly. The rough surface causes uneven toner application and gives text and graphics a ragged look.

Watch out for letterhead stationery. The low-temperature inks used on some letterhead stationery smear if you try to put the paper through your laser printer. Laser printers use a combination of high temperature and intense roller pressure to fuse and permanently bond toner to paper. The high heat causes the low-temperature inks to vaporize so that they smear as they travel through the feed path. Raised-thermograph letterheads also tend to smear when put through a laser printer. Letterheads that have been offset printed, however, should work fine.

Another kind of paper to avoid is the preprinted award certificate (unless the certificate is designed specifically for laser-printer or copier use). The worst offenders are certificates that have gold flakes embedded in their surface dyes. If these metallic flakes come off in your laser printer, you win a trip to your dealer for repairs.

If you prepare camera-ready copy, a smooth, bright-white paper finish for heightened contrast is desirable. Several companies make such paper especially for use with laser printers. This paper costs two or three times as much as ordinary bond, but for important jobs the added cost can be justified.

Tip

Occasionally a laser printer's automatic-feed tray fails to release (or only partially releases) a sheet of paper into the feed path. A misfeed usually results, and the print job stops until you correct the problem. You can reduce the chances of misfeeds in the following ways:

- ❏ Fan all sides of a newly opened package of paper. Fanning helps eliminate static build-up so that individual sheets slip away easily from the rest of the stack.

- ❏ Never overfill the paper tray. Overfilling reduces the effectiveness of the spring-lift, which is vital to proper feed operation. If the paper tray is too full, the rubber take-up wheels inside the printer suffer excessive wear, and the number of misfeeds increases.

- ❏ Feed with the curl side down. Excessive paper curl can cause jams, particularly if the curl lies in the same direction as the rollers.

- ❏ Don't exceed manufacturer's paper specifications for auto-feeding. Overly thick sheets resist proper feeding. Feed heavy paper and card stock manually.

- ❏ Avoid using coated, gummed, or adhesive-backed papers. They can stick to any part of the feed path. These papers also can contaminate the print drum and damage your printer.

Tip

If you plan to reproduce your document on a high-speed copier, print your document on the heaviest paper you can put through your laser printer. Use a 70-pound paper (if available) to eliminate the severe curl you often get from feeding lighter-weight paper across your laser printer's internal rollers at high temperature and pressure. Paper curl is the biggest single cause of jams on high-speed copiers; eliminating paper curl does much to ensure that your print job goes smoothly.

Getting Good Laser Prints

To get consistently good toner bonding on laser-printed copy, use a high-quality paper made especially for laser printers. If you use heavily textured or highly coated stock, you can expect the toner not to fuse properly.

Store your paper in a cool, dry area. Leave paper in its original packaging or place it in a sealed container. Paper is roughly 60 percent water, so the longer paper sits out unprotected, the drier and more brittle it becomes. Toner doesn't adhere well to overly dry paper.

Some LED printers don't generate enough heat to fuse toner properly to certain kinds of papers, especially those with overly smooth or glossy surfaces. To avoid having the toner flake off, set your printer's intensity control to a higher value or change to a paper that has a softer surface texture.

Toner flaking sometimes results from using recharged toner cartridges. Despite hype to the contrary, few remanufactured cartridges contain the same quality toner found in new cartridges. One symptom of a faulty cartridge is toner that rubs off easily.

Note

If you run across a superior toner cartridge that delivers consistent blacks and even toner distribution, set the cartridge aside to use for important printing jobs (where you need superior camera-ready copy or crisp black output for client presentations). However, be sure to store your partially used toner cartridges in a cool, dry place in light-tight containers. Moisture from humidity can cause toner caking, and cartridges left out in the light soon suffer imaging quality loss.

If printing problems persist, you may need to clean or repair the discharge pins in your laser printer. Dirty or damaged discharge pins may cause poor toner deposition, which in turn may cause toner to flake or rub off. Consult the manual that came with your printer for details.

Chapter Summary

In this chapter, you learned how to set up and print your publications using different kinds of output devices. You examined PageMaker's various print options in detail and discovered how to tailor them to meet your printing needs. In the process, you learned how to generate proof prints, do reductions and enlargements, print thumbnails, and tile oversized pages. You gained new insights into the role of printer drivers and APD files. You also learned how to produce color separations and how to download pages directly to film when preparing your publications for offset printing.

You discovered that you can convert PageMaker documents into pure PostScript files for direct processing by a commercial printer or print service bureau. You also saw how to obtain high-resolution offset printing using low-resolution camera-ready masters. Finally, you learned that even the best print job can be ruined by improper paper selection.

This chapter completes your introduction to the mechanics of using PageMaker. In the next chapter, you begin your study of the design process, an essential step on the way to producing professional-looking publications.

IV

Creating Different
Types of Publications

Includes

Planning Page Layouts

Designing a Newsletter

Designing Other Publications

Planning Page Layouts

10

This chapter focuses on designing and laying out your publications. Knowing how to use PageMaker does not make you a successful designer; PageMaker is simply a tool for creating layouts. If you want your publications to look good and appeal to your readers, you must study and practice sound design principles.

No absolutely right way exists to design and lay out a document, but many wrong ways do exist. This chapter helps you avoid the more common pitfalls as you zero in on the right look for your publications. The ideas in this chapter help you produce pages that sparkle with professionalism, even if you are new to the magic of desktop publishing.

Communicating Ideas Effectively

To successfully convey thoughts, arguments, ideas, and feelings to your readers, you have to get them to read your publication. But before people read a publication, they have to notice the publication. Getting people to stop long enough to take notice is increasingly difficult in today's communications-intensive world. The rivalry for reader attention is intense. The following elements are necessary if you are to succeed in getting people to notice any kind of publication:

❑ A publication must be tailored to meet the needs and expectations of its readership. For example, a journal containing nothing but page after page of text in small print could not hope to appeal to the graphic-design community. Similarly, a pamphlet with ornate graphics on every page would have little success among lawyers, who value concise, factual information.

❑ A publication must stand out from the competition. Well-designed publications always have an edge. Few desktop publishers, however, have learned to apply design techniques that can give them that edge. Keep in mind that your publication's appearance sets the tone of its message, even before the first words are read. Like a fishing lure, if your publication has the right look, you get many nibbles and eventually hook a good catch. Without the right look, you are reduced to reciting tales of the readers who got away.

Achieving the Right Look

To help you understand what is meant by the "right look," visualize a page containing nothing but text (see fig. 10.1A). You see a single text block that fills the entire area between the page margins and is fully justified. The unbroken lines of text are hard to read; your eyes must travel across the page without pause, and the layout has no counterbalancing white space. The result is an impenetrable wall of text that is tiring to look at and tiring to read. This look definitely is wrong for almost everything but a deliberately intimidating legal contract.

In figure 10.1B, you see the same text, but with wider margins to allow plenty of surrounding white space. However, because the left-right margins and top-bottom margins are equal and the text is fully justified, the page is monotonously uniform. This look may be right for short formal announcements, but fully-justified text in larger doses turns readers away.

In figure 10.1C the same layout has been improved slightly. The text now is set with unequal margins and ragged-right justification to heighten visual interest. Clockwise from the left, each margin is progressively wider than the last. The top margin is a little wider than the left margin (after binding); the right margin is a little wider than the top; and the bottom margin is widest of all.

The text block in figure 10.1C has been assigned *golden-rectangle* dimensions. A golden rectangle has a length approximately 1.62 times its width (1.61803398, to be exact). This ratio has been used for centuries to design everything from books to buildings (the most famous of which is the Parthenon in ancient Greece). The golden rectangle is pleasing to the eye, and its use in page design makes reading a more enjoyable experience. Although this layout is less imposing than the last, the look still is somewhat formal. This layout is a good choice for books and other long manuscripts.

In figure 10.1D, you see a typical three-column newsletter format. The column rules, reversed running head, and increased white space help make the page more interesting and, therefore, more likely to catch a reader's attention. The subheads help break up the flow of text into easily digestible chunks, and the narrower columns are easy to read. This format has a businesslike appearance without being imposing. This format is the right look for informational publications such as journals and newsletters.

> ### *Tip*
>
> To assign golden-rectangle dimensions to text and graphics easily, create two golden-rectangle boxes (one vertical and one horizontal), using PageMaker's square-corner rectangle tool. Use your rulers as guides to accurate sizing. Copy the rectangles individually to the Clipboard and paste them into your Scrapbook. When you need a golden rectangle for positioning ruler and column guides, use PageMaker's Place command to import the rectangle from your Scrapbook. Be sure to use the Place command. If you copy from the Scrapbook and paste into PageMaker, the rectangles revert to squares when you hold down the Shift key and try to resize them proportionally.

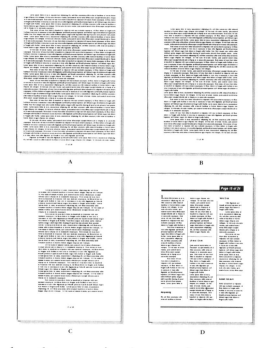

Fig. 10.1

Four different layouts of the same document.

These examples show that even minor layout variations can produce dramatic differences in the appearance of a page. The right look for one publication, however, may be a totally wrong look for another. The trick to achieving the right look for a publication is to experiment with many different layouts until you find one that works best. But experimenting doesn't necessarily mean endless trial and error. You can greatly improve your chances of success if you understand and apply a few universally accepted, basic design principles.

Understanding Structure

Every publication must have structure to accomplish its purpose. A business report, for example, may include supporting charts and tabular data alongside text. If those graphics are arranged haphazardly on successive pages, however, the overall lack of document organization may subconsciously lower reader confidence in the data being presented.

Well-structured pages, on the other hand, inspire confidence even before readers examine the data. For example, many successful advertisements that at first glance seem unstructured actually are laid out according to an underlying grid. The grid directs the structure of the elements on the page. Structure is the key to organizing and presenting your information and getting your message across.

The primary tool for laying out structured pages is the grid. PageMaker enables you to place elements on your pages without regard to a formal grid; however, good design practice entails using some sort of organizational framework to contain your text and graphics. In PageMaker, this framework consists of arrangements of non-printing column, margin, and ruler guides.

You can lay out any kind of grid. PageMaker doesn't constrain your creativity. Consider several things, however, as you formulate your publication's structure:

❑ How large do your pages need to be, and how will they be folded, bound, and distributed? Although PageMaker enables you to produce pages up to 17 by 22 inches, if your printer cannot accommodate paper that large, you have to tile your output to create camera-ready mechanicals.

❑ How wide should you set your margins, and should they be of equal or unequal widths? If you want the image area to be a specific size, you have to pre-calculate margin widths based on paper size.

❑ Should your layouts be symmetrical or asymmetrical, and how will you allocate surrounding white space? If you intend to include bleeds, have you adjusted your page and paper sizes accordingly? (You may have to use larger paper and trim later. If so, check with your printer to see whether you can change paper sizes without increasing production costs.) Also, if you intend to print your publication double-sided, make sure that you leave enough *gutter* space (inner margin) for proper binding.

Note

Most laser printers are not designed to handle large amounts of double-sided printing. Remelted toner eventually can accumulate on rollers and cause internal damage. Have your commercial printer produce any double-sided pages.

Tip

If you occasionally print double-sided pages on your laser printer, let your pages dry at least a couple of minutes before printing on the second side. Waiting gives the toner time to harden and cool and reduces the risk of the toner sticking to the rollers on the second pass through your printer.

❑ Does your publication call for multiple columns? If so, how many columns do you need, and should the number of columns vary from page to page? Must they all be the same dimensions, or can you use variable-width spacing on different pages? If you set variable-width columns, is balancing text and graphics on facing pages for an eye-pleasing arrangement still possible? Should you set text ragged right or fully justified? (If you don't need to justify, set the columns ragged right; they generally look better and are easier to read.) Remember that your columns are the pillars upon which your publication rests—they support your entire layout design.

❑ Should your headlines span multiple columns, or should you confine them to lie within existing column boundaries? How will you distinguish headlines and subheads from surrounding text? What is the most readable type size for your stories, and how much space should you insert between lines and paragraphs? Have you chosen workable type sizes for headlines, subheads, and captions?

Tip

If your headlines span two or more lines, reduce the leading to tighten them up. If your headlines are set in large type, use negative leading values (values less than the existing type size). For example, a two-line, 60-point headline looks much better set with a negative leading of 52 points than with PageMaker's normal 72-points auto-leading setting (equal to 120 percent of type size). See figure 10.2 for an example of negative leading applied to a 24-point headline.

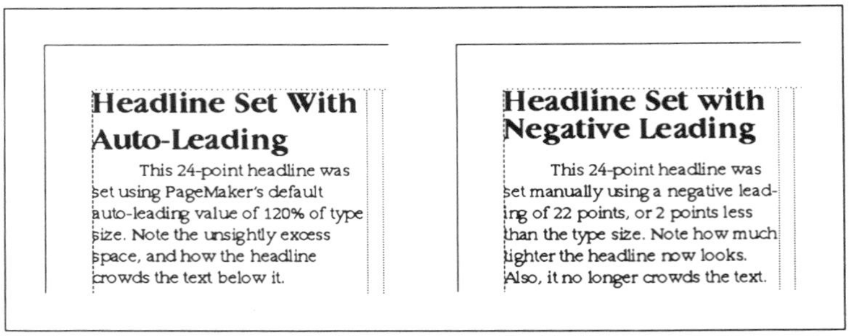

Fig. 10.2

*Assigning negative
leading can improve
the look of headline
copy.*

Headline Set With Auto-Leading

This 24-point headline was set using PageMaker's default auto-leading value of 120% of type size. Note the unsightly excess space, and how the headline crowds the text below it.

Headline Set with Negative Leading

This 24-point headline was set manually using a negative leading of 22 points, or 2 points less than the type size. Note how much lighter the headline now looks. Also, it no longer crowds the text.

❑ How large are your photos and illustrations? Do they fit within column boundaries or span multiple columns? Have you left enough extra space for frames? Where should you place photo and artwork credits—below or vertically alongside your illustrations? (PageMaker enables you to rotate text in 90-degree increments, but be careful not to overuse rotated text in your layouts.) How should you handle illustrations that extend partly into a column? If you have to use *callouts* (outlying captions that refer to different parts of an illustration), is there enough room for them or do you have to alter your layout?

❑ What kinds of design elements do you need, and have you planned for them in your layouts? For example, if you intend to use vertical rules to separate adjoining columns, have you left enough space between columns to include them without crowding the text? How much extra space do you need for headers and footers? Where should you position your page numbers?

❑ Have you planned for consistency? If you use drop shadows with some illustrations, for example, should you use drop shadows with all your illustrations? Are box lines and rule lines of the same thicknesses on facing pages and throughout the document? Are the same type sizes used in the same way on all pages throughout your publication?

Answering these kinds of questions ahead of time helps you set up PageMaker's nonprinting guides to establish a consistent and uniform structure. You then use this underlying framework as a guide for placing text and graphics. A carefully implemented grid prepared in advance does much to give your publications a professional look that otherwise would be difficult to achieve.

Making the Story Fit

The best way to make your stories fit is to monitor character count as you go along. If you determine beforehand how many characters fit on a line and how many lines fit on a page, you can calculate how many characters you should allocate for any story. Remember, to be accurate, your character counts must include punctuation marks, spaces, letters, and numbers.

Be aware that story fit also is affected by other variables, such as using different font types, sizes, and styles, and assigning different line leading and paragraph spacing. As you change these variables, you must adjust character count accordingly. Inline graphics also influence the copy-fitting process.

You occasionally may be tempted to alter a carefully planned layout to make room for a few extra sentences or paragraphs. Don't—almost any story can be made to fit with careful and critical editing. If further editing will hurt your story, make slight adjustments in tracking, word spacing, leading, and hyphenation to achieve a fit. If that fails, you can condense headlines by rewriting them or reducing their size, crop artwork and photos for a tighter fit, reduce the size and spacing of captions and credit lines, and reduce the fixed spacing between paragraphs.

Tip

If a story that needs cutting contains a supplementary topic, extract the supplementary text and set the text apart from the story in a *sidebar*. A sidebar is a separate block of text, usually framed and background-shaded a light gray to distinguish the sidebar from the main story. You then can cut from the main story any transitional text introducing that topic.

As you create your layouts, keep alert for *widows*, single or partial words left dangling at the bottoms of paragraphs or columns. Also watch out for *orphans*, single or partial words or last lines of paragraphs carried over into following columns. Widows and orphans cause breaks in continuity that can interrupt a reader's concentration (see fig. 10.3).

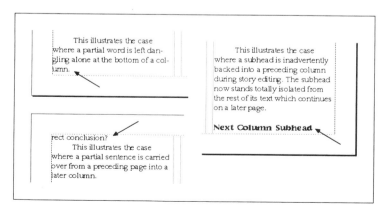

Fig. 10.3

Examples of widows and orphans.

Using White Space

White space is a design element in its own right. You can use white space the same way you use a headline, rule, box, or illustration. Effective placement of white space is as important to your layout as the use of any other design element. Every page should be at least 40 to 50 percent white space. Anything less produces a cluttered look that reduces visual appeal.

The biggest mistake you can make is to try to fit too much onto your pages. Including white space as a mandatory design element helps you avoid overloading your pages with excessive amounts of text and graphics. However, try to confine large patches of white space to one or two areas on a page. Overuse of white space, like overuse of any other design element, detracts from the appearance of your publications.

When laying out your pages, use the path the reader's eye normally follows as a guide when placing white space. The first place a reader usually looks is in the middle of the page, a little less than halfway down from the top. The reader's eye typically travels from there upward, toward the right, then down across the page to the lower left corner, and finally back across the page to the lower right corner, carving out the letter Z in the process.

To use this information when preparing an advertisement or flier, you can place the dominant element, such as a graphic or headline, where the reader first looks—in the upper center of the page. Display your closing statement, such as a sale price or discount coupon, in the lower right corner. Leave plenty of white space in the upper left of the page and elsewhere to reinforce the anticipated path of eye travel (see fig. 10.4).

Fig. 10.4

The reader's eye normally follows a "Z" pattern when looking at a page for the first time.

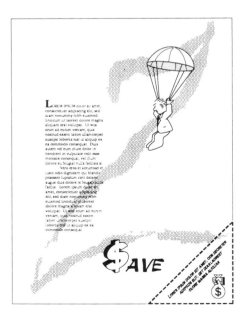

The liberal use of white space contributes to an elegant, expensive look in business documents. A generous amount of white space also achieves an open, casual look in advertising copy. White space also gives you more creative freedom when designing your page layouts. Because white space is light, confine excess white space to the upper parts of your pages.

Tip

When you lay out a publication longer than one page, view your work in the facing-pages mode so that you can see what the reader will see. Look for areas where balance and symmetry are missing and use white space as a compositional element to help correct deficiencies. Remember that the reader never sees only one page unless that page is the front or back cover.

Using Contrast, Balance, and Symmetry

Designers of the most eye-catching publications boldly use contrast to focus attention on their pages. *Contrast* can be a matter of juxtaposing big illustrations beside small ones, fancy lettering beside plain, and dark areas beside light. Contrast also can be as straightforward as using graphics to enliven text (see fig. 10.5). You can use contrast to draw attention to a particular area of a page or to highlight an important item. Contrast often results from your choice of a dominant page element (headline, text, or graphic), but sometimes contrast results from more subtle uses, like setting important text in bold or italic type. Introducing contrast into your publications always makes them more interesting.

Contrast emphasizes disparity; *balance* represents the equal and harmonious distribution of weight within an environment. Because the weights on your pages are made up of visual elements, balance includes the attributes of shape, shade, and size. You can achieve balance in your layouts by offsetting asymmetrical elements with symmetrical ones, darker images with lighter ones, and one large shape with several smaller ones.

Contrast and balance work hand-in-hand. The need for contrast, for example, may dictate a mixture of large and small graphics, but the requirements of balance demand a harmonious arrangement of those graphics on the page.

Fig. 10.5

Strong graphics and bold type can add contrast to pages.

> ### The Luis Pabon
> ### Theatre Dance Company
>
> The Luis Pabon Theatre Dance Company, a concert group of students from the Luis Pabon Dance Arts Centre, was formed in 1974 under the artistic direction of Mr. Luis Pabon. One of Mr. Pabon's continuing goals is to provide entertainment for charitable and community organizations and activites throughout Southeastern Connecticut while at the same time giving his intermediate and advanced students an opportunity to experience the excitement of live performing. Mr. Pabon feels that it's important for all his dancers to obtain stage exposure while dancing as part of a group. Also, and more importantly, he teaches his students to take responsibility for their own lives and careers. The major achievement of the Luis Pabon Theatre Dance company has been to prepare those students who have the desire and ambition to become dancers to successfully enter the world of professional dance.
>
> Since its early beginnings in 1974, the Luis Pabon Theatre Dance Company has performed hundreds of times. The **Stars of Tomorrow Shows** held in both New York City and Las Vegas, the **National Association of Dance and Affiliated Artists Showcase** in New York City, the **Norwich Rose Arts Festival**, the **Country Western Festival**, **Waterford Week**, the **Lebanon Fair**, the **Rochester Fair** in New Hampshire, **Woodstock Fair**, **Willimantic's 150th Anniversary**, **EXPOs '80, '81 and '82**, the **National Banker's Convention** in Lake Placid, New York, and countless benefit shows for organizations and individuals represent only a few of the many performances given in over 15 years of fine family entertainment.
>
> Early in 1986 the Luis Pabon Theatre Dance Company became a National Finalist in both the **Showstopper National Talent** and **Encore National Talent Competitions** where they won six First Place awards. Later that summer they acquired two additional First Place awards at the **Stars of Tomorrow Show National Competition** in Orlando, Florida. During their spectacular 1987-1988 season they captured over 50 First Place awards at the **On Stage America** and **Eastern Performing Arts Competitions** held in New Jersey and Pennsylvania. In starting off their 1988-1989 season, the Luis Pabon Theatre Dance Company won 29 First Place awards at the recent **Star Talent System National Competition** in Bowie, Maryland, earning them the right to compete in the upcoming **Grand Championships** to be held this July in Washington, D.C.

Tip

Always consider balance when laying out facing pages (see fig. 10.6). For example, place running heads and page numbers near the outside margins on both facing pages. This placement balances those pages attractively and makes the running heads and page numbers easier to locate as readers flip through your publication.

Symmetry is the individual and artful arrangement of elements on the page. Too much symmetry, in which everything looks uniform and regimented, can make pages look dull and uninteresting. For example, placing blurbs, quotations, or drop caps in the same spot on every page quickly bores your readers.

Balance brings harmony; symmetry affects mood. An asymmetrical arrangement can exhibit perfect balance, even while dramatically shifting emphasis among elements for heightened contrast (see fig. 10.7). Balancing a layout is like Japanese bonsai, the fine art of pruning and shaping trees. As you contemplate one of these masterpieces, you see that the destabilizing asymmetry of the individual branches is balanced by the wholeness of the tree.

Balanced Facing Pages

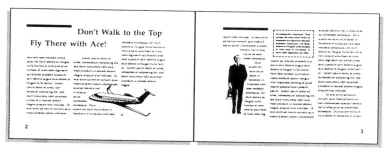

Unbalanced Facing Pages

Fig. 10.6

Balanced pages are more appealing than unbalanced pages.

Fig. 10.7

An asymmetrical arrangement sometimes is most effective.

> ### *Tip*
>
> Asymmetrical layouts are more difficult to manage than symmetrical ones. Symmetrical layouts have an easily identifiable center of gravity on the page about which you can place your elements. The center of gravity for an asymmetrical layout may lie somewhere off the page; you have to use white space as a counterbalancing design element. If you are not practiced at such arrangements, your compositions may look awkward and forced. In your first designs, strive for symmetry in your layouts, and you will enjoy more consistently rewarding results.

Creating Headlines

Without an effective headline, your readers may never consider your convincing argument, discover your well-written insights, or be persuaded to buy your superior product. A powerful headline is the irresistible bait you use to hook a reader's attention.

Make your headlines larger than your body text and set them in a contrasting typeface. Emphasizing headlines in bold type also helps. Headlines must be brief to fit within allowable copy space; however, that doesn't mean they should be dull. Your headlines should announce grandly, admonish severely, sparkle with wit, and call attention to themselves in every way possible. Headlines, like any other text, must be read to be effective. After all, what good is bait on a hook if the bait is ignored?

Here are a few important rules to follow if you want your headlines to work:

❑ Ideal type sizes for headlines range from 48 to 72 points. Headlines set in larger sizes become difficult to comprehend immediately at normal reading distances. Headlines set in smaller sizes lose their impact. This constraint on large type sizes doesn't apply to banners—banners are identifying logos and you can treat them like graphics. This constraint also doesn't apply in cases in which a headline normally is read at a distance of more than about two feet, as with newspapers displayed on a sidewalk newsstand. You need overly large headlines just to catch the attention of the people hurrying by.

❑ Don't capitalize every word in a headline. Capitalize only the most important words, leaving subordinate words in lowercase. Capitalizing every word slows reading comprehension. Never set headlines in all caps unless they are only one or two words long. Text set in all caps is difficult to read because the eye isn't accustomed to seeing words displayed that way. Words are recognized as much by their shapes as by their letters (see fig. 10.8). When you set text in all caps, you eradicate recognizable outlines, leaving only constant-height letter groupings. Using upper- and lowercase letters leads to pattern recognition, which makes the text easier to read.

ALL MERCHANDISE PRICES SLASHED!

All Caps—Difficult to Read

All Merchandise Prices Slashed!

Upper and Lowercase—Easier to Read

Fig. 10.8

The eye uses word patterns as an aid to word recognition.

❑ Don't use overly decorative type unless specifically called for by the theme of your publication. Headlines should contrast with body copy, but not to the point that they become the entire center of attention. A headline's purpose is to stimulate interest in what follows.

❑ Don't use several contrasting headlines on the same page. You don't want your headlines to compete among themselves for reader attention. Only one headline should dominate any given page.

❑ Make your headlines as compact as possible. Kern individual letters as necessary to produce an even appearance, but not so much that serifs touch. Never justify a headline in an attempt to make the headline fit a particular space—justifying usually produces uneven and unsightly character spacing.

❑ In earlier chapters, you learn that you can import text saved in PICT or EPS format and stretch the text to fill a given space. Avoid this practice except for special effect. Stretching text distorts the regularity of the letterforms and reduces legibility.

❑ Above all, make your headlines count by writing them with the reader in mind. For example, don't create headlines such as the following:

XYZ Company Announces New Product for Controlling Baldness

Congress Cites Need for Additional Funding To Help Curb Hunger

Nobody really cares about XYZ Company or Congressional commentary. Such headlines succeed only in producing yawns. Instead, make your headlines interesting by stressing features and benefits or by focusing on strong elements that provoke immediate reader reaction.

For example, you can rewrite these headlines as follows:

New Breakthrough Stops Hair Loss!

Tax Increase Proposed in Fight against Hunger

Let each of your headlines clearly tell a story. Keep in mind that your headlines are likely to be remembered long after their accompanying articles are forgotten.

Tip

Many headlines span multiple columns. You create these headlines as individual text blocks and later drag them into place above their articles. To ensure consistent spacing, use PageMaker's square-corner rectangle tool to draw a box the same height as the space you want between the headlines and your body copy. Store the box on the pasteboard and then drag the box onto your pages when you need to position a new headline. This trick also works for positioning illustration captions accurately.

Using Type Effectively

Mixing different but compatible type styles (for headlines, subheads, and body text) helps break up a page and make the page more interesting. Mixing different type styles is especially important in newsletters and magazines, where dull pages often are dominated by nearby advertisements. You also can reduce the need for expensive color through careful use of bold type and other style variations to provide necessary contrast.

Another effective type-related design element is the *pull quote*. Pull quotes are short segments of text extracted from stories and set apart on the page. Pull quotes most often are set in larger point sizes in bold or bold-italic styles and are bracketed by horizontal rules. Pull quotes highlight important topics of interest and help break up long blocks of text. They also add contrast to your pages (see fig. 10.9).

Sometimes boxing your text with light background shading for increased emphasis works well. Sidebars in magazines and newsletters are typical examples of boxed and shaded text. Often the boxed type is set in a different point size from the main story. For additional impact, use reversed type set against a dark gray or black background. This technique works best with short segments of text set in large point sizes.

Whether you're preparing headlines, subheads, captions, pull quotes, or body text, always pick fonts and type styles that suit your publication's theme. Documents facilisi. Lorem ipsum dolor sit amet, consectetuer adipiscing elit, sed diam nonummy nibh euismod tincidunt ut laoreet dolore magna aliquam erat volutpat. Ut wisi enim ad minim veniam, quis nostrud exerci tation ullamcorper suscipit lobortis nisl ut aliquip ex ea commodo consequat. Duis autem vel eum iriure dolor in hendrerit in vulputate velit esse molestie consequat, vel illum dolore eu feugiat nulla facilisis at vero eros et accumsan et iusto odio dignissim qui blandit praesent luptatum zzril delenit augue duis dolore te feugait nulla facilisi.

Lorem ipsum dolor sit amet, consectetuer adipiscing elit, sed diam nonummy nibh euismod tincidunt ut laoreet dolore magna aliquam erat volutpat. Ut wisi enim ad minim veniam, quis nostrud exerci tation ullamcorper suscipit lobortis nisl ut aliquip ex ea commodo consequat. Duis autem vel eum iriure dolor in hendrerit in vulputate velit esse molestie consequat, vel illum dolore eu feugiat nulla facilisis at vero

blandit praesent luptatum zzril delenit augue duis dolore te feugait nulla facilisi. Lorem ipsum dolor sit amet, consectetuer adipiscing elit, sed diam nonummy nibh euismod tincidunt ut laoreet dolore magna aliquam erat volutpat. Ut wisi enim ad minim veniam, quis nostrud exerci tation ullamcorper suscipit lobortis nisl ut

" Concise but descriptive pull quotes stimulate reader interest. "

aliquip ex ea commodo consequat. Duis autem vel eum iriure dolor in hendrerit in vulputate velit esse molestie consequat, vel illum dolore eu feugiat nulla facilisis at vero eros et accumsan et iusto odio dignissim qui blandit praesent luptatum zzril delenit augue duis dolore te feugait nulla facilisi. Nam liber tempor cum

Fig. 10.9

Well-placed pull quotes can help draw a reader's attention to a story.

identical in every way except the fonts used can look completely different from one another and can convey completely different messages to your readers.

Every typeface has a unique personality (one reason they're called type "faces"). Figure 10.10 shows several typefaces that project different personalities. The examples in figure 10.10 have obvious differences, but even subtle differences in type characteristics often dramatically affect the overall look of a page. Because font selection is critical to the acceptance of your work, take time to study how successful publications are typeset. Becoming type literate helps you improve the effectiveness of your publications.

Tip

When you use tiny type, avoid fonts that combine thick and thin strokes. These fonts look elegant at larger sizes, but they tend to fall apart at smaller sizes. Unless you output your pages on a Linotronic, the thin strokes often break up, making the type difficult to read.

Using Attention-Getting Graphics

Graphics are an effective tool for sparking reader interest. Select your graphics (illustrations, charts, graphs, and so on) to provide additional information to help

Fig. 10.10

*Different typefaces
convey different
impressions.*

readers more fully understand the information you present. However, be careful not to use meaningless illustrations; every graphic should have a specific purpose and should be related to your text.

Place your graphics close to where you reference them in your stories. Many readers skim through publications, stopping to read only those pages where an illustration appears. The longer your readers pause to look at a picture, the better chance you have of getting them to read the accompanying text.

The size of a graphic often affects its placement on the page. You usually can position large graphics at the top or bottom of the page with equally good results. If a graphic is less than a third of the height of the page, however, place the graphic near the top of the page.

Graphics that span multiple columns sometimes cause reader confusion when centered in the middle of the page. Such placement makes finding where a broken column of text continues difficult for your readers. Narrow graphics, on the other hand, usually work well within any column width but are less effective if placed in the exact center of the page. Heavy and dark graphics do best when they sit at the bottom of the page. Light, airy graphics do better near the top of the page.

Tip

When you include several graphics on the same page, make the most important one the largest to help establish the correct hierarchy in your reader's mind.

Avoid framing graphics unless absolutely necessary. Most illustrations can stand alone without boxes around them; adding frames only dilutes their effectiveness. At times, however, you want to frame illustrations for the sake of formality, especially photographs. In such cases, thin, simple frames usually suffice. But other designs also may prove effective (see fig. 10.11). Be careful not to use overly heavy, ornate frames. They draw attention away from the illustrations they contain.

Fig. 10.11

Different frames created within PageMaker produce strikingly different visual effects for the same image.

When a reader stops to look at an illustration, you gain another opportunity to set a hook. Use concise captions with your illustrations to encourage further reading. Captions should relate your illustrations to your stories in ways that stimulate reader interest. The more thought-provoking your captions, the better.

Using Boxes, Rules, and Other Design Elements

Boxes, rules, drop caps, shadows, and other design elements are embellishments that dress up a publication and give the publication a distinctive look. Using design elements is like wearing a colorful tie or a beautiful pair of earrings. They help identify the uniqueness of your publication.

However, design elements shouldn't be used just for the sake of distinctiveness. To be effective, each design element should perform a specific task. For example, if your publication uses running heads on each page, you can create a composite design element by overlaying reverse type on a heavy, black rule. However, the same need also can be addressed in dozens of other ways using many different design approaches. Pick an approach that is best suited to the style of your publication.

Boxes and rules are eminently practical tools. You can use them to set off text and graphics to help bring organization to your pages. Partitioning pages with boxes and rules creates meaningful information groups (such as delineating ad copy from editorial copy) and helps focus reader attention on particular items (such as advertisements, pull quotes, illustrations, and announcements).

Shadows, fills, and reversals enable you to emphasize the relative importance of elements on your pages. They add strong visual accents to blocks of text and graphics. You lightly shade boxed sidebars, for example, to stress the importance of the copy they contain. You use drop shadows to make photos and text leap off the page.

Ornaments are another effective design tool. They range from old-fashioned typographers' ornaments—intricate splashes of artwork—to the modern Zapf Dingbats font characters found in most PostScript laser printers. You can use ornaments decoratively to heighten the visual appeal of your pages or more practically as bullets, check boxes, and stylized pointers to focus information groupings. The choice depends on the nature of your publication. Even when used purely for decoration, however, ornaments always should blend seamlessly with the rest of your publication.

Think of design elements as tools you can use to accomplish specific layout tasks. For example, if your columns crowd one another, you can widen the space between them. You also can place a vertical hairline rule between each pair of column guides, box each column, or apply light background shading to alternate columns. The task in each case is to distinguish more clearly one column from another. You want to make reading the text easier.

> ### *Tip*
>
> Boxed elements generally look best when the spacing between the box and the element contained is equal on all four sides.

You have a multitude of different design elements at your disposal, but that doesn't mean you have to use them all at the same time. In most cases, be conservative. Pick and choose carefully. Don't try to crowd too much onto your pages, or your publication may end up looking like a child's scrapbook.

Keep in mind that design elements have intrinsic character, just as typefaces have personality. For example, thin, double rules used as square-cornered frames add a classical touch to any page. Although they may be suitable for formal business documents, they may be totally inappropriate for other kinds of correspondence, such as wedding invitations, in which the type and illustrations are gently curved. Use design elements to complement your publications, not to compete with them.

> ### *Tip*
>
> Select rule thicknesses to match the stroke weights of your fonts; avoid mixing light-weight rules with strong fonts and heavy-weight rules with delicate fonts. For example, if you use a finely stroked serif font, a thin hairline rule may be your best choice. If you use a boldface sans serif font, a much thicker, heavier rule is called for. If the characters in your typeface combine thin and thick strokes, use a matching double rule with thin and thick lines.

Creating Drop Caps

Book publishers have used drop caps for centuries to introduce chapters or new sections of manuscripts. The key word is introduce. Don't begin every new paragraph with a large initial or drop cap. Drop caps, like any other design element, should be used sparingly. Let them add flair to your pages without overpowering the text.

Capitalizing the first few words in the first line after a drop cap is customary and provides a smooth transition into the text that follows. Modern usage frequently ignores this convention, but as a design technique, capitalizing the first few words in the first line after a drop cap lends subtle sophistication to your pages. If you choose to capitalize part of the first line, reduce the type size of the caps or use small caps to make the transition to the following text more gradual.

Drop caps can be as ornate as the ones used in medieval manuscripts or as sleek as the ones in a modern news magazine (see fig. 10.12). You can place shadows behind drop caps or wrap text around them, as you can do with graphics. You can box them, or have them stand alone. Most often, you want them to rise above the top of a paragraph, but you also can completely embed them in the text. In all cases, when using a drop cap, do not indent the first line of the paragraph.

If you use heavy, black letters as drop caps, or if your drop caps have rounded bases, like O's, U's, and S's, let them sink slightly below the baseline of adjoining text. If your drop caps have square bottoms, however, like E's, H's, and L's, be careful to align them so that their baselines are even with the baselines of adjoining text. Avoid drop caps that hover above the baseline. When in doubt, use a horizontal ruler guide to ensure accurate placement.

Fig. 10.12

Drop caps can add interest to your pages.

To create a drop cap using existing text in PageMaker, do the following:

1. Select the first two lines of the paragraph in which you intend to create the drop cap and manually set the leading the same as PageMaker's auto-leading (unless you already have assigned fixed leading to the entire paragraph). This process keeps your lines from spreading when you enlarge the initial cap.

2. Select the first character of your paragraph and enlarge that character by choosing a new point size from the Type Size menu or Type Specifications dialog box. A point size three times the existing type size usually is a good starting point.

3. Add any styling, such as bold or italic. Choose a different font type if appropriate.

Note

When you first enlarge an initial cap, the upper part of the character may not show on-screen. Switching to another view in PageMaker and back again causes the screen to refresh and properly display the full character.

---

4. Change the first few words of the first line (not the whole line) to all caps. Then manually kern the text immediately following the drop cap for a proper fit.

To create a drop cap using an imported PICT, EPS, or bit-mapped letter graphic, do the following:

1. Import the letter graphic using the Place command from the File menu.

2. Using the Text Wrap command from the Element menu, assign a text-wrap boundary and specify a standoff distance. If you prefer text to conform to the shape of the letter, customize the boundary.

3. Drag the letter graphic into position at the beginning of the paragraph. Work in an enlarged 200 or 400 percent view for accurate placement. Use the leftmost column guide along with a horizontal ruler guide to align the letter with the left edge of the text and the adjoining text baseline. The text reflows around the letter graphic. Make any necessary adjustments to the text-wrap boundary.

4. Delete the first letter of the paragraph (the one you replaced with the letter graphic) and change the next few words to all caps.

Creating Drop Shadows

Drop shadows are offset shaded areas you place behind framed illustrations, text, or other design elements. Drop shadows help create an illusion of depth.

Drop shadows can be any size and shape. You can offset them a little or a lot, and in any direction. Typically, drop shadows are black or gray, rectangular in shape, and slightly offset to focus attention on whatever elements lie in front of them. Because drop shadows create such a strong visual accent, they should be used sparingly, and only where you need to focus reader attention. Drop shadows are used in several illustrations throughout this book. See figures 10.7 and 10.10 for typical examples.

To create a drop shadow, do the following:

1. Select any of PageMaker's rectangular or oval drawing tools and draw a shape the same size or slightly larger than the element to which you want to add the shadow.

Note

If a graphic or block of text to which you want to add a drop shadow is transparent, you first must place a paper-colored shape of the same size behind it. Otherwise, when you add the drop shadow, the dark shading shows through and obscures whatever lies in the foreground.

---

2. Assign the desired shade or color and a border line thickness (or None) to the shape and then drag the shape into position over the original element. Offset the shape slightly in the direction you want the shape to show.

3. With the shape still selected, choose Send To Back from the Element menu. Your drop shadow now is in place. If minor adjustments in size or position are needed, scale or move the drop shadow like any other graphic.

Using Electronic Whiteout

Electronic whiteout is the equivalent of liquid correction fluid, the indispensable white stuff used in offices around the world to make corrections. In PageMaker, electronic whiteout is nothing more than lines and shapes the same color as your paper (usually white). You can use electronic whiteout to do many things, including touching up graphics and adding visual accents to text. One common use for electronic whiteout is to square off the ends of ragged rows of lines or leader dots.

To apply electronic whiteout, draw any shape using one of PageMaker's drawing tools. Assign your shape the color Paper from the Shades menu and a line width of None from the Lines menu. Drag the shape into position to "erase" what lies beneath. You also can use reverse lines as electronic whiteout. Draw a line, assign any width, and then choose Reverse Line from the Lines menu.

Electronic whiteout is a powerful design tool. You can use electronic whiteout to create patterns and designs right in PageMaker. Experiment to discover the possibilities (see fig. 10.13).

Tip

You can create custom electronic-whiteout patterns using reversed text. For example, reversing typed symbols, such as the symbols contained in Zapf Dingbats (a font built into most laser printers), gives you an almost endless variety of shapes to work with for touching up your pages. Symbols and other special type characters also can be combined in many different ways to produce innovative-looking designs. By using different type sizes for these characters, you can control precisely the results you get.

This eye-catching tic-tac-toe game uses simple reversed lines and shapes over a black background.

Use reversed lines over bold type for dramatic results.

You can create complex patterns in just seconds using only PageMaker's basic drawing tools.

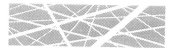

This wave border is a single line of Zapf Dingbats characters (Option-8) reversed and centered vertically along the upper edge of a black rectangle.

Fig. 10.13

Selective use of electronic whiteout adds pizzazz to your publications.

Using Templates

With preformatted templates, you can produce publications more quickly and with less effort than you could if you had to build each new layout from scratch. Well-designed templates also give your publications more consistency. Another advantage is that preformatted templates help employees who have little or no design experience become more productive within a shorter period of time.

Using Prepackaged Templates

Prepackaged templates enable you to create professional-looking documents without spending a long apprenticeship learning advanced design techniques. Because most of the preliminary layout work already is done, all you have to do is drop in text and graphics. With just a little additional customizing, you can produce finished publications in a fraction of the time it otherwise might take. Among the best templates you can find anywhere are the ones from Aldus.

Aldus supplies a collection of basic templates with PageMaker that covers a wide assortment of publishing needs. Included are templates for brochures, business reports, executive summary sheets, memos, newsletters, product specification sheets, some overhead transparencies, and other useful documents. Several of these templates include style sheets that you can import into your own publications. Consider these templates a starter kit and use them accordingly. Build on and refine the templates until you have made them your own.

Aldus also markets several template packages, including Designs for Newsletters, Designs for Business Communications, and Designs for Manuals. These portfolios contain a variety of templates, each saved with specific defaults intended to make them easy to use. Style sheets also are included.

The Designs for Newsletters portfolio, for example, contains 21 different newsletter templates. The manual guides you step-by-step through a detailed practice session to familiarize you with using templates. You then can choose the type of newsletter that most nearly matches your preferred publication style and follow the specific guidelines for placing your text and graphics. Aldus provides character counts for preformatted story lengths so that you can prepare your stories to fit.

Each of the other design portfolios is similar in composition. The Designs for Business Communications portfolio contains several templates in traditional and contemporary formats for each of six different kinds of publications, including proposals, reports, handbooks, overhead transparencies, memos, and business plans. The Designs for Manuals portfolio contains 10 templates designed specifically for preparing books, manuals, and other long publications. Both accompanying manuals are filled with insights and advanced tips aimed at helping you produce quality publications with little or no prior experience.

Creating and Working with Templates

When you create a publication, you are creating a template. To convert your publication into a template, save the publication as a template by clicking **Save as template** in the Save As dialog box.

Before saving your publication as a template, replace existing graphics with shaded boxes and text with dummy text. (The Lorem Ipsum text file included with PageMaker is perfect for use as dummy text; you see the Lorem Ipsum file in many illustrations in this book.) What these placeholders look like doesn't matter, but you should strip them of any meaning so that you can concentrate on the form of your layout instead of on its content. Publication content may change frequently, but your layouts, as dictated by your templates, should change very little. As you create your templates, be sure to make full use of your publication's master pages to handle repeating elements such as rules and non-printing guides.

You replace graphic placeholders with imported illustrations by clicking **Replacing entire graphic** in the Place Document dialog box. When you import graphics this way, PageMaker scales them to fit within the existing placeholder boundaries. Adjust the graphics afterward as necessary to regain original proportions, crop unwanted areas, or configure for optimal printing.

Tip

A convenient template trick when using wrap-around text in publications is to customize the standoff boundaries of your placeholders, making minor adjustments when you import graphics later. If you click the **Replacing entire graphic** button when you import your graphics, the graphics replace the selected placeholders and assume the same standoff boundaries.

Text placeholders work the same way as graphics placeholders. You replace them with your stories by clicking **Replacing entire story** in the Place Document dialog box.

Text placeholders often have specific styles assigned. If you prefer to use an imported style, click the **Retain Formatting** option in the Place Document dialog box. If styles imported from your word processor have names matching styles in the template style sheet, PageMaker uses the template styles. If the names don't match, PageMaker uses the imported styles. If you import your stories as text-only files, PageMaker uses the assigned placeholder styles.

You generally do not import text to replace headlines, subheads, captions, and other short segments. Selecting these elements with the text tool and typing the replacement text is easier. Whatever you type takes on the same styling as the original placeholders.

Templates are easy to create and use. They greatly speed preparing your layouts and cut production time enormously.

Note

When you open a template, open a copy (PageMaker's default selection), not the original. The original remains unaltered for use another time. Click **Original** in the Open Publication dialog box only to modify the template.

Avoiding Layout Mistakes

No rigid rules govern layout design. The layout for one publication may vary enormously from the layout of another, depending on personal taste and the requirements of the publication. New desktop publishers, however, often make several common mistakes. Avoiding these mistakes will help your publication look more professional.

❏ Don't make your columns too wide or too narrow. At either extreme, text becomes difficult to read. Try to keep overall line length around 50 to 60 characters (10 to 12 words) for easiest reading.

❏ Don't use too large or too small a type size. Type that is too large can be overpowering. Extra-large type also limits the amount of information you can include on your pages. Type that is too small makes reading your publication difficult for people with weak vision. Start with 12-point type for body copy and then scale the type size up or down. Do a series of test prints. Try to find a size that is easy to read, yet still fits within the constraints of your layout.

❏ Pick your fonts to match your message. Keep in mind that each font has a unique personality. A delicate typeface with flourishes or extra-thin serifs, for example, conveys sensitivity and sophistication. A chunky sans serif typeface implies a brute force approach to communication. Using the wrong font can drastically reduce the effectiveness of your message. Sometimes variations among similar fonts are subtle. Often, however, even tiny differences become noticeable and profoundly influence reader perception.

❏ Don't mix too many different typefaces or type styles on your pages. Limit yourself to a maximum of three different fonts. Also, avoid mixing different kinds of sans serif faces—they generally don't go well together. Avoid shadow, outline, and underline type styles. The frequent use of such styles is the hallmark of the amateur. Above all, strive for type consistency so that your publications don't look like hastily prepared ransom notes.

❑ Don't use italic type for visual emphasis. Use bold type instead. Italic doesn't stand out on a page unless the word also happens to be in bold. This rule, of course, does not always apply. You have to balance the "look" of a page against the need to make a strong statement. Sometimes downplaying type-style emphasis is more convincing, especially with an objective audience.

❑ Don't crowd your margins. Give your pages room to breathe. Without enough white space, pages look dark and uninviting. They simply don't encourage readers to spend much time on them. Treat margins and other white space as independent design elements. White space becomes an integral part of your layout, and the look of your pages does not seem forced.

❑ Don't type double spaces after periods and colons. Use single spaces. Use double spaces only with monospaced fonts like Courier. Double spaces after periods are a holdover from the days of manual typewriters, in which all typed characters were spaced equally, and double spaces had to be inserted to help the reader pause at sentence endings. Today, most computer-generated type is proportional; the computer uses built-in font metric information to set proper character spacing. This metric information includes the character widths for periods and colons, which are narrower than the widths of other characters.

❑ Avoid using straight apostrophes and quote marks. Use the curly ones instead. Never use double hyphens. Use the longer em-dashes instead.

Type	*To get*
Option-[	"
Option-Shift-[	'
Option-]	"
Option-Shift-]	'
Option-Shift-(hyphen)	—

❑ Don't place graphics having different formats side-by-side on the same page. Avoid mixing bit mapped and EPS graphics, unless you need to mix high- and low-resolution images for special effect. Also be careful about using photographs having different compositions. For example, don't place a close-up portrait photo next to a full-length seated photo. Graphics should complement each other, not clash.

❏ Don't design pages one at a time. Always work with facing pages to ensure proper balance. Also, try not to be overly uniform; otherwise, your publications look sterile.

❏ Avoid making all elements on your pages the same size. One element, whether a headline, block of text, photograph, or graphic illustration, always should dominate the other elements by being larger and bolder. Variations in size tell your readers what element is most important.

❏ Don't print your publications without a final check. Proof your work carefully so that spelling, grammar, punctuation, and factual errors don't slip by. One oversight can spoil an otherwise perfect layout.

Chapter Summary

In this chapter, you learned how to apply good layout and design techniques. You saw that achieving the right look is more than just a matter of style and that success requires careful planning.

You found that document structure is crucial to the development of organized layouts and that white space can be used effectively as a design tool. You learned that typefaces have personality and that graphic elements have character, and you discovered that the way you use them can profoundly influence reader perception. You also learned how to use design elements creatively to enhance your publications.

You discovered that prepackaged templates help you achieve design goals quickly. You also learned how to create your own templates so that you don't have to start over each time. Finally, you learned to avoid the typical mistakes desktop publishers make when laying out publications for the first time.

In the next chapter, you learn how to apply your knowledge and skills to create winning newsletters with strong reader appeal.

Designing a Newsletter

11

Today more newsletters are desktop-published than any other kind of document. Their popularity as quickly digestible sources of specialized information cannot be contested.

Most newsletters are short, averaging no more than 2 to 16 pages. Newsletters typically range from the traditional 8.5-inch-by-11-inch all-text formats to 11-inch-by-17-inch graphics-laden publications.

Newsletters usually display a banner, masthead, and fixed column format. But that does not mean that all newsletters look the same. Even when two publishers use the same template as a starting point, the newsletters they produce usually look completely different from one another.

In this chapter, you learn the basics of newsletter design. You learn how to assemble and lay out the key elements of a newsletter, including the banner, masthead, editorial text, boilerplate, and graphic-design elements. You learn how to work with different column formats and achieve consistency in your newsletter layouts. You also discover ways to apply special visual effects to add interest to your newsletters and make them more appealing to readers.

Designing the Banner and Masthead

The words *banner* and *masthead* frequently are used interchangeably to mean the front-page title or nameplate of a newsletter. However, the masthead is actually the box that contains the name and address of the publisher, editors, writers, and other staff members. The masthead also may contain the issue or volume number, subscription rates, and other pertinent information. You can think of the masthead as being the fine print of your publication (see fig. 11.1).

Fig. 11.1

The Weigand Report newsletter masthead.

The Weigand Report (ISSN 1045-019X) is published 20 times a year by Rae Productions International. A 20-issue subscription is $128 in the United States and Canada, $148 overseas (US dollars). Residents of Connecticut add 8% state sales tax. Bulk rates available upon request.

C. J. Weigand - Editor/Publisher
Jennifer Rae - Copy Editor
Pat Vitagliano - Vit-A-Print Production

© 1990. All rights reserved. Rae Productions International, P.O. Box 647, Gales Ferry, CT 06335. Reproduction in whole or in part without express written permission from the publisher is prohibited. All brand or product names mentioned from time to time in this newsletter are acknowledged to be trademarks or registered trademarks of their respective holders.

Note

The masthead in figure 11.1 shows an ISSN. The ISSN (International Standard Serial Number) is the internationally recognized code for the identification of periodicals, which includes magazines, journals, newspapers, and newsletters.

ISSNs give publishers, subscription agencies, librarians, and computer-based reference services an efficient way to glean bibliographic information about your publication. ISSNs are used when ordering, shipping, billing, and doing other control functions. The U.S. Postal Service also uses ISSNs to regulate certain publications mailed at second-class and controlled circulation rates.

An ISSN uniquely identifies a publication title. If you revise your publication, but don't change the title, the ISSN remains the same.

The Library of Congress assigns ISSNs free of charge. When requesting an ISSN for an existing publication, include a sample issue or copies of the cover, title page, and masthead as appropriate. For prepublication requests, prepare a mock-up showing the identifying parts of your publication. Later you can submit a follow-up copy of the actual publication. The Library of Congress accepts prepublication requests by telephone if publishing deadlines are pending. Additional information is available from the Library of Congress, National Serials Data Program, Washington, DC 20540, (202) 287-6452.

Laying out a masthead is easy. You arrange one or more text blocks to present the information in a hierarchical manner. Box your masthead to set it apart from the main body of your newsletter. The masthead normally appears near the beginning of a newsletter, immediately following the cover page. However, you can place the masthead anywhere you like, even at the back of your newsletter if you want to de-emphasize the information.

Banners are a different story. Whereas you may want to present your masthead in a low-key manner, you always want to make your banner highly visible. Preferably, the banner should be the dominant element on your front page. A banner should be eye-catching enough to attract reader interest, yet succinct enough to tell readers at a glance what your newsletter is all about. In that respect, you can think of your banner as a super headline.

Because the banner introduces your newsletter, you should select an appropriate typeface when designing the banner. The type style you use should complement the publication style of your newsletter. Note that you also can include a logo as part of your banner. If you include a graphic, don't make the graphic too overpowering. You want your banner to stand on its own merits (see fig. 11.2).

Fig. 11.2

The Weigand Report newsletter banner.

Tip

Design your banner in a graphics program like Adobe Illustrator or Aldus FreeHand. These programs enable you to modify the type you use to achieve special design effects, and you can give your banner a distinctive flair. Save your banner as an EPS file and import the file into PageMaker. Importing your banner as a graphic enables you to scale your banner to fit any page size without loss of resolution. The banner in figure 11.2 was prepared in FreeHand, saved as an EPS file, and imported into PageMaker.

Choosing the Right Format

Formats range from single-column sheets to multiple-column pages. Most newsletters use between two and five columns. Again, the choice of format should be dictated in part by style and in part by content.

Using a Single-Column Format

Although a single-column format is used rarely, you may want to use this type of format to emulate typewritten copy for an informal look. When you use a single-column format, you should use Courier or some other monospaced font that accurately replicates typewritten text. Be sure to increase your margins and leading. Increasing the margins makes the column lines a little shorter. That, along with increased leading, makes your copy easier to read.

To achieve a true typewritten look, you also can break one of desktop publishing's cardinal rules and occasionally use underlined type for emphasis. Using underlined type makes your newsletter look like it was produced using a typewriter (see fig. 11.3). It is a familiar look that most readers are comfortable with.

Fig. 11.3

A single-column format designed to look like a typewritten page.

Using Multiple-Column Formats

Multiple-column formats give you greater flexibility when laying out your newsletters. Arranging text and graphics is easier if you use three, four, or five columns per page instead of just one or two. You can introduce more story topics, and the shorter line lengths make your copy easier to read. You also can include more easily a variety of design elements to heighten visual contrast and stimulate reader interest.

A two-column format is the least cluttered and easiest to work with of the multiple-column formats. Although this format is not as flexible as three-, four-, and five-column formats, a two-column format yields a traditional look that is perfect for formal publications.

A three-column format, on the other hand, is currently the most popular format for newsletters. A three-column format is well suited for informal and formal publications and nicely accommodates almost any number of style variations.

A four-column format provides a more academic look than any of the other multiple-column formats. This format is ideal when hard-hitting, specialized information must be conveyed in a concise manner.

A five-column format offers the most flexibility and combines many of the advantages of three- and four-column formats into one exceptionally versatile format. Use a five-column format for periodicals that undergo frequent layout revisions.

Three-, four-, and five-column formats take careful planning to execute, but they enable you to meet rapidly changing publishing requirements on demand. For example, you can fit smaller-size graphics in narrow columns more readily than you can in the wider one- and two-column formats. (More columns also mean narrower columns.) However, you have to avoid fully justifying the text in narrow columns, or you may end up with uneven and unsightly word spacing. Wider columns are a better choice under these conditions.

If your needs are simple and you don't want to spend large amounts of time preparing complex layouts, use a simple two-column format for your newsletters. Because dual columns are fairly wide, you should choose graphics that horizontally span at least a full column's width. Use slim, vertically oriented graphics only if they are half a column or more in height. For three- and four-column layouts, vertical graphics are preferred over horizontal graphics because of the narrower columns.

If you use horizontal graphics, you can spread them over two or three column widths. Vertical graphics should span only one column. However, an exception to this rule applies when using portrait photographs, sometimes called mug shots. You may want to keep mug shots small so that the photos don't dominate your pages. Try fitting two mug shots into one column or five mug shots into two columns.

The choice of column formats greatly affects the placement of headlines. You can confine headlines to lie within single-column boundaries, or you can have headlines span multiple columns that encompass the same story line. When placing headlines within multiple-column layouts, be sure to provide sufficient clearance between each headline and any accompanying graphics. Six to eight lines of text inserted between headlines and graphics should be enough.

Place your headlines in the upper part of the page. Headlines near the bottom of the page lose their impact. Also, avoid having all your headlines start at the same level on all your pages. Too much symmetry is boring.

Tip

When placing headlines in a multiple-column layout, keep the following guidelines in mind:

1. Avoid tombstones—two (or three) headlines placed side by side. For example, a two-column headline next to a three-column headline constitutes a pair of tombstones. Readers may mistakenly try to read the two different heads as one continuous headline and become confused (see fig. 11.4).

2. Extend a story's headline over the entire story. If you have a three-column story, don't use a two-column headline.

3. Make sure that any graphics or photos covered by the headline go with the story. For example, if you have a three-column story about a town council political meeting and a two-column photo of the recent beauty pageant winner, don't run a five-column headline about the town council meeting above both. Readers expect the headline-covered photograph to relate to the story.

Fig. 11.4

Headline tombstones can cause reader confusion.

Entire Town Council Retires

In stormy protest over the Mayor's decision to reinstate the rule requiring that Town Council members reside within town limits, the entire Town Council membership has elected to retire. All members of the council are eligible for a nominal 25% retirement pension. Instead of

New Beauty Queen!

Golden City has a new beauty queen. Debbie Smith was chosen last night to be Miss Golden City as the annual Golden Fair ended a week-long celebration. Miss Smith smiled graciously as she accepted her honors. This was Smith's third straight year of participation in the

When you use multiple columns, you don't have to flow stories down each and every column. A five-column format, for example, doesn't necessarily require five columns of text. Your choice of column formats provides an underlying structure upon which you can build in a variety of ways. You can mix text and graphics over any column structure to achieve an interesting and informative layout. For example, you easily can convert a five-column format into an asymmetrical two-column layout, in which each column of text actually spans two underlying column widths, and the remaining outlying column width accommodates margin notes, pull quotes, or small illustrations.

Using Boilerplate

Boilerplate is text or graphics that remains unchanged from one issue of your newsletter to another. Boilerplate may be a declaration of editorial policy, an

---

Tip

The most difficult task you face when preparing your newsletters is to make everything fit and still have your layouts look good. When planning story lengths and determining the numbers and sizes of headlines and graphics, allow for plenty of extra space. You can manipulate any leftover space to accommodate varying content from newsletter to newsletter. Having plenty of extra space also gives you room to insert additional last-minute material.

---

address line, an order form, your masthead, or your banner. Whatever your boilerplate is, you don't want to reproduce the boilerplate from scratch for each new issue you publish. If you do, you are sure to introduce errors.

Using boilerplate adds consistency to a newsletter. If your boilerplate applies to only one publication, make the boilerplate a part of that publication's template. If your boilerplate is to be used in several different publications, save the boilerplate to your Scrapbook. After that, when you begin a new edition of your newsletter, use PageMaker's Place command to copy all your boilerplates from the Scrapbook onto the pasteboard. Drag individual items onto your pages as you need them.

Tip

Boilerplate text and graphics that you save as separate files for later placement into your newsletters can be difficult to find when you need them, especially if you bury them deep within nested folders on your hard disk. A good way to identify boilerplate files is to prefix each with the letters BP (BP.Editorial Policy and BP.Masthead, for example). The BP prefix groups all boilerplate files together and makes them easy to find.

Achieving a Consistent Look

The formality of business newsletters is enhanced by the regular and consistent placement of text and graphics. Equal margins, centered headlines, justified text, and perfectly balanced layouts all contribute to a dignified look. To stress informality on your pages, do just the opposite—introduce variety into your layouts by using uneven margins, offset headlines, unjustified text, and asymmetrical arrangements. But do so in a consistent fashion. Informality shouldn't breed disorder.

Your choice of typefaces, the placement of special editorial text, and the use of borders, rules, white space, and other design elements are all important factors to achieving consistency.

Using Type and Editorial Text

Try to limit type selection for your newsletters to traditional faces. Some of the modern display faces boast an overly stylized look that impedes reading legibility. Although such highly decorative faces may suit the theme of your newsletter, they can put off readers. Save ornate or unusual type for embellishment purposes only.

Never use more than three kinds of type, and preferably only two, in your newsletters. Also, choose contrasting faces for headlines and body text, or your headlines may not stand out from the rest of the copy. Make sure that your headlines are large enough and that your body text is a readable size. An 11-point or 12-point type usually works well for body text.

For formal newsletters, fully justify your columns of text; otherwise, keep your columns left justified (ragged right). Adjust tracking, word and letter spacing, and hyphenation as necessary to achieve a uniform dispersion of type on the page. (Be careful not to let auto-hyphenation adversely affect headlines.) If you must use all caps, as for acronyms and abbreviations, set them in small caps so that they don't dominate the surrounding text. Also make sure that all your paragraph indents are set the same.

You can add editorial refinements to your newsletters by including introductory text (sometimes called a *kicker*) above main headlines or explanatory text (sometimes called *deck heads* or *subtitles*) just below main headlines (see fig. 11.5). These special headlines help draw readers into a story by highlighting or summarizing what is to follow. When you use kickers or deck heads, set them in smaller italicized type to distinguish them from the accompanying headlines and stories and to emphasize their importance.

Fig. 11.5

Kickers and deck heads can add interest to newsletter headlines.

Bylines are credit lines for stories. Usually, bylines immediately follow story headlines, but sometimes they close stories. For consistency, set bylines in the same type style as your headlines, but in a smaller point size.

Continuations, or *jump lines*, are short sentences at the bottom of columns that tell readers where to find the rest of a story in your newsletter. Like kickers and deck heads, jump lines normally should be set in smaller, italicized type.

If your newsletters are long and include many stories, add a table of contents to the front page to help readers find the information of greatest interest to them. A table of contents also helps stimulate interest in your newsletter. Box or highlight the table of contents. Use a different type style to set the list apart from your stories. Double-spacing the entries in a table of contents also helps differentiate the table from your main text.

Using Borders and Rules

Use borders and rules sparingly to segregate or highlight important text and graphics. Use these graphic elements to add emphasis when emphasis is needed, but avoid overusing them. Otherwise, your newsletters may become cluttered. Most publications look better if you use only a few carefully chosen design elements.

To help focus attention on your pages, consider adding a hairline border around the entire margin. For improved readability, use vertical hairline rules to separate stories in adjoining columns. Use thicker rules to separate horizontal rows of text. Set graphics apart with frames to highlight them but keep the line widths narrow. Hairline rules often are the best choice, unless special emphasis is required.

If you use borders or rules on one page, use them the same way on all pages. Keep the spacing between these elements and any nearby text and graphics consistent throughout your newsletter.

Tip

Boxing a graphic within a graphic to create an insert is an effective way to show how the bigger graphic (usually an enlarged section of the smaller graphic) relates to the smaller one (see fig. 11.6). This technique works especially well with photos. Use at least a one-point line thickness for the frame so that readers notice the smaller graphic.

Don't forget the importance of white space. Think of white space as the one element that can provide the most contrast for your pages. If you visit a museum, the most dominant element is the open space—on the floor and walls. All that open space emphasizes the importance of the few sculptures and paintings on display. If you completely filled the floor and the walls with works of art, how would you ever notice any one statue or painting?

Fig. 11.6

Graphic inserts help to raise the informational content of illustrations.

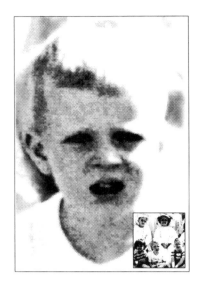

Using Special Visual Effects

Popular visual effects include screens, reverse type, and other custom elements. Like any other embellishment, special effects should be used cautiously. A little design emphasis goes a long way when trying to capture and focus reader attention. Too much of a good thing, however, reduces the appeal of your publication.

Using Screens

You can use screens as backdrops to highlight text and graphics (see fig. 11.7). To create a screen, draw a shape using any of PageMaker's drawing tools and then fill the shape with a selection from the Fill menu. In most instances, you should use the lightest shades —10 or 20 percent. Darker shadings reproduce poorly on a 300 dpi laser printer and obscure whatever lies in front of them.

When you place a screen behind a block of text or an illustration, choose a line width of None from the Lines menu. Unless the screen also is to serve as a frame, you rarely have to add a border. Framed screens generally have less appeal than unframed ones.

Using Reverse Type

In small doses, reverse type can prove effective. When used as a design element, reverse type adds contrast to your pages and calls attention to items of significance. Reverse type also makes locating important information quick and easy (see the

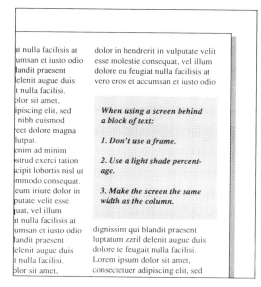

Fig. 11.7

Placing a light screen behind a block of text helps emphasize its importance.

descriptive subtitle in the masthead in fig. 11.2). But in large doses, like the little shepherd boy who cried "wolf," reverse type loses its effectiveness quickly. If too many items compete for attention at the same time, the reader tends to overlook them all.

Because reverse type sometimes is difficult to read, take special care to ensure legibility. Set reverse type in bold, and use sans serif type in large point sizes. Making reversed text bold helps keep individual characters from filling in during printing; setting reversed text in large point sizes helps the text stand out from the dark background. Keep reversed text short and to the point and use upper- and lowercase lettering for better reading legibility.

Using Photographs

Photographs have enormous reader appeal and are especially important for newsletters. Often a photograph can convey more information than many pages of text and certainly more information than most hand-drawn graphics. You already have learned how to resize, reshape, crop, and enhance photographs in earlier chapters. However, you should consider three additional items when using photos in newsletters—dealing with halftones, including captions and credits, and cropping for impact.

Using Halftones

Most newsletters benefit from the inclusion of scanned photographs. But sometimes scanned images are not good enough for important publications. To get crisp, unfuzzy photographs into your newsletters, your commercial printer must strip in the photographs using traditional methods.

If you print scanned images on a Linotronic, you may end up paying as much as if your commercial printer pasted up your photos by hand. TIFF files take such a long time to print on a Linotronic; doing halftone camera shots of your photos and pasting them up in the traditional manner may prove less costly. If you opt for paste-up, scan your photographs anyway and place them in your newsletter as low-resolution files. This placement shows where and how each photo should appear in the final printout and serves as a guide to your printer for image cropping. This guide also helps your printer match each photo with its correct caption.

Using Captions and Credits

When you include photographs in your newsletters, you should provide descriptive captions. Captions help explain your photographs and direct reader attention to the accompanying stories.

Allow space to include a credit line in small type next to each photo. Never use photographs without permission. To be safe, get a signed release from each recognizable person in any photograph you use. Also, make sure that you have written authorization from the photographer.

Cropping for Impact

Photographs and artwork used in newsletters often can be improved by selective cropping. Space generally is at a premium, and cropping helps to conserve space while tightening reader focus.

To *crop* an image is to trim the image on one or more sides, just as if cutting along the edge with a pair of scissors. If you intend to scan an illustration, cropping beforehand means less work later if you have to clean up the image. Cropping also means greatly reduced memory and storage requirements. If you plan to scan an image that already exists in electronic form, you generally can use PageMaker to do the necessary trimming.

Surrounding clutter adds little to an image, generally detracts from reader interest, and impedes getting your message across. Get rid of the clutter. Force each picture to tell a story. A tightly cropped illustration is a more forceful illustration (see fig. 11.8).

You can better visualize the overall effects of cropping by first using a pair of cropping guides to block out specific areas of interest. To crop an image, do the following:

1. Import your illustration into PageMaker. The picture in figure 11.8A, for example, is a piece of bit-mapped clip art.

Fig. 11.8

*Cropping an
illustration for
greater impact.*

2. The guides in figure 11.8B are simple polygons. You create the guides in MacDraw and save them as PICT images to the Scrapbook. You then import these guides into PageMaker, resize them, and click-drag them about on your pages to get a better idea of how you want images to look before actually cropping them.

3. When you are satisfied with the look of an illustration, use PageMaker's cropping tool to trim the excess image (see fig. 11.8C).

4. As often happens when cropping an image, part of the unwanted artwork lies within the cropping boundaries. Use electronic whiteout (a white-filled rectangle with no lines) to hide the excess, in this example the tree leaves (see fig. 11.8D).

5. As you crop an image, you also should enlarge the image. Zeroing in on a smaller area of a picture without simultaneously enlarging the picture yields a smaller picture. The results may be underwhelming at best. If that is what you want, fine. But if you want your illustrations to be noticed, enlarge them after cropping (see fig. 11.8E). Enlarging helps restore enough visual clout to garner reader attention.

Chapter Summary

In this chapter, you learned how to combine the diverse elements of a newsletter into a unified whole and produce pages your readers find appealing. You discovered the importance of design consistency when doing effective layouts, and you learned new ways to enhance the look of your pages.

In the next chapter, you learn how to design many other kinds of publications, ranging from brochures and fliers to catalogs and books.

12

Designing Other Publications

Now that you have mastered the basics of working with PageMaker and learned how to prepare quality layouts, you should consider ways to put that knowledge to work. This chapter provides an introduction to some of the many different publications you can produce using PageMaker. You learn approaches for designing and laying out short and long documents, and you gain insights into preparing successful ads. When you complete this chapter, you will have a thorough understanding of how to use PageMaker to prepare publications on your own.

Working with Short Documents

Short documents often are challenging to create and difficult to produce. You generally intend short documents to induce prompt reader reaction. Whether you want your readers to arrive at an immediate decision, respond appropriately to a sales pitch, or budget time to attend an upcoming event, you must tailor short documents carefully to get your message across and achieve desired results.

Short documents come in many varieties, including overhead transparencies, brochures, fliers, mailers, greeting cards, certificates, and stationery.

Creating Overhead Transparencies

An entire industry has grown up around the concept of desktop presentations. You don't necessarily need specialized software, however, to prepare overhead transparencies. PageMaker does the job nicely.

327

Most overhead projectors are configured to display a horizontal page. To set up your page specifications for making overhead transparencies, do the following:

1. Select **Wide** orientation from the Page Setup dialog box and choose the standard letter-size page from the pop-up Page menu.

2. Lay out any repeating elements, such as borders or company logos, on your master pages.

3. Create each overhead transparency on a separate publication page. Sequence your pages in the same order as your presentation.

4. Print your publication normally. Use clear acetate transparencies made especially for use in copiers or laser printers (to withstand the internal heat of your printer without melting).

Note

PageMaker's rounded-corner rectangles make excellent borders that match the shape of the cardboard holders many companies use to mount overhead transparencies. Figure 12.1 shows a sample overhead transparency.

Fig. 12.1

A mounted overhead transparency created entirely in PageMaker.

Creating overhead transparencies in PageMaker enables you to import high-resolution EPS and TIFF files, apply various Image Control settings to TIFF graphics for added effect, do precision kerning for tighter headlines, and even generate accompanying handouts automatically (by printing pages of Thumbnails). If you do many presentations, convert your overhead transparencies into templates for later use.

Tip

You quickly can shuffle the order of any pages you have created without having to do complex cutting and pasting. To swap two unrelated pages, for example, select everything on the first page and slide the selected elements onto the pasteboard (hold down the Shift key to keep them exactly on a horizontal axis). Turn to the second page and do the same thing, but drag the elements off the page onto the opposite side of the pasteboard. You may find this process easier if you work in the Fit in World view (choose Fit in Window from the Page menu while holding down the Shift key). Drag the first set of elements onto the second page and align them within the page margins (again, hold down the Shift key to keep them from moving vertically). Finally, turn back to the first page and drag the second set of elements onto the empty page. Save your work.

Tip

You can use PageMaker to create multiple presentation overlays without having to duplicate the images and then edit each page. You generate the overlays you need by assigning a color to all the elements that make up an overlay. When you click **Spot color overlays** in the Aldus Print Options dialog box, PageMaker prints a separate page for each assigned color. Stack the resulting transparencies in the desired order, making sure that they are aligned, and tape the edges of the sheets together. By flipping them over one at a time during your presentation, you can show a visual progression of information. Be sure to use transparencies specifically designed to withstand the heat of machine copiers and laser printers.

Creating Brochures and Price Lists

Brochures and price lists are short pamphlets that generally are promotional in nature and designed to sell or promote some item or service. These pamphlets come in many different formats, but most often you see them as 8.5-inch-by-11-inch or smaller size booklets. For these kinds of publications to be successful, your layouts should be spacious and uncluttered.

When designing brochures and price lists, focus first on content; many a company has printed and distributed a sales brochure only to discover later that the designer inadvertently omitted the company address and phone number. Make up a detailed checklist of what should be in your brochure and then proof your publication carefully before printing. Double-check all numbers in all price lists. Transposing two numbers is easy to do and can prove costly.

Your brochure should stress your company's identity. Prominently display your company logo near the front of the brochure and follow the logo immediately by telling your readers what your company has to offer.

Organize products or services into categories but avoid a jumbled look of boxes and rules. Save boxes and rules for highlighting important information such as special discounts or free pickup and delivery announcements.

For tabular material, such as price lists, use the same indents and spacing throughout as much as possible. Clear, logical, and consistent organization of material is crucial to conveying the information successfully to your readers.

Your brochure should have an eye-catching front cover that captures reader interest. Don't list specific products, services, or prices on the front cover. Your goal should be to stimulate curiosity, not provide details. To urge quick response to special offers, list the offers on the back cover as well as inside the brochure. But keep price lists entirely between the covers.

Be as creative as you like when designing brochures, but make every attempt to focus reader attention on your company. A memorable company identity helps to sell future goods and services. Use color when practical for additional emphasis and to help distinguish product categories. For best results, print brochures on a Linotronic ImageSetter. Strip in photos where needed and use high-quality paper for printing.

Creating Handbills, Fliers, and Mailers

Handbills and fliers usually are single-sheet documents printed on one or both sides. When you use handbills and fliers as mailers, you lay them out and fold them in various ways to help guide the reader through the information. Page formats for these mailers are flexible and designed to convey information quickly. Simple black-and-white or two-color reproduction at 300 dpi generally is enough to garner at least a passing interest from potential readers.

Handbills, fliers, and mailers are simple promotional vehicles that usually have a short life span; they often get thrown away as soon as they are looked at. To attract and hold the attention of readers, you want to tie your information to a strong graphic element (see fig. 12.2). The graphic should identify the topic matter immediately. Headlines are important, but they also can be graphic in design. Compose your headlines using decorative or display type—the more decorative, the better. With short promotional pieces, glitz is everything.

The first determination you must make when laying out handbills and fliers is whether you also will use them as mailers. When you design a mailer, you must choose beforehand what kind of folds and how heavy a paper to use. The wrong choices end up costing you extra postage. (Check with your post office to learn the current size and weight restrictions for various kinds of mailings.)

Fig. 12.2

A handbill for a children's benefit performance.

When creating a folded mailer of any kind, do a test fold and measure the results before creating the actual layout. Because folding subtracts usable page space, generally about 1/8th of an inch for each fold, you may have to compensate by offsetting columns of text and artwork. A three-panel letter fold, for example, produces two equal panels and one unequal panel (to accommodate the inside fold).

The most popular mailer is a standard 8.5-inch-by-11-inch, three-panel letter fold. One side of a three-fold mailer is divided into three separate vertical panels: the front cover, the back cover, and the inside first fold. The second side typically presents a panoramic display when the mailer is fully opened. This side becomes your interior spread and is where your main message goes.

To create this type of mailer, perform the following steps:

1. Open a new PageMaker publication. Select double-sided and facing pages. Set initial publication size to three pages so that you can view the two pages you work on side-by-side. Delete the unused page when you finish composing your layout.

2. Set the side and top margins to 2.5 picas.

3. Set the bottom margin to 3 picas for a balanced, eye-pleasing appearance.

4. Choose **Wide** orientation, unless you plan to produce a mailer composed of all horizontal panels. In that case, set the page orientation to **Tall** and work with rows instead of columns.

5. Assign three columns to your pages and adjust the spacing of the column guides to compensate for the folds so that you can properly center individual panel displays. (A column spacing of 3 picas or 0.5 inches works well in most cases.)

6. Design the front cover. On the cover, you try to persuade the reader to open your mailer and discover what is inside. Keep the front cover simple. Try to elicit reader interest by using a strong visual element such as a headline or graphic.

7. Lay out the inside first fold. This panel serves as your introduction. Use this area to expand on the theme of the front cover. Because the reader sees the first third of your interior spread at the same time, try not to have the two panels clash.

8. Lay out your interior spread. Almost any arrangement of text and graphics is permissible, but try to keep your message concise and hard-hitting. Avoid including too much material and make your text large enough to be read easily. For best results, confine columns to individual panels, keep paragraphs short, and break up long text with subheads. Use illustrations and photos when appropriate to provide contrast and heighten reader interest.

Tip

Center short hairline rules between columns in the top and bottom margins of your inside spread. Draw the rules just long enough so that just the tips of these lines print on a laser printer without being clipped off. Use these rules as guides to ensure proper folding of your mailers after printing. Your readers do not notice the rules because they lie exactly along the folds of the opened mailer.

---

9. Finally, lay out your back panel. On the back, place your company name and address, and any pertinent ordering information. If your piece is a self-mailer, use this panel for the mailing and return addresses and move the company data and ordering information to your interior spread.

Tip

If you prepare invoices, announcements, and other kinds of mailers so that the mailing address shows through the window of a #10 envelope, try switching to a #9 envelope. The insert then has less side-to-side and top-to-bottom movement that can cause part of the address not to show through. Your trifold sits snugly in place so that the postman can read the correct destination ZIP code every time.

Creating Greeting Cards

Everyone enjoys getting greeting cards and, with PageMaker, you now can create your own. If you start with an 8.5-inch-by-11-inch sheet, you can assign any of several different folds to produce an attractive card. A standard "french" or double-fold format is a good starting choice because of its familiar look and because this format accommodates inserts nicely. This double-fold format also enables you to print all your panels on one side of the paper.

To create a double-fold greeting card, perform the following steps:

1. Set up your page using two columns and split the page horizontally with a pair of ruler guides. Column spacing and the distance between horizontal ruler guides should be roughly 3 picas to accommodate folds.

2. Split each resulting quarter-panel horizontally and vertically with ruler guides. This produces four sets of crosshairs. Use the intersections of the ruler guides as a guide for centering text and illustrations. You initially set page margins to zero; otherwise, the page margins can prove unnecessarily distracting. If you later find that you are having difficulty centering objects, draw a frame in each panel as an additional guide. After you position your text and graphics, delete these extra boxes.

3. Center your text and graphics in each panel. Note that everything in the upper two panels should be placed upside down as displayed on-screen. (These panels become right side up when you fold your card into fourths.) PageMaker rotates text in 90-degree increments, making the placement of the greeting easy. You must make the inversions of graphics within your drawing program before saving and importing the images. See fig. 12.3 for a sample greeting card layout.

4. The right paper can make or break a card. Print greeting cards on 70-pound stock for best results. Paper heavier than 70-pound weight doesn't fold easily, and paper lighter than 70-pound is too flimsy to stand upright after being folded. Use 4 3/8-inch-by-5 3/4-inch envelopes to mail your cards.

Fig. 12.3

A double-fold Christmas greeting card.

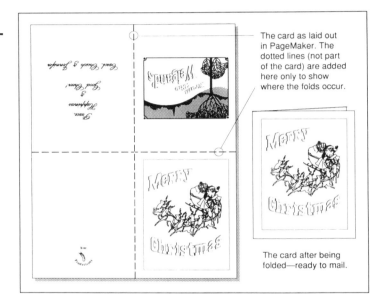

The card as laid out in PageMaker. The dotted lines (not part of the card) are added here only to show where the folds occur.

The card after being folded—ready to mail.

Creating Certificates

Most people appreciate occasional, well-deserved recognition for an achievement or job well-done. Certificates and awards are a popular way of delivering this recognition to others. To prepare a certificate in PageMaker, execute the following steps:

1. Choose a **Tall** or **Wide** page orientation for the kind of certificate you want to produce. Set all page margins to 3 picas (0.5 inch).

2. Design a frame using PageMaker's drawing tools or import one from a separate drawing program. Size the frame so that the outer border lies just within the page margins.

3. Type and center your text on the page. Use an appropriate mix of font types, sizes, and styles to suit the message. Be sure to include signature and date lines near the bottom of the certificate. Draw these lines using PageMaker's straight-line tool.

4. Import any graphics, including logos and seals, and place them in their proper locations on the page. To further dress up your certificate, import and enlarge a bit-mapped Paint or TIFF graphic. Place the graphic behind the text using PageMaker's Send To Back command. Next, lighten the graphic to a faint shade of gray using PageMaker's Image Control dialog box. This process creates an interesting visual backdrop that is appealing and professional-looking.

5. Print your certificates on minimum 70-pound paper stock. If you routinely prepare many certificates or awards, seek out companies that supply special certificate paper. Certificate paper comes in a variety of styles preprinted with frames. Be sure to buy certificate paper specially made to withstand the internal heat of machine copiers and laser printers. Also avoid the kind of certificate paper that has embedded gold specks; the gold specs can flake off inside your laser printer and cause damage.

Creating Stationery and Business Cards

PageMaker is an excellent design tool for creating personalized stationery. For example, you easily can include a logo on letterhead stationery or a signature on business cards. You can prepare a set of templates in advance for different kinds of correspondence and print letters and envelopes as needed. Or you can have a commercial printer print your stationery, including matching envelopes and business cards, in eye-catching color on the paper of your choice.

The greatest challenge when designing letterheads, envelopes, and business cards is to produce a design that works equally well on all three document sizes. Start by arranging each element (return address, photo, logo, or other graphic embellishments) identically on all three pieces. Keep in mind that your envelope design should not intrude into the area reserved for postage or the recipient mailing address.

You need to allow at least a 0.25-inch margin on all sides of your design for text and graphics to remain within the imaging area of your laser printer. Vary the placement of elements on all document sizes until you arrive at a satisfactory arrangement that not only looks good, but also exhibits design consistency.

For stationery, stick with standard 8.5-inch-by-11-inch paper and number 10 envelopes. Nonstandard sizes generally cost more and can be more difficult to produce. Business cards should always be 3.5 by 2 inches (21 by 12 picas). Lay the cards out 10 up to a page (five cards down and two across) to save printing costs; this arrangement yields 500 business cards for every 50 sheets you print. Print business cards on a minimum 100-pound paper stock.

To create a set of business cards in PageMaker, do the following:

1. Configure a single, **Tall** oriented, letter-size page with 0.75-inch side margins and 0.5-inch top and bottom margins.

2. Divide the page vertically into two halves using a ruler guide and then reset your ruler zero point to the upper left corner where the page margins intersect.

3. Drag a horizontal ruler guide to each 2-inch ruler mark to divide the page horizontally into five sections. This process produces 10 boxes made up entirely of non-printing guides into which you can place repeating text and graphics.

4. Draw short hairline rules at all margin and ruler-guide intersections and at the four page-margin corners to facilitate cutting your business cards after printing. Make these rules no longer than 1 pica.

5. Drag additional ruler guides onto your page to create 1-pica margins inside each box. You can use slightly smaller margins, but a minimum 1-pica margin looks best on a business card. Toggle the Snap To Guides Menu command on and use PageMaker's square-corner rectangle tool to draw a dashed rectangle along the inner margins of each card. Also draw a solid rectangle along the outer margins. These rectangles function as visual aids to help you center your business card layout. Your basic business card format is complete. Save your layout as a template for future use.

6. Next, produce your final design by typing the text, placing any logos or graphics, and adding any other design elements. Lay out just one business card. Place the card in the box in the upper left corner of the page (see fig. 12.4).

Fig. 12.4

A business-card template showing the layout of the first card.

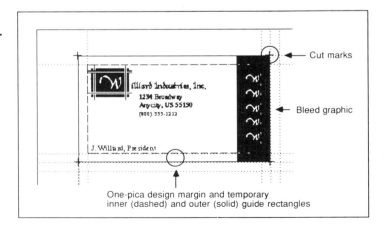

7. When you are satisfied with the layout, select all the elements of your card, including its margin rectangles, and copy them to the Clipboard. Repeatedly paste the contents of the Clipboard back onto your page, each time dragging the contents into a different box. The rectangles snap to the margin guides to center the elements within the box. You also can Option-paste the first time, drag to the next box, and then continue Option-pasting to place the remaining cards in the column. Repeat for the second column.

8. When your page is full, select and delete all the margin rectangles. Print your cards and cut them using the hairline rules as cutting guides. Your business cards will look as good as the finished sample in figure 12.5.

Fig. 12.5

The final printed business card.

Managing Large Publications

Some large publications are easier to produce than others. For example, after your initial layout is completed for a long tract composed mainly of text, little effort is needed to produce the final document. PageMaker enables you to generate a table of contents and index quickly and chain print the publications in your book list.

Many large publications, however, mix text and graphics in various ways and require extensive planning and careful management to avoid production problems. Some of the many types of large publications you may be called upon to produce include pamphlets, booklets, reports, proposals, catalogs, and directories.

Pamphlets and booklets are much like brochures, but lack the usual sales pitch and promotional graphics. Any graphics you include are used mainly to illustrate and supplement the text. Pamphlets can be thought of as short books and require much the same approach when preparing the layouts.

Reports and proposals, on the other hand, can be short or long and can exhibit a variety of formats. Although some government reports consume thousands of pages, academic, business, and technical reports usually are more modest. These reports may range from a few dozen to several hundred pages. Such publications rely frequently on diagrams and photos to supplement the text and often include detailed tables, charts, and graphs. Many reports include an executive summary or abstract to provide an overview of the contents. Proposals are similar in nature to reports, but their formats are aimed more specifically at winning support (usually financial) for some undertaking.

Catalogs generally exhibit a thorough mix of text and graphics. They can be the most difficult of the large publications to produce, unless you standardize your layouts ahead of time to provide an orderly and consistent placement of text and graphics. Often you can create catalogs and update old ones easily by using templates. PageMaker's capability to link external text and graphics to a publication also helps streamline catalog production efforts. Although catalogs are considered budget periodicals, they sometimes can be quite large and complex to produce.

Directories range from everyday telephone books and registers to specialized listings of companies and products. The variety of subject matter is endless, but the format is generally similar—two or more columns with stylized type to differentiate one entry or listing from another. Directory publishing is really database publishing. You translate data stored in spreadsheets or databases into tab-delimited text and then import that text into PageMaker for layout and formatting. Your main concern is ensuring that the formatting remains consistent throughout for the proper display of information (see the Additional Tips and Techniques section of this book).

Layouts for large publications vary considerably, depending on content. Your first consideration when you take on the job of producing a large publication is to select a style of presentation appropriate to the subject matter. For example, technical books entail a method of presentation that is different from that of novels. You have to format these two kinds of books differently. Similarly, you format self-help training manuals differently from law books and encyclopedias differently from dictionaries (even though both may be organized alphabetically).

Before you get started, identify common elements in your layout for inclusion on your master pages. Then ask questions like the following to help decide on an appropriate overall format:

❑ If you have chapters, how should you define your chapter heads?

❑ Does your publication require multiple levels of headlines? If so, must the headlines be individually numbered, as in many textbooks and manuals?

❑ Should you use running heads throughout your publication? If so, what information should they contain?

❑ How are you going to handle the placement of any accompanying graphics or illustrations?

❑ Should you prepare different sections as separate publications?

Publications composed entirely of text, like novels, are easier to lay out than publications containing many illustrations. However, even when your page layout requirements appear simple and straightforward, be sure to pay close attention to the details of type selection, leading, paragraph spacing, and other typographical concerns. Only in that way do you obtain consistently good results.

Large publications often require forewords, introductions, acknowledgment pages, copyright pages, tables of contents, indexes, and bibliographies. You also may have to deal with footnotes, glossaries, and appendixes, all of which may require different formatting. In every case, you need to estimate page counts accurately, determine page sizes, and select binding methods before beginning your layouts.

To achieve consistency, create and assign styles to different parts of your publications. You will have fewer corrections to make later because of formatting errors. Combine sections you prepare as separate publications into a book list for easy document management.

If you set up your master pages properly in each publication to handle repeating elements, your final proofing goes more smoothly. Remember that you always can turn off master page elements on any one page to customize that page.

Preparing large publications often presents special challenges to the uninitiated. The sheer complexity and magnitude of such publishing tasks seems daunting. However, if you carefully plan your projects, things generally go well. Break up large publications into smaller, easily manageable documents. Also prepare comprehensive checklists to cover each stage of production. Use these checklists religiously to ensure that you don't overlook anything.

Designing Successful Ads

PageMaker is an ideal tool for preparing ads because of its inherent flexibility. You can work like a graphic designer, moving items here and there on your pages until you find a satisfactory, pleasing arrangement. You also can work like a copy editor, composing and editing text until the words fairly leap off the page.

Ads represent a special category of short documents. In advertising, almost every kind of layout design has been tried, discarded, and tried again. Highly successful ads have ranged from tiny images centered in a sea of white space with nothing else on the page, to pages crammed full of text carefully composed to look like regular articles and news items. However, many ads using these same techniques have proven equally disastrous. In short, no one formula works every time.

Your biggest constraint when designing ads is space. You generally are limited to one page and often to just a small portion of a page. Your graphics must be appropriate to your message, and your message must be concise. Tight copy is essential. You have to convey information compactly in a way the reader understands immediately, and you have to sell features and benefits while urging the reader to action. The whole purpose behind ads is getting readers to commit. Whether that commitment is to buy a product, join a cause, or vote a particular way does not matter. If the call to action works, and your ad elicits the desired response, then the ad is deemed successful.

In earlier chapters, you learned the basics of good layout design for newsletters and other publications. Those lessons apply equally to creating effective ads. The following are additional things to keep in mind:

- ❑ Isolate the most important selling point and make that point into a headline. Your headlines should offer something of value to your readers. Follow strongly worded headlines with supporting leads that help pull the reader further into the copy that follows.

- ❑ Make sure that each line of a multiple-line headline makes sense. Be careful about the words you use and how you position them. Don't, for example, write a two-line headline with the phrase "Enjoy Retirement in" on the first line, leaving "Sunny Arizona" dangling on the second line. Instead, let "Enjoy Retirement" stand alone on the first line as a complete thought that the reader can immediately assimilate. Then reinforce that upbeat introduction with "in Sunny Arizona" on the second line to complete your message. Appending the word "in" to the first line changes an otherwise positive phrase into a confusing question mark for the reader.

- ❑ If your copy calls for subheads, make the subheads tell a complete story. Prepare your subheads to get your message across, even if your readers read none of the accompanying text. Many readers scan the headlines and subheads, stopping to read the ad copy only if they become sufficiently intrigued.

- ❑ In your ad copy, support any claims you make in your headlines. Don't disappoint your readers by using headlines in "bait-and-switch" fashion. Deliver on what you say by expanding on the headline. Prove your claims before readers can mount arguments. For example, don't write a headline that announces "End Baldness with Nobald," and go on to tell how shiny and thick-looking your hair becomes when you use Nobald without addressing the issue of baldness. Explain convincingly how and why Nobald ends baldness.

- ❑ If you cannot squeeze everything of importance into your ad, include a coupon for a free brochure. Use the brochure to list additional details and close the sale. Use your limited ad space to urge the reader to clip and mail in the coupon.

❑ Don't forget to double-check your ads before printing. Many an ad has failed because the price of the product or the phone number wasn't included.

Chapter Summary

In this chapter, you discovered that you can produce a wide assortment of publications with PageMaker. You explored several different approaches for designing and laying out short and long documents, including overhead transparencies, brochures, mailers, greeting cards, certificates, personal stationery and business cards, pamphlets, books, reports, proposals, catalogs, and directories. You also learned how to compose winning ads. In the appendixes, you find some additional hints and tips that may prove useful to you in your work.

Your training in how to use PageMaker on the Macintosh is complete. You now possess the basic skills necessary to start producing publications on your own. You should find desktop publishing a challenging and rewarding activity and PageMaker a most able assistant.

Additional Tips and Techniques

In this section, you find an assortment of valuable tips, techniques, and recommendations that are not included in earlier chapters. Because these items are not arranged in any special order, feel free to browse. You may find something that helps you use PageMaker more productively.

Avoiding Production-Time Heartburn

One hard-edged, cardinal rule you don't want to violate, ever, is making changes on production time. This rule applies to everything from hooking up a new hard drive to installing new INIT software. If you make changes on production time, you are going to suffer down time, guaranteed. Getting up and running again almost always takes a grossly disproportionate amount of lost time.

Wait to do periodic System software updates and hardware configuration changes until after a day's work is done. After hours is the best time to make changes, anyway. You won't be distracted by ringing telephones or anxious customers. Also try to make changes early in the week. Sundays through Thursdays are good because you always have the next day when stores are open and you can get help if needed.

Be sure to back up everything in sight before you start implementing changes. If disaster strikes, you have a much easier time recovering. A little common sense is all you need to avoid having everything go wrong at the worst possible time.

Dealing with System Errors

System errors often occur when you do something that takes you "outside" PageMaker. To reduce your chances of losing data, save your work regularly.

Always save your work before opening a desk accessory, switching to another program under MultiFinder, or printing from a currently open document.

Dealing with Computer Gremlins

If you experience frequent system crashes, frozen applications, unexplained printing difficulties, or other unreliable and slow system operation, the problem may be due to one of the following possible causes:

❑ You may be under attack by one or more viruses.

❑ You may be using conflicting INIT software.

❑ You may have a damaged Desktop file.

❑ Your Parameter RAM (PRAM) may be corrupted.

❑ Your System file may be damaged.

❑ You may have too small a System Heap size.

If problems continue after you verify that your system is virus-free (using a good viral-detection software) and you eliminate any potential INIT conflicts (by removing suspect INITs from your System folder), the next step is to rebuild the invisible Desktop file. Hold down the Command and Option keys as you restart your Macintosh (or as you quit from an open application). Rebuilding the desktop eliminates superseded directory information, including leftover icons for programs no longer present.

If rebuilding doesn't work, try zapping the PRAM (PRAM, or Parameter RAM, is a small amount of memory that operates off the internal battery to keep the time, date, and various Control Panel settings current). To zap the PRAM, press Command-Option-Shift while selecting the Control Panel desk accessory from the Apple menu. Zapping the PRAM resets it and clears any scrambled data.

If things still don't work, the culprit may be a damaged System file. The System file plays a key role in all computing operations. So, when things go wrong, as they sometimes do, the System file often is the first to become corrupted. The correct way to replace a damaged System file is to trash the file (you first have to reboot using the replacement System disk as your start-up disk). Then run Apple's Installer utility to install a fresh replacement. Don't just drag the System file from disk to disk. The System that Apple distributes contains code for all Macintosh models. Using the Installer strips out any excess and potentially troublesome code that is not needed for your particular configuration.

The last step, if all else fails, is to check your System Heap. The System Heap is the block of memory allocated to the System at start-up. If the Heap is barely large enough to manage your installed collection of fonts, desk accessories, INITs and CDEVs, with little or no room left over for unexpected program demands, you may experience problems. To check how much memory is used by the System, choose About Finder from the Apple menu. The dark portion of the System bar represents actual memory used. The light portion represents available or free memory. The total is the System Heap. If less than 25 percent free memory is available, you need to increase the size of the Heap.

Unfortunately, Apple doesn't give you a way to increase the size of the Heap. Fortunately, CE Software does. HeapFixer, an obscure little utility that comes free with most CE Software products, enables you to adjust Heap size quickly and easily. You don't have to be experienced to use HeapFixer. Keep in mind, however, that increasing System Heap size also decreases the amount of memory available to run other programs and may prove limiting if you are using a one-megabyte machine. For more information about HeapFixer, write or call: CE Software, P.O. Box 65580, West Des Moines, IA 50265, (515) 224-1995 or (800) 523-7638.

If you encounter a stubborn problem that rebuilding the desktop, zapping Parameter RAM, resolving INIT conflicts, and increasing Heap size don't fix, the culprit most likely is the System file. Start-up using a backup System disk, trash the corrupted System file off your hard disk, and replace the corrupted file with a clean copy. You are up and running again in just minutes.

To create a backup System disk, first install and configure a fresh System file on your hard disk. Be sure to use Apple's Installer utility. After you have configured your newly installed System, copy the System and Finder onto a clean disk. Lock the write-protect tab. This disk becomes your instant-recovery backup System disk.

Note

Lock all master floppy disks when you take them out of the box and before using them the first time. For your protection, many vendors now ship program disks write-protected. If you catch a virus, the virus can infect any unlocked disks inserted into your computer. To lock a disk, slide the write-protect tab up so that you can see through the hole. After you lock a master disk, keep the disk locked. A drop of SuperGlue on the write-protect tab helps ensure that the tab remains in the locked position.

Recovering from a Crash

If you have an emergency and cannot save current changes, you can use PageMaker's mini-save feature to recover your data. Use the following steps to effect a recovery:

1. Reboot your Macintosh and reopen PageMaker.

2. Choose Open from the File menu and look for the name of your file.

3. Select and open the file. PageMaker substitutes the last mini-saved version. After that document is open, you can revert to the last version you saved previously with the Save or Save As command. Choose Revert from the File menu.

4. If you haven't saved your document for the first time yet, look for a file named PMF000 in your System folder and open that file as an original publication. The file is PageMaker's mini-saved version. If you have accumulated several of these mini-saved files, the one you want to open is the one with the largest PMFXXX, in which XXX represents a sequential three-digit number.

Backing Up Intelligently

Everyone knows, or should know, that working without backups is like walking a high-wire without a safety net. However, equally as important to actually doing backups is the method you use to do your backups. Keep in mind that page-layout documents can be enormously complex. Consequently, the tiniest "gotcha," whether a power failure, system error, or random attack by computer gremlins, can spell disaster if your document or publication gets zapped.

Even if you take care to save and back up regularly, going so far as to store duplicate copies of your files off site, disaster still can strike. If a file you are working on becomes corrupted without your being aware of it, you may end up saving the corrupted version over your good original and then not be able to open the file again (or perhaps open the file, but not be able to access all the data). If you also back up the damaged file to one or more archives, overwriting earlier saved versions, every one of those copies also becomes corrupted. Recovery of your data in any kind of usable form may be out of the question.

So here's the trick. Stagger your backups. As you work, periodically save documents to at least three different locations, but only to two locations at one time. For example, the first time you do a Save, save to your internal hard disk and then to an external hard disk or floppy. Your working file then becomes the second copy saved. The next time you do a Save, save to your external hard disk (or floppy) and then to a third disk. The third version becomes your active file. The next time you Save, you conclude by saving back to your internal hard disk once again.

If you stagger backups this way, when a problem does arise you lose only as much work as you have completed since your last Save. If you find yourself working on exceptionally large or complex publications, consider increasing the number of staggered backups. String out your backups to encompass four, five, or even six different disk locations. But save to only two locations at one time (save often and periodically check documents to verify their integrity). Never replace or copy over all previous versions of a document at the same time. By sequentially backing up your work in this fashion, you may avoid having to completely redo a major project.

Using a Holding Folder

If you occasionally use the trashcan in haste, you know how easily you can discard an important file you later discover you need. The solution is to place an empty folder next to the trashcan and name the folder "Holding." After that, every time you start to place a file in the trashcan, place the file into the Holding folder instead. Make this a habit. When your day's work is done, or at the end of the week, go through the Holding folder and weed out any files you are absolutely sure that you want to get rid of.

This approach gives you a second chance to decide whether you want to hang onto an important file. This technique is a simple and nearly foolproof way to avoid inadvertent file deletions, and keeps you from having to go through the trouble of trying to recover lost data later.

Avoiding Power-Outage Data Losses

To protect your work, consider getting a UPS (uninterruptable power supply). If a power failure occurs, the battery reserve gives you enough time to save your files and shut down gracefully without losing any data. A UPS also protects your equipment from power surges, spikes, and various under- and overvoltage conditions.

Even if you do not use a UPS, you always should use a surge suppresser. Surge suppressers screen out line noise and voltage fluctuations and keep power spikes from getting through.

You also should feed all power to your equipment through a fused power strip. With a power strip, you can completely remove power to your equipment when lightning storms occur. Simply pull the plug out of the wall. Keep in mind that no protection device can withstand a direct lightning hit.

Always disconnect your modem from the incoming phone line when your computer is shut down. Otherwise, a power surge coming down the phone line still can zap your computer.

If you use two or more protection devices, daisy-chain them together. Ideally, you want to feed a surge suppresser off a power strip, a UPS off a surge suppresser, and your computer equipment off a UPS. That way, a 50-cent power-strip fuse protects a $50 surge suppresser, which in turn protects a $500 UPS. The UPS, last in the defense chain, protects your $5000 computer system. Hopefully, the 50-cent fuse blows first, and so on up the line. That way you protect your high-value items with low-value ones.

Avoiding Disk Fragmentation Slowdowns

Disk fragmentation results from the scattering of bits and pieces of code so that files occupy noncontiguous blocks on your hard disk. This fragmentation occurs normally as you add or remove files and as files grow or shrink in size. Unfortunately, the more scattered the pieces, the longer it takes to access the data. A badly fragmented hard disk may begin to respond like cold molasses—slooooooooowly.

The surest way to eliminate disk fragmentation is to back up all your files, erase (reinitialize) your hard disk, and then copy the files back onto the disk. This process is tedious, especially when working with large-capacity hard drives, but is 100 percent effective. Note that doing a mirror backup and restore (for example, with a tape drive) does not work because you end up replacing fragmented file pieces exactly where they were before.

To avoid disk fragmentation slowdowns, back up and restore your hard disk at least every couple of months.

Solving SCSI Problems

Apple's SCSI (Small Computer System Interface) implementation does not always work properly. When you make a hardware change, for example, you invariably find that you have to manipulate your equipment line-ups exhaustively to get things working again. This assumes, of course, that you have several kinds of SCSI devices daisy-chained together.

SCSI problems can be difficult to resolve. SCSI performance depends on the types of devices in the chain, their internal characteristics (including, but not limited to termination), and the order in which you connect the devices. Other factors include the hierarchy of assigned addresses, the types and lengths of cables used, and the tightness of the connections. Enough variables exist that juggling even a few of them to get a reliably functioning arrangement can prove to be a major headache.

If you have only one or two devices in your chain or if all your equipment is the same type (for example, hard disks from the same manufacturer), you can expect few difficulties. However, try to mix and match several different kinds of equipment from various vendors, and you may find yourself having to experiment with multiple alternative configurations to get everything working properly.

As an aid to troubleshooting, here is a five-point checklist for resolving SCSI problems:

1. First, be sure that you give each device in the chain a unique SCSI address ID (use only numbers zero to six). If you inadvertently assign the same ID number to two devices, you experience severe operating difficulties and may lose some or all of your data. Note that most hard-drive manufacturers set internal drives to address zero at the factory.

2. Ensure that you begin by terminating only for the first and last devices in the chain. Keep in mind that most internal hard disks come already terminated. Some devices include external termination switches, a modern convenience that makes changing settings easy. But you also may have to use plug-in terminating resistors (they look like single- or double-ended SCSI connectors). If you add new equipment to your chain, remember to reposition, as necessary, the external terminating resistors.

3. Verify that all cable connections are made snugly. Loose connectors can cause intermittent failures. Also, make sure that no sharp bends exist in any of your cables to crimp internal wiring. Do not rule out the possibility of a defective cable or connector—these kinds of problems are more common than you think. Try to keep the total length of your SCSI chain to less than 18 feet (which includes the electronic signal paths through each device). A chain that is too long can overload the bus and cause failures.

4. If you have everything hooked up properly and you still experience problems, try juggling SCSI address assignments. A few devices work only if set to a specific SCSI ID number. Some devices respond to different address settings depending on the connection sequence of the equipment in your chain. Try altering the sequence to find an arrangement that works.

5. As a last resort, change the termination configuration. Add or remove terminating resistors, working from the outermost device of your chain inward. You may have to violate Apple's basic guidelines to get everything working properly. Some SCSI chains work only when terminated at one end instead of both ends.

As you work your way through the above steps, change only one thing at a time. Test your results thoroughly before making more changes. Also, write down everything you do. Otherwise, you may lose track of the changes you make and end up having to try the same non-working arrangements over again.

Understanding Viruses

Nothing is more devastating than to get hit with a malicious viral attack. Viruses are insidious little rascals that enjoy a well-deserved reputation for being able to bring production work to a sudden and total halt. If you do not set up some form of impenetrable defense well in advance, you can expect someday to get ransacked. No one is immune.

The computer viral threat looms large on the horizon for the 1990s. As we enter the new decade, perpetrators actively are waging new assaults on innocent and unsuspecting computer users. And the number of viruses in circulation is escalating. Although no one fully understands what goes on in the minds of individuals who set out to do this kind of criminal mischief, one thing is certain—viruses are going to get worse before they get better.

Viruses are bits of computer code that covertly attach themselves to programs. Unpredictable results may occur after a virus is unleashed. Applications may function unreliably or freeze altogether; routine tasks may take longer to execute; computers may crash unexpectedly and often; start-up disks may fail to boot properly; files may explode in size and eventually become inaccessible; documents may not print properly—in short, your entire system may behave erratically or become totally unusable.

Methods of viral transmission vary, but sharing or downloading public domain or pirated software is still the surest way to become infected. If you download a contaminated file from a BBS or across a network, you easily can infect your hard disk. A virus also can remain hidden in a compressed file. The virus remains completely undetectable (and impotent) until the file is uncompressed. After the virus is released, however, the virus becomes infectious.

Some viruses lie dormant for an extended period (determined in advance by the programmer) only to activate days, weeks, or even months after initial exposure. Keep in mind that the goal of every virus is to go completely unnoticed while replicating until the maximum amount of spread has occurred.

Make no mistake—it is all-out war, and you are the target. Even well-intentioned viruses, like the famous "World Peace" message of a couple of years ago, can do extensive damage. After all, you have enough difficulty writing legitimate code without also trying to make viruses "bug-free."

So what can you do? In brief, do not trust any external contact with your computer system. Test everything before using it. That includes commercial software, which may arrive in its shrink-wrapped box already infected (which has happened on more than one occasion). Use a good viral-prevention software to unmask invaders and prevent infection.

After you initially verify that your system is clean, install a viral-prevention software and keep the software active at all times. Make multiple backups of new programs and continually back up all your work files. Always keep the write-protect tabs on master disks locked. And, most importantly, after you establish an effective system of safeguards, absolutely never bypass the system. The one time you ignore your defenses could be the one time you end up getting clobbered.

A Virus-Protection Primer

Antiviral products generally include one or more of the following kinds of features: virus prevention, virus detection, and virus eradication. These products recognize attempts by viruses to replicate and effectively stop them from spreading.

The best virus-prevention software takes a generic approach to virus identification and thus provides a broad safety net that can unmask new invaders before they gain a foothold. The downside to this approach is that certain legitimate file-altering evolutions occasionally may trigger false alarms.

Virus-detection software can scan floppies and hard disks to search for infected files. They detect viruses based on known characteristics. Virus-detection programs are, by nature, viral-specific and must be upgraded constantly to recognize every new virus that comes along. Although virus-detection programs identify all known viruses, they, unfortunately, cannot protect you from new or unknown ones.

Consider, for example, a new virus that lies dormant, programmed to activate itself weeks into the future. Even with the most up-to-date version of the very best viral-detection software, you still could wind up with this new virus on your hard disk. If no one has heard of this virus yet, its identifying characteristics cannot be known. Therefore, no viral-specific code can be written to detect the virus. When the dormancy period ends, the virus activates and, of course, quickly infects your hard disk—unless, that is, you previously installed a generic viral-prevention utility. Such a program can block the virus after activating and prevent the virus from spreading.

Note

Trojan horses, programs specifically designed to destroy data, also are making the rounds of the Macintosh community. Unlike viruses, which replicate and spread from disk to disk and across networks, Trojan horses are stand-alone programs that do damage only when they are run; they do not reproduce themselves automatically. Trojan horses typically masquerade as ordinary applications, seemingly harmless, but maliciously destructive when unleashed. Most antiviral products block the spread of Trojan horses.

Viral-eradication software also is viral-specific by nature. After a known virus has been detected, eradication programs attempt to remove the virus and repair any damage that may have been done. This procedure is tricky at best, and often produces "twice altered" applications. Such applications may not perform reliably after undergoing repairs. In a production environment, however, the use of viral-eradication software could make a difference in getting a crucial job out on time. But, even when viral eradication works, you should consider viral eradication only a temporary solution.

Some antiviral products support more than one category of features. Understanding when and how to use which program is the key to establishing an effective protection barrier. Some come with INITs that you install after verifying your disk is free from infection. These INITs prevent subsequent infection (or reinfection) and also include the capability to generically detect new viral strains. Some scan floppies for infected files but recognize only known viruses; they cannot protect you against the unknown variety. To be fully protected from viruses, you need to use a good viral-prevention utility, or you can become infected with a new virus suddenly and without warning.

Proper use of antiviral software can eliminate completely the risk of casual infection. But you do have to use the software. Ask yourself how much your data is worth. Then add to that the cost of your software holdings. Also, assign a value to the estimated time you may spend recovering from an unexpected viral attack. You find that the numbers speak eloquently for themselves.

Pick a good antiviral software to use as your first line of defense against viral attack. Check all new floppies prior to using them for the first time and do occasional backup scans of your hard disk. Using an automatic disk-scanning utility also is important when sharing files with others, as within an office or user-group setting. You ensure that any disks you pass along are not infected by known viruses.

Setting up an organized system of defense affords several layers of protection and more opportunities to contain potentially crippling viruses before they spread. Adhere strictly to safe computing practices and you may avoid becoming a victim.

Getting Clean OCR Scans

When OCR-scanning flimsy documents such as magazine or newspaper clippings for eventual inclusion in your publications, the reverse side of the page sometimes shows through and produces random litter during scanning that can confuse OCR software and lead to errors in character recognition. If you try to compensate by lowering the contrast or brightness settings, you may get an even less accurate scan.

A better approach is to back your documents using a piece of dark card stock. This technique eliminates any print show-through and enables you to use your preferred scan settings. Note that this trick also produces cleaner machine-copied documents.

Placing Stubborn TIFF Files

You may encounter a TIFF graphic that PageMaker does not accept (currently dozens of different TIFF formats exist, several of which are proprietary to specific scanners). To get around this problem, open the recalcitrant file into a compatible graphics program like Zedcor's DeskPaint, LetraSet's ImageStudio, or Silicon Beach Software's Digital Darkroom. Resave the file from there as a new TIFF file to regenerate the graphic in a revised TIFF format that PageMaker recognizes.

Adding Signatures to Documents

For that special personal touch, try including handwritten signatures in your documents. If you have a scanner, including signatures is easy. Sign your name on a sheet of paper as you normally would, but make your signature a little larger than usual for a cleaner scan. Then, scan your signature as line art at a medium resolution of 150 or 200 dpi.

Save your scan as a TIFF file. When you place your signature into PageMaker, proportionally resize the signature down to increase the printing resolution. You can assign your signature any color, such as blue, if you print your documents as color separations. If you import your scan into a high-resolution drawing program like Adobe Illustrator or FreeHand, you can trace an outline of your signature, fill the signature with any shade or color, and save the signature as an EPS file. Your signature looks good when scaled to any size.

Creating Spatter Patterns

Spatter patterns work great as screened backgrounds. You do not have to buy expensive clip art collections to get spatter patterns. All you need is a toothbrush, a bottle of ink, a few sheets of paper, and a scanner.

Dip the toothbrush into the ink and then run your finger along the bristles so that the ink spatters on the paper. After the ink dries, scan the images you created and save them as TIFF files. Import into PageMaker for final cropping, screening, and placement.

Drawing Quick White Lines

You can avoid the multistep process of drawing individual lines, selecting the lines, moving them into position over a black background, and choosing Reverse Line from the Lines menu. Draw lines in place to start with by using PageMaker's double- or triple-line styles. Because the spaces between the lines are opaque, they show up as solid white lines against the black background.

Another Drop Caps Technique

Creating drop caps and auto-wrapping text around them without leaving Page-Maker is a snap. To use this drop cap technique, do the following:

1. Type the character you want in its own text block.

2. Assign the desired type styling.

3. Select the text block using the pointer tool.

4. Copy to the Clipboard.

5. Paste to the Scrapbook.

6. Using PageMaker's Place command, open the Scrapbook and click to place the character.

7. Click the pointer tool to cancel placing additional Scrapbook images.

Your drop cap is now a PICT graphic. You can scale the drop cap like any other graphic and assign a custom text-wrap boundary. The character still prints at full type resolution.

Creating Check Boxes in PageMaker

A quick way to make check boxes for forms or other kinds of documents is to type *n* as a Zapf Dingbats character. This produces a solid black box. Select the box and assign an appropriate type size. Choose Outline from PageMaker's type-style menu. When you print your publication, you get a perfect checkbox every time.

Using Zapf Dingbats Arrows

Desktop publishers frequently use arrows in their publications to highlight important topics. Arrows are very useful as typographical accents. Surprisingly, however, good-looking arrows often are hard to come by. Most general purpose clip art packages include a few arrows, but there never seems to be quite enough of a selection to meet every need.

You may be surprised to learn that you already have a generous assortment of more than three dozen designer arrows immediately available to you—and they're absolutely free. You do not need to buy expensive specialty font and clip-art packages. Zapf Dingbats, a PostScript typeface built into most laser printers, has all the arrows you may ever need.

Figure T.1 shows the keystroke combinations for the 38 Dingbats arrows accessible from the standard keyboard. Four more hidden arrows are accessible only by using one of the many commercial and public domain keyboard-character viewing utilities. You can get interesting results by applying different type sizes and styles to individual arrows.

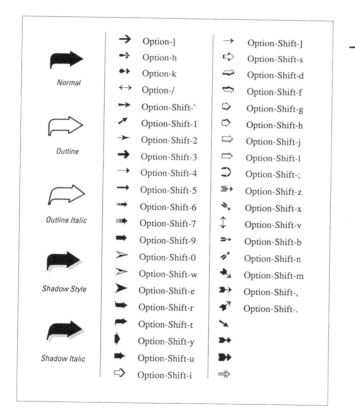

Fig. T.1

Zapf Dingbat arrows.

Using Turn-of-the-Century Images

Useful clip-art borders can be difficult to find. Most often you see ordinary-looking Paint or EPS images that contribute little to a publication. However, a few good collections are available if you know where to look. Among the best are the old-fashioned piece borders released in TIFF format by The Underground Grammarian. One of the most attractive borders is Artemis, a lovely graphic that is entirely faithful to that genus of flowering herb. Each piece in the collection is a separate drawing. You assemble the pieces within your page-makeup program to create borders of any size or shape. You also can use individual pieces as spot decorations, section dividers, screened artwork, and so on.

The Underground Grammarian is famous for its unrivaled digital collection of turn-of-the-century Typographers Ornaments. Their border elements exhibit the same uniqueness. Unlike most commercial clip art, a remarkable richness of detail and an exquisite elegance characterizes each piece. The Underground Grammarian is highly recommended for adding a special touch of timeless grace to your most important publications.

For more information, write or call: The Underground Grammarian, P.O. Box 203, Glassboro, NJ 08028, (609) 589-6477.

Using Smart Quotes Intelligently

Smart quotes, a convenience built into some programs, converts straight apostrophes (') and quotes (") to the curly variety (') and ("). However, this feature isn't entirely foolproof. Backspacing to make typing corrections sometimes results in errors.

To get around this problem, use QuicKeys from CE Software. QuicKeys' Alias command enables you to reassign the hard-to-type curly apostrophes and quotes to more readily accessible keystroke combinations. Get in the habit of using the new key assignments. That way you always get what you expect.

For example, try reassigning the curly apostrophe Option-Shift-] to the straight apostrophe (') key, and the left and right curly-quote marks Option-[and Option-Shift-[to the less confusing Shift-[(left square bracket) and Shift-] (right square bracket) key combinations. After that, when you hit the straight apostrophe key, you get a curly apostrophe instead. And when you hit Shift-[or Shift-] you get the matching curly quotes. For those few times you need curly brackets { }, turn QuicKeys off to type them and then back on again.

Detecting Rivers of White

"Rivers of white," a term familiar to desktop publishers, describes wiggly lines of white space that sometimes meander down a page if you have overly wide word spacing. These rivers, however, may not be apparent immediately to the untrained eye.

To better visualize how text sits on the page, try viewing your printed copy sideways. Hold the page out away from you so that the page lies eye-level in a nearly horizontal plane. Subtle imperfections like tiny rivers of white suddenly leap out from the otherwise even background gray distribution of text. You may want to tighten word spacing or tracking or substitute a more suitable typeface.

Checking Documents for Creation Fonts

If you use a utility like Suitcase from Fifth Generation Systems to manage screen fonts, you easily can determine which fonts were used to create any PageMaker document, even if you don't have those fonts installed. By installing only the minimum required screen fonts (Chicago, Geneva, and Monaco) into your System file and letting SuitCase handle the rest, you quickly can verify font availability before printing.

The trick is to close all font suitcases before opening the document you want to check in PageMaker. Then only the fonts used to create that document (plus any fonts permanently installed in your System) are listed in the menu. The names of missing fonts are grayed out to indicate that they are not available. This graying out tells you exactly which fonts you need to print a given document.

Do this check before downloading to a Linotronic or other high-resolution output device to avoid mistakes like missing or wrong fonts—errors that can increase per-page printing costs dramatically.

Staying in Shape with DataShaper

DataShaper is a PageMaker database-publishing import filter. If you use PageMaker to publish directories, catalogs, parts and price lists, schedules, mailing labels, and so on, DataShaper is indispensable. DataShaper enables you to apply PageMaker text attributes to any database or spreadsheet field as you import the information into your publications. This capability eliminates the need to do tedious line-by-line formatting afterward. You only have to assign the desired text attributes once. After that, PageMaker applies the formatting for you automatically. For more information about DataShaper, write or call: ELSEWARE, 4708 Burke Ave. North, Seattle, WA 98103, (206) 547-9623.

Tracking with PMtracker

PageMaker lists only a few track-kerning choices on its Track menu. When you make a selection, the tracking you assign to selected text is determined by the characteristics built into the current font. You cannot vary these settings.

With PMtracker, you can overcome this limitation by revising the track-kerning parameters for any font you use. The revised parameters enable you to refine and improve tracking to meet the most demanding and rigorous publishing requirements. PMtracker stores the revised information in PageMaker's Kern Tracks file. After you revise a set of tracking parameters, you make Track menu selections normally; PageMaker uses the new settings for the selected fonts.

PMtracker enables you to adjust the spacing increments for all typefaces from any font library. An interactive visual display makes getting your revised settings right on the first try easy. PMtracker also includes an easy-to-use Kern Pair Editor for updating the kerning pair assignments within your fonts. Taken together, these two powerful tools enable you to calibrate character spacings to achieve output with a typeset look.

For more information about PMtracker, write or call: EDCO Services, 12410 North Dale Mabry Hwy., Tampa, FL 33618, (813) 962-7800 or (800) 523-8973.

Using High-Resolution Printers and Paper

High-resolution, plain-paper printers are becoming less expensive and therefore more fashionable. However, you should consider several significant trade-offs before rushing out to buy one.

First, these printers sometimes output documents slowly. Positioning all those extra dots takes a lot more processing time (and printer memory) than on lower-resolution, 300 dpi machines.

Second, most of these printers do not use an Adobe PostScript interpreter, which raises a host of unanswered questions concerning software compatibility.

And third, despite their increased output resolution, these printers remain incapable of generating perfectly registered color separations. For high-quality color output, you still have to use a high-end color prepress system or print your pages directly to film on a Linotronic L300.

Another factor to consider is the kind of paper you should use with these machines. The paper should handle the placement of fine toner dots without loss of image quality. Otherwise, any potential gains in resolution are offset immediately by scattering and pocketing of the toner. So forget using ordinary copier paper—it doesn't hold a crisp image. You need a smooth, bright-white paper to get decent camera-ready copy or presentation-quality prints. Such paper generally is harder to find than ordinary, run-of-the-mill brands, but the results this paper produces are well worth the effort it takes to track the paper down.

Among those papers specially made for producing camera-ready copy and client presentations, CG Graphic Arts Supply's LaserEdge paper consistently proves itself the top performer. No other paper compares to LaserEdge at any price. Depending on the kinds of jobs you do, the paper you choose does make a difference. For more information, contact: CG Graphic Arts Supply, 481 Washington St., New York, NY 10013, (212) 925-5332 or (800) 342-5858.

Improving Laser-Printed Output

You can get blacker blacks for crisper camera-ready copy by applying a non-glossy spray fixative to your pages. Use the same kind of spray that artists use for fixing charcoal, pastel, and pencil artwork. You can find cans of fixative spray in any art supply store. Lightly spray your pages to bring out highlights but don't overspray or your toner may streak.

Checking Laser Printer Performance

Commercial graphic arts firms regularly run control strips through their processors to determine the condition of the equipment. These control strips usually are pre-exposed pieces of photographic material that are designed to indicate problems or weaknesses in the processing system. Large commercial shops may run as many as four control strips a day.

You also can use a control strip to verify proper printer performance (see fig. T.2). With a control strip, you can monitor the gradual degradation of image quality that results from normal printer use and detect potential problems before they adversely affect production output.

To prepare your control strip, design a page that includes each of the following:

❑ The smallest, lightest weight type your system can set

❑ The largest and heaviest type you generally use

❑ A paragraph of text set using various font types and styles

❑ The thinnest line your printer can reproduce

❑ Several 1/4-inch shaded bars that extend horizontally the full width of the page. The first bar should be solid black. The remaining bars should be screened using progressively lighter shades of gray.

❑ Several 1/4-inch shaded bars oriented vertically on the page. The first bar should be solid black.

❑ A sample scanned photograph. Use typical middle-of-the-range scanner settings.

❑ One or two geometric shapes to check for linearity and page alignment

The best time to produce a software control strip is when you are sure that your laser printer is operating at peak efficiency. The ideal time is when your printer is new or immediately after your printer has been cleaned and serviced. After you prepare your software control strip, the first print you make becomes the standard by which you judge all later prints. Be sure to use a good-quality toner cartridge—one that yields reasonably solid blacks.

You can use your control strip to evaluate new paper and film products and periodically check the performance of your laser or ink-jet printer. Inconsistencies in toner deposits from left to right across the page may be caused either by a low-toner condition or the toner becoming caked due to moisture. Ghosting (the image repeats itself on the page) generally is caused by a worn imaging drum. If the print image shows shadows, excessive fill-in, or streaking, the problem may be a build-up of stray toner on or near the charging wires, a dirty transfer corona wire or transfer guide, or dirty discharging pins. On LED printers, this condition also can be caused by dirt on the LED Imaging head. Consult your printer's manual for specific information about other problem conditions.

Adding Color with Kroy

An easy way to add dazzling color to your PageMaker documents is to use a Kroy Kolor Processor. This remarkable machine applies a combination of heat and pressure to bond color ink from foil transfer sheets into the black toner on your laser-printed or photocopied pages. The transfer sheets come in a wide variety of colors, including gold and silver metallics, that are perfect for dressing up invitations, certificates, awards, report covers, business cards, personal stationery, and other important documents.

Because you manually have to feed each sheet to add color, use of the Kroy Kolor Processor is limited to small production runs. The results you get, however, are so extraordinary that, if your printing requirements are modest, you should consider this alternative to using a commercial printer. To obtain more information about the Kroy Kolor Processor, write or call: Kroy Sign Systems, 14555 N. Hayden Rd., Scottsdale, AZ 85267, (602) 948-2222 or (800) 729-5769.

Easy Binding with Unibind

A quick, easy, and effective way to bind your publications and give them a uniformly elegant look is to use a Unibind Thermal Binding Machine. Several models are available, but all work on the same principle. Place your publication pages into a one-piece Unicover and insert the Unicover into the machine. The machine applies controlled heat to melt an inlaid thermoplastic adhesive that binds the pages and cover firmly together. In seconds, you can produce a perfect, durable binding that enables even the thinnest documents to lay perfectly flat when open. You even can later reheat the binding to add or remove pages.

The Unibind system is far superior to most small-production binding tools. As with the Kroy Kolor Processor described above, if your printing needs are modest, consider this alternative to paying a commercial printer to prepare your bindings. To obtain more information about Unibind Thermal Binding Machines, write or call: Unibind Systems, 7900 Capwell Dr., Oakland, CA 94621, (415) 638-1060.

Keeping Uncle Sam Updated

You are expected to send two complete copies of every copyrightable work you publish to the Library of Congress. If you fail to do so, you may be subject to a hefty fine. The U.S. Copyright Act states that all works published in the United States are subject to mandatory deposit. Submissions get placed in Library of Congress collections or used in national library programs. Additional information is available from the Copyright Office, Library of Congress, Washington, DC 20559.

Keeping Updated with *ThePage*

A continuing source of reliable information about PageMaker is *ThePage*, a monthly subscription journal that provides coverage of PageMaker and other desktop publishing tools. The contents are well-illustrated (*ThePage* is subtitled "A Visual Guide to Using the Macintosh in Desktop Publishing") and the information is presented in an organized and concise manner. For a free sample issue of *ThePage*, write to: ThePage, P.O. Box 14493, Chicago, IL 60614.

Better *Before & After*

An excellent source of practical, hands-on insights about using PageMaker is *Before & After*, a full-color newsletter published by PageLab, a highly regarded graphic design firm with clients that include Apple, Aldus, and Adobe Systems. Each issue of *Before & After* contains detailed and fully illustrated step-by-step design techniques that you can apply immediately to your own work. For a free sample issue of *Before & After*, write to: Before & After, 331 J St., #150, Sacramento, CA 95814.

Going On-Line for Information and Support

For additional help and information about PageMaker, go on-line with CompuServe and join the Aldus Forum. Just type *GO ALDUS* at the prompt. The forum is free, except for your connect time. You have access to a complete collection of PageMaker Technical Support Notes and an assortment of the most current APD files. The Forum also has a message board that enables you to exchange personal insights and information with other users, many who are qualified PageMaker experts. You can ask difficult technical questions and get prompt, in-depth answers, often directly from the folks at Aldus. For more information, write or call: CompuServe, 5000 Arlington Center Blvd., Columbus, OH 43220, (614) 457-8600 or (800) 848-8990.

Another on-line data source is MacNet, a part of the expanding Connect Information Service. Aldus maintains a free forum on MacNet, in which they post up-to-date technical support notes, APDs, and other useful files and information. Aldus representatives, however, do not provide on-line conference support or take part in interactive technical discussions. The MacNet interface consists entirely of familiar windows and icons, exactly like those on your Macintosh desktop. For more information, write or call: Connect, 10101 Bubb Rd., Cupertino, CA 95014, (408) 973-0110 or (800) 2-MACNET.

The newest of the on-line services is America Online. Like Connect, America Online consists entirely of familiar Macintosh windows and icons. Unlike Connect, America Online is set up to handle real-time conferencing. Special forums and chat rooms enable you to carry on conversations with other users just as fast as you can type. America Online has an excellent desktop publishing forum with a continuing, dynamic interchange of useful information. They also have a large library of templates, utilities, and other software of particular interest to desktop publishers and to Macintosh users in general. To request additional information and free trial software, or to join America Online, write or call: America Online, 8619 Westwood Center Drive, Vienna, VA 22182, (800) 227-6364.

Another on-line service is the Macintosh Exchange on BIX (Byte Information Exchange). One conference of the MacExchange (mac.desktop) is devoted entirely to self-publishing. The flat-fee subscription pricing contrasts favorably to the other services' hourly usage charges. For further information about BIX and the Macintosh Exchange, call (800) 227-2983.

Staying Current with *The Weigand Report*

If you found this book helpful, you may want to subscribe to *The Weigand Report: The Working Newsletter for Macintosh Professionals*. This newsletter delivers essential information for communicators, desktop publishers, and small-business users.

If you use a Macintosh to help with your daily publishing tasks, this newsletter is for you. In every issue, you find practical hands-on tips and techniques, industry insights, and timely decision-making information.

The Weigand Report looks at the world of desktop publishing as it exists for the mainstream user. If you are new to the field of computer-aided publishing, this newsletter provides the information you need to compete successfully. If you are an experienced user, this newsletter helps you refine old skills and acquire new ones. You keep abreast of the latest developments in your field, and you get concise product evaluations that enable you to make sound buying decisions.

The Weigand Report carries no advertising. Subscription fees cover all costs, including First Class postage. An order form you can use to subscribe to *The Weigand Report* is included in the back of this book.

Quick Reference

This section is for users who have forgotten a PageMaker procedure and need to access the information quickly. Step-by-step instructions take you through basic procedures—from opening publications to printing.

Some steps present more than one method for achieving the same result. These alternative procedures are introduced by "Or." Choose the method with which you are most comfortable.

Working with Files

Opening Publications

1. Choose New from the File menu to open a new publication.

2. Choose Open from the File menu to open an existing publication or template.

   Or, double-click on the file in the Finder.

Reverting to the Last Saved Version of a Publication

1. Choose Revert from the File menu.

2. Click OK.

Saving Publications

1. Choose Save from the File menu to save an existing publication to the original file.

2. Choose Save As from the File menu to save a new publication, to save an existing publication under a new name or to a different disk location, or to save a publication as a template (or a template as a publication).

Viewing Your Publication

1. To view your publication's actual size, choose Actual Size from the Page menu.

2. To view your publication reduced to 75 percent of its original size, choose 75% Size from the Page menu.

3. To view your publication reduced to 50 percent of its original size, choose 50% Size from the Page menu.

4. To view your publication reduced to 25 percent of its original size, choose 25% Size from the Page menu.

5. To view your publication reduced in size to fit entirely within the publication window, choose Fit In Window from the Page menu.

6. To view your publication reduced in size with the entire pasteboard visible within the publication window, choose Fit In Window from the Page menu while holding down the Shift key.

7. To view your publication enlarged to 200 percent its original size, choose 200% Size from the Page menu.

8. To view your publication enlarged to 400 percent its original size, choose 400% Size from the Page menu.

9. To toggle between Actual Size and Fit In Window, click the part of the screen you want centered in the viewing window while holding down the Command and Option keys.

10. To toggle between Actual Size and 200% Size, click the part of the screen you want centered in the viewing window while holding down the Command, Option, and Shift keys.

Hiding the Toolbox and Window Scroll bars

1. To hide the toolbox, deselect the Toolbox command under the Windows menu.

2. To hide the publication window's scroll bars, deselect the Scroll Bars command under the Windows menu.

3. To redisplay the toolbox or scroll bars, choose the appropriate menu command from the Windows menu.

Working with Graphics

Drawing Tools

1. Click the square-corner rectangle, rounded-corner rectangle, oval, diagonal-line, or perpendicular-line icon in the toolbox.

2. Click the page or pasteboard with the selected tool and drag to draw a square-corner rectangle, rounded-corner rectangle, oval, or line.

3. Hold down the Shift key while dragging to make rectangles into squares, ovals into circles, and diagonal lines into exact multiples of 45 degrees.

Assigning Line Widths and Fill Patterns

1. Select graphic elements with the pointer tool (select only graphics drawn using PageMaker's drawing tools).

2. Choose a line width or line style (or None) from the Line menu under the Element menu to assign that width or style to the borders of the selected elements.

3. Choose a shade or pattern (or None) from the Fill menu under the Element menu to assign that shade or pattern to the fill areas of the selected elements.

Reversing Lines and Border Shapes

1. Use the pointer tool to select a line or shape drawn with PageMaker's tools.

2. Choose a line thickness or line style from the Line menu under the Element menu.

3. Choose Reverse Line from the Line menu.

Resizing and Reshaping Graphics

1. Click the graphic with the pointer tool to select it.

2. Click a reshaping handle and drag. Release the mouse button when the graphic is the desired size and shape.

3. To resize a graphic proportionally, hold down the Shift key while dragging the reshaping handle.

4. To resize an imported bit-mapped (Paint or TIFF) graphic for the best printing resolution, hold down the Command key while dragging the reshaping handle. (The graphic must have been imported using the Place command under the File menu.)

Changing the Corner Radius of Rectangles

1. Use the pointer tool to select the rectangles.

2. Choose Rounded Corners from the Element menu.

3. Click the desired corner-shape icon.

4. Click OK.

Importing New Graphics

1. Choose the Place command from the File menu in the layout view to open the Place Document dialog box.

   Or, choose the Import command from the Story menu in the story view to open the Import To Story Editor dialog box.

2. Select the file you want to import from the document-selection window.

3. Click the **As independent graphic** button.

   Or, if an insertion point exists in your text, click the **As inline graphic** button to import the file as an inline graphic.

4. Click OK.

Linking Graphics

1. Choose Links from the File menu to display the Links dialog box.

2. Click the Link options button to display the Link Options dialog box.

3. If no graphic is selected, set Link Options defaults. If a graphic is selected, set Link Options for that graphic.

4. Click OK.

Updating Graphic Links

1. Use the pointer tool to select the graphic you want to update.

2. Choose Links under the File menu to display the Links dialog box.

3. Click the **Link info** button to display the Link Info dialog box.

4. Choose an update file from the document-selection window and click the **Link** button to link the file to the selected graphic.

5. Click OK.

Cropping an Imported Graphic

1. Click the cropping tool icon in the toolbox.

2. Click the imported graphic with the cropping tool to select the graphic.

3. Center the cropping tool over a reshaping handle.

4. Click and drag in the direction you want to crop the graphic.

Centering a Cropped Graphic

1. To move or center a cropped graphic within its boundaries, click the graphic with the cropping tool.

2. Continue holding down the mouse button. The cropping tool changes into a grabber hand.

3. Drag the grabber hand while still holding down the mouse button to adjust the display.

Modifying Scanned and Bit-Mapped Images

1. Select the graphic to be modified.

2. Choose Image Control from the Element menu to open the Image Control dialog box.

3. Click the **Black and white** button to modify black-and-white images.

4. Click the **Screened** button to vary the contrast and brightness of black-and-white images, to adjust individual gray levels for gray-scale images, or to change screen assignments for both kinds of images.

5. Click the **Gray** button to individually adjust gray levels for gray-scale images (only if you are using a Macintosh II).

6. Adjust image contrast and brightness by scrolling the **Contrast** and **Lightness** scroll-bar arrows or by clicking the bar-graph window to adjust the graph display (the **Screened** or **Gray** button should be selected). Note that each bar represents a different gray level and can be adjusted individually when modifying gray-scale or screened black-and-white images.

7. Click one of the four special-effect icons located above the bar graph to apply the indicated effect (from left to right: **Normal, Negative, Posterize, Solarize**).

8. To change the screen assignment, click the **Screened** button.

9. To apply a dot-screen to your image, click the dot-screen screen icon. To apply a line-screen to your image, click the line-screen screen icon.

10. To change screen angle or lines-per-inch settings, type new values directly into the **Angle** and **Lines/in** fields.

11. Click the **Apply** button to view the effects of your modifications.

12. Click the **Reset** button to undo your modifications.

13. To better view your graphic, click the title bar of the Image Control dialog box and drag the dialog box to another spot on-screen.

14. Click OK.

Substituting Graphics

1. Use the pointer tool to select the graphic to be replaced.

   Or, use the text tool to select the inline graphic to be replaced.

2. Choose the Place command from the File menu in the layout view to open the Place Document dialog box.

   Or, choose the Import command from the Story menu in the story view to open the Import To Story Editor dialog box.

3. Select the file you want to substitute from the document-selection window.

4. Click the **Replacing entire graphic** button.

5. Click OK.

Working with Pages

Selecting Page Sizes

1. Choose Page Setup from the File menu to open the Page Setup dialog box.

2. Make your selection from the pop-up Page menu. The page dimensions appear in the **Page dimension** fields.

3. To use a custom page size, type the desired page dimensions into the **Page dimension** fields.

4. Click the **Tall** or **Wide** button to set the page orientation.

5. Click OK.

Setting Margins

1. Choose Page Setup from the File menu to open the Page Setup dialog box.

2. Type new margin settings into the **Margin** fields.

3. Click OK.

Turning Pages

1. To display a page or set of facing pages, click the corresponding numbered page icons in the lower left corner of your publication window. Scroll the page icon display, if necessary, by clicking the arrows at either end of the display.

   Or, choose Go To Page from the Page menu and type the desired page number into the **Page number** field.

2. To display your master pages, click the left or right master page icons in the lower left corner of your publication window.

   Or, choose **Left master page** or **Right master page** from the Go To Page dialog box.

Viewing Facing Pages

1. Choose Page Setup from the File menu to open the Page Setup dialog box.

2. Click the **Double-sided** and **Facing pages** option check boxes.

3. Click OK.

Assigning Automatic Page Numbers

1. To have PageMaker number all your pages, type the Command-Option-p (small p) key combination on both master pages for double-sided publications and on the right master page for single-sided publications. (Make sure that the Caps Lock key is toggled off.)

2. To have PageMaker number individual publication pages, type the Command-Option-p key combination on just those pages you want numbers to appear. (Make sure that the Caps Lock key is toggled off.)

Setting the Number of Pages in an Existing Publication

1. Choose Page Setup from the File menu to open the Page Setup dialog box.

2. To change the beginning page number, type a new beginning page number into the **Start page #** *field.*

3. Click OK.

4. To change the total number of pages, choose Insert Pages or Remove Pages from the Page menu and type new values into the Insert Pages or Remove Pages dialog box fields.

5. Click OK.

Setting the Number of Pages in a New Publication

1. Choose Page Setup from the File menu to open the Page Setup dialog box.

2. Type a beginning page number into the **Start page #** field.

3. Type the planned total number of pages for your publication into the **# of pages** field.

4. Click OK.

Selecting Elements

1. Click the pointer tool icon in the toolbox.

2. Click the element you want to select or drag a selection rectangle completely around the element.

3. To select more than one element, hold down the Shift key while clicking on successive elements or drag a selection rectangle completely around the elements.

4. To select an element from within a stack of elements or one that lies behind an overlapping guide, click the element's location while holding down the Command key. Each successive click selects a different item in the stack.

5. To select all items on a page, choose Select All from the Edit menu.

Deselecting Elements

1. To deselect all currently selected elements, click a blank area of the page or pasteboard or click the pointer tool icon in the toolbox.

2. To deselect one or more elements from a group of currently selected elements, click each element in turn while holding down the Shift key or draw a selection rectangle around the elements while holding down the Shift key.

Hiding Master Elements

1. To hide the master elements on a publication page, deselect the Display Master Items command under the Page menu.

2. To redisplay the master items, choose Display Master Items from the Page menu.

Changing the Stacking Order of Elements

1. Select one or more elements with the pointer tool. To select an element buried within a stack, hold down the Command key and click repeatedly until the desired element is selected.

2. To move selected elements to the bottom of the stack, choose Send To Back from the Element menu.

3. To move selected elements to the top of the stack, choose Bring To Front from the Element menu.

Moving Elements on the Same Page

1. Select the elements to move using the pointer tool.

2. Click one of the selected elements and drag the elements as a group to their new location on the page.

Moving Elements to Another Page

1. Use the pointer tool to select the elements you want to move.

2. Choose Cut from the Edit menu.

3. Turn to the new page and choose Paste from the Edit menu. The elements reappear on the page.

4. While the elements are still selected, drag the elements to their new location.

   Or, choose Paste from the Edit menu while holding down the option key. The elements reappear on the new page at exactly the same coordinates as they were located on the old page.

   Or, drag the elements onto the pasteboard, turn to the new page, and drag the elements back onto the new page.

Working with Rulers and Guides

Displaying Rulers

1. To display the rulers, select the Rulers command from the Options menu.

2. To hide the rulers, deselect the Rulers command from the Options menu.

Using Ruler Guides

1. Click the pointer tool in the horizontal or vertical ruler and drag to get a horizontal or vertical ruler guide.

2. Continue holding down the mouse button and drag toward the center of the viewing window. The ruler guide follows along. Use the ruler tick marks to accurately position the guide on the page.

3. To reposition a ruler guide, click the ruler guide with the pointer tool and drag while holding down the mouse button.

4. Choose Snap To Rulers from the Options menu to activate the "magnetic" properties of the guides.

Resetting the Ruler Zero Point

1. Display the rulers by selecting the Rulers command from the Options menu.

2. Unlock the zero point if locked by deselecting the Zero Lock command from the Options menu.

3. Click the pointer tool on the crossed-lines icon in the upper left corner of the window where the rulers intersect.

4. Hold down the mouse button and drag the zero point to a new location on the page.

5. Release the mouse button.

6. To relock the zero point, select the Zero Lock command from the Options menu.

Selecting Units of Measure

1. Choose Preferences from the Edit menu to open the Preferences dialog box.

2. Choose the desired unit of measure from the pop-up Measurement System menu.

3. To set a different unit of measure for the vertical ruler, make a selection from the Vertical Ruler pop-up menu or type a custom point size into the **Custom points** field.

4. Click OK.

Using Column Guides

1. Choose Column Guides from the Options menu to open the Column Guides dialog box.

2. To specify the number of columns you want, type a whole number between 1 and 20 into the **Number of columns** field.

3. To specify the spacing between columns, type a numerical value into the **Space between columns** field.

4. Click the **Set left and right pages separately** checkbox if you are viewing facing pages and want to use a different column arrangement on each page.

5. Click OK.

6. To reposition a column guide, click the guide with the pointer tool and drag while holding down the mouse button.

Using Snap To Options

1. To precisely align text or graphics to ruler tick marks, choose Snap To Rulers from the Options menu.

2. To precisely align text or graphics to column or margin guides, choose Snap To Guides from the Options menu.

3. To turn off either of these options, deselect the appropriate menu command under the Options menu.

Moving Guides to the Front or Back

1. Choose Preferences from the Edit menu to open the Preferences dialog box.

2. Click the Guides **Front** or **Back** button.

3. Click OK.

Locking Guides

1. To prevent the inadvertent movement of column and ruler guides, choose Lock Guides from the Options menu.

2. To unlock the guides, deselect the Lock Guides command under the Options menu.

Copying Master Guides

1. Turn to the page or facing pages to which you want to copy the master guide arrangement.

2. Choose Copy Master Guides from the Page menu.

Working with Text

Creating Text

1. Click the text tool icon in the toolbox.

2. Click between a pair of column guides to create an insertion point.

3. Type your text. The text wraps between the column guides.

   Or, click and drag the text tool to create a text block of a specific width. When you type your text, the text wraps to that column width.

   Or, choose Edit Story from the Edit menu.

4. Type the text into the Story Editor window.

5. Choose Place from the File menu, close the window, or click anywhere in the layout view to display the text-placement cursor.

6. Place the text as a story into your layout.

Opening the Story Editor

1. Triple-click a text block with the pointer tool. The Story Editor window opens.

   Or, click a text insertion point in your story.

   Or, select a range of text.

2. Choose Edit Story from the Edit menu. The Story Editor window opens.

3. To open a new Story Editor window, choose Edit Story from the Edit menu with no insertion point in any text block and no text selected in any story.

Spell-Checking Stories

1. Open the Story Editor.

2. Choose Spelling from the Edit menu.

3. Click the **Search Selected text, Current story**, or **All stories** button as appropriate.

4. Click Start.

5. During spell-checking, click **Ignore** to ignore a flagged word.

6. During spell-checking, click a replacement word in the Suggested-replacements window, or type a replacement word in the **Change to** field and click **Replace** to effect a correction.

7. To add a replacement word to the user dictionary, click the **Add** button.

8. Make sure that the word is spelled exactly as you want the word to appear.

9. Click OK.

Finding, Changing, and Replacing Text

1. Open the Story Editor.

2. Choose Change from the Edit menu.

3. Click the **Search Selected text, Current story,** or **All stories** button as appropriate.

4. Enter the text you want to find, change, or replace into the **Find what** field.

5. Enter the text you want to substitute into the **Change to** field.

6. Select the **Match case** and **Whole word** options to search for exact matches. Leave either or both of these options unchecked as appropriate.

7. Click the **Attributes** button to define additional search criteria based on paragraph styles and font types, sizes, and styles.

8. Click OK to return to the Change window.

9. Click the **Find** or **Change all button** for the type of search you want to conduct. Click the **Change** button after each find to effect a change and pause momentarily, or click the **Change & find** button after each find to effect a change and then continue searching.

Resizing and Reshaping Text Blocks

1. Click the text block with the pointer tool to select it.

2. Click a windowshade handle and drag to lengthen or shorten the text block without changing its width.

3. To reshape the text block, click a corner reshaping handle and drag. Release the mouse button when the text block is the desired size and shape.

Rotating Text

1. Click the text block with the pointer tool to select it.

2. Choose Text Rotation from the Element menu.

3. Click the icon representing the desired text orientation.

4. Click OK.

Selecting Text

1. To select a range of text, click the text tool to create an insertion point.

2. Drag through the text while holding down the mouse button.

   Or, click the text tool to create an insertion point and then hold down the Shift key and click the text tool at the end of the range.

3. To select a word, double-click the word with the text tool.

4. To select a range of words, double-click the first word and then drag through the remaining words while holding down the mouse button.

   Or, double-click the first word in the range, hold down the Shift key, and click the text tool on the last word in the range.

5. To select an entire paragraph, triple-click the text tool anywhere within the paragraph.

6. To select an entire story, click the text tool anywhere within the story to create an insertion point and choose Select All from the Edit menu.

Deleting Text

1. Select the text to be deleted using the text tool.

2. Press the Delete (Backspace) key or choose Clear from the Edit menu.

   Or, choose Cut from the Edit menu to remove the text from your document and leave a copy of what was removed on the Clipboard.

Greeking Text

1. Choose Preferences from the Edit menu to open the Preferences dialog box.

2. Type a point size below which you want Greeking to occur into the **Greek text below** field.

3. Click OK.

Changing Type Specifications

Changing Font Sizes

1. Use the text tool to select the text to be changed.

2. Choose Size from the Type menu.

3. Select a new font size from the Size submenu.

   Or, choose Type Specs from the Type menu.

4. Select a new font size from the pop-up Size menu in the Type Specifications dialog box.

Or, type a new point size into the **Size** field. Tenth-point type sizes are permitted.

5. Click OK.

Changing Font Types

1. Use the text tool to select the text to be changed.

2. Choose Font from the Type menu and select a new font type from the Font submenu.

   Or, choose Type Specs from the Type menu.

3. Select a new font type from the pop-up Font menu in the Type Specifications dialog box.

4. Click OK.

Changing Type Style

1. Use the text tool to select the text to be styled.

2. Choose Type Style from the Type menu.

3. Select a style from the Type Style submenu.

   Or, choose Type Specs from the Type menu to open the Type Specifications dialog box.

4. Select a new type style by clicking the appropriate **Type Style** checkbox in the Type Specifications dialog box.

5. Click more than one option to assign multiple styles simultaneously.

6. Click OK.

Assigning All Caps and Small Caps

1. Use the text tool to select the text to be styled.

2. Choose Type Specs from the Type menu.

3. Select **All caps** or **Small caps** from the pop-up Case menu in the Type Specifications dialog box.

4. To revert to your original type styling, select **Normal** from the pop-up Case menu in the Type Specifications dialog box.

5. Click OK.

Reversing Type

1. Use the text tool to select the text to be reversed.

2. Choose Type Style from the Type menu and select **Reverse** from the Type Style submenu.

   Or, choose Type Specs from the Type menu to open the Type Specifications dialog box.

3. Click **Reverse** from the Type Style checkbox.

4. Click OK.

Assigning Superscripting and Subscripting

1. Use the text tool to select the text to be super- or subscripted.

2. Choose Type Specs from the Type menu.

3. Select Superscript or Subscript from the pop-up Position menu in the Type Specifications dialog box.

4. To revert to your original type styling, select **Normal** from the pop-up Position menu in the Type Specifications dialog box.

5. Click OK.

Formatting Text

Setting First-Line Indents

1. Use the text tool to select the paragraphs to be indented.

2. Choose Paragraph from the Type menu to open the Paragraph Specifications dialog box.

   Or, choose Indents/Tabs from the Type menu to open the Indents/Tabs ruler.

3. Type the desired first-line indent value into the **Indents first** field.

4. To set a normal indent from the Paragraph Specifications dialog box, type a positive value.

   To set a hanging indent from the Paragraph Specifications dialog box, type a negative value. (Note that you first must type a larger positive value in the **Indents left** field to create enough room for the hanging indent.)

5. To set a normal indent from the Indents/Tabs ruler, drag the first-line indent marker to any spot along the ruler to the right of the left-indent marker. The first-line indent marker is the small upper triangle at the left end of the ruler. The left-indent marker is the small lower triangle at the left end of the ruler.

To create a hanging indent from the Indents/Tabs dialog box, drag the first line indent marker to any spot along the ruler to the left of the left indent marker. (Note that you first must move the left indent marker to the right to create enough room for the hanging indent.)

6. Click OK.

Setting Left and Right Indents

1. Use the text tool to select the paragraphs to be indented.

2. Choose Paragraph from the Type menu to open the Paragraph Specifications dialog box.

   Or, choose Indents/Tabs from the Type menu to open the Indents/Tabs ruler.

3. To set left and right indents from the Paragraph Specifications dialog box, type the desired left and right indent values into the **Indents Left** and **Indents Right** fields.

4. To set the left indent from the Indents/Tabs ruler, drag the left indent marker to any spot along the ruler. The left-indent marker is the small lower triangle at the left end of the ruler.

   To set the right indent from the Indents/Tabs ruler, drag the right-indent marker to any spot along the ruler. The right-indent marker is the left pointing arrowhead at the right end of the ruler.

5. Click OK.

Setting Tab Stops

1. Use the text tool to select the text to which you want to assign tab stops.

2. Choose Indents/Tabs from the Type menu to open the Indents/Tabs ruler.

3. Click **Reset** to remove any assigned tab stops from the ruler.

   Or, to use the existing tab stops, adjust them one at a time by dragging them to new positions along the ruler.

4. Remove any default tab stops you don't want by dragging them off the ruler.

   Or, choose **Remove tab** from the pop-up Position menu.

5. Click the **Left, Right, Center,** or **Decimal** tab icon for the kind of tab stop you want to set.

6. Choose the kind of leader style you want from the pop-up Leader menu. You can assign dots, dashes, a solid line, custom, or none. To set a custom leader style, type one or two characters of your own choosing into the leader field.

7. Click anywhere along the ruler to make the tab marker appear.

   Or, choose Add Tab from the pop-up Position menu.

8. Drag the tab marker to the desired position along the ruler. Use the value displayed in the **Position** field to check placement accuracy.

   Or, choose Move Tab or Repeat Tab from the pop-up Position menu.

9. Click OK.

Adding Paragraph Rules

1. Use the text tool to select the paragraphs to which you want to assign paragraph rules.

2. Choose Paragraph from the Type menu to open the Paragraph Specifications dialog box.

3. Click the **Rules** button to display the Paragraph Rule dialog box.

4. Select the **Rule above paragraph** and **Rule below paragraph** options as appropriate for your layout.

5. Select rule attributes from the pop-up Line Style and Line Color menus.

6. Specify the line width and the amount of left and right indent.

7. Click the **Options** button to open the Paragraph Rule Options dialog box.

8. Type the amount of distance above and below the baseline for your rules into the **Top** and **Bottom** fields.

9. Check the **Align to grid** box to have following and adjoining paragraphs align to your vertical grid. Enter the current leading value in points into the **Grid size** field.

10. Click OK.

Spacing Paragraphs

1. Use the text tool to select the paragraphs for which you want to change the spacing.

2. Choose Paragraph from the Type menu to open the Paragraph Specifications dialog box.

3. Type the desired spacing values into the Paragraph Spacing **Before** and **After** fields.

4. Select the desired options to keep your paragraphs intact (**Keep lines together**), force paragraphs to begin a new column or page (**Column break before** and **Page break before**), and tie their movement to a certain number of lines of a following paragraph (**Keep with next xxx lines**).

5. Click OK.

Controlling Widows and Orphans

1. Use the text tool to select the paragraphs to which you want to assign widow and orphan control.

2. Choose Paragraph from the Type menu to open the Paragraph Specifications dialog box.

3. Click the **Widow control** and **Orphan control** check boxes. Enter the number of lines that you want to apply to each option.

4. Click OK.

Justifying Text

1. Use the text tool to select the paragraphs to be aligned.

2. Choose Alignment from the Type menu.

3. To left-justify your text, choose Align Left from the pop-up Alignment submenu.

4. To right-justify your text, choose Align Right from the pop-up Alignment submenu.

5. To center-justify your text, choose Align Center from the pop-up Alignment submenu.

6. To fully justify your text, choose Justify from the pop-up Alignment submenu.

7. To force-justify the last line of your text, choose Force Justify from the pop-up Alignment submenu.

   Or, choose Paragraph from the Type menu to open the Paragraph Specifications dialog box.

8. Choose the appropriate Alignment Left, Right, Center, Justify, or Force Justify command for the desired alignment.

9. Click OK.

Adjusting Word and Letter Spacing

1. To adjust the word spacing of a story, use the text tool to create an insertion point in the story.

2. Choose Paragraph from the Type menu to open the Paragraph Specifications dialog box.

3. Click the **Spacing** button to display the Spacing Attributes dialog box.

4. Type the desired word-spacing values into the **Word space Minimum**, **Desired**, and **Maximum** fields. All field values must fall within the range 0 to 500 percent.

5. Type the desired letter-spacing values into the **Letter space Minimum**, **Desired**, and **Maximum** fields. **Minimum** field values must fall within the range -200 to 0 percent, and **Maximum** field values must fall within the range 0 to 200 percent.

6. Click OK.

Typing Non-breaking Spaces

1. To type an Em space, simultaneously press Command-Shift-M.

2. To type an En space, simultaneously press Command-Shift-N.

3. To type a thin space, simultaneously press Command-Shift-T.

4. To type a fixed space, simultaneously press Option-Space bar.

5. To type a non-breaking hyphen, simultaneously press Command-Option-(hyphen).

Kerning Type Automatically

1. Use the text tool to select the range of text to be kerned.

2. Choose Paragraph from the Type menu to open the Paragraph Specifications dialog box.

3. Click the **Spacing** button to display the Spacing Attributes dialog box.

4. To have PageMaker kern your text, click the **Pair kerning** check box.

5. In the **Auto above points** field, type the point size above which you want auto-kerning to be applied.

6. Click OK.

Applying Track Kerning

1. Use the text tool to select the range of text to apply tracking.

2. Choose Track from the Type menu.

3. Select a tracking value from the Track submenu.

   Or, choose Type Specs from the Type menu to open the Type Specifications dialog box.

4. Select a new tracking value from the pop-up Track menu in the Type Specifications dialog box.

Kerning Type Manually

1. Use the text tool to create an insertion point between two characters you want to kern.

   Or, use the text tool to select the range of text to be kerned.

2. To remove space, press the Delete (Backspace) key while holding down the Command key. Repeat to remove additional increments of space. Press the Delete and Option keys to remove space in smaller increments.

3. To add space, press the Delete (Backspace) key while holding down the Command and Shift keys. Repeat to add additional increments of space. Press the Delete, Option, and Shift keys together to add space in smaller increments.

Removing Applied Kerning

1. Use the text tool to select the range of text from which you want to remove all assigned kerning.

2. Press the Command-Option-K key combination. All assigned kerning is removed.

Assigning Fixed Leading

1. Use the text tool to select the text to be changed.

2. Choose Leading from the Type menu.

3. Select a new leading value from the Leading submenu.

   Or, choose Type Specs from the Type menu.

4. Select a new leading value from the pop-up Leading menu in the Type Specifications dialog box.

5. To specify a leading value other than those values listed in the pop-up menu, type the new value directly into the Type Specifications dialog box **Leading** field. Tenth-point sizes are permissible.

6. Click OK.

Assigning Automatic Leading

1. Use the text tool to create an insertion point in your paragraph.

2. Choose Leading from the Type menu.

3. Select Auto from the Leading submenu.

   Or, choose Type Specs from the Type menu.

4. Select Auto from the pop-up Leading menu in the Type Specifications dialog box.

5. To change the way PageMaker computes auto-leading, choose Paragraph from the Type menu to open the Paragraph Specifications dialog box. Click the **Spacing** button to display the Spacing Attributes dialog box.

6. Type a new value into the **Auto leading % of point size** field.

7. Click the **Proportional** or **Top of caps** leading method button.

8. Click OK.

Wrapping Text Around Graphics

1. Select the graphic around which you want to wrap text.

2. Choose Text Wrap from the Element menu to open the Text Wrap dialog box.

3. Click the rectangular-wrap icon (the middle icon) to set a rectangular graphic boundary.

4. Type desired standoff values into the **Standoff Left, Right, Top,** and **Bottom** fields.

5. Click a text flow icon to set the desired pattern of text flow.

6. Click OK.

Creating a Custom Text-Wrap Boundary

1. Select the graphic that has a text-wrap boundary you want to customize.

2. To change the shape of the boundary, click any diamond reshaping handle with the pointer tool, hold down the mouse button, and drag the handle to a new position.

3. To create additional handles, click anywhere along the text-wrap boundary.

4. To move a text-wrap boundary segment, click the line segment with the pointer tool, hold down the mouse button, and drag the segment to a new position.

5. To prevent the screen from being redrawn each time you make an adjustment, hold down the space bar until you have completed editing the boundary.

Using Automatic Hyphenation

1. Use the text tool to select the paragraphs to be hyphenated.

2. Choose Hyphenation from the Type menu to open the Hyphenation dialog box.

3. Click the **Hyphenation On** button and the **Manual plus dictionary** or **Manual plus algorithm** button to have PageMaker hyphenate your paragraphs automatically.

4. To turn auto-hyphenation off for selected paragraphs, click the **Hyphenation Off** button.

   Or, leave the **Hyphenation On** button selected and click the **Manual only** button.

5. Click OK.

Inserting Discretionary Hyphens

1. To add a discretionary hyphen to a word, click the word with the text tool to create an insertion point where you want the hyphen to appear.

2. Type the hyphen while holding down the Command key. The hyphen remains invisible until PageMaker splits the word.

3. To delete a discretionary hyphen from a word PageMaker has split, click with the text tool just after the hyphen to create an insertion point and then press the Delete (Backspace) key.

4. To delete a discretionary hyphen from a word PageMaker has not split, use the text tool to select the letters on both sides of the hyphen and then retype the letters.

Updating the User Dictionary

1. Choose Hyphenation from the Type menu to open the Hyphenation dialog box.

2. Click the **Add** button to display the Add Word To User Dictionary dialog box.

3. Select a user dictionary from the pop-up Dictionary menu.

4. Type the words you want to add or delete into the **Word** field. Be sure to click the appropriate **Add** button (**As all lowercase** or **Exactly as typed**) if adding a word.

5. To make corrections, first remove the words and then add their replacements.

6. Insert tildes (~) into words when you want PageMaker to hyphenate the words. Type one, two, or three tildes to indicate the ranking preference of your hyphenation choices. If you don't want a word to be hyphenated, type a tilde before the word.

7. Click OK.

Adjusting the Hyphenation Zone

1. To adjust the width of the hyphenation zone (the area at the end of an unjustified line of text in which PageMaker hyphenates words), choose Hyphenation from the Type menu to open the Hyphenation dialog box.

2. Type a new value into the Hyphenation Zone field.

3. Click OK.

Importing and Exporting Stories

Importing a New Story

1. Choose the Place command from the File menu in the layout view to open the Place Document dialog box.

   Or, choose the Import command from the Story menu in the story view to open the Import To Story Editor dialog box.

2. Select the file you want to import from the document-selection window.

3. Click the **As new story** button.

4. Click the appropriate options to retain the original story format, convert straight quotes and apostrophes to curly ones, or import style tags.

5. Click OK.

Autoflowing Text

1. Choose Autoflow from the Options menu.

2. Place your text in the layout view. PageMaker autoflows your story and creates additional pages and columns as necessary to hold the text.

3. To stop autoflowing text, click the cancel button. To resume autoflowing text, click the arrow symbol in the column windowshade handle.

4. To semi-autoflow imported text, hold down the Shift key when clicking with the text-placement icon.

5. To change text-flow modes from automatic to manual, or manual to automatic, hold down the Command key while clicking with the text-placement icon.

Replacing a Story

1. Use the text tool to create an insertion point in the story to be replaced.

2. Choose the Place command from the File menu in the layout view to open the Place Document dialog box.

   Or, choose the Import command from the Story menu in the story view to open the Import To Story Editor dialog box.

3. Select the file you want to import from the document-selection window.

4. Click **Replacing entire story**.

5. Click OK.

Replacing Selected Text

1. Use the text tool to select the range of text to be replaced in the story.

2. Type the new text.

   Or, paste the text from the Clipboard.

   Or, choose the Place command from the File menu in the Layout view to open the Place Document dialog box.

Or, choose the Import command from the Story menu in the Story view to open the Import To Story Editor dialog box.

3. Select the file that contains the replacement text from the document-selection window.

4. Click **Replacing selected text.**

5. Click OK.

Inserting Text into a Story

1. Use the text tool to create an insertion point in the story for the new text.

2. Type the new text.

   Or, paste the text from the Clipboard.

   Or, choose the Place command from the File menu in the Layout view to open the Place Document dialog box.

   Or, choose the Import command from the Story menu in the Story view to open the Import To Story Editor dialog box.

3. Select the file containing the text you want to insert from the document-selection window.

4. Click **Inserting text.**

5. Click OK.

Exporting Text

1. Use the text tool to select the text or story to be exported.

2. Choose Export from the File menu to open the Export dialog box.

3. To export the entire story, click the **Entire story** button.

4. To export a selected range of text, click the **Selected text only** button.

5. Select an export file format from the File Format Selection window.

6. Assign a name to your exported file and a disk destination.

7. Click OK.

Using Styles

Applying Styles

1. Use the text tool to select the paragraphs to which you want to apply a style.

2. Choose Style Palette from the Windows menu to display the Styles Palette. Click a style in the Styles Palette list to apply that style to the selected paragraphs. Hold down the Shift key when you click to preserve any existing overrides.

   Or, choose Style from the Type menu. Select a style name from the Style submenu to apply that style to the selected paragraphs.

Defining and Editing Styles

1. Choose Define Styles from the Type menu to open the Define Styles dialog box.

2. To define a new style, click **New** to open the Edit Style dialog box. To edit an existing style, click the name of the style to be edited and then click **Edit** to open the Edit Style dialog box.

   Or, if the Styles Palette is displayed, click the name of the style to be edited (click **No style** to create a style) while holding down the Command key. This action opens the Edit Style dialog box.

   Or, from the Style submenu (choose the Style command from the Type menu), click the name of the style to be edited (click **No style** to create a style) while holding down the Command key. This action opens the Edit Style dialog box.

3. If defining a new style, assign a name to your style by typing the name into the **Name** field. Choose a style name from the **Based on** pop-up menu if your new style is to be based on an existing style.

4. Click **Type** to open the Type Specifications dialog box. Set the desired type specifications and click OK.

5. Click **Para** to open the Paragraph Specifications dialog box. Set the desired paragraph specifications and click OK.

6. Click **Tabs** to open the Indents/Tabs dialog box. Set the desired indents and tabs and click OK.

7. Click **Hyph** to open the Hyphenation dialog box. Specify the desired hyphenation attributes and click OK.

8. Click OK to return to the Define Styles dialog box.

9. Click OK to save the style.

Copying Styles

1. Choose Define Styles from the Type menu to open the Define Styles dialog box.

2. Click **Copy** to open the Copy Styles dialog box.

3. Click a publication or template name in the list.

4. Click OK to import that publication's or template's style sheet and return to the Define Styles dialog box.

5. Click OK to save the updated style sheet.

Deleting Styles

1. Choose Define Styles from the Type menu to open the Define Styles dialog box.

2. Click the name of a style in the style list.

3. Click **Remove** to delete that style.

4. Click OK to save changes to your style sheet.

Working with Book-Length Publications

Generating a Table of Contents

1. Use the text tool to select each paragraph you want to include in your table of contents.

2. Choose Paragraph from the Type menu to open the Paragraph Specifications dialog box.

3. Click the **Include in table of contents** option.

4. Click OK.

5. When you are ready to generate your table of contents, choose the Create TOC command under the Options menu to display the Create Table of Contents dialog box.

6. Type a title into the **Title** field.

7. Click the **Replace existing table of contents** if updating an older version.

8. Click **Include book publications** to generate a table of contents for all publications in your current book list.

9. Choose the desired page numbering Format option and enter any special formatting into the **Between entry and page number** field.

10. Click OK.

Generating an Index

1. Use the text tool to select the text you want to appear as an index entry.

2. Choose Index Entry from the Options menu to display the Create Index Entry dialog box. Your selected text is displayed in the first **Topic** field.

3. If adding the entry to an existing topic, click the **Promote/Demote** button to cycle the entry to the second or third field.

4. Click the **Topic** button to display the Select Topic dialog box.

5. Choose a topic for your entry and click the **Return** button. Hold down the Command key at the same time to return to the Create Index Entry dialog box without deleting your original entry. If you forget to hold down the Command key, retype your entry into the second or third **Topic** field as appropriate.

6. Enter any special spellings for your entries into the corresponding sort fields to ensure correct sorting of your index.

7. Assign any special style formatting by clicking the appropriate Reference override options.

8. Click OK.

9. When you are ready to generate your index, choose the Create Index command from the Options menu to display the Create Index dialog box.

10. Click **Replace existing index** if updating an old version.

11. Click **Include book publications** to index all publications in your book list.

12. Click **Remove unreferenced topics** to remove index topics from other publications that do not appear as entries or cross-references in your current publication.

13. Click the **Format** button to display the Index Format dialog box.

14. Configure your index formatting using the active display at the bottom of the dialog box as a guide.

15. Click OK.

Working with Color

Applying Colors

1. Use the pointer tool to select the graphics to which you want to apply a color. Use the text tool to select the text to which you want to apply a color.

2. Choose Color Palette from the Windows menu to display the Colors Palette.

3. Click a color name to apply that color to your text or graphics.

Defining and Editing Colors

1. Choose Define Colors from the Element menu to open the Define Colors dialog box.

2. To define a new color, click **New** to open the Edit Color dialog box. To edit an existing color, click the name of the color to be edited and then click **Edit** to open the Edit Color dialog box.

   Or, if the Colors Palette currently is displayed, click the name of the color to be edited while holding down the Command key to open the Edit Color dialog box directly.

3. If defining a new color, assign a name to your color by typing the name into the **Name** field.

4. Click the appropriate **RGB, HLS,** or **CMYK** color model button to select the color model with which you prefer to work.

5. Adjust the color scroll bars to achieve the desired color.

   Or, type the known color values directly into the color fields.

   Or, click the **PANTONE** button to display the PANTONE Color dialog box. Make PANTONE color choices by clicking a color or typing the corresponding number into the **PANTONE CV** field.

6. Observe the top half of the color display to view color changes. The bottom half of the color display shows the original color you started.

7. Click the bottom half of the color display to restore color settings to their original values.

8. Click OK to return to the Define Colors dialog box.

9. Click OK to save the color settings.

Editing Colors with the Apple Color Picker

1. Choose Define Colors from the Element menu to open the Define Colors dialog box.

2. Hold down the Shift key and click **Edit** in the Define Colors dialog box to open the Apple Color Picker dialog box.

3. Click and drag around the wheel to change the color hue.

4. Click and drag inward (toward the center) or outward (toward the rim of the wheel) to change the color saturation.

5. Scroll the scroll bar up or down to change color brightness.

   Or, type the known values for your new color directly into the **Hue**, **Saturation**, and **Brightness** (or **Red**, **Green**, and **Blue**) fields.

   Or, scroll the **Hue**, **Saturation**, and **Brightness** (or **Red**, **Green**, and **Blue**) values using the arrows to the right of each field.

6. Observe the top half of the color display to view your new color changes. The bottom half of the color display shows the original color.

7. Click the bottom half of the color display to restore color settings to their original values.

8. Click OK to return to the Define Colors dialog box.

9. Click OK to save the color settings.

Copying Colors

1. Choose Define Colors from the Element menu to open the Define Colors dialog box.

2. Click **Copy** to open the Copy Colors dialog box.

3. Click a publication or template name in the list and click OK to import that publication's or template's color palette and return to the Define Colors dialog box.

4. Click OK to save the updated color palette.

Deleting Colors

1. Choose Define Colors from the Element menu to open the Define Colors dialog box.

2. Click the name of the color.

3. Click **Remove** to delete the color.

4. Click OK to save changes to the color palette.

Printing Your Publications

Changing Output Devices

1. Select Chooser from the Apple menu.

2. Click a printer icon to select that printer.

3. Close the Chooser window.

4. Choose Print from the File menu to open the Print To dialog box.

5. Select the matching Printer APD from the pop-up Printer menu.

6. Click OK.

Changing Printer Drivers

1. Choose Print from the File menu while pressing the Option key.

2. The series of dialog boxes for the Apple Driver appears.

Printing Multiple Copies of a Publication

1. Choose Print from the File menu to open the Print To dialog box.

2. Type the desired number of copies into the **Copies** field.

3. Click **Collate** to automatically collate your output.

4. Click **Reverse order** to reverse the normal order of printing pages.

5. To print copies of only a specific page range, type the beginning and ending page numbers into the **From** and **to Page range** fields.

6. Click OK.

Setting PostScript Print Options

1. Choose Print from the File menu to open the Print To dialog box.

2. Click the **PostScript** button to display the PostScript Print Options dialog box.

3. Select desired options by clicking the appropriate check boxes and buttons.

4. Click OK.

Generating Proof Prints

1. Choose Print from the File menu to open the Print To dialog box.

2. Set the desired page range.

3. Click the **Options** button to display the Aldus Print Options dialog box.

4. Click **Proof print**.

5. Click OK.

Scaling Page Output

1. Choose Print from the File menu to open the Print To dialog box.

2. Type a value between 25 and 1000 percent into the **Scaling** field. Pages printed at less than 100 percent size are reduced and centered on the paper. Pages printed at greater than 100 percent size require tiling.

3. Click OK.

Smoothing Bit-Mapped Graphics

1. Choose Print from the File menu to open the Print To dialog box.

2. Click the **Options** button to display the Aldus Print Options dialog box.

3. Click **Smooth** to smooth bit-mapped graphics during printing.

4. Click OK.

Generating Spot Color Overlays

1. Choose Print from the File menu to open the Print To dialog box.

2. Set the desired page range.

3. Click the **Options** button to display the Aldus Print Options dialog box.

4. Click **Spot color overlays**.

5. Click **Knockouts** if knockouts are desired.

6. Click **Crop marks** if crop marks are desired.

7. Click OK.

Substituting Fonts

1. Choose Print from the File menu to open the Print To dialog box.

2. Click the **Options** button to display the Aldus Print Options dialog box.

3. Click **Substitute fonts** to replace New York, Geneva, and Monaco bit-mapped fonts with Times, Helvetica, and Courier laser fonts during printing.

4. Click OK.

Printing Thumbnails

1. Choose Print from the File menu to open the Print To dialog box.

2. Click **Thumbnails**.

3. Type the desired number of thumbnails (up to 64 per page) into the **Thumbnails per page** field.

4. Click OK.

Tiling Page Output

1. Choose Print from the File menu to open the Print To dialog box.

2. Click the **Options** button to display the Aldus Print Options dialog box.

3. Click **Tile** and click the **Manual** or **Auto overlap** button for manual or automatic tiling.

4. To control what part of the page is tiled during manual tiling, reset the ruler zero point on your page to where you want the upper-left corner of the tile to start (repeat for each tile).

5. To control automatic tiling, specify the amount of image overlap by typing a numerical value into the **Auto overlap** field.

6. Click **Crop marks**.

7. Click OK.

Dealing with a Commercial Printer

Use the following checklist as a guide when dealing with commercial printers, quick printers, and print-service bureaus.

1. Before deciding on a commercial printer, do some comparison shopping. Prices and quality vary enormously within the printing industry. Examine samples of each print shop's work before committing your project. Try to find a commercial printer knowledgeable about desktop publishing.

2. Discuss your project in detail with each printer to determine the most cost-effective way to do the job. Ask specifically about different grades of paper. Paper is often your biggest expense, and the quality and cut of paper used can greatly influence the final cost of your job.

3. Ask for advice. Most commercial printers are happy to help, but are reluctant to volunteer suggestions or information unless asked. Get recommendations before you begin your project—you can end up saving time and money.

4. Specify the exact work to be done and obtain written, signed bids from each of the commercial printers whose services you are considering. You may find that costs at one location vary considerably from those at another location. If yours is a repeat-type job, such as a newsletter, obtain new bids periodically to ensure you are still getting a fair deal. Most printers gladly provide estimates with the understanding that the estimates may be exceeded by as much as 10 percent. If your job is a big one, or if you are on a stringent budget, arrange for a written contract. Don't forget to ask about discounts.

5. Agree beforehand on a firm schedule and identify drop-dead dates (absolute deadlines). Expect to pay premium surcharges for rush jobs. Also, expect to pay extra for any last-minute changes. Rush jobs and last-minute changes can double an estimated bill.

399

6. When you deliver a job to a service bureau for Linotronic printing, include a cover sheet or a Read Me file on disk to eliminate guesswork. List the following information:

   ❏ Your name, company name, address, phone number, purchase order or job number, and any other required billing information. Indicate when, where, and how the job is to be delivered.

   ❏ The names of your publication files and any accompanying documents (such as original TIFF scans). Indicate the disks on which the files are stored and specify which pages you want printed.

   ❏ The names and type styles of all fonts used. If your commercial printer doesn't have the required fonts, you must supply the necessary screen and printer versions. Be careful not to violate licensing agreements when doing so. In such cases, convert your publications to pure PostScript files so that the printer fonts are not accessible. If you choose to convert to PostScript, you should check beforehand to verify which fonts are resident in the output device. If a publication font is already resident in the destination printer, don't include the printer version in your PostScript file, or you may overload the printer's memory.

   ❏ The programs used to create your publication files. Be sure to include program version numbers. Also include the version numbers of the System and Finder used. To avoid printing anomalies, use the same version of the System and Finder as your commercial printer uses or be prepared to supply your System and Finder on disk with your publication files.

   ❏ How you want your documents printed. If in color, specify the pages and colors.

   ❏ Any special instructions.

7. If your job is to be printed on a Linotronic ImageSetter, or if you include photos to be stripped in separately, supply a sample laser printout of the publication. The sample serves as a guide to the operator. Provide a rough copy if you don't have access to a laser printer.

8. Always keep a backup of all files and documentation. Your backup copy is your salvation if your originals get damaged or lost (it does happen).

9. Proof your work carefully before delivering it to the printer. Arrange to see photocopies of the mechanicals or the actual bluelines before final printing takes place. Proof these copies just as carefully as your originals.

10. Check the job thoroughly before accepting it. After you sign for a job, it's yours. The printer is relieved of all responsibility. If an error is discovered later, you may have to pay extra to have the error corrected.

B

Installing PageMaker
and Configuring
Your System

PageMaker 4.0 requires a minimum of 1M of memory to operate, and at least 2M is recommended. Because PageMaker is more than 1,500K in size, the program does not fit fully into memory on a 1M machine. Program data transfers back and forth between your hard disk and computer memory during use. Although you can run PageMaker on a 1M machine, doing so is inefficient and time consuming.

Because PageMaker is larger than 1,500K in size, the program doesn't fit on one 800K or 1.44M floppy disk. PageMaker comes encoded in installable segments on separate disks. An Aldus Installer/Utility does the installation automatically. The installer utility loads the software onto your hard disk and then joins the individual segments into a fully functional program at the conclusion of the installation process.

You cannot drag-install PageMaker onto your hard disk like you do most other applications. Many of the files you need, including the program itself, are in compressed format. The installer utility decompresses these files during installation.

The installation procedure is simple: all you do is double-click the PageMaker Aldus Installer/Utility or Install Control icon. You find them on the disk labeled Disk 1. PageMaker prompts you to insert the remaining disks as necessary until the installation is complete. If you become confused at any point, click the installer screen **Help** button for information on how to proceed.

Before installing PageMaker, review carefully the chapter titled "Installing Page-Maker" in your *Getting Started* manual.

The following are some key points to remember:

❏ You must run the installer from floppy disks. You cannot copy the individual parts of the PageMaker program to your hard disk and run the installer there. To be safe, however, never use your original disks. Lock them immediately after you open the package (slide up the disk lock tabs so that you can see through the holes).

❏ Make a mirror backup copy of each disk. Store the original disks in a safe place and do the installation using your backups. Make sure that the backups are exact copies of the originals. For the installation to work, the names of your backup disks must be the same as the original disks.

❏ Before you begin, read the ReadMe file included on Disk 1. The ReadMe file contains important installation data and other late-breaking information that may have been omitted from the manuals. Print a copy of the ReadMe file for ready reference. You also see this file at the beginning of the installation process.

❏ If you are updating PageMaker from an earlier version, relocate earlier software into a separate folder or remove the software from your hard disk. You can run earlier versions of PageMaker from the same hard disk as later versions.

❏ If you receive error messages during the installation indicating that PageMaker is having problems, and the cause is not readily apparent, you may have a corrupted or outdated System file. You also may have conflicting INITs loaded into memory. Start over again after placing a fresh, current System onto your hard disk. Also remove all INITs from your System folder, including any virus-protection INITs (be sure to check your PageMaker disks first using an anti-viral program). The installation should go smoothly. Drag the INITs back into your System folder when you are done.

Warning

Make sure that you have only one System and Finder on your hard disk. Otherwise, you are sure to encounter problems, including system crashes, during the installation process and later during normal program operation.

❑ During installation, PageMaker enables you to choose which import/ export filters you want to install. Shift-click within the list to make multiple selections. These filters enable you to import stories from and export stories to word processors and other applications. Be sure to install the Story Import filter. This filter enables PageMaker to place stories from other PageMaker documents without having to open those documents separately and cut and paste the information. Also be sure to install the Smart ASCII Import filter. This filter enables you to process text-only files.

❑ During installation, PageMaker also enables you to choose which APD (A Printer Description) files you want to install. These files contain information specific to the types of printers you use. The printers don't have to be connected to your system for PageMaker to use the data. Install only those APD files that correspond to the kinds of output devices you intend to use. Installing all the APD files wastes disk space.

❑ Check your hard disk ahead of time. The total installation normally requires about 7M of available hard-disk space. After the installation is complete, remove any files you are sure that you don't need to free up extra space on your hard disk.

❑ During the installation, a TeachText file titled Aldus Installer History is created and stored on your hard disk. This file provides a history of PageMaker's installation and documents the files installed and what problems, if any, were encountered. Save this file in case you have difficulties you need to resolve later with Aldus' technical support department.

❑ If you do run into problems, the Diagnostics menu in the Installer utility enables you to run several tests on your Macintosh. The results of these tests are documented in another TeachText file titled Aldus Installer Diagnostics. You can use these tests to locate duplicate files, verify your System configuration, identify any damaged fonts or duplicate font ID numbers, and list INITs and other System software to help eliminate possible conflicts.

Running PageMaker under MultiFinder

As MultiFinder opens new programs, it partitions the available memory depending on what each program indicates it needs to run properly. Occasionally, however, these allocations are not large enough to handle such memory-intensive tasks as working on excessively long or complex documents. One indication of a PageMaker low memory allocation is that PageMaker may unexpectedly quit. If this happens more than once, try increasing the amount of memory that MultiFinder sets aside to run PageMaker.

To increase the amount of memory available to PageMaker, quit to the Finder desktop while still operating under MultiFinder. Click the PageMaker icon to select it, and choose Get Info from the File menu. In the Get Info window, change the number in the **Application Memory Size** box to reflect the desired memory increase (see fig. B.1). Assigning 2,500K generally reserves enough extra memory for most tasks.

Be careful not to make the new number smaller than the value in the **Suggested Memory Size** box or PageMaker cannot operate. Close the Get Info window to save your changes. When you next open PageMaker, MultiFinder partitions an amount of operating memory equal to your setting. To return to PageMaker's default memory setting, leave the **Application Memory Size** box empty when you close the Get Info window.

Fig. B.1

PageMaker's Get Info window.

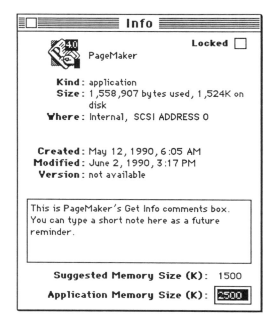

Index

407

D

E

M

N

Q

R

S